D0205696

THE
Sentimental
NATION

The Sentimental Nation

The Making of the Australian Commonwealth

John Hirst

OXFORD
UNIVERSITY PRESS

253 Normanby Road, South Melbourne, Victoria, Australia

Oxford University Press is a department of the University of Oxford. It furthers the University's objective of excellence in research, scholarship, and education by publishing worldwide in

Oxford New York

Athens Auckland Bangkok Bogotá Buenos Aires Cape Town Chennai Dar es Salaam Delhi Florence Hong Kong Istanbul Karachi Kolkata Kuala Lumpur Madrid Melbourne Mexico City Mumbai Nairobi Paris Port Moresby São Paulo Shanghai Singapore Taipei Tokyo Toronto Warsaw

and associated companies in Berlin Ibadan

OXFORD is a trade mark of Oxford University Press

First published 2000
Reprinted 2001

National Library of Australia

Cataloguing-in-publication data:

Hirst, John, 1942–.
The sentimental nation: the making of the Australian Commonwealth

Bibliography.
Includes index.
ISBN 0 19 550620 0.

1. Federal government—Australia—History. 2. Australia—Politics and government. 3.—History—20th century. I. Title.

321.020994

Edited by Cathryn Game
Indexed by Russell Brooks
Text and cover designed by Polar Design Pty Ltd
Typeset by Polar Design Pty Ltd
Printed by Kyodo Printing Co. Singapore Pte Ltd

Published with the assistance of the National Council for the Centenary of Federation.

To the 422,788 Yes voters who have no other memorial

What is this movement based on but sentiment? When you see strong-minded men—men of intelligence—being carried away by sentiment, watch them. A strong-minded man governed by sentiment is more dangerous than a hysterical woman.

J. H. Want, New South Wales Assembly, 1897

While not desiring to underrate the sentimental aspect, we are a practical people and our pockets are the first consideration in this great question.

Richard Baker, Adelaide Town Hall, 1 August 1895

With regard to Australian federation … the sentimental side will prove to be the practical, or the basis of the practical.

Andrew Inglis Clark, Federation Conference, February 1890

Contents

Illustrations

Acknowledgments

Archivists and librarians around the country have given me efficient and courteous service. I thank in particular the staff of the Mitchell and Dixson Libraries in Sydney, the La Trobe Library in Melbourne, and the Manuscripts Room in the National Library, Canberra.

Bruce Davidson, the librarian of Parliament House, Melbourne, gave me access to the memorial to the Victorian voters in the federation referendum. Beryl Armstrong, the librarian at Australian Unity, which holds the records of the Australian Natives Association, was most welcoming and cooperative.

When I was writing in Melbourne and needed information quickly from other cities, I received willing assistance from Peter Cochrane in Sydney, Mark Orford and Catherine Hirst in Canberra, Michael Connor in Hobart, and Alex McDermott in Adelaide.

I have received advice and useful leads from my historian colleagues: Geoff Bolton, Graeme Davison, Ken Inglis, Bev Kingston, and John Williams. Allan Martin lent me a copy of his path-breaking MA thesis on George Reid and the politics of New South Wales in the 1890s. George Winterton was my adviser on constitutional matters. Bob Birrell and Michael Roe read chapters on which I was keen to have their advice. Stuart Macintyre read it all and made numerous helpful suggestions.

Introduction

> It is sometimes forgotten that it is much easier to surrender than recall autonomous rights. The question for us now is whether we are prepared to allow any other Government than the one we are accustomed to, and can control, to interfere with our lives or interests. What is offered in exchange? Intercolonial free-trade? That may be obtained without federation. Security against invasion? A simple agreement would suffice to secure that …
>
> *Why Federate?* by Democrat, Adelaide 1897[1]

Self-governing communities do not readily surrender their powers. The Australian federalists of the late nineteenth century were acutely aware that previous federations had been formed to meet an external threat. Sometimes they fantasised about how much easier their task would be if an enemy fleet appeared off Sydney Harbour or at Port Phillip Heads. The smart money said that until there was such a threat federation would never be accomplished.

It took three attempts before the six self-governing colonies agreed to form a national government. In 1883 the Victorian Government launched a campaign for federation that produced only a very weak coordinating body, the Federal Council. New South Wales and South Australia did not join it. This was truly a Clayton's union. None of its four members—Queensland, Victoria, Tasmania, and Western Australia—had a common border.

In 1889 Sir Henry Parkes, the Premier of New South Wales, launched a one-man campaign for federation. He was the grand old man of Australian politics, a survivor from the mid-century battles for self-government and democracy. His campaign was initially remarkably successful. Delegates appointed by the colonial parliaments attended a Convention in Sydney in 1891 and agreed on a constitution, which was drafted by Sir Samuel Griffith, the Premier of Queensland. But there was strong opposition to the constitution in Parkes's own colony of New South Wales, and the scheme collapsed.

A much broader federal movement appeared in 1893 proposing a novel procedure for nation-making. The people of the colonies, rather than the parliaments, would elect another convention, and the constitution it drew up would be put to the people at referendum for their acceptance or rejection. This unique mechanism was put in train in 1897. A new Convention met and, although it was meant to begin afresh, it kept Griffith's draft and made modifications to it. This constitution was put to the people of the six colonies during 1898–1900 and eventually accepted by all. It was enacted by the British parliament in 1900 and came into force on 1 January 1901.

The union was accomplished peacefully without external threat or internal coercion. Of course. After all, this is Australia. So because this is Australia, shouldn't we understand federation as a natural process of evolution?

The colonies were founded separately, but from the 1880s intercolonial ties were strengthening. Big business was operating across the colonial borders. Working men moved from colony to colony depending on where the prospects for work were best. The railways were joined: Sydney–Melbourne in 1883; Melbourne–Adelaide in 1887; Sydney–Brisbane in 1889. Churches, trades unions, and professional bodies formed intercolonial associations. It is easy to think that federation was simply government catching up: a more unified society needed a national state.

But these six separate governments were already operating on a national scale. They were running the intercolonial train service. Since the 1850s they had run a national telegraph network and a national and international mail service. They had passed uniform legislation to keep out the Chinese. They combined to pay for the building of forts at strategic points on the coast. The gun batteries at Albany in Western Australia were constructed by the Victorian Government and manned at first by South Australian soldiers. The six governments standardised time across the continent into three zones in 1895. No progress had been made on a common tariff, but this too did not require federation. A customs union, the preferred option of business, would do the job.

Of course there would be advantages in a national government. Things can always be done better. But self-governing communities will not yield up their powers merely for advantages. We have to find the force that was compelling them to do so.

Cause

1
Destiny

> Though Australians will federate in their own interests yet, from the point of view of world history, the chief importance of Federation will be in its being a necessary step in the progress of civilized man.
>
> William Gay to Alfred Deakin, 9 March 1895

> *Oh, fair Ideal, unto whom*
> *Through days of doubt and nights of gloom*
> *Brave hearts have clung, while lips of scorn*
> *Made mock of thee as but a dream*
>
> J. Brunton Stephens, 'The Dominion', 1883

God wanted Australia to be a nation.

Among the thousands of federalists who believed this were the two men who worked hardest to achieve it. They received their due reward. Edmund Barton became the first prime minister of the new Commonwealth and Alfred Deakin the second.

God and success: these may appear to make this an un-Australian story, but it became so in the end, for few Australians now know who Barton and Deakin were, and none believes God played any part in federation. Among historians it is a common view that the creation of the Commonwealth was not much more than a business transaction.[1]

It is no surprise that Deakin believed he was doing God's will in working for federation. To fathom the divine, to discover its purpose for the world and his duty in it, were the preoccupations of his life.[2] He discarded Christianity in his teens and turned to spiritualism and its seances. He saw through that too, but continued the struggle to reach the supernatural realm and receive guidance from it. As prime minister, he was still listening for voices, watching for signs, and pondering what fortune-tellers had told him. He wanted to be a poet, a prophet, a preacher, or a recluse, and half resented his political success for robbing him of his vocation. No matter what political office he held, he devoted hours of each week to his secret life of meditation and writing; he composed poems, reflections, prayers, and theological and philosophical treatises, all unseen by anyone, except the poems that he presented to his wife on her birthday and their wedding anniversary.

Until the moment he was nominated for a seat in the Victorian Parliament, Deakin had never thought of being a politician. He did not know the location of the electorate he was to contest and had never set foot inside it. But he could not help succeeding in politics. He was handsome, eloquent, personable, and quick-witted; he could read rapidly and remember everything and do business quickly. He was a member of parliament at 22, a minister at 26, leader of the liberal party and deputy premier at 29. If God perversely wanted him in politics, there must be something God wanted him to do there. Deakin found his calling in federation. In his private writings, he marked the assembling of the conventions and the results of the referendums with prayer. For himself Deakin prayed that he might be obliterated, annihilated, humiliated, crucified—if that's what his service required.[3] In this he was to be disappointed; he was dogged by success.

From 1891 Edmund Barton led the federation movement in New South Wales. He and Deakin became friends through the bond of the federal cause. They were not alike. Deakin was a progressive liberal, but Barton was temperamentally a conservative. Deakin agonised over religion, while Barton remained a conventional, unenthusiastic Anglican. Deakin was a teetotaller and semi-recluse; Barton's best hours were those spent drinking and conversing in his club. Deakin took no interest in sport; Barton has the distinction of being the only prime minister to have been an umpire in first-class cricket. In his youth Barton had been a player, but he was soon much too portly for that. Deakin kept fit by skipping and bike-riding; he took his bike with him to the Adelaide Convention in 1897.

Barton had a fine presence, but he was not quite handsome. Deakin described him as possessing a fine head, good features, beautiful, glowing eyes, and then a falling away to a large jowl, which represented for Deakin some failing in character.[4] Barton did not overexert himself at politics or his business of law; he had the reputation of being lazy. The crises in his life arose from drinking too much alcohol and possessing too little cash. Yet he was transformed by the federal cause. He gave himself to it utterly, and in launching the campaign for a Yes vote at the 1898 referendum he declared 'God means to give us this Federation.'[5]

What attracted God to Australian nationhood? He wanted Australia to put aside its divisions and be united because He was guiding humankind to a better future. For most people, God was still the all-powerful figure of Christian belief but now He was more benign following His commitment to the march of progress and the laws of social evolution. For Deakin and

Edmund Barton and Alfred Deakin, probably taken when Barton was Prime Minister and Deakin his deputy.

others who were idealists in the German philosophical tradition, God was not at all the figure of Christian belief. He was the Spirit or Force or Principle leading humankind to higher forms of life and deeper understanding. Evolutionary social thinking, with authority borrowed from Darwin's biology, was strong among both orthodox and heterodox believers. God and evolution were an irresistible mix.

The Christian beliefs that nothing happened unless God willed it and nothing prospered without His blessing left their mark on the constitution. The churches bombarded the Constitutional Convention of 1897–98 with petitions requesting that God be acknowledged. More petitions with more signatures were received on this issue than any other. Federation occurred when the churches were at the peak of their influence, and the Protestant churches were looking to make Australia into a Christian Commonwealth.

The Convention delegates would have preferred to stick to a strict separation between church and state, which was exactly what the Protestant churches were now contesting. No matter what their own views—and most were believers—the delegates knew that religion was always a hot potato. But on this occasion the usual source of contention did not exist. Catholics and Protestants were united in wanting God in the constitution. So rather than offend such a large constituency, the delegates made the constitution read that the people were 'humbly relying on the blessing of Almighty God' when they decided to form the Commonwealth.[6]

Nation-making had become a progressive cause well worthy of divine favour because in Europe it represented an escape from tyranny and foreign domination. Liberals and democrats everywhere yearned for Hungary, Poland, and Italy to be free. Hungary and Poland produced martyrs and moments of hope, but they remained captive until the end of World War I. Italy's liberation in the ten years after 1860 was the miraculous, inspiring success. Three powers had held her in thrall. Large parts of the north were controlled by the Austrian empire; the south was ruled by a particularly cruel and vicious Bourbon king whose regime was described by Gladstone as 'the negation of God erected into a system of government'; and the Pope, the declared enemy of liberalism and nationalism, was the temporal ruler of a large swathe of territory in the centre of the peninsula. The unification of Italy was achieved by the King of Piedmont in the north who employed, at arm's length, the free-wheeling soldier of fortune, Garibaldi. With his band of red-shirts he conquered the whole of the south in a whirlwind campaign, sent the Bourbon King of Naples packing, handed over his conquest to his patron, and went into temporary retirement on his island in the Mediterranean. He wanted nothing for himself.

Garibaldi was the model patriot of the age, admired all around the globe. In Melbourne money was raised by public subscription to present him with a ceremonial sword to mark his victory over the King of Naples. In Sydney on

The nation begins with prayer: the Anglican Archbishop of Sydney reads prayers in the pavilion, Centennial Park, Sydney, 1 January 1901.

his death in 1882 a crowd of 10,000 gathered in the Exhibition Building to mourn him. Both movements were organised by the local Italian community.[7] When federation was achieved, Sydney's Italian community contributed a float to the inaugural procession that featured a bust of Parkes surrounded by Italian soldiers, two of them dressed like Garibaldi's red-shirts.

The enthusiasm for Italian unification in Britain and Australia was partly because the most recalcitrant enemy of unification was the Pope. Protestants

The Italian float in the federation procession, Sydney, 1 January 1901.

gained added satisfaction from hating the Pope when he placed himself so firmly against a progressive cause. Garibaldi was fiercely anti-clerical, and several times, with and without the support of his royal patron, he launched campaigns to free Rome from the Pope. He fought valiantly to defend the short-lived Roman republic proclaimed in 1848, the year of revolutions throughout Europe. He was defeated then by the Catholic powers of Austria and France, which came to the Pope's rescue. It was only in 1870, when France was preoccupied by its war with Prussia, that the King of Piedmont, now King of Italy, was finally able to take Rome.

Garibaldi visited Australia briefly. Between revolutions and campaigns it was his habit to take ordinary work. After the collapse of the Roman republic, he passed through Australian waters as a ship's captain but landed only on a Bass Strait island where his ship took on water. He made more of an impact when he contributed to a debate in the New South Wales Parliament on state aid to church schools. His views were solicited by David Buchanan, a member opposed to aid to Catholic schools. He read to the parliament Garibaldi's letter: 'The principal obstacle to human progress is the priest … I trust in God that you will not suffer the presence of this human reptile in your beautiful virgin country; and if anyone says there must be liberty to all, answer him that you will not give liberty to vipers, assassins and crocodiles, and the Romish priest is worse than all of these.'[8]

In Australia the liberal hope was that the new state schools would take children of all denominations and so put an end to old-world feuding. The refusal of the Catholic Church to support this project and its demand for state support for its own schools seemed to non-Catholics illiberal, unprogressive, and unpatriotic, the local equivalent of the Pope clinging to his Italian territories and imprisoning Italian patriots.

Mazzini was the ideas man for Italian unification and the theoretician who made nationalism into a worldwide progressive cause. He had a troubled relationship with Garibaldi. Mazzini wanted united Italy to be a republic created by popular risings of the people; Garibaldi, although he learnt his nationalism from Mazzini, was prepared to work for unity under the best prospect available, the King of Piedmont. Because he was always promoting risings and revolution, Mazzini could not safely live in Italy, and he spent most of his life in exile in London. He had his moment of glory on Italian soil as one of the rulers of the Roman republic.

Mazzini reacted against the French Revolution's stress on rights. He believed humankind would reach its best by accepting the bonds of living in associations, which were the God-given nations. God had allocated a special mission to each nation; Germany's was the development of thought; France's was action; Italy's was thought in unison with action. Once all the nations had been given the freedom to develop their mission, they would then come together in a federation of nations, which would establish peace and carry humankind to a higher stage of development. Nationalism of this sort was not chauvinistic; every lover of mankind had an interest in the freedom and development of every nation. Garibaldi took this view and fought for France against Prussia in 1870.

Deakin was a great admirer of Mazzini and defended him against the charges that he was an irreligious and irresponsible revolutionary promoting from his exile the overthrow of every form of government.[9] As a young man Deakin distilled his thought into a catechism for use in the Sunday School run by the Progressive Lyceum, the organisation of Melbourne spiritualists. Deakin was the Conductor who led the service; the children, divided into different circles, gave the responses:

CONDUCTOR:	What does History disclose to us?
AURORA CIRCLE:	Man's trials
SUNBEAM CIRCLE:	Man's conquests
MOUNTAIN CIRCLE:	Man's progression
ALL:	The progress of civilisation
CONDUCTOR:	What are the ascending grades of organised life?
AURORA CIRCLE:	The individual
SUNBEAM CIRCLE:	The family
MOUNTAIN CIRCLE:	The nation
ALL:	Nations are individuals in the family of Man.

The questions then elicited the distinctive character of each nation. Mazzini had made Britain responsible for industry and colonies; Deakin, as was more common, made their contribution political freedom.

CONDUCTOR:	What will be the probable future of national existence?
ALL:	Each nation will perfect itself harmoniously in its own sphere, until all are blended into a superb whole.
CONDUCTOR:	Does that perfection involve the loss of nationality?
ALL:	Not in its true sense; they will be distinct in their offices, but united in their cooperation like the various limbs and organs of the body
CONDUCTOR:	Is then Humanity in reality a Unity?
ALL:	Yes, even as God is. Its many members mutually assist each other; they are governed by an intelligence and a sympathy, which the same in every race, blends the millions of mankind in one holy brotherhood, of aim and being.[10]

Deakin was always the eclectic; these ideas remained part of his thinking—certainly the connection between nationality and social evolution and God as God of the nations—but he did not become a Mazzinian. His attachment to entities that Mazzini did not recognise—the British race and the British Empire—was too strong. The Italian's true disciple in Australia was Andrew Inglis Clark, one of the two men who arrived at the 1891 Convention with a constitution already written.[11] It was this constitution from which Samuel Griffith composed his draft. Had Clark drawn up a constitution according to his heart's desire, he would have provided for an independent republic because, true to Mazzini, he believed each nation had its character and mission and that Australia could not fully develop its potential while it was in any way subordinate. In a poem on a future Australian flag, which like all his other poems remained unpublished, he wrote:

Australia, thou alone
Our sovereign lord shall be
No other land shall own or claim
Thy children's fealty.[12]

Among the inner group of founding fathers he was the only republican.

The Federation Conference, Melbourne, 1890. The best informed delegate was the smallest—Andrew Inglis Clark is at the left of the back row. Parkes is standing in the centre; Griffith is standing behind him to his right.

Andrew Clark was born in Hobart in 1848 when convicts were still being transported to Van Diemen's Land. In his early twenties he gave up both the Baptist religion of his mother and the career his father had marked out for him in his engineering workshop. He studied law and, like Deakin, spent his life thinking through for himself the big questions of God, morality, and immortality, experimenting with spiritualism and theosophy on the way. He was philosophically an idealist, and his religion was the cause of humanity. Unlike Deakin, he was not a good performer before an audience. He was tiny, only five feet tall, a dwarf among the giants of the Convention, and he did not speak well. When the 1891 Convention was settling the actual words of the constitution, he moved around the chamber collecting opinion from delegates and trying out options, and then reported the results to Griffith.[13] He was at his best in a small circle, and his Hobart home became in effect the first university of Tasmania where young men met to hear and debate papers read by their 'padre', as they called Clark. He and his circle were a new force in Tasmanian politics, introducing the liberal and democratic principles established much earlier in Australia (which being then solely a geographical entity did not embrace Tasmania). Clark served as Attorney-General in reforming governments in the 1880s and 1890s, and introduced his modification of the proportional representation scheme developed by the Englishman Thomas Hare, the Hare–Clark electoral system.

From his adolescent years Clark had idolised the United States, the home of liberty, and Italy, which had been united by dashing and passionate patriots. Even in Hobart he found ways to put himself in touch with these countries. When their warships called at the port, he befriended some of their officers. He kept in touch with Luigi Blotto of the *Garibaldi* by writing in Italian, a language he was still learning.[14] Then just before the 1891 Convention assembled, he had the chance of a round-the-world trip, his first time away from Australia. As Attorney-General, Clark had to go to London to conduct a case in Her Majesty's Privy Council, which enabled the Mazzinian republican to make a pilgrimage to Italy and the United States.

There are poems in honour of both countries in his papers. The poem on the United States is couched in general terms; the nation is hailed as the beacon of liberty:

The light that leadeth onward
The nations in their quest
For an ampler, clearer vision
Of freedom's radiant face …

The poem on Italy is a long, detailed account of his response to the places he visited. Clark was a most unusual Italian traveller. He did not want to see the ruins of ancient Rome, which was barbaric, or the treasures held by the Pope, who was an enemy of liberty, progress, and true religion. He wanted to stand where the heroes of unification had fought and bled. His poem conveys the thrill he still felt at such extravagant devotion and such willingness to die. One of the shrines he visited was the prison where the patriot Ruffini had died. Fearing he would be forced to betray his comrades, Ruffini had taken a nail from the cell wall and 'pierced his throat and sealed his lips for evermore'. Mazzini was for Clark still the Master; at his tomb 'every rod of earth is holy ground', and from it pilgrims bear away new faith for 'the eternal war between the flesh and spirit, to obtain and hold possession of the world'. The poem ends with a salute to his heroes:

Thus ever have the saviours of the world
Behind the things that seemed to other men
Eternal facts, seen truthful dreams
That others would not see

Until the facts in fragments at their feet
Fell down, and in the face of all men stood
Revealed the visions which the prophets saw
And followed unto death.

This encapsulates the idealist philosophy. The material world—the world of fact—which seems so solid, actually takes its form from 'dreams', the Ideal as it is revealed to those who are attuned to its message, the prophets and the heroes. For Clark and for Deakin federation was a dream that it was their business to make real. Deakin insisted that the cause would require men to go to the extremes that attracted Clark: 'the devotion that will annihilate self', 'suffering, valour and sacrifice'.[15]

The satisfactions the two men gained from their own work for federation were deeply hidden; they would never claim, even in the privacy of their notebooks and diaries, to be heroes. Deakin's prayers insisted that he did not want success for himself. The man who believed that he was playing the hero's part and had no compunction in claiming it was Sir Henry Parkes.[16]

Clark and Deakin were unusual in having a fully worked philosophy to support federation, but federalists generally looked on it as a holy or noble or sacred cause, which would carry the people to a higher form of life. When Barton was criticised over his tactics for advancing federation he refused to answer his critic in detail: 'I decline', he said, 'to scuffle with you on the steps of the Temple.'[17] When federal parliamentarians first took their place inside the temple, which was for the moment Parliament House, Melbourne, one member was immediately disappointed. Circulars had been issued extolling the virtues of candidates for the speakership of the House and presidency of the Senate. This crude canvassing was not the much-promised higher life.[18]

That rather metaphysical notion had meanings that were plain enough. Federation would supplant the mutual suspicion and hostility between the colonies with brotherhood, a widening of human sympathy, which was the hallmark of moral progress. The petty and provincial concerns of colonial politics—the struggle over roads and bridges; the endless deputations to ministers begging favours—would be replaced by a politics that dealt with a national life and the fate of a whole people. For the Tasmanian federalists this was a particularly strong allure. Backward and most deeply marked by the convict stain, Tasmania would be cleansed and invigorated by its incorporation into a wider national life.[19]

Federation itself—the means by which Australia was to become a nation—wore a progressive air. It represented so clearly a stage in social evolution from simple to complex forms. It was by federation that men envisaged that the British Empire, the Anglo-Saxon race, the English-speaking peoples, and finally the world would be united. Mazzini's federation of nations was a widely held vision. Tennyson, the poet laureate, sang of 'the parliament of man, the Federation of the world'.[20] In Melbourne the eccentric bookseller E.W. Cole launched an active campaign in its support. The tokens he produced for advertising carried a variety of messages on the theme. He confronted Australians' race prejudice and told them

Medallion carrying the message of world federation by the bookseller, E.W. Cole.

that black and white would have to be joined: 'The people everywhere whom we do not know are as good as the people that we do know.'[21]

In looking for the motives for Australian federation, historians usually are far too instrumental in their thinking. The Commonwealth Government was given power over various subjects, and the puzzle of why federation occurred is reduced to ranking these subjects in order of importance. Was federation chiefly to secure a customs union, or a united immigration policy, or a national defence? To federalists none of these things was sacred; the whole forty-two powers given to the Commonwealth did not together make federation sacred. It was the making of the nation, apart from anything it might do, that was sacred. Of course various interests were to be advanced or, in some cases, threatened by federation, and the impact of federation would vary according to the form it took. That form became a matter of prolonged dispute, which sometimes appears fully to constitute the federal movement. But these interests did not create the desire to be a nation; they merely responded to it opportunistically.

Because federation was a sacred cause, poetry was considered the most appropriate medium to express its rationale and purposes. It was poetry's role to deal with what was noble, profound, and elevating. There are innumerable federation poems by hundreds of different hands.[22] The nation was born in a festival of poetry. Historians have noticed the poems, but have not known quite what to do with them. Most of them are valueless as poetry. One leading scholar, introducing his bibliography of federation sources, declared: 'It seemed kinder to spare us all any inventory of the poems, "poems" and verse.'[23] He thus removed from consideration the best guide to the ideas and ideals that inspired the movement. Readers of this book are not to be spared, although a sample of the poems will be sufficient since their themes are very similar. The poets were great plagiarists; or to put it another way, they gave their variations on well-established themes.

The evidence offered by the poets that God or destiny intended Australia to be a nation was in the first place physical. They forgot Tasmania (which was inconsiderate since it was always keen about federation) and saw the nation-to-be as a single geographical unit, a whole continent with only natural boundaries. This was a special benediction. Other nations had artificial frontiers; Australia's were the sea. A common word for the sea in this role was 'girdle' and in its verbal form 'girdled' or 'girdling' or 'girt'. 'Advance Australia Fair', written by Peter McCormick in 1878 and now the national anthem, uses 'girt' and assumes the implications of the sea boundary do not have to be spelled out, recording merely: 'our home is girt by sea'.

The social uniformity within the continent also marked out Australia for nationhood. The people were of one blood or stock or race; they spoke the same language; they shared a glorious heritage (Britain's), the most celebrated part of which was political freedom, which had been extended in Australia to all men so that the country was the freest on earth; the people were also of the one religion (which ignored the Protestant/Catholic divide, although it was not regionally based as it was in the United Kingdom and in Canada). This unity was also put down to God or destiny, overlooking the British Government, their undoubted instrument, which had claimed the whole continent and determined the composition of its population.

The best federation poem, written very early (1877), does not argue that Australia should be one, but assumes it and deals instead with the ideal becoming real. It is the most powerful expression of the idea that union was Australia's destiny. The author was James Brunton Stephens, a headmaster at a Brisbane state school. He had taught in the bush, which he hated, and obtained a transfer to Brisbane with the approval of Samuel Griffith, then Minister of Education. He wanted to be close to a good library and other literary men. When Griffith became Premier in 1883 Stephens had a senior post in the Premier's office, organised, it is said, by the Governor's daughter, who admired his poetry.[24]

His federation poem was called 'The Dominion of Australia: A Forecast':

She is not yet; but he whose ear
Thrills to that finer atmosphere
Where footfalls of appointed things
Reverberant of days to be,
Are heard in forecast echoing
Like wave-beats from a viewless sea,
Hears in the voiceful tremors of the sky
Auroral heralds whispering, 'She is nigh'.

The middle part of the poem develops an elaborate comparison between the silent force carrying Australia to its destiny and the underground rivers that some experts assumed must run under the parched lands of the outback and which one day might be released to make the desert bloom.

So flows beneath our good and ill
A viewless stream of Common Will,
A gathering force, a present might,
That from its silent depths of gloom

At Wisdom's voice shall leap to light
And hide our barren feuds in bloom,
Till, all our sundering lines with love o'ergrown,
Our bounds shall be the girdling seas alone.

When Parkes opened his campaign for federation in his famous speech at Tenterfield, he quoted from this poem.[25] He did well to quote from Stephens' poetry rather than his own. At the time he launched his campaign he was revising the proofs of his next book of poems, *Fragmentary Thoughts.* Unlike Clark and Deakin, he was quite willing for the public to see his efforts. In the preface to *Fragmentary Thoughts*, he said with his usual mock humility that he would be happy to be judged no great poet, but lest anyone dare to make that judgment he reproduced a letter from his friend Lord Tennyson that praised his efforts, how guardedly Parkes probably did not notice. In Brisbane a few days before his Tenterfield speech, he had refused to disclose his federal plans to the *Courier*'s reporter but had been very willing to discuss poetry.[26] He passed the proofs of his poems to the journalist for his opinion. Parkes declared Stephens to be the best poet in Australia, a compliment Stephens returned in his review of *Fragmentary Thoughts*, which contrived to be favourable without pronouncing definitely on the quality of the poems.[27]

In his new collection Parkes rehearsed a standard theme in 'The Flag':

God girdled our majestic isle
With seas far-reaching east and west,
That man might live beneath this smile
In peace and freedom ever blest.

He was a much better phrase-maker in his speeches.

As federation became a firm proposal, it met opposition as well as the old indifference. The poets identified the forces that frustrated it as selfishness, greed, and faction, by which they meant a sinister political combination. Men were damaging the union already created by God. The symbols of this divisiveness were the customs houses on the colonial borders, which were hated not as a commercial inconvenience but as a moral outrage. So to reveal the Australian nation, men had to repent and return to God. In a Christian culture this was a powerful theme. It was best expressed by William Gay in his sonnet 'Federation', written in the early 1890s:

From all division let our land be free,
For God has made her one: complete she lies

Within the unbroken circle of the skies,
And round her indivisible the sea
Breaks on her single shore; while only we,
Her foster children, bound with sacred ties
Of one dear blood, one storied enterprise,
Are negligent of her integrity.—
Her seamless garment, at great Mammon's nod,
With hands unfilial we have basely rent,
With petty variance our souls are spent,
And ancient kinship under foot is trod:
O let us rise, united, penitent,
And be one people,—mighty, serving God!

Deakin used this poem to conclude the great speech with which he launched the Yes campaign in Victoria for the 1898 referendum.[28] He had come to know Gay well, although only by letter. He admired his poetry and, since Gay was a follower of German idealist philosophy, they had much in common. Gay was a young Scotsman who came to Australia in 1888 for his health's sake.[29] In the 1890s he was dying of consumption and was bedridden. In his letters to Deakin he frequently says he can write no more because he is coughing blood and terribly weak, although 'if I choose I can make my handwriting appear quite vigorous'.[30] The philosopher

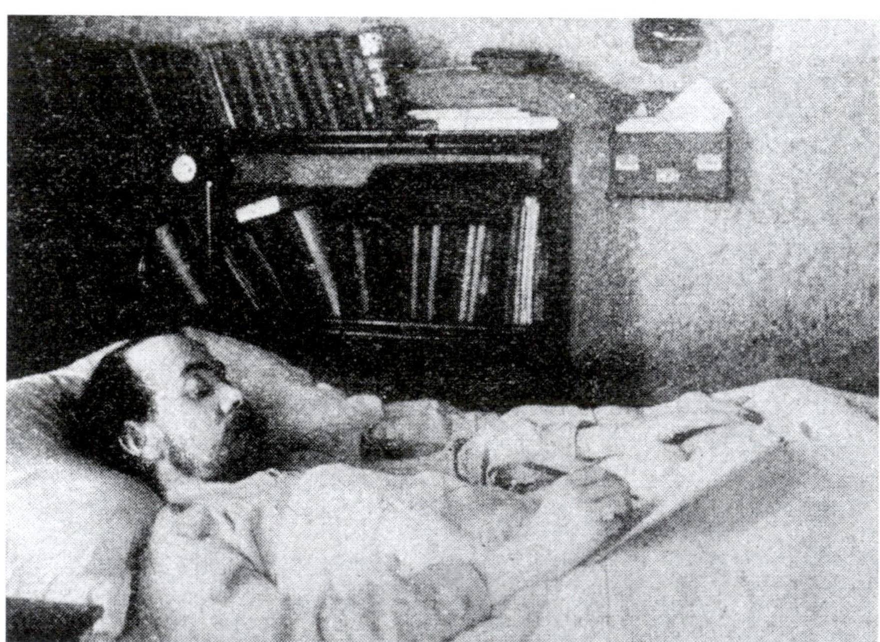

William Gay, federation poet, on his deathbed.

made the most of his sickness; it sharpened his reflections on suffering, gratitude, and immortality.

Gay was nursed by Mary Sampson, a state school teacher, in her Bendigo home. Twice Gay asked Deakin to interfere on their behalf with the Education Department so long as it did not conflict with 'even your lightest principle', first to see that Mary was not transferred away from Bendigo and second that she would not lose her job when they married. Gay sent three sonnets to show how deep was his affection, but explained that the marriage would be one of the spirit and the affections only.[31] Deakin was very ready to help, but the pair decided after all not to marry. Gay died late in 1897 aged 32. Deakin's great speech was given in Bendigo a few months later so the effect of quoting Gay was enhanced because he could declare his 'grave is not yet green in your midst' and his poem was a message from 'dying lips'.

According to the poets, the prospects for the new nation were unrivalled. Australia had no ancient feuds, no privileged caste, no bar to anyone making money from its abundant resources; it was a land of freedom and opportunity. Always imagined as female, Australia was young, pure, virginal. The themes are present in 'Advance Australia Fair', although again rather minimally. Australians are young and free; the land is rich in opportunities—golden soil—which are open to those ready to work: wealth for toil.

A focus on the future was almost obligatory since the nation's origins were disreputable and it could not yet boast of the customary feats of nationhood. 'Advance Australia' had long been the motto of the nation-to-be. It appeared under the unofficial coat of arms of kangaroo and emu, in common use since the 1850s. Above the kangaroo and emu was the rising sun.[32]

There was a constant insistence that no blood had been spilt in this land. This is a puzzle to us who are now so conscious of the violence done to the Aborigines. In part the claim could be made because the slaughter was simply being forgotten, although the forgetfulness was more complete in the early twentieth century than in the nineteenth. It was possible to know well enough what had happened on the frontier and still see Australia as pure. In *Fragmentary Thoughts* Parkes wrote of the Australian flag: 'It bears no stain of blood and tears/Its glory is its purity.' In the same volume is a poem that gives a chilling account of the murder of an Aboriginal boy by settlers on the Hawkesbury in 1794. He was tied hand and foot, dragged through a fire until his back was horribly burnt, and then thrown into the river and shot.

Loud talk ye of savages
As they were beasts of prey!—
But men of English birth have done
More savage things than they

The unofficial coat of arms of the coming nation: the Adelaide Arcade, 1885.

The two thoughts remain unconnected. It was easy not to make the connection when Aborigines were not seen as part of the future nation since they were dying out and in any case unworthy of its citizenship. Furthermore, when they spoke of no blood spilt, the poets had in mind the European experience of warfare ravaging the land and being constantly renewed.[33]

The best poem on Australia as a new world free from all the ills of the old was written by John Farrell. He was a brewer turned journalist and poet.[34] In the late 1880s he edited and produced most of the copy for a radical Sydney newspaper that supported land nationalisation along the lines of Henry George's single tax. Parkes admired his writing, although he did not support his politics, and helped him to a job as editor of the *Daily Telegraph*.[35] Griffith corresponded with Farrell over his own plans for radical social reform, a phase in his career that soon passed.[36]

Farrell's poem is more insistent and defiant than the norm, which reflects his own radicalism and the occasion of its writing. In 1883 the British Government quietly shipped to Australia a group of Irish nationalists who had informed on their comrades and so secured their conviction for murder. There was outrage in Australia when the plan became known. Informers were hateful to the local Irish, and everyone was touchy about Australia being treated as England's dumping ground. The men were not allowed to land. Farrell's poem was conceived as a message to the British. It was titled simply 'NO'.[37] The reproaches to Britain that begin and end the poem are omitted in what is quoted here, as they were when it was reused in the campaign for federation.

We have no records of a by-gone shame,
No red-writ histories of woe to weep:
God set our land in summer seas asleep
Till His fair morning for her waking came.

He hid her where the rage of Old World wars
Might never break upon her virgin rest:
He sent His softest winds to fan her breast,
And canopied her night with low-hung stars.

He wrought her perfect, in a happy clime,
And held her worthiest, and bade her wait
Serene on her lone couch inviolate
The heightened manhood of a later time …

The sexual theme was never more explicit. The men worthy to take Australia, the 'manful pioneers', leave Europe only when freedom has dawned there.

They found a gracious amplitude of soil,
Unsown with memories, like poison weeds,
Of far-forefathers' wrongs and vengeful deeds,
Where was no crown, save that of earnest toil.

They reared a sunnier England, where the pain
Of bitter yesterdays might not arise:
They said—'The past is past, and all its cries
Of time-long hatred are beyond the main …

'And, with fair peace's white, pure flag unfurled,
Our children shall, upon this new-won shore—
Warned by all sorrows that have gone before—
Build up the glory of a grand New World.'

From the 1880s the purity of this new world increasingly took the form of a purity in race. It is common now to denounce the White Australia policy as racist and nothing more. It was certainly racist, but it also embodied the hopes for Australia as a better world. By excluding the 'inferior' races, the dignity of labour and a decent standard of living would be preserved, caste divisions avoided, and social harmony maintained. Australia was not only to be better Britain; it was also to be a better new world than the United States, which flouted its principles of equality in its treatment of the Negroes.

Before the Commonwealth was established, the colonies had acted together to exclude Chinese and other Asians. Federation was not needed to make the White Australia policy, but that policy was the most popular expression of the national ideal that inspired federation.

The new Commonwealth did not seem designed to build up a grand new world since it was to have limited powers. In the 1890s Australia was

The colonies had cooperated to exclude the Chinese: even for this heavy work they are represented by female figures. (*Melbourne Punch*, May 1888)

gaining a reputation for progressive social and economic legislation, but this was and would remain chiefly the responsibility of the states. Only at the last minute was the Commonwealth given power over old-age pensions and interstate industrial disputes.

It was in the name of the federation that the founders most clearly expressed their sense that Australia represented a new dispensation.[38] The name 'Commonwealth' was suggested by Parkes at the 1891 Convention and was taken up enthusiastically by Deakin, who lobbied the delegates on its behalf. Some were wary of the name because it had been used by Oliver Cromwell for the English republic established after the execution of Charles I. One or two were attracted to it for this reason. After being narrowly adopted by the Convention's constitutional committee, the term won general acceptance in the Convention and outside it because it embodied an Australian view of the nature of government. The state existed not to aggrandise an elite or to embark on conquest, but to serve the common weal, the common good. It was this view of government that was to make the Commonwealth much larger than its formal powers implied.

During the 1890s affection for the term grew, and there was no question that the Convention of 1897–98 would stick with it. A feeble opposition continued, chiefly from people who saw it as committing the new state to an expansive role; they denounced the word as socialistic or communist.[39] One persistent critic asked why had Australia abandoned a straightforward territorial title for a 'verbose, unmeaning and unnecessary title … which implies no tangible entity, but a mere abstract, social—something'.[40] When Queen Victoria saw the word 'commonwealth' she thought 'republic'. Her ministers had to assure her that Australians meant no disloyalty by the name before she signed the Constitution into law.

The entry that won the New South Wales Government prize for a poem celebrating the inauguration of the Commonwealth deals with its name. These are its best lines:

Free-born of Nations, Virgin white,
Not won by blood nor ringed with steel,
Thy throne is on a loftier height,
Deep-rooted in the Commonweal!

The author was George Essex Evans, a Queenslander, and, like Brunton Stephens, accommodated on the government payroll. He was the Toowoomba registrar of births, marriages, and deaths. Had the judges known how much help he had received in composing the poem from his patron Alfred Deakin, they might not have given him the prize. Deakin rewrote a number of lines, and the poet accepted all these corrections. Then on consideration he decided he preferred his own version. But it was too late to restore the poem to its original form. As requested by Evans, Deakin had already had it published in the Melbourne *Argus*. Evans wanted the poem to be in the public arena before Rudyard Kipling's poem on the new Commonwealth arrived. If, as he thought quite likely, they pursued common themes, he did not want to be accused of plagiarising Kipling.[41] He need not have worried. Kipling's poem, as we shall see later, was entirely different from any Australian production.

So the poem entered for the competition was the version published in the *Argus*. It is due to Deakin that it begins 'Awake! Arise! The wings of dawn/Are beating at the Gates of Day!' Evans had written: 'Awake! Awake!'

On 1 January 1901 and for the days before and after newspapers gave over a large part of their space to poetry. There was Evans's prize-winning poem; a new poem by Brunton Stephens, which again reworked the 'she is not yet' refrain of his 1877 work, now very well known; and the words of the anthem sung at the inauguration, which had been written by John Farrell, the author of 'NO'.

These poets are now almost entirely forgotten. The poets of the turn of the century who are remembered, honoured, and read are Banjo Paterson and Henry Lawson. They have helped to define the Australian nation. They were newcomers in the 1890s. The critics, while acknowledging the appeal of their work, regarded it as light, ephemeral verse. Paterson's poems had sold in the thousands, but would anyone keep the book on their shelves? He lacked the nobility, the profundity, and moral elevation thought proper to poetry. Brunton Stephens, who had himself fled from the 'horse-horse-horse' talk in the bush, was generous about Paterson's achievement, but could not believe that poems about racecourses and backblocks life would endure. He regarded William Gay as the true, new poet of the 1890s.[42] Evans conceded that Paterson was a master of the bush ballad, but thought Stephens would always be acknowledged as the founder of the national literature.[43] Of course no one in the 1890s ever imagined that a whole nation could come to treasure a Paterson poem about a Snowy River horseman and a Paterson song about a sheep-stealing swagman.

Historians examining what part nationalism played in the creation of federation find it hard to imagine the founding fathers reciting 'The Man from Snowy River' and assume that nationalism's role was small.[44] They overlook the whole school of nationalist poetry that flourished from the 1870s, whose leading practitioners were in a double sense the established poets of the time. Their reputation stood high, and they were encouraged and supported by leading colonial politicians who became founding fathers of the Commonwealth. When Griffith took to translating Dante he sent his efforts to Brunton Stephens and Essex Evans for their professional criticism.[45] The flier advertising Gay's book of sonnets carried endorsements from Parkes, Barton, and Deakin.[46] When Gay produced a book of essays on federation he attracted contributions from Deakin, Clark, and Griffith.[47]

The nationalism of these poets was a civic nationalism, concerned with the state and the principles and values it should protect and advance; its symbol was female, a young virginal goddess in the classical tradition. The nationalism that grew from Paterson's verse was social and masculine, concerned to honour men of the outback and their values. It was the civic nationalism, now lost to sight, that inspired the federation movement. It was dignified, earnest, Protestant, not raffish, Irish–Catholic or working-class.

In 1977 Australians were asked at referendum to choose a national anthem. 'Waltzing Matilda' was the best known and best loved of the candidates, but when it came to the point a majority found it inappropriate for an anthem. They chose instead 'Advance Australia Fair', not well known and with indifferent words, but in so choosing they put themselves in touch again with the makers of their Commonwealth.

2
Identity

Without a country you have no name, no identity, no voice, no rights, no membership in the brotherhood of nations.

Mazzini[1]

The desire for recognition and a secure identity is a prime force in the movements to create nations.[2] Australian historians who doubt the force of national feeling in federation have looked to economics to reveal the selfish motive behind it. They overlook the motive that is quintessentially selfish and integral to nationalism: the desire for identity and status.[3] The federalist who was most revealing about this was Samuel Griffith.

Griffith came to Australia as a boy of eight.[4] His father was a Congregational minister who gave his bright son a good education in the hope that he would follow him into the ministry. But Griffith would not be bound by his parents' narrow puritanism. His ambition was to become pre-eminent in the law, rich, and famous. There was no open rupture with his parents; the young man kept his exploits with women and drink secret, and outwardly conformed. He took to drinking when he was at university in Sydney; at home in Brisbane during vacations he went with his parents to teetotal meetings. From the start there was something unruffled in his progress. Until his father died he attended the Congregational church and then he switched to the Anglican. Religion did not mean much to him. He invested far more in the Masonic lodge, the codes of which he studied as assiduously as the law and where his advancement was equally rapid.

In politics he was a liberal, the protector of the small farmer, the working man, and the kanakas on the sugar plantations. He was a man of principle, a legal philosopher in politics who could not rouse a crowd but who could argue a case from first principles. He pursued his personal ambition in politics with the same rectitude, as if he were taking only what was his due. He appeared not to see the contradictions and improprieties involved in serving the people and himself. Others noticed and gave him the nickname 'Oily Sam'. In parliament he opposed the importation of kanakas, yet in court he was prepared to defend a ship's captain against a charge of kidnapping kanakas. When he was persuaded that the sugar industry could not

Samuel Griffith as Lieutenant-Governor, displaying all his honours.

survive without kanakas, he abandoned his opposition to them. As Premier he directed the government's legal business to himself and brought his political career to an end in 1893 by getting himself appointed Chief Justice, but only after parliament had increased the salary.

He liked the trappings as well as the substance of success. At 21 he designed the coat of arms that he hoped would be his; at 41 he secured it when he was made a Knight of the Order of St Michael and St George. One of the jobs of Queensland's Agent-General in London was to lobby the Colonial Office for honours for Griffith. After gaining his knighthood, he wanted to be promoted to Knight of the Grand Cross. Once he was Chief Justice, he set his sights on being Lieutenant-Governor as well. On formal occasions he delighted in wearing all his badges and ribbons. He was always well dressed, a tall, spare, dignified figure.

Fortunately Griffith's own estimate of his abilities was correct. He was the most learned lawyer in the country and a superb draftsman. Since the general opinion was that Griffith deserved a high place, he reached his pre-eminence not too much damaged by his efforts to push himself forward. His was a calm self-confidence.[5] Everyone admired the patience and consideration he displayed in steering the constitution through the 1891 Convention. He was rightly proud of his work, but ready to accept improvements and admit mistakes.

It was entirely characteristic that Griffith planned to travel to the Sydney Convention in the Queensland Government's steam yacht, the SS *Lucinda*. When the weather turned bad, he went by train, but the yacht still made the journey and Griffith had the use of it in Sydney. He entertained the delegates on board and took the drafting committee cruising on the Hawkesbury while they got the constitution into proper shape, prompting one of its critics to describe it as a 'whisky and paste' production.[6]

On great occasions, when Griffith was called on to detail the advantages of federation, he spoke, quite uncharacteristically, in a personal and heartfelt way. He said, 'I am tired of being treated as a colonial.' Even when the English were being considerate, he continued, they could not hide their disparagement of the colonist. In the eyes of the world, Australians were nothing but children while they remained colonials. As a nation, they would meet the rest of the world as equals, and the status of every Australian would be raised.[7]

As Premier of Queensland, Griffith was well aware of the difficulties involved in intercolonial cooperation and the advantages union would bring. He was a conscientious administrator. Yet at the deepest level, he wanted federation not so that public affairs might be handled differently, but so that he might be someone different. His assiduous application and lobbying for honours could not prevail against one barrier: there would have to be an Australian nation before Samuel Griffith ceased to be a colonial.

Griffith wanted to constitute an independent Australian nation that would remain in the empire, but without being subordinate to Britain; the only link to Britain would be the Crown. Britain would be an equal and an ally, and all the people of the empire would share a common citizenship. This arrangement was not formally achieved until the passage of the Statute of Westminster in 1931. Legally Griffith could not produce that outcome in 1901, but he had it in mind as he drew up the constitution. When Australia became independent, the constitution did not have to be changed.

Griffith took great satisfaction from the fact that immediately the Commonwealth was established the colonies were to be reconstituted as its states. So the word *colony*, the badge of inferiority, would no longer be used by Australians talking of themselves, nor, Griffith hoped, by other people, particularly the English, in talking about Australia and its people.

In England *colonial* meant 'second-rate' or at least suspect. Australians laboured under a double handicap because *Australian colonist* also suggested 'convict', or the descendant of convicts, or the associate of convicts and their descendants. The Australian rule was not to talk about the convicts—unless to insult New South Wales in intercolonial feuding—but Australians knew that the world had not forgotten. They were very anxious to find and parade signs that the stock had not degenerated despite this taint. Victories over England at cricket were very comforting.

Australians were annoyed by and sometimes angry at British disdain, but they could not easily reject or ignore Britain. Most of them admired Britain and its civilisation and wanted British interest and approval. By the late nineteenth century there was more British interest in the colonies than there had been thirty or forty years before, when the colonies were widely viewed as an encumbrance, but old attitudes persisted. Simple ignorance abounded. People in Britain did not know the names of the various colonies or their location. Letters arrived with bizarre addresses: 'Melbourne, near Sydney, Victoria'.[8] Visitors to England were asked where they learnt to speak English.

In the 1880s the leading colonial politicians, among them Samuel Griffith, were brought into a new relationship with British ministers and officials as they sought to influence the empire's defence and foreign policies. The men who were accustomed to govern their own societies were cast into the role of lobbyists and petitioners at the metropolis. Frequently they found it a frustrating and humiliating experience. They felt themselves very much the colonials. 'We are children', said Griffith, 'dependent on a superior people.'[9] They thought the British did not care enough for them. If their submissions were rejected, their first response was to assume it was because they and the people they represented were mere colonists.

The leading politicians gave as one of the advantages of federation that the colonies would speak with one voice and more notice would be taken of them as a nation. Britain would no longer ignore them. Australians generally would benefit from this increased stature and strength, but so would they in a very particular way as their representatives and spokesmen. They would cease to be colonial politicians. They might be Australian statesmen. It was notable that the founding fathers, having declared that they must limit Commonwealth power and keep the states strong, immediately transferred to the Commonwealth parliament in 1901.

The man who hoped to lead the new nation as Prime Minister was Henry Parkes, an intention clearly indicated by the frequency with which he disclaimed it. He was the best known politician in Australia and the only Australian politician well known in Britain, but he still knew the hurt of being colonial.[10] It was part of his success as a politician that he could fuse his own pursuit of a greater glory with the emancipation of a whole people. In the series of speeches with which he launched his campaign for federation he promised to remove humiliation and slight and bring dignity and pride.

> Instead of a confusion of names and geographical divisions, which so perplexes many people at a distance, we shall be Australians, and a people with 7,000 miles of coast, more than 2,000,000 square miles of land, with 4,000,000 of population, and shall present ourselves to the world as 'Australia'.
>
> We shall at once rise to a higher level; we shall occupy a larger place in the contemplation of mankind, the sympathies of every part of the world will go out to us, and figuratively, they will hold out the right hand of fellowship. We cannot doubt that the chord awakened by such a movement will be responded to in the noble old country where our forefathers' graves are still. All England has awakened with sympathy to this movement through its press.
>
> We shall have a higher stature before the world. We shall have a grander name.[11]

These are the desires that make nations.

It is difficult for us to imagine them at work as we look at the Commonwealth constitution. It does not read as if colonial subjection is being thrown off. In the first place the Australian constitution is encased within an Act of the British parliament. Yet the whole of it—the constitution proper and the Act of Parliament—were Australian productions. When Canada federated in the 1860s, Canadian politicians agreed on broad principles of the union, which they took to London for British officials to make into a constitution that was put to parliament for approval. The draft that Andrew Clark brought to the 1891 Sydney Convention was already in the form of a British Act of Parliament.[12] Griffith used this as his base. No one imagined that British officials would contribute as much as a word to the document.

The Canadian constitution was provided by the British for Canada, and its amendment remained in British hands. The Australian constitution was drawn up in Australia and provided for amendment within Australia. The constitution needed British authority to take effect, but all the British had to do was pass it unaltered through their parliament and thereafter have nothing further to do with it. There is an air of defiance here.

The document was designed to provide for Australian control of Australian affairs. Since federation was a union under the Crown, the provision that the Crown could disallow acts of the Australian parliament had to be there. No one expected it to be used much, if at all. The power of veto was almost a dead letter in regard to the colonies. But why does the Crown feature so prominently at the very heart of the new government? The constitution says that the executive power of the Commonwealth is vested in the Queen and is exercisable by her Governor-General and that the Governor-General is head of the armed forces.

Griffith wrote those words and defended them. They were criticised at the Convention. Henry Wrixon, a Victorian lawyer, said it looked as if Australia was to be a Crown colony, not a self-governing nation, a sentiment echoed many times since. A number of delegates wanted the constitution to make clear that all the executive power of the monarch was to be wielded by ministers responsible to parliament. Griffith's defence was that in law the monarch had those powers; Australia could not expect to remove them, and there was no need for it to do so: in its working the constitution would follow English conventions.

But Deakin pressed him. In Britain there was no written constitution. Australia was writing a constitution but omitting the most important parts of British practice from it. Griffith had trouble seeing the point, although he said he was trying. He was quite definite that 'responsible ministers' could not be included because that was a term unknown to the law. Finally he offered to include some words of reassurance. Executive power would still lie with the Governor-General, ministers would be appointed at the pleasure of the Governor-General, but they would be 'the Queen's Ministers of State for the Commonwealth', which would indicate that they were to be just like British ministers. It was something, but not enough to save the constitution from misrepresentation and savage criticism during the campaign to have it adopted.[13]

Here is Griffith the lawyer at work, and it is hard to see the man who was sick of being a colonial. On other matters it is very evident. He insisted that the states could not communicate with London except through the Governor-General and that they be given the power to alter the office of Governor—their link to the Crown—without Britain's approval. This would ensure that Australia faced the world as a single entity and would never have to bother the British again on constitutional matters. The link to the Crown would be solely a matter for the Commonwealth and controllable by amendment to the constitution. Neither of these provisions was necessary to secure the benefits of union. One gave offence to the states, and the other appeared disloyal. Griffith got them through against stiff opposition. In 1897–98, there was no one who thought them worth fighting for, and they sank without trace. After federation, much to London's annoyance, the states did insist on having access to the British Government, and the governorships did not pass into the states' control until 1986.

The closest thing to a declaration of independence in Griffith's constitution is the limitation on appeals from Australian courts to the Privy Council in London. Constitutional cases and those affecting wider British interests would still go there, but all the private cases could go no further than a new Australian high court. This was a declaration by the lawyers, who were the largest occupational group at both conventions, that they were as good as English lawyers. They were incensed by the suggestion that Australia could not provide judges as learned, experienced and impartial as the English judges. They were not impressed by the quality of some of the English judges and their rulings. Clark had conducted a case before them (on the trip that had enabled him to visit his beloved republics, Italy and the United States). When he arrived in London, the English solicitor retained by the Tasmanian Government told him that it was important to secure a 'good' court as sometimes old fossils showed up on the bench. Clark went to check out the court and found only one of four judges was awake.[14] At the 1897 Convention Josiah Symon, the leader of the South Australian bar, condemned the court by quoting a Privy Council judge. Lord Westbury reported that he had asked another judge why he never came to sit on the Privy Council. He replied, 'I am old and deaf and stupid.' 'That's nothing,' said Westbury. 'Chelmsford and I are very old, Napier is very deaf, and Colville is very stupid, but we make a very good court of appeal none the less.'[15]

Griffith supported the limitations on appeals, but typically his words were guarded. He said he was opposed to appeals going to the Privy Council as it was presently constituted.[16] He was hedging because his attitude could well change if there should be a new supreme court for the empire and should judges from all over the empire be eligible to sit on it. He was taking a central part in the formation of the Australian nation, but his ambitions were not limited to Australia. He was still pursuing imperial honours. Just before Parkes opened his campaign for federation he was contemplating leaving Australia and standing for a seat in the House of Commons. His researches to establish that he was a descendant of Welsh kings were continuing.

The repackaging of himself as Welsh is one of the more puzzling aspects of this enigmatic man. Coming to Australia as a boy of eight, Griffith could have identified strongly with Australia. He was sometimes taken to be native born.[17] His parents were English, and his childhood memories were of England. He was born in Wales, but he had no memory of it because he left before his first birthday, when his father completed a four-year stint as the minister of the *English* Independent Chapel at Merthyr Tydfil. Griffith is a Welsh name, but his father and mother did not identify themselves as Welsh, nor did his siblings. The Welsh ancestors had left Wales some generations previously.

On his first trip to Britain Griffith visited his birthplace briefly and was unimpressed with the 'grimy and dirty' town. On his second trip he did not visit Wales. On his third, when he was Premier of Queensland, a banquet in his honour was given at Merthyr Tydfil. The town was pleased to have a notable son, but the Welsh connection was something that Griffith himself cultivated assiduously from middle age. He wanted to be known in England as Welsh, which was not quite as good as being English, but it indicated very definitely that, although he was a colonial, he did not suffer that extra disadvantage of being colonial-born.

A colonial was suspect for leaving the mother country and being ready to live in a crude society with doubtful associates. The native-born colonial was a degree more alien, lacking the anchor of metropolitan birth and the instincts that were assumed to flow from it. The immigrant colonists, under suspicion themselves, could lord it over the native-born because of the immigrants' superior birth and metropolitan experience. The native-born responded with apology or boasting.

The process began in early New South Wales. In 1824 Hamilton Hume, applying for the job of exploring southwards from Sydney, claimed that he had the necessary skills, 'although an Australian'.[18] (He was actually much superior in bushcraft, and in dealing peacefully with Aborigines, to the

Englishman Hovell to whom he was yoked.) For the boasting, which was equally pathetic, witness a native-born lad, returning from London, declaring he had seen there nothing as fine as Coopers Stores in Sydney.[19] An official discrimination was practised against the native-born since immigrants were favoured by the Colonial Office in land grants and government employment. A native-born wing was part of the movement to achieve self-government.

Self-government for eastern Australia was achieved in the 1850s at the same time as hundreds of thousands of new immigrants arrived to dig for gold. So the day when the native-born would predominate was postponed. In Victoria the new immigrants completely swamped the existing population. For the next thirty years Victoria was run by the gold-rush immigrants. Government, the law, the churches, the press, the trade unions, the schools, and university were in their hands. A native-born man holding a position of importance was a rarity. When Australians were in the presence of men of authority, they heard English, Scots, or Irish accents. Then in the 1880s the children of the gold-rush immigrants reached their twenties. The message that greeted them as they came of age was that they were inferior to their parents. But they were not so inferior that they accepted this slur without protest. Out of this battle of the generations came one of the great forces for federation.

Dealing in stereotypes is now frowned on; creating stereotypes was then the duty of a social commentator. Assessing the fitness of races and the quality of national characters was the preoccupation of the social sciences. The characteristics of the native-born that made their future doubtful were widely agreed on: a love of sport, a disinclination to mental effort, lack of respect for authority, and persistent swearing. Books, learned articles, editorials, and speeches elaborated on these failings, added speculations on the effects of climate and the environment, physical and social, and produced forecasts, more or less insulting, of the future Australian character.[20]

The Collins Street doctor who offered consultations by post on sexual complaints had every warrant for claiming that it was the native-born who were particularly likely to have wasted their vigour and yielded themselves to the temporary sweet allurements of vice. His advertisement read: 'Look at our Australian youth! See the emaciated form, the vacant look, the listless hesitating manner, the nervous distrust, the senseless, almost idiotic expression. Note his demeanour and conversation, and then say, is that a man to leave his footprints on the sands of time?'[21]

The easiest way for the native-born to combat the slurs was to turn the tables on their accusers and claim that the native-born were superior to their

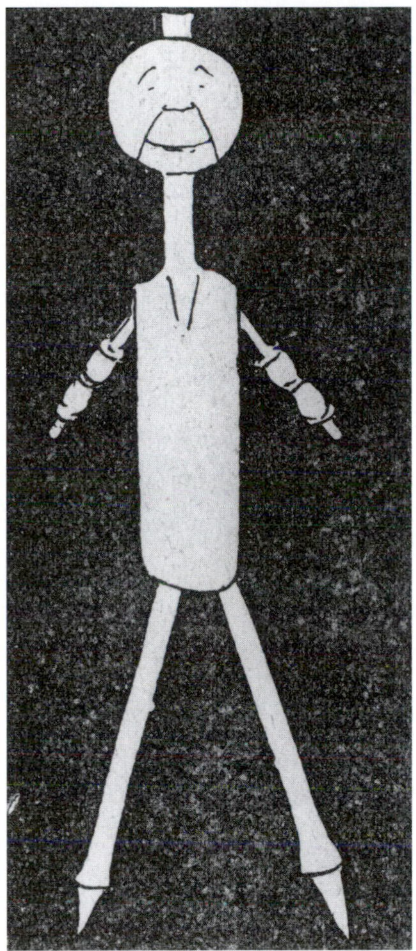

The coming race: *Quiz* in Adelaide comments on the 1894–95 Test Matches.

parents. A few took this line, which quickly led to slanging matches. Most defenders of the native-born stayed on the defensive, producing arguments against the charges. One pamphleteer denied all the failings except the swearing, explaining that a young man saying 'bloody' meant no more than the 'Good gracious' of a lady. Another writer conceded that sporting events were well attended, but produced evidence to show that two-thirds of the crowd at cricket matches were immigrants. Who, after all, taught Australians to like cricket? All the native defenders complained about stereotyping. What about the Australians who were excelling at British universities or were barristers and doctors? Of course it was those who wanted to be more than sports-mad bloody rebels who most resented the slurs.[22]

The exchanges between the generations showed how touchy both sides were. In discussing larrikins, a country newspaper editor accused them of being cowards who only attacked in packs, and put down their behaviour to the lack of respect of the native-born for their elders. He wanted parents to demand instant obedience and use the rod more. A native writing in response claimed that the editor had demonised them all—apparently we are all larrikins. If that were so, the crime rate would be higher, when actually the native-born have a very low crime rate and are the best in the world! And we are not cowards. Although in a peaceful country there is not great opportunity for heroism, natives have risked their lives for their mates in mine accidents. He was pleased Australian children showed more independence. He himself had not been beaten by his parents, and he ascribed whatever virtue he possessed to this fact. Of course, said an immigrant defender of the editor, that explains his arrogance and boasting. Their fathers made the colony, and the boys claim all the credit. The editor denied he was attacking all youth; he was attacking larrikins, who were a blot on Australia's reputation. Is the native champion claiming that there are no larrikins or that they should not be mentioned?[23]

The native champion in this exchange was an office-holder in a branch of the Australian Natives Association. This organisation was the most effective response of the native-born to the institutional and cultural power of the immigrants. Far more offensive than their counter arguments was their running an association to which no one else could belong.[24]

The Natives Association began modestly in Melbourne in 1871. It expanded rapidly in the 1880s, not at first in Melbourne but in the goldfields towns. In the 1870s eleven branches were formed; in the 1880s, 118.[25] Ballarat became the largest branch and the headquarters of the organisation. Nowhere else in Australia was there such a concentration of substantial towns as in Victoria's gold country, nor such a sharp line between immigrant and native-born. The towns had sprung into life at a single instant in the early 1850s; the young immigrants who founded them married in the late 1850s; their children reached adulthood in the 1880s.

The organisational strength of the Association came from its being a friendly society of the usual sort. For a small weekly payment friendly societies provided free medical consultations and sickness and funeral benefits. They were a mixture of an insurance scheme and a men's club. Each member had a voice in the running of the scheme: doctors would tender for the right to service the members and their families, and the members would decide which doctor to accept—and haul him over the coals if he did not give good service. Doctors did not like the friendly societies; they thought too many of their members could afford to pay full fees. There were some business and professional men among the Natives, but the bulk

"FOR LOVE."

Larrikin (executing a step).—"IS MY DARLING TRUE TO ME?"
Larrikiness.—"YES, THY DARLING'S TRUE TO THEE."
Larrikin.—"THEN PAY FOR THESE BLOOMING DRINKS."

The coming race in its ugliest guise: a larrikin and larrikiness.

of the membership came from the lower middle class (clerks, teachers, salesmen) and the skilled working class.[26]

The Natives competed against the societies that had come from Britain: the Oddfellows, Manchester Unity, the Foresters. These societies wrapped up the insurance scheme in secret proceedings, initiations, passwords, and the wearing of regalia. The Natives set their face against all of this; their proceedings had a republican plainness and were conducted with open doors. They boasted that they were a 'national' organisation by which they meant taking no notice of religious and class differences. ('National' carried the same meaning when it was used as the name of the first state schools.) One of the Association's rules was that there should be no religious discussion or allusions likely to excite sectarian feelings.[27] It was acting on the widespread desire that old-world divisions should not be reproduced in the new. In its early years the Natives attracted a substantial Catholic following, but it later fell away as the Catholic Church pressured its members to join Catholic friendly societies.[28]

Local branches met fortnightly. After the sick visitors had reported on whether all those receiving sickness benefits deserved them and after the insurance business was completed, the members devoted themselves to self-improvement. This took the place of the ritual mumbo-jumbo of the old societies. They debated, listened to readings and lectures, and ran mock courts. As young men with their way to make, most of them educated only to primary level, they did want to improve themselves. They also wanted to demonstrate that they were not the stereotypical Australian.

The on-going moral debate in the Association was whether to conduct raffles and sweeps.[29] They did raise large sums for charities, but they also identified the Natives with that other national failing, gambling. It was a matter for great scandal when a mother complained her son had learnt to drink at a Natives 'smoke social'.[30] At a Bendigo branch meeting Mr Lewis proposed that in order to pursue the higher objects of the Association, no intoxicants be served at its social functions. The Natives never wanted to be that pure. The motion was overwhelmingly lost. Mr Murphy withdrew his amendment to add after the word 'intoxicants', 'except the best brands'.[31]

Whatever other responsibilities they had assumed, the young men still thought a lot about young women. While pursuing self-improvement, they found a way to discuss the delights and perils of courtship. The favourite case dealt with in their mock courts was breach of promise, that is, promise to marry. They also debated whether there should be a tax on bachelors and whether married life was better than single. As a progressive organisation, the Natives considered admitting women as members or sponsoring a separate women's organisation. The board of directors was doubtful about both schemes. Single women earned less and tended to go to doctors more than men. They were a poor risk for a health scheme. In 1900 after years of debate the Association founded the Australasian Women's Association.[32] So the Natives remained a men's club.

In the 1880s the Association gave a new meaning to the word *national.* It began to foster pride in things Australian. The Natives promoted the cause of Australian literature and lobbied for the teaching of Australian history in schools. It supported the widow of Marcus Clarke, the author of *For the Term of His Natural Life*, in her efforts to produce the complete works of her husband.[33] Its journal published patriotic verses of the usual standard. The editor of the journal, Jefferson Connelly, a Bendigo lawyer, produced the best of them on the theme of Australia as a new beginning:

So let the Autumn of the old world's strife
With crowded weary souls oppressed by caste
Be here the gladdening spring of free new life,
As broad and unconfined as our blue sky,
Thus makes brave seed time in the hearts of men,
And there shall be a harvest grander yet
Than e'er our earth has known.[34]

This verse embodied the Natives' vision of an Australian nation, their civic nationalism. The new nation would protect and extend a society that offered freedom and opportunity and was free of the division and strife of the old world.

The honouring of Australia Day is the work of the Natives Association. New South Wales celebrated 26 January, but it was not celebrated anywhere else. At the suggestion of the Association, the Victorian Government organised with the governments of other colonies the first national celebration of the day in the centenary year, 1888.[35]

It was a running joke in the Natives Association that they were not the black natives that outsiders sometimes took the term to mean. But those natives were indigenous and hence of symbolic use to the Association. Its members sometimes called their social functions corroborees and appropriated Aboriginal motifs when they were looking to decorate a room in totally Australian style. The refreshment booth at a ball might take the form of an Aboriginal mia-mia.[36] At one conference it was proposed that a boomerang badge be used to identify members. The opposition to any signs or regalia was always strong, and this proposal was laughed off by the suggestion that members should appear in a loincloth of gum leaves.[37] There was no engagement with the Aborigines. In the twentieth century, after federation was achieved, their welfare did become one of the Association's national causes.[38]

The Association grew in a hostile environment. It was accused of ignoring the achievement of the immigrant generation who had given the colony its wealth and its democracy. The Natives responded by showing them elaborate deference, inviting representatives to their banquets and toasting their health, and supporting homes for old colonists. Because it was concerned with Australian culture, the Association was accused of disloyalty to the British Empire and aiming at independence. It was painstaking in constantly affirming that it was loyal and sought only a respected place for an Australian nation within the empire.

Although accommodating and temperate with its critics, it would never yield on its rule that only the native-born could belong. Whatever the Natives said, adherence to this rule had the appearance of claiming superior worth. The rule was contested by a few members within the Association on the grounds that it ran counter to their own national agenda. Why exclude immigrants who shared their national aspirations, especially those who came as babes in arms and children who knew no other home? These moves were always decisively rejected. Members had some trouble formulating arguments against them because they were so flabbergasted. They blurted out that the Association just wouldn't make sense without the rule.[39] Indeed it was not they who first identified the native-born as a special group. They had transformed a point of dishonour into a mark of distinction. Branches that had fudged the rule were told to comply.

The Association paraded the successes of the native-born. During the 1880s several of its own members became members of parliament. The MP in whom they took the greatest pride was Alfred Deakin, who became a sort of mascot of the Association.[40] Deakin was a member, although not active in its affairs, but fully identified as a native-born Australian and shared its nationalist ideals. In 1887, when he was only 30, he led the Victorian delegation to the first Colonial Conference in London. Deakin acquitted himself splendidly and refused the knighthood offered by the British to all the colonial leaders who did not yet have one. (Griffith had gained his the year before.) This refusal marked him as an Australian advocate who would not be seduced by baubles.

Deakin, like the Association that honoured him, was not opposed to Australia's connection to the empire. He was critical of the snobbishness and self-obsession of London's high society; he thought they would have to reform themselves before London could be a worthy capital of the empire he had in mind: a free association of nations of equal standing.[41] This was Griffith's aim too, except that Griffith still thought he might have a place at the centre of the new empire. Deakin had no desire to live anywhere but in his native land.

Deakin went on refusing knighthoods. He even refused an honorary degree from Oxford University, to the chagrin of the vice chancellor, who told him no one had ever refused before, except a man who thought payment was required. No payment was required, he explained, but Deakin still refused.[42] His refusal of English honours was not simply a nationalist gesture; he would have refused even Australian honours if such had existed. He could not have faced the Almighty if he had taken something for himself. However, he did keep the letter of congratulations sent by the Natives on his return from London in 1887. Jefferson Connelly, the lawyer–poet who was now its president, told him: 'It has probably never occurred that the whole body of the young men of a country accepted their representation by one man with such unanimity and looked forward to the outcome with such eager confidence.'[43]

Deakin welcomed home, surrounded by a wreath of wattle.

From the early 1880s the achievement of federation became the preoccupation of the Natives Association. It is not enough to say that it supported federation and campaigned for federation. The Natives *needed* federation. If federation were not achieved, the Association would have failed. Its journal echoed Mazzini in explaining why federation meant so much: '... we are fighting for nationhood—for the right to call ourselves a people; for the right that should be ours by birth—to be called by name and to make that name shine amongst the nations—"Australia".'[44]

FEDERATION

PROSPERITY. UNITY. PEACE.

Australian Natives' Association.

CERTIFICATE OF MEMBERSHIP

This is to Certify that Mr James Corbett
of Mortchup was elected a Member of
the Carngham Branch No 198
on the 25th day of June 1900

President.
Board of Directors

General Secretary

The Australian Natives Association displays its commitment to federation.

Federation could not be gained solely by an appeal to the native-born. They constituted a majority of the population, but many were below voting age. Among adults, immigrants were still a substantial proportion. The unifying appeal was to Britishness, an identity shared by immigrant and native-born. But by the logic of blood and birth, which all accepted, no one had a better claim to own the Australian nation than those born in it. By creating an Australian nation, the native-born would have the final victory over those who had thrown doubt on their origins.

The Natives were well aware of the contradiction of a national organisation having members in only one colony. From 1882 they committed themselves to becoming an Australia-wide organisation.[45] Some branches in other colonies formed without the Association's assistance as members moved there from Victoria. This gave them branches at Charters Towers in Queensland, at Zeehan on the west coast of Tasmania, and at Kalgoorlie, Fremantle, and Perth. Visits from Association leaders and officials helped to launch the organisation in Adelaide, Hobart, and Launceston.[46]

Sydney was resistant to this Victorian export, and much money and effort were expended on forming a branch there. In this much older society, which had not been swamped by the gold rushes, the native-born were already well integrated. Twenty years earlier, natives had been Premier and Leader of the Opposition. Here the complaint that the Natives' birthplace rule was divisive had more force. At their second attempt, the Victorians established an organisation in Sydney in 1888, but it had to agree to allow as members immigrants of ten years standing who identified with Australia.[47] Here as in Adelaide the organisation attracted men of more established reputation who were nationalists and supporters of federation.[48] In Victoria young men made their name in the Association and then were elected to parliament. In Adelaide and Sydney the first presidents were MPs.

In no other colony did the organisation reproduce its Victorian success, which owed so much to that colony's peculiar demographics. Still, in January 1890, the Association was able to gather delegates from all mainland colonies in Melbourne to debate the issues involved in forming a federal constitution for Australia. It was the first body to do so. The politicians began the following month. From the time federation was seriously mooted, the Australian Natives Association was the only organisation to give it consistent and committed support. Barton kept a list of its branches beside him for reference.[49]

The economic interpretation of federation cannot explain such as commitment. In attempting to explain the Natives Association this interpretation reaches its nadir. It describes the Association as a middle-class body—business and professional people—pursuing federation for economic advantage. This is wrong about its social composition and wrong about its driving dynamic.[50]

The committed federalist leaders—Parkes, Deakin, Griffith, Barton, Clark, and others—and the Natives Association were pursuing a sacred ideal of nationhood. They can be thought of as both selfish and pure.

Selfish, in that the chief force driving them was the new identity and greater stature they would enjoy—either as colonists or natives—from Australia's nationhood. Pure, in that the benefit they sought did not depend on the particular form federation took. In a sense any federation would do. They knew of course that interests had to be conciliated and other ideals not outraged; they shared some of these themselves. But they were not mere managers or lobbyists; underneath all the negotiation and campaigning there was an emotional drive. Those who considered only economic and provincial interests when they contemplated federation understood this quality in the federalists. They called them federation-at-any-price men, enthusiasts, or sentimentalists.

It might be objected that these enthusiasts were only a minority. Sometimes the test for the role of national feeling in federation has been how widespread it was. So relatively low turn-outs for the choosing of Convention delegates and at the referendums have been used to indicate that national feeling played a small part in federation. But the role of national feeling is not to be measured by taking the pulse of the community at large. Nationalism has always possessed one section of the population first—whether poets or intellectuals or a new middle class or local officials of an empire. They become passionate for the nation, while the mass of the people remain attached to their chiefs, villages, or provinces and can see no benefit in creating a new government. Nationalism in its creative phase is a minority movement.

3
Barriers

But though our Austral Land is one, and one our tongue and lore,
We're barred apart, though one in heart,
by the curse of the Customs' door.

William Carrington, 'United We Will Be'[1]

It was a tribute to the liberality of the British Empire that it allowed the Australian colonies to treat each other as foreigners. Customs houses stood at both ends of the bridges across the River Murray, each bearing the sign 'Her Majesty's Customs'. One was HM Customs, Victoria; the other HM Customs, New South Wales. Queen Victoria had to consent to this multiplication of herself in order that the colonies should exercise to the full the powers of self-government.

The duties levied by the border customs houses were a great nuisance to the inhabitants of the border territories, especially those along the Murray, where settlement was dense and much business was done across the river. Most intercolonial trade, however, went by sea and did not cross a land border. When these goods came to port the customs officers regarded them as just as foreign as those coming from overseas and made them pay the same duty.

It might be thought that Britain was more stupid than liberal in allowing these barriers to develop. That would be unfair. A British minister had done his best to prevent it. Henry George, the third Earl Grey, Secretary of State for Colonies from 1846 to 1852, was one of the most conscientious and far-sighted men to hold that office.[2] Those qualities made him highly unpopular in Australia. Instead of doing what was normal and customary, he was forever dreaming up special schemes of his own. When Victoria demanded to be separated from New South Wales, he refused to agree

Her Majesty's Customs House at Wahgunyah on the Victorian side of the River Murray in the 1890s; Her Majesty also had a customs house at the other end of the bridge in Corowa, New South Wales.

until some provision was made for an Australia-wide government. Already South Australia and New South Wales levied different customs duties. If Victoria, carved out of New South Wales but closely connected to it, began levying its own distinctive duties, these differences would become a great drag on economic development.

To prevent this, Grey produced an elegant plan. A common Australian tariff, based on that of New South Wales, would be set by a British Act of Parliament; to alter it the colonies would have to meet in a General Assembly, whose constitution was also to be laid down in London. This plan was not well received in the colonies. Just as they were about to gain full powers of self-government, the imperial power was putting new shackles on them. Victoria did not want in the same instant to be separated from New South Wales and then rejoined to it. South Australia did not want to associate with the convict east. Tasmania and South Australia thought New South Wales would dominate the Assembly. When Grey made an adjustment to the system of representation in the Assembly, it did not please New South Wales. There was no national feeling to welcome a national government.

Grey inadvertently created a proto-nationalist feeling by one of his other policies, an expedient unworthy of him: the reintroduction of convict transportation. The men to be sent were allegedly reformed characters because they had spent some time in the new penitentiaries. Grey called them exiles. The colonists called them convicts and set up an intercolonial movement to resist them. After Grey had perpetrated this outrage, anything he proposed was to be resisted. The parliamentary Opposition at Westminster took up the colonists' complaints about the federation plan, and Grey was forced to drop it. Transportation stopped when Grey lost office with a change of government in 1852. He did leave a lasting legacy in Australia, however, for when he agreed that squatters could have leases for their land he insisted that Aborigines should retain the right of access to it.

For the next fifty years the colonies attempted to organise for themselves what Grey had offered to provide for them: a common tariff. Until the 1880s there was no serious proposal for federation. The plan was to form a customs union for which the model was the customs union of the German states—the Zollverein—formed in 1833. On the solid foundation of a customs union, a federation might later be formed, as it was in Germany in 1871. The chief lobbyists for a customs union were the chambers of commerce in the capital cities. The Melbourne chamber was the most active. After the gold rushes, Melbourne was the country's largest city and port, and its merchants and financiers were those most involved in intercolonial business. They had most to gain by the tariff barriers coming down.

The colonies came closest to agreement on a customs union in 1863. Representatives of New South Wales, Victoria, South Australia, and Tasmania agreed on a common tariff, which was to be kept secret until the treasurers of the four colonies presented it to their parliaments simultaneously, on 2 June at 4.30 p.m. Only the South Australian Treasurer kept to the arrangement. The scheme collapsed because New South Wales and Victoria could not agree on how the proceeds of the uniform tariff were to be distributed.[3]

Victoria had the simplest plan: each colony should keep what it collected at its ports. That would mean that Victoria would keep the tax on those goods landed in Melbourne and sent into southern New South Wales, which was much closer to Melbourne than Sydney. New South Wales understandably did not want the Victorian Government to keep taxes levied on its citizens. It proposed that all the revenue collected by the uniform tariff be put into a common pool and distributed to the colonies according to their population—or that some special adjustment be made for the goods sent from Melbourne across the Murray. Victoria refused to consider any of the New South Wales proposals. So New South Wales refused to be held to the agreement on the common tariff, and the scheme collapsed.

At this time there were no customs houses operating along the Murray. In the mid 1850s, just before the colonies achieved self-government, the governors of the three south-eastern colonies reached a customs agreement for the River Murray, which had become an important artery of commerce with the development of paddle steamers. Again it was British officials who took the larger view. They agreed that South Australia should collect customs duties on goods shipped up the river, with the proceeds to be divided between New South Wales and Victoria. Goods crossing the river where it was the boundary of New South Wales and Victoria would pay no duties.[4]

The second part of the agreement was based on the assumption that the flow of dutiable goods north across the river equalled the flow southwards. Very soon, as Melbourne pushed its geographical advantage, that ceased to be so. The Riverina was becoming a province of Victoria. All its spirits, tea, and tobacco came through Port Melbourne, and the Victorian Government pocketed the duties levied on them. Whatever happened with regard to a customs union, New South Wales was determined that Victoria should not continue to enjoy this advantage. At any time New South Wales could open customs houses along the river and start collecting duties, but it preferred to obtain its revenue by direct dealing with the Victorian Government, since collecting duties at the river would antagonise its southern citizens. They were already talking of breaking away from New South Wales, a movement Victoria encouraged.[5]

The case was getting desperate. In the early 1860s Victoria was building a railway to reach the Murray at Echuca. That would give Melbourne and its port a commanding hold over the river districts. The two governments exchanged the sort of diplomatic notes that lead to war. New South Wales reminded Victoria that the border was the southern bank of the River Murray. New South Wales would be within its rights to treat all voyages along the Murray as journeys through New South Wales. Goods passing from Echuca to Swan Hill, both ports on the Victorian side, would be liable to pay duty as imports into New South Wales! Victoria reminded New South Wales that until the last minute the border between the two colonies was to have been the Murrumbidgee, not the Murray. Only by some shady intrigue had New South Wales acquired the Riverina and deprived Victoria of what geographically, economically, and politically belonged to her. As to the current border, it might be on the southern bank, but Victoria would never yield to New South Wales the right to control navigation. Until that claim was withdrawn, there could be no negotiation.[6]

Since Victoria would not come to a settlement, New South Wales opened its customs houses and began to collect duties aggressively. It required Mr Hopwood, the ex-convict who had put Echuca on the map, to pay a huge bond in order to operate his punt.[7] The bond would be forfeit if he ferried smuggled goods to the New South Wales side. It insisted on its right to search all river boats and to seize them if duty had not been paid on their cargo.

The Victorian Government decided to meet this challenge with force. It sent a party of armed police to the river under the control of Inspector Hare.[8] They travelled all the way to Echuca by train, the last rail having been laid a few days before. Hare placarded the town with the message that he would protect all Victorian boats from search and seizure. He met the New South Wales customs officer, Mr Gordon, and in a gentlemanly fashion they informed each other of their instructions. Gordon's orders were to seize all boats. Hare's were to protect boats against seizure. Hare asked Gordon what he would do if he (Hare) prevented him from seizing goods. Gordon replied, 'I would have to shoot anyone who interfered with me.'

Hare determined to meet this challenge. He informed Gordon that he would be shipping goods from the Victorian side along the river and invited him to be present. As the boat was about to leave the shore, Gordon approached declaring, 'I seize this boat in the name of the Queen.' Hare (who held a commission from the same Queen) replied, 'If you put a foot in, I will throw you overboard.' Gordon decided he should telegraph Sydney for further instructions. Sydney backed down. Although it yielded no rights, it decided not to interfere in river navigation. Goods entering New South Wales proper (as distinct from the river) would still have to pay duty.[9]

The collection of duties created much irritation as well as hindering commerce. Travellers were frisked and their luggage searched. Female travellers were searched by male customs officers. One of these lost his cap in the river after a husband took exception to the way he was searching his wife. Mr Gordon announced that the Echuca punt could operate only in civil service hours. Bullockies and drovers who arrived at the river before 10 a.m. or after 4 p.m. had to wait. The punt was finally seized by Mr Gordon for carrying smuggled goods, namely a box labelled 'glass', which turned out to hold perfume and painkiller. Gordon allowed the punt to continue to carry the mail coach, but all other traffic was suspended while he consulted Sydney. Again his government backed down, but at this point negotiations between Sydney and Melbourne began.[10]

It took two years for the governments to reach agreement. Victoria agreed to pay New South Wales a fixed annual sum in lieu of customs duties levied

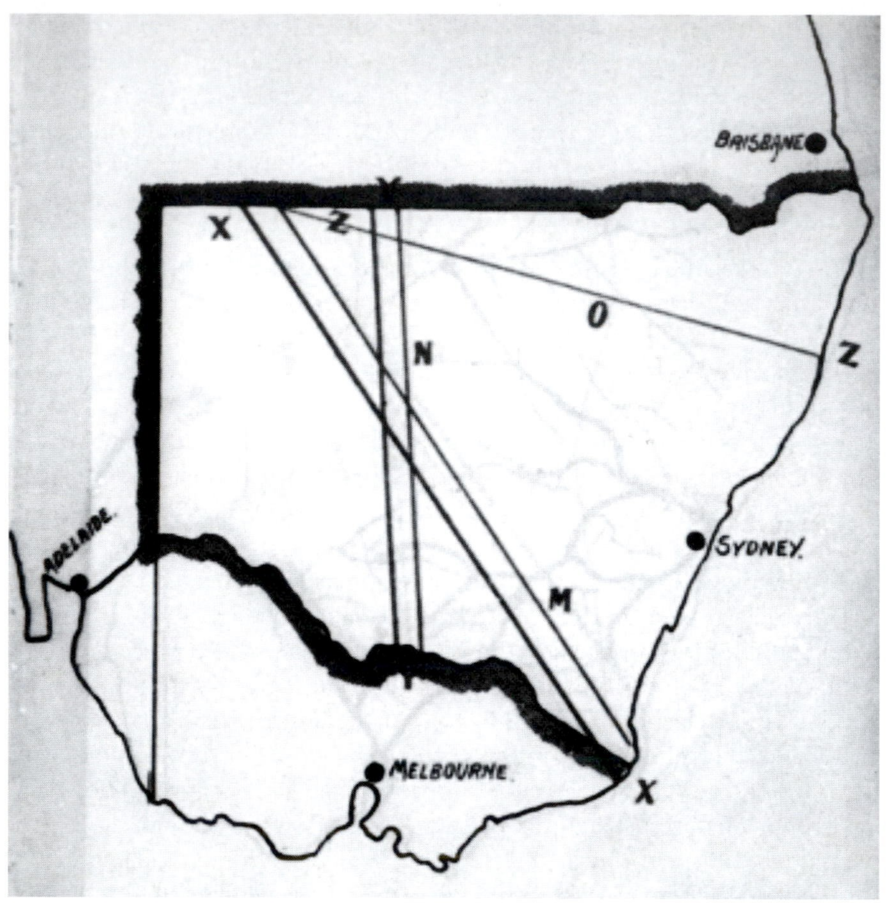

XX—Line dividing the parts of New South Wales lying closer to Melbourne from those lying nearer to Sydney.

YY—The like, as to the parts of our Colony nearer to Adelaide than to Sydney.

ZZ—The like, as to the parts of our Colony nearer to Brisbane than to Sydney.

MNO—Boundary lines of the Reduced New South Wales which would continue to trade with Sydney if Railways were federated.

Sydney's nightmare: federation allows rival capitals to capture New South Wales trade. (L. F. Heydon, *Prudence in Federation*, Sydney, 1897.)

at the border. New South Wales agreed that it did not have exclusive right to control river navigation. The agreement lasted for five years (from 1867 to 1872), was renewed briefly, and then broke down with mutual recriminations about foul play. From 1873 until federation the customs houses operated at the Murray River border. The Riverina settlers, who still did most of their business with Melbourne, were incensed that the New South Wales Government did not reach a settlement with Victoria, but Sydney now had in view the ultimate solution to the Riverina problem. Its railways were heading southwards; the lines reached Albury in 1881 and Hay in the western Riverina in 1882. By offering special low rates for the carriage of goods, the New South Wales railways would induce the settlers to export their wool and import their stores through Sydney rather than Melbourne.

The Victorian assault on the Riverina and the threat to reopen the question of who owned it left a lasting fear of dismemberment in New South Wales. When Parkes launched his federation campaign, he envisaged the new national government controlling the sparsely settled outback in the north and west, encouraging its development, and eventually creating new states. This idea did not reach the 1891 Convention; his fellow New South Wales delegates scotched it immediately.[11] They did not want the national government reshaping Australia for fear that it would partition New South Wales because on three sides, not just in the Riverina, a good portion of its territory was closer to other capitals than to Sydney. So in the Constitution the boundaries of the states were strongly protected. They could not be altered except with the consent of the state parliament, and then, to make doubly sure, a referendum of the people was required as well.

After the mid 1860s, a new and more profound difficulty stood in the way of an Australian customs union. The difference between New South Wales and Victoria over the Riverina was a straightforward clash of interest; when Victoria moved to adopt a protective tariff, the differences between the colonies took on an ideological dimension.

Free trade was the orthodox policy, endorsed by the best economists and followed by Britain. Tariffs were to be used to raise revenue but not to foster local industries. Prosperity achieved by that route was a mirage. To direct resources to industries that could not face foreign competition was to hamper economic development. Protection also gave privileges to some citizens and denied liberty to all. If the state put a tariff on imported boots, it was giving boot manufacturers official protection against competition and forcing everyone to pay a higher price for boots. Boot manufacturers would become a privileged caste; whenever they got into difficulties, they would persuade the state to raise tariffs further and make everyone pay even higher prices for boots.

If citizens were to have equal rights, the state could not play favourites in the economy. That was the doctrine of British liberalism. In Britain it had scored great victories. In 1832 the liberals had reduced the political power of the great landowners by widening the franchise and giving more representation to the great new towns. In 1846 they had removed the landowners' economic privilege by abolishing import duties on foreign grain. No longer did the poor have to pay more for their bread to keep up rents on the great estates. Against this impressive intellectual edifice and these great victories, the Victorian protectionists dared to proclaim a different doctrine. The British political world was turned topsy-turvy. In Victoria liberalism became synonymous with protection. The Victorian liberals were opposed to political privilege; they were indeed thorough democrats, which British liberals were not. They were protectionists because they wanted to produce a secure living for the people. The small farmers who liberals hoped would replace the squatters needed protection from imported South Australian grain. Tariffs on British manufactured goods would assist local factories, which could then give jobs to disappointed gold-diggers.

Victorian liberals became more confident that their doctrine was correct because its opponents were the rich: the merchants who wanted no bar to imports; the squatters who sold wool on a world market and did not want to pay more for imports; and the bankers who financed the squatters. They all told the liberals that protection could not bring prosperity, but they would, wouldn't they? The same message came from every person with any pretence to education. Protection was a delusion, attractive only to ignoramuses and demagogues. The intellectual case against protection did present problems to those liberals who knew the laws of political economy. They took comfort from John Stuart Mill's allowing that protection might be used to enable industries to start. But when protection became permanent, Mill warned that in Victoria, as elsewhere, it created vested interests damaging to the public good.[12]

Victorian protection found its philosopher in David Syme, the redoubtable Scot who edited the Melbourne *Age*.[13] He wrote a book to demolish the central principle of the free-trade doctrine: that the state had no role in shaping the economy. Through the pages of the *Age* he gave liberals their intellectual armoury and their battle tactics. He exercised an unparalleled influence. Syme was personally responsible for converting Alfred Deakin to protection. Deakin was fresh from university, and Syme had hired him to write occasionally for the *Age*. The two men discussed the matter on and off for months, and then in an instant the light dawned for Deakin. He remembered where and when it happened; it was evening, and they were walking across Princes Bridge.

Free trade and protection were not simply ways of pursuing economic interests. Both promised prosperity. They were rival philosophies that men espoused with religious fervour. Free-traders had a vision of international harmony. An open world economy would not only bring prosperity to all but also remove the prime cause of wars. Protectionists had a vision of national greatness. They wanted to keep out foreign competition and build up local industries so that the nation would have a strong and diverse economy. Australia would never be a great and secure nation if it grew only wool and wheat.

The question of protectionism versus free trade was a moral issue. Protectionists called those who imported goods selfish and unpatriotic. Free-traders called factory-owners who demanded protection privilege-seekers and monopolists.

Protection became law in Victoria only after a fierce political struggle.[14] The Legislative Council elected on a narrow property franchise was known to be hostile to it. To make it harder for them to resist, the government tacked protection to its annual Appropriation (Budget) Bill. The Council refused to pass the Bill and so denied the government supply. This was the situation Australia faced in 1975. In 1865 it was played out very differently. The Governor backed the government and assisted it to obtain funds by a shonky arrangement with the banks. The Governor was recalled whereupon a new crisis ensued as the Assembly sought to pay him a pension as a reward for supporting the popular cause. The crisis was finally resolved by the Assembly removing protection from the budget Bill and the Council agreeing to pass it separately.

The Legislative Council put up a determined resistance to all the great liberal measures: cheap land, protection, mining on private property, and payment of members. The campaign for payment of members led in 1877 to a second constitutional crisis even more severe than the first. These traumas had their effect on the Australian constitution. The Victorian liberals at the 1897–98 Convention were the most determined to provide a mechanism for resolving deadlocks between the two houses. On the other side, conservatives ensured that tacking controversial matters on to the budget was forbidden.

Victoria's adoption of protection made its rival, New South Wales, more determined to stick to free trade. Sir Henry Parkes, now ashamed of his early, brief dalliance with protection, was its standard bearer. The senior colony was less likely to be tempted into protection. It had fewer people and much more good land than Victoria. The further expansion of the pastoral industry kept it prosperous. The sale of its public lands to pastoralists was a prime source of government revenue. One reason why protection was attractive to Victorian governments was that having less land to sell they looked to higher tariffs to raise revenue.[15]

Although New South Wales did not systematically protect manufacturing industries, they developed none the less and not very differently from

NEW SOUTH WALES: *I say, old man, why should there be a fence between good neighbours like you and me? Let's knock it down and the others will soon follow suit.*
VICTORIA: *No fear! Not so long as you keep that there pig to threaten my cabbages.*
The Victorian 'cabbage garden' fears the trade policy of its rival. (*Bulletin*, 9 November 1889.)

Victoria's. Whether factories and workshops grew depended as much on the size of the market and the protection afforded by distance from other suppliers as on tariffs. (Despite all the upheaval they occasioned, the Victorian tariffs were not very high.) But the champions of the rival philosophies had to see profound differences between the two colonies. They tortured statistics to demonstrate that one had more factories and greater prosperity than the other, and to make more profound points about the quality of society, they used the statistics of crime and insanity.[16]

Victoria raised and widened its tariff several times. In 1878 it introduced a tariff on a new item: not an overseas import but the sheep and cattle that walked through Queensland and New South Wales to the River Murray crossing places and then to Victorian fattening paddocks and the abattoirs. This was the great trade route of inland Australia, linking three colonies and until this moment taking no account of their borders. To disrupt it with a stock tax seemed to non-Victorians mean and vindictive. This tax made Parkes see red. Here was protection in all its barbarity and inhumanity, turning neighbours into enemies and taxing the people's food.[17] In England it had been bread that was taxed; in Australia it was equally outrageous to tax the chop.

Representatives of the colonies continued to meet to discuss a common tariff and a customs union. The discussions were not extensive. As soon as proceedings began at the 1870 conference Victoria announced that the common tariff would have to be protective like its own. Free-trade New South Wales declared that it could have no part in such a scheme. Victoria then attempted to make a customs union of itself, Tasmania, and South Australia. The two smaller colonies declined. Victoria's terms were outrageous: the other two colonies would have to accept the Victorian tariff in toto and agree that only the Victorian Parliament could alter it.[18]

At the 1880 conference Graham Berry, the demagogic liberal Premier, read a lecture to New South Wales on how it was not strictly true to its free-trade principles. Some of its duties were quite high and could be considered protective. There was thus no question of principle involved in New South Wales agreeing to a protective tariff along Victorian lines. Victoria, on the other hand, was completely principled in its attachment to protection, which it would never give up. Victoria refused even to begin discussions with the other colonies on a common tariff.[19] This arrogance was long remembered against it.

How could a common tariff policy ever be reached? The Melbourne Chamber of Commerce wanted Victoria to moderate its protectionist ardour. That seemed unlikely: import duties, including the stock tax, went on rising. The *Age* wanted all other colonies to become protectionist. Then an Australian union could be formed on the basis of internal free trade and protection against the world. There were encouraging movements in this direction. In the 1880s and 1890s South Australia, Queensland, Tasmania, and Western Australia moved to higher duties, chiefly to raise more revenue. In none of them was there as strong a protectionist movement as in Victoria, and their duties were not as high as Victoria's. But these changes did not produce complete harmony. The protectionists in these colonies wanted to protect their industries against Victoria's. Industries in Victoria were now well established, and manufacturers, having fully met local needs, were looking to sell their products in the other colonies. If the factories and workshops of Adelaide and Brisbane were to get a good start, they would need to be quarantined for a time from Victorian competition. The latecomers to protection wanted protection against the world and their neighbours; they could not be in favour of immediate intercolonial free trade.

In New South Wales free trade would never be readily abandoned. In the mid 1880s a protectionist movement emerged and was met by an organisation to defend free trade. The protectionists were based in the bush and were chiefly interested in protecting small farming, a late developer in this pastoral society. They also expressed the anti-Sydney feeling of country people and collected strong Catholic support because the free-trade leader was Sir Henry Parkes, the champion of Protestantism and the author of the Education Acts that deprived Catholic schools of their funding.

The New South Wales farmers needed protection from grain imported from South Australia and Victoria. So like their counterparts in the other colonies, the New South Wales protectionists were not in favour of immediate intercolonal free trade, although in principle they supported a united Australia with protection against the world. Nor had they yet defeated the Sydney free-traders, who would never consent to join a customs union if it were to be ruled by the Victorian heresy.

After 1880 the colonial governments gave up trying to reach agreement on a customs union. The politicians divided their attention between something much larger—federation—and something much smaller—trade treaties between pairs of colonies. They had no guarantee that the federal movement would be a success and much to suggest that it would fail. Meanwhile treaties among the colonies would bring immediate economic benefit. And trade treaties could be the road to a customs union. And a customs union might lead to federation.

Tasmania was the colony most anxious to make treaties.[20] The other colonies' chief business lay in exporting primary products overseas. Tasmania's primary products—its fruit, hops, oats, potatoes, and timber—relied on markets in Australia. When Victoria went protectionist Tasmania

Intercolonial travellers faced baggage searches until 1901. (*Australasian Sketcher*, 4 October 1887.)

became more reliant on Sydney's market. If New South Wales went protectionist, Tasmania would be in dire straits.

In 1885 Tasmania persuaded Victoria to sign a treaty. Tasmania would drop its duties on Victorian clothing, footwear, and harness in return for Victoria accepting its primary products. The flaw in this arrangement was that Victorians also grew hops, fruit, and oats and cut timber. They set up a clamour against the treaty. Its carriage through the parliament could not have been in better hands. The man to advocate the opening of a chink in Victoria's protective wall was Graham Berry, the old protectionist leader. He said Tasmania's production was tiny and would have little or no impact on the Victorian market; if there was an adverse effect it should be borne for the greater good of getting Victorian manufactures into other markets. To no avail. On this matter the government's majority disappeared, and the treaty was dropped.[21]

Queensland with its tropical products looked a more likely partner for Victoria. Queensland sugar, in which much Victorian capital was invested, was facing competition from European beet sugar. In 1886 the Victorian Premier floated the idea that sugar might be let into Victoria free in return for Victorian products being accepted into Queensland. There was no point, he said, in asking Queensland to accept manufactured goods since it was moving to place a protective tariff on these, but it could take Victorian wheat, wine, and oats. The parliamentary representatives of the Darling Downs farmers moved quickly to scotch that idea. They would not allow their constituents to be ruined by the Victorians in order to prop up the sugar planters. Even Queensland wine found a defender in the Queensland Parliament, although one member was prepared to say that the extinction of that industry would be no loss. Nothing more was heard of the treaty.[22]

There were numerous attempts at treaties. The only other one to move beyond the preliminary stage was between New Zealand and South Australia in 1895. Its unravelling followed the usual pattern. The New Zealand parliament altered the treaty so that South Australian wine would pay half duty rather than none and refused any concession on fruit. The South Australian Parliament threw out the free admission of New Zealand oats and barley; the local growers of these products not being willing to sacrifice themselves to get South Australian wine into New Zealand. After the two parliaments had dealt so summarily with what their governments had negotiated, there was no treaty left.[23]

A step-by-step approach to a customs union would not work either. The colonies were not complementary in their production. They covered large areas and produced a similar variety of products. But more importantly, their governments were at the mercy of democratic parliaments. There was scarcely any grouping that could be called a party in the modern sense, and the highly disciplined voting to which we are accustomed was unthinkable. Members then would not support governments that were attacking the livelihoods of their constituents. The governments that made the treaties were serving the general interest of their people, but when the losers in these deals had such opportunity for disruption, governments could make no headway.

Although the politicians had abandoned it, the Melbourne Chamber of Commerce still pursued the customs union. If Australia had become a nation by first forming a customs union, the name of Benjamin Cowderoy would be inscribed in our history books. He was the secretary of the Chamber of Commerce for twenty-five years and was responsible for the customs-union campaign. He negotiated with chambers in the other colonies, organised conferences, and lobbied governments. Cowderoy was one of those stalwarts who come to embody the institution they serve; he *was* the Chamber of Commerce. When he retired as secretary in 1889 the council of the Chamber had his portrait painted in oils and presented it to the National Gallery. He stayed on as a member of the council since he was a businessman in his own right: an expert land-valuer and dealer. In 1893–94 he was the Chamber's president.[24]

In 1883 Cowderoy produced a pamphlet detailing the unsuccessful efforts of the chambers of commerce and the colonial governments to achieve a customs union or more limited commercial agreements.[25] But this exercise did not dislodge from Cowderoy's mind the notion that Australia would be united first by a customs union. Nothing would draw him away from this plan, not even his own demonstration of its failures. Nor did his own or his chamber's failures in the next fifteen years have any effect. Defeated again and again, he would simply try harder.

In the 1880s the Chamber of Commerce had a new ally, the Chamber of Manufactures.[26] In the great battle over the tariff, merchants and manufacturers had been on opposite sides. But the Chamber of Commerce had had to reconcile itself to Victoria's attachment to protection. It was still in principle in favour of free trade, and it campaigned for a customs union to secure free trade within Australia. The Chamber of Manufactures also wanted intercolonial free trade and, in addition, protection against the world. That outcome of a customs union the Chamber of Commerce was prepared to wear.

The two chambers cooperated and in the late 1880s organised intercolonial conferences of chambers of commerce and manufactures that passed resolutions in favour of a customs union. These resolutions must

A failed father of Australian union: the oil painting of Benjamin Cowderoy of the Melbourne Chamber of Commerce.

not be set down as resolutions in favour of federation. When these businessmen declared for a customs union, they meant a customs union.[27] They were explicitly opposed to working for federation; that might be an ultimate goal, but a customs union must be established first.[28] Benjamin Cowderoy had an unhappy time as president of the Chamber of Commerce because he failed to prevent a revival of interest in federation.[29]

The merchants and manufacturers were opposed to the federal movement because they thought federation was too difficult. The politicians who talked of federation were wasting everyone's time; they would not achieve it, and meanwhile the immediate benefits that could be secured by a customs union were being lost. These men were, as they boasted, practical men, and they wanted results.

One can see why practical men were drawn to this approach. Everyone agreed that a customs union would be part of a federation. The poets quite as much as the businessmen wanted to abolish the border customs houses. Since agreement on customs policy would have to be secured to achieve federation, why not reach agreement on that first? Reduce the size of the problem; don't write a constitution, negotiate a commercial treaty; move step by step.

The merchants and manufacturers fantasised that they would themselves reach agreement on a customs union and show the politicians the way.[30] This they were totally unable to do. Their resolutions in favour of a customs union papered over their differences and led to no detailed plan. When the manufacturers met in 1887, the Adelaide representatives dissented from the Victorian plan for a customs union because they feared the Victorians.[31] When the merchants met in 1888, the Sydney merchants registered their dissent from its resolutions.[32] They wanted no part of a customs union that would adopt a policy of protection against the world. That was not the wish of the Melbourne Chamber of Commerce, but Sydney knew that Melbourne merchants did not speak for Victoria. No progress was being made to resolve this difficulty. The intercolonial conference of chambers of commerce in 1869, twenty years before, had ended in the same way: a resolution for a customs union from which Sydney delegates dissented.[33]

Dealing only in economic interest, the chambers could not reach agreement about the larger economic interest that union would serve. The practical men did not produce the customs union; it was the work of poets, politicians, and patriots, and came as a by-product of the creation of a nation, about which businessmen were not prone to dream.

Movement

4
Confusion

There are in the life of nations periods when processes are silently at work, which the mass of living men never see, and which are only detected by the clearest sighted and the most philosophic observers.

Sir Henry Parkes, New South Wales Assembly, 21 November 1888

As the poets sang, Australia was pure, set apart, free from old-world rivalries and wars. That this was due to physical isolation or divine favour were pleasing illusions. Australia enjoyed its peace because the old-world power responsible for the continent was much more powerful than the others.

From the 1880s British supremacy was under challenge. In 1884 Bismarck, Chancellor of the new united Germany, reversed course and announced that he would be claiming territory around the globe. He planned to have an overseas empire as Britain and France did. Bismarck's new interest in colonies made Britain and France even more interested in colonies. The three powers began a contest to seize territory. Britain also faced an economic challenge from Germany and the United States, which, having industrialised later, were more efficient in the old industries of iron and steel and more adept than Britain at the new industries of chemicals and electricity. In a more hostile world, British policy-makers and exporters began to think that the colonies might be their salvation.

In April 1883, before Bismarck officially announced his interest in colonies, the Premier of Queensland, Thomas McIlwraith, moved to forestall him. Suspecting that Bismarck might have designs on New Guinea, McIlwraith ordered the police magistrate at Thursday Island to go to Port Moresby and claim the eastern half of the island for the Queen. McIlwraith did not want a hostile power controlling the northern shores of Torres Strait, a vital shipping lane for Australia, and especially for Queensland.[1]

In the politics of Queensland, McIlwraith was Griffith's great rival. He was a bold entrepreneur with his own fortune invested in pastoral property and mining ventures. He was captivated by the prospects of Queensland's development and scorned the limitations that Griffith wanted to place on it. His policy was to permit kanakas to work the sugar plantations and to allow

ANNEXATION—CARRYING THE BENEFITS OF CIVILIZATION INTO NEW GUINEA. Gladstone, the British Prime Minister, took the same view of Queensland's annexation as the radical Sydney *Bulletin*: a cartoon by Hop published on 9 June 1883.

private companies to build railways in return for grants of land along their route. The colonists in the south favoured Griffith's approach, but this did not tell against McIlwraith when they learnt of his daring New Guinea coup. He became an Australian hero.

But would the British Government accept the new territory from his hands? The Secretary of State for Colonies was not unsympathetic, but the government was led by Gladstone, the great liberal statesman who believed in free trade and economy, and who was opposed to further growth of the empire. When his good friend Sir Arthur Gordon, High Commissioner for the Western Pacific, told him that McIlwraith was interested in New Guinea as a source of cheap black labour—which might well have been the case—his mind was made up. Queensland's annexation was disallowed.

Indignation and rage swept through the Australian colonies. This was the nightmare moment for loyal colonists. The mother country was betraying them.

At the same time the Victorian Premier James Service was picking up rumours that France intended to occupy the New Hebrides (now Vanuatu). That would give a potentially hostile power another base near Australia (France already held New Caledonia). It would also put a Catholic power in charge of the islands' Presbyterian missions, which were staffed and supported by Victorian Presbyterians. They were a powerful lobby, demanding action of Service and rousing public opinion against the French.

The French were already sending small numbers of convicts to New Caledonia. In July 1883 news came that 20,000 of the worst convicts were to be sent there, and if New Caledonia could not accommodate them all, the New Hebrides would be taken for the same purpose. Convicts escaping from New Caledonia were a minor nuisance to New South Wales and Queensland; now there would be more escapees, but that was not the cause of the Australian outrage at the French proposal. The super-sensitive Australians could come to only one conclusion: the French must believe polluting the South Pacific with convicts did not matter because it had a notable precedent for doing so. Australia's convict origins were being thrown in its teeth.

Service now led a movement to persuade Britain to annex all the islands, from New Guinea to Fiji, including the New Hebrides, New Ireland, and New Britain. He and McIlwraith planned a national convention of the colonies to put more pressure on Britain and to plan a federation, because Australia needed a national government to deal with this crisis. The new government would provide Britain with the funds to administer the islands (the expense of new possessions was always a worry to Gladstone) and eventually take them over as Australian territory. At

McIlwraith's insistence, Service took over leadership of the cause. 'Federation and all the islands' was his slogan.

A determined move to create a federation had commenced. It was prompted by fear of external threat and so fitted the common pattern of federation movements. It was most unusual, however, in that a principal aim of the colonies planning a federation was to involve the imperial power more closely in the defence of their interests. Australia would speak to Britain with one voice and not be denied.

This was not the way Australian federation was meant to have happened. The expected—the natural—course of events was that as the colonies grew stronger they would have less need of Britain; they would combine into a nation that would look after itself and gradually break its ties with the mother country.

The new external threats, coming before Australia could deal with them on its own, were very destabilising. Something new had to be done, but since old assumptions had been overturned, the colonists were floundering, divided over what they should do, unsure where their plans would lead, and thinking the worst of schemes different from their own. A nation with ties to Britain seemed to many a contradiction in terms. They could not comprehend it or refused to accept it. No one could be confident of what it would be like. Would membership of the empire assist the new nation, or would the new nation be made to minister to Britain's interests? Some thought that to form a nation must threaten loyalty to the empire; others that a nation within an empire could be no true nation.

Broadly the colonists took up three positions on Australia's future. The imperial federationists, responding to a movement initiated in Britain, wanted to bind Britain and its self-governing colonies together in a federation. The nationalists loyal to the empire wanted to create an Australian federation within the empire. This was Service's position and that of nearly all the founding fathers of the Commonwealth. The independent nationalists wanted a federation outside the empire, if not now, then sooner rather than later.[2] In different ways all wanted to escape colonial inferiority and gain greater security and recognition. They were closer to each other than they imagined.

The imperial federationists wanted to stop a drift to separation and to give the colonies more influence over imperial policy. To independent nationalists they were traitors. The nationalist spirit was to be quenched, and Australia yoked to wicked imperial purposes. The new tree, just coming into bud, was to be torn up by the roots. Indeed, halting the rise of Australian nationalism was initially one of the aims of the local Imperial Federation League. Its founding president in Victoria was worried by the

LITTLE RED RIDING HOOD AUSTRALIA: *O, Grandmother, what nice imperial teeth you have!*
GRANNY DOWNING STREET: *All the better to eat you up with, my little colonial dear.* (Phil May, *Bulletin*, 23 April 1887)

Australian Natives Association. The Natives might express loyalty to the empire, but their harping on Australian virtue and cultivating an Australian sentiment could have only one result. He reasoned that since the first generation born in Australia could not have the same love for Britain as those born there, a concerted effort was needed to hold it to the empire.[3] He could not imagine that love for an ideal Britain might become stronger than for the real one. The league was supported by well-off and successful immigrants (some of them now returned to Britain) who did not want to see the next generation wreck their patrimony.

The nationalists who denounced the imperial federationists reacted to the word *imperial* and refused to look at *federation*. The imperial federationists were not simply scampering back to Mother; they wanted to have some control over Mother. A federation is a union of equals. The imperial federationists in Melbourne showed their independence by refusing to remit subscription fees collected locally to England.[4]

The imperial federationists soon dropped their opposition to Australian federation and supported a double federation—of Australia and of the empire—with some ambiguity over which should occur first. That made them more interesting to the loyal nationalists who wanted an Australian nation to remain within the empire and exert a strong influence over its foreign and defence policies. They concluded, however, that imperial federation simply could not deliver what it promised. Imagine an imperial parliament sitting at Westminster: how many seats would Australia have? It might be able to put its case, but it could be easily swamped and forced to support policies against its interests. And what if the teeming millions of India were to have seats as well and vote on Australian migration policy? The loyal nationalists wanted not only to secure the strength of the empire connection but also the right to insist on some policies, with the unstated threat that Australia would leave the empire if need be.

After the notion of an imperial parliament had been subject to such severe criticism, the imperial federationists dropped it. Instead they said the British people around the globe should be able to develop some satisfactory mechanism to bind the empire together; perhaps an imperial council where leaders of all the self-governing colonies would meet. This brought them closer to the position of the loyal nationalists.[5]

Until Australia was obliged to make a decision on its connection with the empire, there was widespread sympathy for the independent nationalist position. If you believed in Australia's future, you could not imagine it remaining forever subordinate to the mother country. When its population was greater than Britain's or when it was as great as that of the United States, it could have no position other than as an independent nation. To imagine a republican future for the country was almost an obligation of patriotism.[6] In this sense many Australians were practically loyal and theoretically republican. A scattering of people in high positions were declared republicans, but this did not cause outrage because for the moment loyalty to the empire was very strong and there might be a time—it could be quite soon—when republicanism was perfectly appropriate.

But separation from Britain was clearly not appropriate in the mid 1880s, when only Britain could put a stop to the Germans and the French, and empire loyalty was still strong. Everything was happening too soon. The independent nationalists knew deep down that immediate separation was not a realistic option, but they could not bring themselves to support closer ties with the empire. For some, like the Irish, this was because they hated Britain; for others it was because they loved Australia and what it might become, and in those dreams an old-world empire simply had no place. Since the independent nationalists had no sure path to follow, they were highly volatile, looking for ways to register their dismay.

The independent nationalists had some connection with a fourth group, the radical republicans. These were almost all newcomers to Australia, working-class immigrants of the 1880s who brought republicanism with them from Britain. They were republicans not because they were Australian nationalists—they were fresh off the boat—or because they considered separation from Britain the best course for Australian foreign policy, a subject in which they took no interest. They were republicans because the ideal society should be republican, just as it should be socialist. They objected to the Queen because of her privilege and wealth.

In Sydney in the mid 1880s there was a lively counterculture of these people, socialists, republicans, free thinkers, and land nationalisers. Louisa Lawson fell in with them when she came to Sydney in 1883, leaving her husband behind in the bush. When her son Henry joined her he was immediately caught up in radical activity. He could scarcely avoid it since the cranky old printing press that produced the *Republican* was housed in his mother's cottage.[7]

Henry was a true nationalist. He was born in Australia and knew the rhythms and heartaches of country life:

Our Andy's gone to battle now
'Gainst Drought, the red marauder:
Our Andy's gone with cattle now
Across the Queensland border.

He also knew the Australian ideas that would have to be exploded before socialism had a chance: 'They lie, the men who tell us for reasons of their

Mother and son: Louisa and Henry Lawson.

own/That want is here a stranger and that misery's unknown.' In 'The Song of the Republic' he insisted on a choice that the loyal nationalists said did not have to be made:

Sons of the South, make choice between
(Sons of the South, choose true)
The Land of Morn and the Land of E'en,
The Old Dead Tree and the Young Tree Green,
The land that belongs to the lord and the Queen,
And the land that belongs to you.

The strength of the different views on Australia's future varied in the different colonies, as did the strength of national feeling generally. In Victoria national feeling was strongest and almost uniformly loyal. Its society was now remarkably cohesive and gave strong support to its Premier's campaign for federation. The bitter political divisions between liberals and conservatives were over. They combined in a grand coalition, which Service led and which governed throughout the boom decade of the 1880s. Working men, who had acted with their employers to obtain and defend protection, had an assured place in the polity. They were strong enough to prevent governments from spending on immigration. So in Victoria there was no importation of radical republicans; they went to New South Wales and Queensland, whose governments were still subsidising immigration.

The divide in Victorian society was between the immigrant generation still in control and the native-born. This social division had prompted the formation of the Imperial Federation League, which only in Victoria operated as an organisation, but on the annexation issue the Australian Natives were enthusiastically supporting their elders. Their long campaign for federation began with their rallying around Service, who was a Scots merchant.

Service did not appear loyal when he was denouncing the imbecility and laziness of English cabinet ministers, views that came fairly readily to a Scotsman. The Colonial Office certainly thought him disloyal. But he was loyal to his ideal of empire, which was one that would protect the interests of all its parts. Service was a strong supporter of the Imperial Federation League.[8]

Even before his Convention met, Service found New South Wales lukewarm. Its government had joined in the protests to Britain about New Guinea and the French plans, but there was little enthusiasm for Service's demand that all the islands be annexed. Sydney had nearly all of the Australian trade with the islands and saw no need for them to be owned by Britain for business to continue. In the free-trade colony opinion was less hostile to Gladstone's free-trade and no-annexation government, which Service was denouncing as criminally negligent. The New South Wales Government was more obviously loyal to Britain; in the parliament and among the people independent nationalism was much stronger than in Victoria.

New South Wales also had its own patriots who saw no need for an Australian nation because New South Wales was a nation or would become so. Their leader was old John Robertson, who made his name as a radical land reformer in the 1850s. He had a simple formula for Australian union: the colonies that had left New South Wales should return to it. Victorians hated him for calling their colony 'a cabbage garden'. From Robertson and the geebung patriots came the greatest suspicion of Victoria. The upstart colony, the bully boy of the group, was now playing the nationalist card for its old ends: a national protection policy, a rearrangement of colonial borders, and a general plundering of New South Wales.[9] Certainly national protection was still a Victorian ideal, and the *Age* still talked of taking the Riverina, but Service was passionate about federation because he feared that the opportunity of creating a new nation free of big-power conflict was slipping away.

The Convention met in Sydney in November 1883. The proceedings began with a dispute over what this gathering should be called. Service and McIlwraith had called it a *Convention* because they wanted it to plan a constitution. The government of New South Wales preferred the less exalted term *conference*. The New South Wales delegates lost that battle, but they were able to water down Service's proposals. Instead of demanding that Britain claim all the islands, the Convention requested that it prevent all other powers from doing so, except for New Guinea, which they were united in thinking must be British. This was still a bold enough claim to outrage both Gladstone and Bismarck. The Convention planned not a true federation but a federal council composed of representatives from the various parliaments, which could pass laws on a few matters of common interest. The two major matters were relations with Pacific Islands and the influx of criminals; the others were minor matters like fisheries and serving court summonses across the colonial borders. There was to be no federal government and no federal budget. The vexed issue of the tariff was not tackled at all.

New South Wales delivered two near-fatal blows to the Federal Council: it ensured that it had few powers and then refused to join it. Some of its opponents in New South Wales claimed that any federal body would threaten the colony's interests. It was to appease these that the Council's powers had been reduced. But reduced too far, said the other objectors. New South Wales might deign to submit to a true federation but not to a pipsqueak council. This was the argument advanced most forcibly by Sir Henry Parkes. He was out of office and had played no part in the 1883 Convention. He himself had proposed a federal council in 1881, but now he claimed that the Federal Council would impede the formation of a true federation.[10]

More than two years elapsed before the Federal Council was operational. It held the first meeting of its inglorious career at Hobart in January 1886 with no delegates from New South Wales or South Australia. Meanwhile, by the agreement of the Convention, Service continued to lead the movement for the annexation of the islands.

Gladstone's stocks plummeted further in Australia in 1884 when Bismarck took the northern half of New Guinea. So McIlwraith had been right all along—except that Bismarck might well have been provoked by the Australian doctrine that only Britain could claim Pacific islands. Unbeknown to the Australians, the British Government was on the point of claiming all of eastern New Guinea when Bismarck declared his interest. The two powers then agreed to partition the territory, with Britain taking the southern half. Britain could not afford to offend Bismarck because it needed German support for its control of Egypt, where the French were its opponents. Of considerations like these, which weighed heavily on British policy, Service was completely oblivious. He demanded that Britain reverse the German takeover of northern New Guinea.

The British were attempting to satisfy the Australians over the French threats in the Pacific. Since the colonists evidently disliked convicts so much, the British urged them to accept a French offer that would allow France to claim the New Hebrides in return for abandoning convict transportation.

Only New South Wales would accept this deal. The other colonies wanted no French convicts and no French annexation, and could not understand why Britain could not secure both. So the issue dragged on, with Service watching the French narrowly and firing off a withering cable to the mother country when danger loomed. He wished he could do more. He developed the odd argument that the colonies were handicapped by their membership of the empire; otherwise they could have taken on the French directly.[11] This might have been seriously meant and not just a threat to push Britain into action. Later in the 1880s the Victorian Government did briefly contemplate landing its own troops on the New Hebrides.[12] Service was not a diplomat or a careful weigher of the balance of power; the founder of Australian foreign policy was a passionate nationalist angry that Britain was ignoring Australia. In Sydney's governing circles, they thought he was mad, which is how nationalists appear to those who are not.[13]

In 1885 the government of New South Wales found the opportunity to show how its approach to Britain was different from Victoria's. The Premier, William Dalley, a Catholic and the child of Irish convict parents, offered New South Wales troops to serve with British forces in the Sudan.[14]

Gladstone's government, although opposed to more imperial entanglements, had been drawn deep into the internal affairs of Egypt whose government it was propping up. It was involved in the suppression of a Sudanese revolt against Egypt led by a Muslim leader, the Mahdi. When the Mahdi killed General Gordon, an upright and pious servant of the British Empire, Gladstone had to yield to the clamour that Gordon be avenged and the Mahdi's movement crushed.

His government wished that New South Wales had not made its offer to join in, but felt it could not refuse. A gracious acceptance was sent, to which the Queen added her own message of thanks, and Sydney went wild with the excitement of fighting, of being accepted by Britain, of becoming known in the world. Two hundred thousand people, two-thirds of the city's population, turned out to see the troops leave. In Britain the offer brought surprise and pleasure; the colonies were loyal after all and perhaps the empire might become one fighting force. When Dalley died three years later, the Imperial Federation League in Britain arranged for a tablet to be erected in St Paul's Cathedral that honoured him as a defender of the empire. He was more than that, or rather he was redefining the empire. His offer of troops was also a test: Will you accept us? Are our soldiers worthy to fight with yours? Are we colonists or partners? It was also an implied contract: since we are willing to fight for you, you must be prepared to defend and protect us.

The Sudan contingent departs from Sydney.

So Dalley's help had a similar purpose to Service's protests, which Service immediately recognised. He offered a Victorian contingent, which was politely refused, as were the offers from South Australia and Queensland. Swallowing his disappointment, Service saluted Dalley as a statesman who had 'precipitated Australia in one short week from a geographical expression to a nation'. Not for the last time, national self-confidence was boosted by participation in Britain's wars.

The enthusiasm for the New South Wales contingent was unbounded, but not universal. Sir Henry Parkes opposed it. It was hard for him to allow that a national movement was worthy if he were not at its head, and, furthermore, Dalley was an old opponent. His chief objection was the sending of the men without parliamentary approval, but he also sounded like an independent nationalist when he said there was no need for Australia to risk its sons in a doubtful war of aggression when there was so much to be done at home. At this time Parkes was out of parliament and rapidly approaching his third bankruptcy. He had tried again to set himself up as a commercial agent, but politics was the only trade at which he excelled. Members of parliament were not paid, but ministers were paid handsomely. That thought must have been in his mind when he stood at a by-election as an opponent of Dalley's policy. He won the seat narrowly, but that should not be taken as a vote against the contingent, for constituencies welcomed the chance to be represented by a leading politician.

By that time parliament had given retrospective approval to the contingent. Only two members opposed it outright, but twenty-three were ready to censure the government for acting without parliamentary approval, and behind that move lay more covert opposition to the contingent itself.

The most damaging critic of the Sudan contingent was the Sydney *Bulletin*, which was just getting into its stride as the first national weekly. Under the slogan 'Australia for the Australians' it wanted nothing to do with the rottenness of Britain and its empire. Like the radical republicans, the *Bulletin* borrowed much of its policy from British radicalism but found its own distinctive Australian voice. Radicalism was a rollicking send-up of all that was sacred. The Queen, the empire, Government House, knighthoods, the churches, men in top hats: all were regularly pinioned by sharp paragraphs and lampooned in cartoons.[15]

The *Bulletin* argued against the contingent, but it also poked fun at the 800 men who had been gulled into this absurd enterprise. It took a great risk, for what if the soldiers should perform great feats of valour and die in defence of the empire? The joker's luck held. The men saw scarcely any action and spent most of their time guarding navvies building a railway. Gladstone had no wish to prolong this war and soon found a need to transfer the British troops to India to guard the frontiers against Russia. Dalley wanted to send his men with them, but the feeling in the colony was that if there was to be a war with Russia the men of New South Wales should be at home. So they came back to Sydney after only four months away. The *Bulletin* was merciless. No enemy dead, no heroes, no widows and orphans to benefit from the Patriotic Fund, no trophies except a donkey. After such a huge anticlimax, the expedition became difficult to defend. The independent nationalists became very cocky about the mistake of sending troops to an imperial war.[16]

Meanwhile the willingness of Australians to contribute troops gave encouragement to British policy-makers who were developing plans for integrated imperial defence. Colonies had developed their defences haphazardly; they were now to be reviewed and colonies encouraged to reorganise for a more efficient and better coordinated effort. For sea defence, the Admiralty wanted the Australian colonies to abandon their minuscule navies and contribute funds to secure a larger British fleet to operate in Australian waters. This was the issue that would bring the conflict over Australia's future to a head.

It was listed to be settled at the first Colonial Conference held in London in 1887 to coincide with Queen Victoria's jubilee. Gladstone had lost office; the conference invitations came from a Conservative Government led by Lord Salisbury. The Conservatives had long been more enthusiastic about the empire than the Liberals, and in holding the conference they were responding to the new concern to bind the empire more firmly together.

Griffith, Premier of Queensland since 1883, was the senior Australian representative. Parkes, who was again Premier of New South Wales, sent others to represent his colony. Service was present as elder statesman, having given up the premiership of Victoria for the sake of his health the year before. Deakin led the Victorian delegation, which was a striking fulfilment of a prophecy made to him seven years before by a spiritualist medium that before long he would be in London representing Victoria before the highest tribunal of the land. This was the clearest sign he had received that he was being directed for some great purpose.[17] He rose to the occasion and was the most defiant of the Australians when the Prime Minister and the Secretary of State for the Colonies tried to talk them out of their obsession with the New Hebrides.

Deakin's response to Salisbury's worldly-wise, condescending speech became legendary. Quite full accounts were leaked to the press. Griffith, who was overshadowed by Deakin at the Conference, hinted that Deakin himself had boosted his reputation by this means.[18] Here is part of the speech as Deakin gives it in his own book:

> We were reminded that the French were a proud, high-spirited and powerful nation, perfectly prepared to defend their rights by war if necessary. Had then the colonists come thousands of miles to learn that Great Britain was no longer proud, nor high-spirited and was not prepared to defend the rights of her people or to resist unjust demands? If so, it was a most unfortunate but very impressive manner of teaching the lesson ... the people of Victoria would never consent to any cession of the islands on any terms.[19]

Salisbury displayed more admiration than annoyance at his speech being answered point for point in this *tour de force*. Deakin reports—and here his vanity got the better of him—that a few nights later Salisbury forced his way through a packed drawing room to whisper to him that the ambassador in Paris had been given instructions not to yield to the French.

The dispute still remained. On this matter Deakin took home no great victory, but he was received as a hero none the less. To have their representative confront the British Prime Minister, to see him speak uncompromisingly for Australia: this was enough to convince the Victorians that there was no danger in the imperial relationship and that a nation within the empire would give them all they could want.[20]

The Conference accepted that the colonies would contribute to the cost of new cruisers for Australian waters. The ships would be under British command but could not be removed from Australian waters even in time of war without the colonies' consent. The agreement had to be ratified by the colonial parliaments. The *Bulletin* was confident they would reject a deal that it alleged the British had secured by bribing the delegates with knighthoods.[21]

The Victorian Parliament accepted the arrangement unanimously. In New South Wales and Queensland the independent nationalists put up a determined opposition supported by reputable daily newspapers, the *Daily Telegraph* in Sydney and the *Courier* in Brisbane, as well as the disreputable *Bulletin*. In New South Wales after an all-night sitting eighteen members voted against the Naval Bill and fifty for. The Noes gave three cheers for Australia to which the Ayes responded with cheers for Old England. The Queensland Assembly refused to pass the Naval Bill. Griffith was mortified. He had been closely involved in the negotiations over the plan and at the Conference had played a mediating role in the settling of the terms. Now his own parliament disowned him and the agreement he had made in London. He thought of resigning and sounded out the views of the Secretary of State for Colonies. He absolved Griffith from any imputation of bad faith and urged him not to resign.[22]

The opponents of the naval agreement had only to oppose. They did not want imperial entanglements hobbling the nation's development, but they were not strong on what the colonies should do instead. Many, refusing to accept that circumstances had changed, simply repeated the old truisms that Australia was safe and would soon be a large nation well able to look after itself. They argued that the British connection was more a handicap than a benefit since Britain would drag the colonies into wars in which they had no interest. The supporters of the scheme admitted that this was a risk, but it had to be taken since the colonies now did face dangers that they could not handle alone. The opponents also retreated into irresponsibility: they said the defence of the colonies was Britain's responsibility; after all, she reaped a huge benefit from her Australian trade and investment; it's her worry, not ours. Some opponents attempted to depict this payment as a tribute that Britain was exacting from unwilling colonists, similar to the taxation that had driven the Americans to revolt.[23]

A few accepted that Australia faced new dangers and opened serious discussion about how it could survive alone. Robert Thomson treated the subject in his *Australian Nationalism: An Earnest Appeal to the Sons of Australia in favour of Federation and Independence of the States of our Country*, published in Sydney in 1888. He argued that Australia was already able to cope with a hostile landing on its shores but to be safe it would need to develop a strong navy. Quite small countries—such as Denmark and Chile—managed this. Australia should not be fazed by the presence of European powers; a clever diplomacy would play them off against each other.

Of these ideas only an Australian navy was regularly discussed. Loyal nationalists were happy to contemplate it, but now was not the time to build it. The colonies were not yet united, and the expense would be tremendous. The British Navy offered first-class defence at a very cheap price. To loyal nationalists, future prospects were not blighted by this arrangement with the mother country.

They were equally unmoved by the warning that Britain was entering on these arrangements with the colonies because she was in decline or under threat. This was a hard notion for colonists to comprehend. Britain became greater the further they were removed from her. Service and Deakin both seemed genuinely to believe that Britain could override the French and the Germans if only she tried harder. It was mere inertia that kept Australia from getting what she wanted. Deakin had a schoolboy belief in the invincibility of the British. He yearned for another Raleigh or Drake to stand up boldly for England, his school books not having told him how circumspect was Elizabeth, their Queen, in her dealing with other powers.[24]

How could the loyal nationalists calmly assess Britain's purposes or the possibilities of independence when they were so flattered by Britain's new interest in the colonies? Normally nationalism implies complete independence. But when Australian nationalism burgeoned there was the prospect that the imperial power would reorganise its empire so that its self-governing colonies would have the same status as itself. The desire for recognition and the ending of colonial status could be assuaged both by the forming of the nation and by its remaining in the empire.

If the loyal nationalists did perceive that Britain's interest in a reorganised empire flowed from its relative decline, the recognition was soon obliterated by the thought of the huge strength the empire would possess when it was a partnership between Britain and the new nations overseas. And after the British everywhere were united, the Americans might combine in an alliance of the Anglo-Saxon race, which would control the world for peace.

The defeat of the Naval Bill in Queensland was not a true indication of the strength of independent nationalism. An election was imminent, and the Opposition decided to humiliate Griffith. Their argument that such an important matter should not be determined until after the elections allowed Opposition members who supported the plan to vote against it. Griffith might still have carried the measure if some of his own supporters had not been lukewarm about it.[25] The naval scheme did not determine the outcome of the election. Griffith was vulnerable because he had had been in office for five years, a period that had included a drought, and because he had proposed new taxation to offset declining revenues. The two sides competed to be more anti-Chinese than the other. Griffith strengthened his appeal to working men by declaring that the new issue for politics was the equitable division of wealth. But naval policy was discussed. McIlwraith, returning to lead the Opposition, was quite definitely opposed to it. Australian defence should have been settled in Australia. Griffith, denounced as an imperialist, became increasingly defensive and quiet on the issue.[26]

It is an amazing election. Of the two men competing to lead Queensland, one was a capitalist toying with republicanism; the other a loyalist toying with socialism. McIlwraith won. Soon after the election he organised his following into a National Party whose program, although not asking for separation, wanted to cultivate an Australian national spirit and form a federation with no imperial veto on Australian legislation. Its motto was 'Alliance not dependence'.[27] The independent nationalists were in charge of one of the colonies. Queensland continued its refusal to participate in the naval scheme. McIlwraith, the buccaneer capitalist, was the darling of the Sydney republicans and of independent nationalists everywhere.[28] Even in Victoria a new spirit briefly stirred. At the 1888 Australian Natives dinner five members refused to honour a toast to the Queen. 'Do you want a republic?' the chairman asked, and received an unexpected answer. 'Yes,' they replied. 'Yes.'[29]

5
Prophet

You (and you only) will for ever live in history as the originator and creator of the movement which will change these colonies into a nation.

Lord Carrington to Henry Parkes, 11 September 1890

I doubt if any serious historian believes that some sort of federation would not have been established in Australia at about the beginning of this century if Parkes had lived out his life as a labourer in Warwickshire.

W. G. McMinn, 1991[1]

The strengthening of independent nationalism in New South Wales took place as Parkes returned to the premiership for the fourth time early in 1887. With the death and retirement of his old rivals, he stood alone, a giant surviving from the heroic age when self-government and democracy were won. He looked like a seer, with his strong worn face, long beard, and white luminous hair. When he opened his mouth, the effect was spoiled. His voice was screechy; he dropped and misplaced his aitches; his talk was full of himself and made worse by ludicrous attempts at humility. His pretences were so transparent that he was called a humbug rather than a hypocrite. The *Bulletin* dubbed him 'the great high ham'. But although it was very easy to see through Parkes, it was impossible to ignore him. He could still command an issue, relate the ordinary to the significant, sway an audience, and destroy an opponent.

Because he had not gone to London for the Queen's jubilee, Parkes had to deal with the attempt by the radical republicans to disrupt the local celebrations. In June 1887 he watched helplessly from the stage of the Sydney Town Hall as republicans created mayhem at a public meeting called to discuss how the event should be honoured. Neither he nor the other worthies on the stage could gain a hearing. This was the second meeting on the jubilee. Republicans had taken over the first and voted down a plan to give school children a picnic in honour of the Queen, which they denounced as a threat to democratic values. The mayor hurriedly closed the meeting and called another. To keep the republicans out special invitation cards were printed, but republicans forged them and so were able to occupy all the strategic spots in the hall and orchestrate such a torrent of boos, hisses, and groans that the meeting never began.

The worthies retreated to an upstairs room. Parkes delivered a scathing denunciation of these disloyal wreckers, and the group planned a third meeting to remove this stain from the colony's reputation. A huge crowd

Putting down republicans: the Governor, his wife, and leading citizens protected by police at the loyalty meeting (above); a would-be republican speaker (below). (*Town and Country Journal*, 25 June 1887.)

did come to the third meeting, but only the use of hundreds of police, volunteer soldiers, sportsmen, and university students (in those days reliable upholders of law and order) kept the republicans suppressed and allowed demonstrations of loyalty. The following day at Parkes's insistence the Assembly declared its unalterable attachment to the laws and institutions of the British Empire.

Parkes had already moved to cripple the radical republican movement by closing the theatres on Sunday evenings. Entertainments were forbidden on Sundays, but meetings had been allowed, an opportunity that the republicans had seized. With church services the only competition, they had gathered large crowds at their theatre meetings. They were now forced to meet outdoors.[2]

Publicly Parkes appeared bent on suppression. Privately he acknowledged that 'young active intellects' were being drawn into republicanism and the new movements for social reform and was not altogether unsympathetic to them.[3] He read Henry George's works and was patron of the poet John Farrell, the author of 'NO', who started the land nationalisation journal. Parkes himself declared for female suffrage in 1887.[4] Louisa Lawson, who had turned the *Republican* into a feminist paper, asked him in 1889 for a government position for her poet son. The Premier's response was to summon the impoverished young poet to his office. This was of course a meeting of two poets. The elder Henry spoke approvingly to young Henry about his poems, but does not appear to have found him a job.[5]

The social ferment of the 1880s was similar to that of the 1840s and 1850s when the issues were transportation, self-government, and democracy. Then it was Parkes who was the radical poet, the journalist starting a reforming newspaper, and the republican. In 1850 he had served briefly in Dr Lang's League to secure 'the entire freedom and independence' of the Australian colonies. After the jubilee was fittingly celebrated, the loyal Premier showed he had not forgotten the part of the independent Australian nationalist, of which he had given intimations in his opposition to the Sudan contingent.

In 1888 he supported McIlwraith's Queensland Government in its demand that the colonies should be able to veto the appointment of a governor of whom they disapproved. This followed the attempt by the Colonial Office to appoint as Governor of Queensland Sir Henry Blake, a low-born former police magistrate who had been involved in suppression of Irish disturbances. Worse still, he had a son in Brisbane who was out of work and recently married to a barmaid. After the Queensland protest, the Colonial Office pressured the hapless Blake to resign, but it refused to grant colonies a veto over appointments. In their eyes, to lose control of the man who was to protect imperial interests in the colony was a step towards separation. Parkes denied this and insisted that the growing strength of its national life entitled Australia to this consideration. He passed a motion supporting this principle through the Assembly. Only two members opposed it because they wanted complete separation from Britain.[6] In Victoria only three members of the Assembly supported the Queensland position, the rest joining in singing 'God save the Queen'.[7]

During the anti-Chinese agitation in 1888, Parkes issued the nearest thing to an Australian declaration of independence. Britain always had some misgivings about the Australian desire to restrict Chinese immigration. It did not want to offend China or impose restrictions on Chinese who were British subjects. But it recognised the strength of Australian feeling on the subject and was working closely with the colonies to find a mutually agreeable mode of procedure. Then Parkes declared he would act unilaterally against the Chinese. He was under great pressure: there were boats in the harbour carrying Chinese immigrants, and parliament was besieged by a large crowd, led by the mayor, demanding action. He rushed through new tough anti-Chinese legislation in a day and, quite gratuitously, cast Britain as Australia's opponent: 'Neither for Her Majesty's ships of war, nor for Her Majesty's representative on the spot, nor for the Secretary of State for the Colonies, do we intend to turn aside from our purpose, which is to terminate the landing of Chinese on these shores forever.'[8]

He created a sensation. The *Sydney Morning Herald* said these were wild and foolish words that in a calmer moment Sir Henry would regret.[9] But he did not. Within a few days he issued his speech as a pamphlet and defended every word of it. With these performances the independent nationalists began to claim Parkes as their own.[10] Robert Thomson, the native-born author of *Australian Nationalism*, was ready to forgive him all his past trickery and accept him as teacher and prophet of the Australian nation.[11]

A loyal nationalist, dismayed at Parkes's attack on Britain, said there seemed to be two Sir Henrys.[12] The *Bulletin* also saw two. It thought Parkes in his secret soul was still a republican who aspired to play the part of a Cromwell or a Washington, but would remain the loyal monarchist because what he liked most was power.[13]

What was the old man up to? He was even prepared to use the *Bulletin* slogan: 'Australia for the Australians'.[14] Fortunately he kept his letters, which enable us to follow his thinking.

Parkes welcomed the growing strength of national feeling, but was afraid of its independent element (which he appeared to be encouraging).

The other Henry Parkes: the minstrel as depicted by Phil May in the *Bulletin*. The dog is Francis Abigail, Secretary for Mines.

If matters were allowed to drift, separatism and republicanism would soon be too strong for Australia to remain within the empire. Action of two sorts was needed. Australia must be united to give it the institutions of strong national life so that the rich would no longer want to go 'home' and the best minds would have an arena worthy of them. The nation must have a strong, independent identity, inferior to no other, and capable of attracting the allegiance of all its citizens. Such a nation would remain in the empire but only if the empire was fundamentally reorganised. There should be a Council of Empire, made up of representatives of its self-governing nations and colonies, which, beginning as a consultative body, would assume executive power for the empire's defence and foreign policy. Some such arrangement was needed to persuade all the subjects of the

Queen that they were equal citizens of the empire. Just striking up 'God save the Queen' would no longer work.

Parkes prided himself on being able to detect the deep movements in society and knowing when action would lead to success. He was sure Australia was now close to a transforming moment in its history.[15] In 1889 he himself took action on both fronts. He launched his campaign for federation and put his plans for the empire direct to Salisbury, the British Prime Minister.[16]

Parkes's political strategy was to put himself at the head of the independent nationalists and so head off the movement to separation from the empire. He would create a strong, independent nation, and Salisbury would meanwhile reorder the empire so that Australia could be offered a place in it to which the independent nationalists could not object.

Parkes was a loyal nationalist, but of a different sort from the Victorians. They were happy to see the nation created by a growth in membership and powers of the Federal Council and were reassured by the Colonial Conference that Britain would listen to Australia. Parkes, aware of the more separatist nationalism in his own colony and Queensland, wanted more arresting action: an immediate move to nationhood and a more thorough-going change to the British Empire.

Continuing the approach he had taken during 1888 and 1889, Parkes conducted his federation campaign as if he were an independent nationalist. If his vision of a strong nation within a cooperative empire was to be realised, the independent nationalists had to be won over. In his first speech at Tenterfield, he spoke ten words on Australia retaining its ties with the empire, but gave no reasons why it should. In the second he said if Australia was loyal to England, England had to be loyal to Australia and treat her properly as a nation. This was the closest he came to discussing the plan he had posted to Salisbury a few days before. In the speeches that followed he did not mention the empire at all. Australia was to federate to meet its destiny, to be a great nation, proud and independent, respected around the world.[17]

Parkes had told Salisbury that the way Britain responded to a more assertive Australia would determine whether Australia remained in the empire. A reply from Salisbury could not be expected for some time. So Parkes himself was not sure as he spoke whether he was launching a nation within an empire or one that might soon be outside it. He was much given to day-dreaming about himself in heroic roles, and the thought that one day he might have to stand by Australia and renounce England had not left him.[18] Uncertain whether he could be both loyal Englishman and Australian nationalist, Parkes was an ambiguous figure of great political drawing power, a fitting father for that supreme ambiguity, a nation within an empire.

For himself, Parkes wanted the honour of founding a nation and being its first prime minister. One writer has suggested that Parkes's move is a classic case of an old man facing death wanting to leave a substantial monument behind him.[19] We can do better than speculate because Parkes himself confirms the hypothesis in a poem on his seventieth birthday:

What task of glorious toil for good,
What service, what achievement high,
May nerve the will, re-fire the blood,
Who knows, ere strikes the hour to die!

The next decade of time and fate,
The mighty changes manifold,
The grander growth of Rule and State,
Perchance these eyes may yet behold!

He waited four more years before he made his move. He would have to hurry to be first prime minister, although he was far from being in decline. His wife having died, he had recently married his mistress, and she was pregnant with their fourth child.

Parkes planned to federate the colonies single-handedly. There would be a 'movement', but he would head it. 'I', he boasted, 'could federate these colonies in twelve months'—a remark recorded by Lord Carrington, the Governor of New South Wales, just as he was about to begin. In his own colony there was much opposition to federation, but Parkes did not commence by winning it round. He was confident that his timing was right and that he could carry his colony with him. He did not consult with, nor even inform, his cabinet about his federal plans. He would play the hero's part and lead Australia to its destiny. He was a great admirer of the historian and philosopher, Thomas Carlyle, the author of *Heroes and Hero-worship*. Indeed Carlyle while he lived was one of the famous people in England whom Parkes claimed as a friend. He learnt from Carlyle that great men of prophetic insight and strength of purpose lead humanity forward.[20]

He unveiled his federal plan first to the Premier of Victoria, Duncan Gillies, who had replaced Service as the leader of the coalition government.[21] Victoria was the largest colony and the keenest about federation. Parkes proposed to Gillies in a private letter that the colonies should appoint delegates to a convention, which would draw up a constitution for the nation and discuss the nation's relationship with Britain. He assumed that his overture would be welcomed. At the centennial banquet in Sydney in 1888, Gillies had encouraged Parkes to take the lead in federation.

Victoria's leaders had decided that since New South Wales was so diffident about federation, especially when proposed by Victoria, the next move would have to come from the mother colony. Now that Parkes had made a move, Gillies rebuffed him. He told Parkes that he should bring New South Wales into the Federal Council. If all the colonies were represented in the Council and its powers expanded, this would be a sure and steady route to federation. To attempt a full federation immediately was building castles in the air.

Gillies was a cautious, practical man, miffed at Parkes wanting to commandeer the federal movement that New South Wales had previously spurned. Indeed there appeared to be good grounds for caution. Parkes gave no reasons why his colony would now support federation and no explanation of how all the barriers to federation could be overcome. The free-trade Premier of New South Wales did not mention the difficulty of the tariff in writing to the Premier of protectionist Victoria. Parkes's own record on federation was dubious, although Parkes himself of course could justify every twist in it. He had proposed a federal council and then opposed it when proposed by others. Only the year before he had outraged the other colonies by planning to change the name of New South Wales to Australia. Gillies suspected that Parkes's move was a stunt, which might serve temporarily to boost him but almost certainly would damage the federal cause. The counter move of welcoming him into the Federal Council would test his sincerity.

Parkes would have nothing to do with that 'rickety' body, the Federal Council, and in any case, he said, it was beyond his power to persuade his colony to join it. Nor did he want to move cautiously to federation; he had political and personal reasons for brooking no delay. Giving out that he was on holiday, he sailed to Brisbane to lay his still-secret plans before its National Party Government. He took with him, as well as the proofs of his next poetry book, a report from Major-General Edwards of the British Army into the defences of the Australian colonies. The report recommended that the colonial forces should be federated, a conclusion that Parkes might have encouraged the major-general to reach. Parkes himself was far above thinking of federation in narrow utilitarian terms, but for a few weeks he worked the argument that federal military forces required a federal government.

In Brisbane he met separately with McIlwraith and Griffith, and laid his plans before a cabinet meeting. McIlwraith had retired from the premiership because of ill health, but was still a power in the land. The new Premier was Boyd Morehead. Parkes had a much better reception in Queensland than he had received from Gillies. The Queensland ministers were surprised, sceptical about his chances, but supportive. Griffith and McIlwraith were both encouraging. What Parkes told McIlwraith and his followers about the relations of the new nation with Britain is not recorded. They would have been more ready to accept him as federal leader because he had supported their claim to a veto in the appointment of governors. Parkes now had allies. It was time to go public and put pressure on Gillies.[22]

He planned to return to Sydney by train. The first town over the border was Tenterfield, which happened to be one of several centres Parkes had represented in parliament in his long career. He stopped there, and at a banquet in his honour held at the School of Arts he gave the speech that launched his public campaign. When Parkes was given the title 'father of federation', his Tenterfield oration took on a legendary status. It was described as reverberating around Australia and creating new enthusiasm for union.[23] In truth the speech is not memorable in its language, and it did not create a great deal of interest; in some places it was not reported at all. The press comment was not generally favourable: Parkes was criticised as vain in wanting to lead the movement and arrogant in wanting the other colonies to abandon the Federal Council, which was federation's best hope. When Parkes returned to Sydney, he still had his work to do.

He now told all the premiers his plans, which led to South Australia and Tasmania endorsing Victoria's position that New South Wales should join the Federal Council. Parkes was not deterred. He was confident that the issue would be settled by the deep desire of the people for union, not by the men who happened to hold public office. He planned, in his own words, to appeal from the governments to the people.[24] His aim was to bring the people to an awareness that their nation already existed; all the barriers between them were artificial; they were one in blood and sentiment, and ready now to claim their national destiny and put colonial inferiority behind them.

His awakening call was made in a series of speeches, which were duly reported in newspapers throughout the colonies.[25] He also organised his network of friends and connections in the colonies and in England to comment favourably on his campaign, which made further newspaper copy.[26] His South Australian contact, William Rounsevell, moved a motion of support in the local Assembly.[27]

The English dimension was important. In Australia it was easy for press and politicians to depict Parkes as vain, insincere, and arrogant, but when the metropolitan press—that is, the London press—and English notables declared that Parkes was a statesman and his cause worthy of support, he became harder to ignore.[28]

Parkes gave equal attention to ensuring that his scheme was not destroyed within New South Wales, where opposition to federation was very strong. He

'FEDERATION' IN THE AIR OR G.O.M. [GRAND OLD MAN] PARKES ON HIS HIGH HORSE AGAIN.
A cartoon by 'Hop' from the *Bulletin*, 23 November 1889.

himself was the leader of the free-trade party, and federation looked likely to destroy free trade. It would deliver intercolonial free trade, but since five of the six colonies were protectionist, the policy of a united Australia would be protection against the world. Sydney would no longer be a free port. Within Parkes's cabinet were some young Turks, for whom the old man had never been free-trader enough because he blurred the line between a revenue and a protective tariff. They were alarmed that their chief, without consulting the cabinet, had committed the government to a course that would deny them the chance to bring New South Wales to free-trade purity. Parkes was scornful of their grumblings and assumed, correctly, that he could carry them with him. He gave much more attention to the Opposition.

The protectionist party, as it boasted, was the party of national union much more than the free-traders. It could assume that its policy would become the policy of the nation. But although the protectionists wanted federation, they did not want it now. Their strength lay in the country, and their constituents were protectionists because they wanted to exclude from the New South Wales market the wheat, flour, and chaff of Victoria and South Australia. They could contemplate intercolonial free trade only after New South Wales industries had time to grow under a protectionist regime.

The party seemed on the point of achieving that. Its support had grown rapidly, and it expected that after one more election it would be in power. The Opposition's line on Parkes's federation proposal was that it was a cunning diversion designed to take the fiscal issue out of New South Wales politics just as the free-traders were about to go down to defeat and ignominy. They accused Parkes of being a secret protectionist in order to spread alarm in the free-trade ranks, but they had no intention of allowing this closet protectionist to divert them from their course or take the credit for leading Australia to union. They heaped up reasons why this was not the man nor this the hour for federation.[29]

George Dibbs, the leader of the protectionists, was an avowed republican, which made him less rather than more disposed to support Parkes. He was interested in Australian union, but not as a federation.[30] For the present he played the party game and throughout Parkes's federal campaign took his job to be to harass Parkes and destabilise the federal movement any way he could. He safely declared that the protectionists would support Parkes's national plans if he declared himself to be a protectionist.[31]

Given the misgivings among the free-traders, had the Opposition been united Parkes would have been defeated at home before his national crusade was under way. To ensure that the Opposition was not united Parkes secretly contacted a few of its leading men who he thought were keen enough about federation to defy the party line and follow him. With Edmund Barton he had protracted negotiations. Within the space of a fortnight they wrote to each other five times and met twice. They were fellow conspirators, negotiating across the party divide and keeping their colleagues in the dark. They were risking much for the noble cause. At the same time they were both

Chambers
29th Oct 1889

My dear Sir Henry Parkes

Of course I have read with the deepest interest everything which the papers have published of your conferences with the public men of Queensland on the subject of Federation for Australia. I cannot doubt any more than you do that ~~such~~ a Federation to be effective must be armed with the most complete powers of a General Executive and Parliament in matters of National – I use the word by way of distinction

Parkes's first success: Barton from the Opposition agrees to support him.

speaking publicly, watching how each other developed the line they had discussed in private. Their confidence in each other grew. Barton's willingness to speak publicly in support of Parkes and in defiance of his party was the beginning of his career as a leading federalist. The bond between the two men made Parkes's federal campaign possible.

Parkes and Barton decided that the tariff difficulty, the chief obstacle to federation, should be resolved after federation and not before it. Until this moment everyone had assumed that it had to be solved as a precondition of federation. The Parkes–Barton formula was that the nation should be created first and all parties be prepared to accept whatever tariff policy its parliament determined. But Barton was a party man too, and he had to be careful that Parkes had not laid a trap for him. Federation might take some time; meanwhile he and his party must be free to continue their advocacy of protection for New South Wales. Of course, said Parkes; whatever could have led you to think otherwise?[32]

When this was settled, Parkes gave the second in his series of speeches on federation. Delivered to his constituents at St Leonards on the north shore of Sydney Harbour, it is of much more significance to the success of federation than the Tenterfield speech. He explained the strategy in an arresting and alarming way. He declared that the 'question of free trade and protection was trifling compared with the necessity and the grandeur and the duty of giving to Australia an Australian Government'.[33] *Trifling* was his word. The leader of the free-trade party, which had just won two elections on a free-trade cry and was gearing up for a life-and-death battle with protection, had declared free trade to be a trifle. Alarm became panic. Had the old man lost it completely? It was only at a third meeting, two nights later, when Barton and Parkes spoke together under the auspices of the Australian Natives Association, that the strategy emerged more clearly. Free-traders and protectionists who accepted the strategy were still to fight for their creed before and after federation.[34] Both Parkes and Barton on subsequent occasions had to reassure the party faithful on this score.[35] To the faithful it continued to look like betrayal, and in a sense it was; fiscal creed was to be put at risk in order to create the nation.

The speeches in which the strategy was explained were published in the other colonies. Parkes's St Leonards speech created great interest in Melbourne.[36] And yet the new idea struggled to live against the prevailing wisdom; it kept getting lost or being misunderstood, downplayed or wilfully misrepresented, particularly as it was filtered through the press of the other colonies.[37] Still, these speeches must have made Gillies as Premier of protectionist Victoria more willing to deal with Parkes. He clearly was not demanding that federation occur on a free-trade basis. In his formal communications with the premiers Parkes did not allude to the strategy explicitly; he spoke of all subordinate issues and party disputes being set aside, and of New South Wales seeking no guarantees.

Parkes's campaign was a success; Gillies and the other premiers could not ignore him. However, they were determined that Parkes should not bypass the Federal Council. They suggested that representatives from New South Wales should meet with the Federal Council to discuss Parkes's plan. Parkes still refused. He was persuaded to yield by his Governor and the Queenslanders. The Queensland Premier, Boyd Morehead, gave him a formula he could accept: he was to meet with the members of the Federal Council simply as representative men of their colony. Morehead, McIlwraith, and the Governor assured him from their soundings that if he agreed to do this he would be master of the situation and able to proceed with his plan for a convention. McIlwraith was particularly influential, and in a trip to Sydney and Melbourne, he exerted himself on Parkes's behalf.[38] The plan to move quickly to federation emanated from the two colonies where independent nationalism was strongest.

As Carlyle complained, historians are reluctant to accept the importance of great men or heroes. They think they have their measure; they reduce them to mere instruments of wider forces. Australian historians recently have written expressly to downplay Parkes's role in federation.[39] The fact that he could not browbeat the other premiers into doing as he wished is part of their case. But look closely. Parkes is told he must join the Federal Council. He refuses. He is told he should discuss federation with the Federal Council. He refuses. He is invited to discuss federation informally with the members of the Federal Council as representative men. He accepts. And what happens to this informal meeting? It transmutes into the Australasian Federation Conference; it debates in public; its thirteen members are surrounded by more than fifty representatives of the press who fill the papers with reports of its deliberations;[40] it recommends that the parliaments select delegates to write a constitution. The wording of the key resolution for union is settled by Parkes and Gillies, who four months earlier was telling Parkes he had to join the Federal Council and take federation one step at a time.

As with all good conferences, the outcome of this was one was settled in advance of the formal meetings. When Parkes arrived in Melbourne he met Gillies and Deakin and showed them the resolutions he planned to move. The Victorians noticed immediately that the resolution for union did not include the words 'under the Crown'. They were worried about the strength of the independent nationalists and that Parkes had seemed to be courting them. From the outset they wanted it settled that the nation would be loyal to the empire. Parkes willingly accepted the correction and amended his draft. But the omission was almost certainly not accidental.[41]

Just before he left for Melbourne Parkes had received a reply from Salisbury about his plan for an Empire Council. It was friendly and accepted that the bonds of the empire would hold only if the colonies could reach their aspirations within it, but unyielding on Britain never sharing executive power. Taking Parkes to be advocating a form of imperial federation, Salisbury summoned up the standard bogey of the Asian parts of the empire holding nearly all the seats in an imperial parliament. Parkes would have to write again to set him right.[42]

Parkes gets his way: moving the resolution for union at the Federation Conference, Melbourne, 1890; to his left is Thomas Playford of South Australia, who took Parkes on and lost. (*Illustrated Australian News*, 1 March 1890.)

Parkes's own fervent wish was that the new nation be a union under the Crown. But by keeping the issue open, pressure might have been put on Britain to agree to his Empire Council scheme and the independent nationalists kept onside. Parkes in his initial letter to Gillies had wanted his convention to consider Australian federation 'in relation to the other groups of colonies and in relation to the central power of the empire'; that is, the scheme he had put to Salisbury. But the meeting place for the conference was loyalist Melbourne, and the Victorians did not want any debate.

At the great public banquet that marked the opening of the Conference, the toast to a united Australasia was given by James Service, elder statesman of Victoria.[43] Well informed, one might think, but he had not comprehended the Parkes strategy. He declared that the 'lion in the way' of federation was the fiscal problem. 'The Conference must either kill the lion or the lion will kill it.'

When Parkes rose to reply he was greeted rapturously. This was a message to the other delegates, some of whom were still very wary of Parkes—or were they too on their feet, waving handkerchiefs, cheering wildly? The man who had been pilloried a few months before as charlatan and opportunist had made himself into the prophet of the nation. It is for this moment that the conclusion of Deakin's unmatched pen portrait of Parkes is most apt: there was in him the substance of the man he dressed himself to appear.[44]

Deakin on Parkes

First and foremost of course in every eye was the commanding figure of Sir Henry Parkes, than whom no actor ever more carefully posed for effect. His huge figure, slow step, deliberate glance and carefully brushed-out aureole of white hair combined to present the spectator with a picturesque whole which was not detracted from on closer acquaintance. His voice, without being musical and in spite of a slight woolliness of tone and rather affected depth, was pleasant and capable of reaching and controlling a large audience. His studied attitudes expressed either distinguished humility or imperious command. His manner was invariably dignified, his speech slow, and his pronunciation precise, offending only by the occasional omission or misplacing of aspirates. He was fluent but not voluble, his pauses skilfully varied, and in times of excitement he employed a whole gamut of tones ranging from a shrill falsetto to deep resounding chest notes. He had always in his mind's eye his own portrait as that of a great man, and constantly adjusted himself to it. A far-away expression of the eyes, intended to convey his remoteness from the earthly sphere, and often associated with melancholy treble cadences of voice in which he implied a vast and inexpressible weariness, constituted his favourite and at last his almost invariable exterior. Movements, gestures, inflexions, attitudes harmonised, not simply because they were intentionally adopted but because there was in him the substance of the man he dressed himself to appear. The real strength and depth of his capacity were such that it was always a problem with Parkes as with Disraeli where the actor posture-maker and would-be sphinx ended or where the actual man underneath began. He had both by nature and by art the manner of a sage and a statesman.

His abilities were solid though general, as [were] his reading and his knowledge. Fond of books, a steady reader and a constant writer, his education had been gained in the world and among men. A careful student of all with whom he came in contact, he was amiable, persuasive and friendly by disposition. A life of struggle had found him self-reliant and left him hardened into resolute masterfulness. Apart from his exterior, he was a born leader of men, dwelling by preference of natural choice upon the larger and bolder aspects of things. He had therefore the aptitude of statecraft of a high order, adding to it the tastes of the man of letters, the lover of poetry and the arts, of rare editions and bric-à-brac, of autographs and memorials of the past. His nature, forged on the anvil of necessity, was egotistic though not stern and his career was that of the aspirant who looks to ends and is not too punctilious as to means. He was jealous of equals, bitter with rivals and remorseless with enemies …

Deakin, *The Federal Story*, pp. 26–7.

In his speech Parkes praised the Queen and declared that there would be no separation from the empire. He spoke on this theme with a fulsomeness entirely absent from his previous federation speeches. To show that obstacles to federation could be overcome, he proclaimed most memorably: 'The crimson thread of kinship runs through us all.' He then set out the tariff strategy, using the same word that had brought him so much trouble in his St Leonards speech: a 'common tariff is a mere trifle compared with the great overshadowing question of a living and eternal national existence', but he made clear that he was still a fervent free-trader who would nevertheless trust the national parliament to settle the tariff problem. Now everyone who mattered understood the strategy. The biggest difficulty was not to be solved. Federation was to be reached not incrementally but by a leap of faith. It was to be achieved by trusting in the nation that it would create—or rather formalise, because, according to Parkes, the nation already existed.

When the Conference began, some of the delegates objected to Parkes's approach. Interests had to be considered and could not be swept aside by appeals to national sentiment. Victoria clearly had an interest in federation since she was looking for wider markets, but the South Australians were worried that their new industries were not ready to face Victorian competition, and the Western Australians could not afford to lose their customs revenue. Deakin conceded that Victoria had been and was self-interested. What had to be done was to make other colonies see how their interests would be served by union. But fortunately interests were not the only force in play. National sentiment was strong and could be encouraged further, and that would help them over their difficulties.[45]

Andrew Clark, the republican scholar from Tasmania, made the most profound contribution to the discussion. On the authority of the historian E. A. Freeman, he contested the dichotomy between sentimental and practical politics. The so-called practical politician often missed the heart of the matter because he was determined not to be sentimental. Freeman had written: 'men's feelings, their hopes, their memories, their loves, their hatreds, in a word, their sentiments, go for a great deal in human affairs.' 'With regard to Australian federation', said Clark, 'the sentimental side will prove to be the practical, or the basis of the practical.'[46] This was the best defence of Parkes's approach.

There was general agreement that the tariff 'lion in the path' was no longer so fearsome. A minority still doubted whether Parkes's strategy would be acceptable, but thought federation was worth having even without a customs union. All were agreed that a constitution should now be drawn up, and since no one expected that the constitution would contain a tariff, Parkes's call to establish the nation first and settle the tariff afterwards was to be followed.

There was no dissent about the union being under the Crown. Only Parkes remained uncertain. The resolution for union that he moved included the words 'under the Crown', put there by Gillies and Deakin, but in a long speech he did not refer to them. Tom Playford, the bluff, earthy South Australian, noticed the omission and queried Parkes's loyalty. He received a withering reply, but then Parkes, putting on his seer's mantle, said that since quite trivial circumstances can sometimes cause great slippages, Australia might not always live under the English flag. He hastened to say that he hoped this would not be so. He prayed it might not be so. But yet it might be otherwise. And maybe 'as many very respectable and reputable citizens dream', we might form a nation by ourselves.[47]

Since Parkes was such a consummate politician, one always does him the credit of looking for a political purpose in this constant desire to leave the matter open. He did still want something out of Salisbury. But could it be that he simply could not help himself? One cannot know where the ambiguity of the politician ended and the ambiguity of the actual man underneath began.

Playford made a more subtle attack on Parkes when he opined that the federal cause was handicapped because it was in the hands of leading statesmen whereas all great reforms sprang from the people. Parkes could not let that pass. In all he knew, in all that he had read, there was always 'the people and their leaders'. Now for the first time he heard of 'statesmen and their drivers'. In fact there was not one movement for the benefit of mankind that did not at first arise 'in some pregnant far-seeing human mind'.[48]

That was the justification for the role he took. He knew he was a great man; he knew also that lesser men always put barriers in the way of the far-seeing. These were the certainties that powered his will.

The Convention to write a constitution met in Sydney in March 1891 with Parkes in the chair. The meeting had to be held in Sydney because Parkes had had a carriage accident and could scarcely walk. It was unthinkable that the Convention be held without him, so the seven delegates elected by the parliaments of each colony and the three delegates from New Zealand attended on him. The New Zealanders were present more as observers, although they took full part in the proceedings. For the moment at least New Zealand was not interested in federating with Australia.

Parkes did not take a very active part in the proceedings. He exerted himself to secure the name 'Commonwealth', and he gave the federal

'The Lion in the way' of federation: a cartoon by Hop published on 22 February 1890. The *Bulletin* was still opposed to federation under the Crown.

movement one of its enduring slogans at the Convention banquet with his toast to 'One People, One Destiny'.

In the space of five weeks, to their great surprise, the delegates were able to agree on a constitution. They debated general principles for two weeks and worked in committees for one; they gave Griffith and his assistants the

Easter break to finalise the draft, which they accepted with only minor alterations in the last week. In its fundamentals it is the constitution we have today: a House of Representatives representing the people (the men, that is, who possessed the vote in the colonies); a Senate in which the states had an equal number of representatives (to be elected by the state parliaments); specified powers given to the federal parliament and the rest remaining with the states; and a High Court to interpret the constitution. All this was borrowed from the United States and readily agreed to.

The problem with the copying was that the delegates had no use for the separate election of a president and an executive independent of the legislature. Most wanted to retain the British or Westminster system, to which they were accustomed, of ministers sitting in the parliament and being responsible to it. That system gave pre-eminence to the lower house of parliament, to which ministers were responsible and where the purse strings were controlled. But the delegates from the small states did not want to see the Senate's powers weakened to accommodate responsible government. The compromise on the Senate's powers was that it could make suggestions on money Bills, not amendments.

Griffith's solution to the problem of marrying American federalism with responsible government was to leave options open to allow new practices to evolve. To the delegates who wanted British responsible government enshrined in the constitution, he replied that the British constitutional tradition was evolutionary. Out of deference to him, the constitution said that ministers may sit in parliament, not that they had to.

Parkes's strategy on the tariff was embodied in this constitution and in that of 1897–98. The constitution would establish the parliament, which would determine the tariff, at which point free trade between the colonies would commence. This was Parkes's greatest contribution to federation: that he gave to all the federalists the strategy that brought success. He did play the hero's part. His historian detractors make their task easy by not discussing the strategy at all. It did not of course guarantee success. Both protectionists and free-traders would have to think that their policy had a chance of being adopted by the nation. The danger was that the confidence of one side might destroy that of the other.

At the 1891 Convention, it was the Victorian protectionists, frequently thought of as the keenest nationalists, who were most reluctant to accept Parkes's strategy of trusting the nation. Deakin made a strenuous effort to secure some guarantee that Victorian industries would not be harmed if the federal tariff should be lower than the Victorian. Of course this could not be granted.[49]

The 1891 Constitution was transmitted to the various parliaments with instructions to seek the approval of the people. How the people's approval was to be gained was not specified: the options canvassed were a general election on the issue, a referendum, or the election of a special ratifying convention. Some members were worried that the parliaments were not to consider the constitution, but Griffith insisted they must not be given that chance or all their work, with its delicate compromises, would unravel.

Between the holding of the Federal Conference in February 1890 and the assembling of the Convention in March 1891, Australian society passed through a transforming experience. When Parkes had predicted that some crisis was at hand, he was thinking of relations with Britain. The crisis turned out to be a clash between capital and labour. In August 1890 a maritime strike snowballed into something like a general strike. Unions had been growing rapidly in the 1880s, gaining easy victories in good times; as employers faced declining returns they wanted to call a halt to the union advance. When the two sides clashed, the unions suffered a great loss. The workers, bitter in defeat, vented their anger on the governments that had sided with the employers. Deakin in Melbourne, Parkes in Sydney, and Griffith in Brisbane had all organised special constables to cope with the crisis. While he was writing the constitution at the Sydney Convention in 1891, Griffith was directing troops by telegraph in an even more bitter shearers' strike. These men were not unsympathetic to the workers, but they were determined to maintain law and order and to preserve the right of employers to hire non-union labour, which is what broke the strikes. The workers' response was to create labour parties to ensure that in future they controlled governments.

The crisis affected the fortunes of federation. The new labour parties were preoccupied with wages and working conditions and were suspicious of federation or outrightly hostile to it. Among the ranks of labour were the radical republicans of the 1880s, who were opposed to any union under the Crown. On the other hand, the wider movement of independent nationalism lost its momentum. It had been buoyed by optimism about Australia's prospects. A country with a depressed economy riven with class warfare did not look so ready to claim its independence. Among the property-owning class there was a closing of ranks, most notable in Queensland where independent nationalism had been strongest. At the 1888 election Griffith and McIlwraith were in dispute over relations with Britain; in 1890 they formed a grand coalition that crushed the unions and marginalised the Labor Party. McIlwraith conceded that the naval subsidy should be paid to Britain. Griffith decided that the needs of the sugar industry required that kanakas continue to be imported.

THE LABOUR CRISIS. CAPITAL: '*See here, my man, one of us must either go back, or else lie down and let the other walk over him. Now, which of us shall it be?*' A cartoon from the *Bulletin*, 16 August 1890.

A union under the Crown would continue to have opponents but only from the margins of political life. Parkes no longer had to fear that he was confronting a force that would make the existing empire connection untenable. The need for ambiguity had passed. After the 1890 Conference Parkes wrote to Salisbury a second time about his Empire Council scheme. After the 1891 Convention he wrote to the Queen to report that although discussion of a constitution almost invited consideration of other forms of government, only one speech had been made that was inconsistent with the most ardent loyalty to Her Majesty's throne and person.[50]

The exception came from Dibbs, the Leader of the Opposition to Parkes's government in New South Wales. In a typical piece of mischief-making he said that limiting appeals to the Privy Council amounted to a declaration of independence, the course he favoured.[51] The following year when he was in London he accepted a knighthood. On being chided for abandoning his republican principles, he explained that the Queen had offered the honour personally and he could not refuse a lady.

6
Limbo

Federation is as dead as Julius Caesar.

Sir John Robertson, 1891

Parkes had conjured up a convention and got it to write a constitution. His federal plans were then wrecked by a backbencher in his own parliament and, what was worse, from his own party.

George Reid had entered the New South Wales Assembly in 1880. He was briefly a successful minister of education, but then he held aloof from the battle of the ins and the outs. He devoted himself to his law practice and the good life. At 45 he was still unmarried. He was becoming grossly fat; he was always eating cakes and lollies, even during the sittings of parliament. He attended parliament irregularly, claiming that to listen to the drivel that passed for debate would drive anyone mad. His own speeches were forceful, intelligent, and well considered. In the rough house of the Assembly he was one of the few who maintained gentlemanly standards. Outside, before his electors of East Sydney, he spoke in a colloquial, slangy style and was quite happy to be crude.

'Who's the father, George?' yelled an interjector as he rested his great belly on the verandah rail of the pub from which he was addressing his constituents.

'You must be', said Reid, 'since it is all piss and wind.'

Deakin, who disliked him intensely, regarded him as the best platform speaker in Australia. Parkes scorned him as an uncultivated clown who did not read books. Reid said he had told Parkes that he did not read in order

George Reid, 1898.

to escape Parkes's literary talk, which consisted of his boasting of the famous authors he knew.

In 1891, when Reid decided to become more active in politics, he was not content with half measures. Just as the Constitutional Convention was assembling in Sydney he told a meeting of his constituents that he would destroy Parkes. After Parkes's Convention had finished its labours, he announced that he would destroy its constitution.[1] He planned to destroy it in the parliament; he rejected absolutely the notion that parliament should merely pass on the constitution for the people's verdict.

Reid was, like Parkes, a free-trader. He had written a book of essays on free trade that had been highly regarded in England. His objection to Parkes was that he was not free-trader enough. He still used the customs to raise too much revenue. Instead he should impose direct taxation on land and income and so be able to establish true free trade. If Parkes was not prepared to take the free-trade party in this direction, he would.

His chief objection to federation was that it would destroy free trade. Parkes was betraying the cause he claimed to support. With five of the six colonies protectionist, there could be only one outcome of his policy of trusting the nation. At the Convention New South Wales offered poetry and eloquence; the other colonies sent hard bargainers. While Parkes was proclaiming that he sought no guarantees for New South Wales, Deakin was scheming to defend Victorian industries. For free-traders to trust the nation was like a teetotaller setting up house with five drunkards with the question of beverages to be decided later. Why did New South Wales have to yield to the protectionist colonies? She was young, beautiful, wealthy, and full of promise, whereas Parkes was treating her like a middle-aged, ill-tempered spinster whom he wanted to marry off at any price. How pleasing this sally must have been to old John Robertson, chief of the New South Wales patriots, who chaired the meeting where Reid made this attack.

To the constitution itself Reid had abundant objections. He was the first of many who had an easy time attacking something so alien to the liberal and democratic tradition of a British community. The people had gained their liberty by fighting upper houses, and now a new, strong upper house was being created. And against all democratic principle, the tiny state of Western Australia would send to it the same number of representatives as New South Wales. Reid was not persuaded that the Senate's being confined to suggestions on money Bills lessened its power. The two large states would provide the bulk of the revenue, and the four small states would decide how to spend it.

Griffith made Reid's task easier by refusing to insist on responsible government and giving in black-letter law so much power to the Governor-General. Behind the entrenched upper house, Reid raised the spectre of a revitalised monarch. And worse. This all-powerful Governor-General was to receive his instructions from the Queen. The new nation would be ruled from Downing Street! This constitution was a travesty; not a charter for a free people but an attack on their liberties.

Three weeks after Reid's first attack, Barton spoke in defence of the constitution.[2] He began the long grind of explaining the principles of a federal system—he would do this hundreds of times in the coming years. The Senate was not a conservative upper house of the sort liberals and democrats had fought against. It too represented the people but as they were grouped in states. The small states would never agree to federation unless they had equal representation in the Senate. The Convention unquestioningly recognised their equal sovereign status by allowing each to send the same number of delegates, and the constitution would have to follow the same principle for one of the houses.

As to the scare about the Governor-General, Reid was either a very poor lawyer or deliberately misleading. Everyone knew that the powers of the Governor-General would in practice be exercised on the advice of ministers. Reid was raising the alarm because the conventions of responsible government were not written into the constitution, but they were not written into the colonial constitutions either.

It was a very good speech. Parkes, who was on the platform, moved thanks for a magnificent address in support of the noblest of causes. Deakin and Griffith, reading the press reports, were delighted that Reid had been so completely refuted.[3] The one weakness of the speech was that it had to be delivered at Manly, well away from Sydney's radicals and labourites, who would have shouted it down. They too were convinced that the federal constitution was an attack on the people's liberties.

Reid replied to Barton where he had spoken before, in the heart of Sydney, and was cheered uproariously.[4] He retracted nothing, although he was a little more cautious in dealing with constitutional questions. He insisted reasonably enough that the nation's founding charter should embody the real principles of their government. It might be true that the colonial constitutions did not explicitly provide for responsible government, but they did not confer on governors the powers given to the Governor-General. Mostly he kept to the safer ground of speculating how their hard-nosed neighbours would use the constitution to plunder New South Wales. The real force of his speech was its immediate endorsement by Dibbs, the protectionist Leader of the Opposition. Speaking after Reid, he promised that as soon as parliament met he would combine with Reid to defeat Parkes and the constitution.

Parkes's cabinet now revolted against its leader. Ministers had borne Parkes launching the federation campaign without consulting them and in secret collusion with Barton, a leading figure of the Opposition; they had even accepted that neither they nor the parliament could amend the constitution on its way to the people's endorsement, but they were not going to let Parkes destroy them in the cause of federation. They insisted that he must yield in the face of this attack. The old magician was finally brought to earth.[5]

When parliament met, Parkes tried to take the wind out of Reid's sails by announcing that parliament could recommend changes to the constitution that would go to a second convention and then to the people. Reid still launched his attack. Parkes countered by announcing that federation would no longer be top priority in his program for the session. It was not enough. Reid and some other dissident free-traders crossed the floor to support a no-confidence motion moved by Dibbs. The government survived only on the casting vote of the speaker and went to the people.

Parkes being destroyed by the Frankenstein of his own creation. A cartoon by Hop, *Bulletin*, 6 June 1891.

Parkes would have liked federation to have been the issue at the election, but it could not override the battle over free trade and protection. Barton, with Parkes's support, did win a seat campaigning as a federalist first and a protectionist second. This was the election, June 1891, when Labor made its stunning debut, winning thirty-five seats and immediately holding the balance of power. It was neutral on the tariff issue and uninterested in federation; its concern was to transform the living conditions of the workers. It supported Parkes until he refused to insert an eight-hour-day provision in a mining Bill when it switched allegiance to Dibbs and the protectionists. Parkes, disappointed over federation and worn out, seemed almost to court defeat. Barton met him with resignations written out not only of his government but for his own seat. 'What is to become of Federation?' said Barton. Parkes replied, 'You are young and strong—you must take up Federation.'

Of course Barton had already 'taken up' federation, but this was his warrant for assuming the leadership of the cause. To many his next act appeared to betray it. He joined Dibbs's protectionist government, which, by introducing tariffs directed against the other colonies, created another barrier to federation. Barton obtained undertakings from Dibbs that the tariffs would not be high and that he would have a free hand to seek parliamentary consideration of the Convention's constitution. Yet this action seemed at odds with the independent line he had taken at his election. To free-traders it confirmed that federation was not a noble national cause but a device for imposing protection on New South Wales.

Barton as bandit cloaking protection with federation: the view of the free-trade *Daily Telegraph*, July 1898 (election edition), recalling the 'betrayal' of 1891.

It was more than a year before Barton introduced the constitution to the parliament. Parkes, who in the event had not resigned his own seat, berated him for the delay and denied that he had given him the leadership. Barton chided Parkes for demoting federation from top priority. The two men had a nasty falling out. The bond that had launched the federal campaign was broken. While the constitution languished in New South Wales, there was no point in the other colonies proceeding.

The collapse of the federation movement coincided with the collapse in the economy. Severe depression set in from 1891 and was followed by a long drought. In 1891 wool prices sank to their lowest point ever. In Melbourne, where the depression was worst, unemployment reached 25 per cent. Between 1891 and 1893 most of the building societies and banks collapsed, destroying or locking up the modest savings of ordinary people and paralysing commerce.

Deakin, like other leading politicians, had been at the heart of the land boom mania of the 1880s. He was chairman of directors of the City of Melbourne Building Society, which was an older and more reputable society than most, but it still went under. Deakin lost his own and his father's savings. In prayer he wrote, 'Disaster has overtaken me at last, O God, and upon me lies in some degree the responsibility for disaster to many others.' He led a penitential life in the 1890s, refusing ministerial office, returning to the law (which he hated) to recoup his own and his family's finances, and devoting himself to federation.

The London money market temporarily lost faith in Australia. The collapse of the economy and its financial institutions confirmed the doubts it had been harbouring since the late 1880s that Australia was borrowing too much and not investing wisely. In April 1891, just as the Convention dispersed, the Victorian Government was rebuffed when it tried to raise a loan. Borrowing in London was central to the operation of government in Australia. British capital built the railways and other developmental works. As loan funds dried up, governments had to stop their construction works. With the depression, ordinary government revenue also shrank. Harsh economies had to be made and new taxation imposed. This is when Australians began to pay income tax. At all costs, interest on the debt had to be met and the money market reassured about government solvency and efficiency.

This restructuring was carried through by governments that were liberal and progressive, not conservative. Conservatives were keen about cutting public spending but not good at imposing taxation on land and income. Despite the stringency, these governments expanded the role of the state. They founded state banks, repurchased land for closer settlement, started agricultural departments to promote the new industries of dairying and frozen meat, and set up arbitration courts and wages boards. The new Labor Party was a supporter of state activity, but nowhere did it govern. In still-fluid parliaments, liberal governments in New South Wales, Victoria, and South Australia depended on Labor to varying extents.

The 1890s was also a decade of democratic progress. The democracies established in the 1850s were hobbled and half-hearted. When all men had been given the vote, property holding was retained as a voting qualification, so those who owned land in several electorates had more than one vote. Strong upper houses, either elected by property-holders or nominated by the Governor, regularly rejected popular measures. In the 1890s the new Labor Party and the radical liberals raised the cry of 'one man, one vote', and plural voting, as it was called, was finally abolished. South Australia had never allowed it. Maintaining its progressive reputation, this colony in 1894 was the first to introduce votes for women. In the more backward Tasmania and Western Australia votes for all men were introduced for the first time. Since democracy was now being taken seriously, upper houses not elected by the people came under serious attack, and there were many advocates of the referendum as the authoritative expression of the people's will.

The federal cause had to make its way in this environment and was of course affected by it. Those who see federation as primarily a business settlement consider that the depression gave the stimulus it needed for success. Since a single economy with a national government would be a better credit risk, business and government now had solid reasons for wanting federation. Some go further and argue that federation should be understood as a restructuring of the economy and the creation of a system of government that could resist the new forces of socialism.

Little evidence has been produced to support these claims. The most revealing evidence on this issue is something that did not happen.

In 1894 Dibbs, the protectionist Premier of New South Wales, proposed a new plan for union that was designed to please the markets.[6] He had been closely involved in the financial crisis. In 1892 he had gone to London to reassure the markets about Australian solvency (this is when he received his knighthood); in March 1893 he went bankrupt; and in May 1893 he deftly used government backing to save the remaining New South Wales banks even against their will.

He argued that the 1891 constitution followed the US model too closely in leaving most powers with the states. They would still run their railways and compete with each other for border trade. They would still compete in London to raise loans. He proposed a complete union of New

South Wales and Victoria: one railway system, one public debt, one revenue (including the proceeds of land sale and lease), and a single representative in London to deal with loan business. The local parliaments would remain to deal with subordinate matters, fully under direction of the centre. For the moment the other four colonies were excluded. They would join later on terms set by the union. There was to be no nonsense of equal representation for the states.

If such a plan had been adopted, the financial crisis could have been credited with forcing Australian union into an entirely different path. In fact the plan received almost no support. The *Insurance and Banking Record* liked it. Oddly, the *Bulletin* found it attractive because it was hard-headed and free of Parkesian heroics. But it was just these qualities that made it unattractive to committed federalists. They wanted to make the whole of Australia into a nation. Dividing the nation and leaving the smaller states the options of being coerced into union or languishing outside it was simply abhorrent. The Victorian Government was wary of being reabsorbed into New South Wales. Times were not so hard that reunification had to be agreed to. The Dibbs plan is the great non-event of the federal story.

So what did happen?

At first interest in federation almost completely disappeared. In principle the case for federation strengthened. A united Australia would have weathered this storm much better. In practice federation was no help at all. The failure of Parkes's initiative had confirmed the view that federation was extraordinarily difficult and would take a long time. Quick remedies were needed. The Federal Council still existed; New South Wales could join it and its responsibilities could be expanded. A customs union could be formed, and, failing that, reciprocal treaties between particular colonies could be agreed. All these ideas had their advocates.

Despite all its previous failures, the Melbourne Chamber of Commerce took up the customs union plan in February 1893. Its secretary, Benjamin Cowderoy, still believed that this was an easy, practical project. This time the Chamber was determined to succeed. Before it approached the other colonies, it planned to build a solid base of support in Victoria. It called into conference the Chamber of Manufactures, the Royal Agricultural Society, the Trades Hall, and the Australian Natives Association. They quickly agreed on the benefits of intercolonial free trade and immediately fell out over what customs duty the union should levy. The manufacturers and the Trades Hall insisted on protection against the world. Cowderoy objected that this would damage their chances with the other colonies. He suggested that the protectionists reserve their right to insist on that policy, but allow a declaration in favour of a customs union to go forward. They refused. They wanted tariff policy to be defined.

The Chamber of Commerce then offered a definition that it hoped all could support: the tariff of the union 'should be based upon the present existing tariffs of the various colonies'. So it could be anything: the Victorian tariff or the New South Wales tariff! That placated the manufacturers, but not the Trades Hall, which abstained on the vote. It would support only a policy committed to protection. Not deterred by this dissension, the Chamber of Commerce obtained agreement for a further conference to draw up a tariff that Victorian delegates would present to an intercolonial conference. This proposal never left the realm of fantasy.[7]

None the less, the Chamber pressed Patterson, the Victorian Premier, to open negotiations with the other colonies for a customs union. He had the chance when the premiers met in an emergency conference in May 1893 immediately after the worst week of the banking crisis.[8] Banking was its chief business. Dibbs failed to persuade the other premiers to follow him in giving the banks government guarantees. Patterson had dealt with the crisis by enforcing a bank holiday for a week, which had made the panic worse. Instead the premiers agreed to uniform bank legislation in the future. Downer of South Australia was to draft it, but he was defeated soon after and the plan lapsed. Intercolonial free trade was reached late in the proceedings. Dibbs, not in a cooperative mood, said New South Wales was not ready for it. He could not abandon the duties he had recently introduced directed against agricultural produce from Victoria and South Australia. They were assisting farming to grow in the pastoral colony. There seemed no way to solve this conundrum of New South Wales and a customs union: protectionists in that colony would fear intercolonial free trade; free-traders would fear protection against the world.

In the second half of 1893 leadership on Australian union in Melbourne passed from the Chamber of Commerce to the Australian Natives Association.[9] The branches in Melbourne and its suburbs formed a special organisation to reawaken interest in federation. They made Deakin its president. It canvassed the views of the key interest groups: the Chamber of Commerce, the Chamber of Manufactures, the Agricultural Society, and the Trades Hall. The Natives did much better than the Chamber of Commerce in holding this coalition together. They could present themselves as neutral players, having nothing to gain out of federation except federation itself, and since federation now meant federation by Parkes's method, the tariff issue did not have to be resolved. The Natives next brought together every political association and interest group in the city and achieved agreement on the formation of a Federation League. About forty groups were represented in a meeting without parallel: employers and workers, free-traders and protectionists, radicals and conservatives, teetotallers and publicans. This diverse group then had to agree on the rules and platform of the League. If Deakin was looking to do penance, he found it in the hard grind of holding these groups together.

In July 1894 the League was finally constituted. The Chief Justice was the president. The secretary was Richard Toutcher, who had been secretary of the Natives federation organisation. The formation of the League was a triumph for the Natives. When they first took up federation in the early 1880s they were still being mocked and reviled; now everyone was prepared to accept their leadership.

The whole process had taken almost a year. It established in Victoria that the union was to be political before it was economic. The Chamber of Commerce and other business groups had to drop their insistence that a customs union be first priority; they were placated by the Federation League's commitment to reducing barriers between the colonies in the interim. The union was to be by federation, not unification. No group before it joined the Federation League demanded that the powers of the central government be more than was granted in the 1891 draft. This provided for Commonwealth power over banking, the option to take over state debts, and of course intercolonial free trade once a tariff had been agreed, which was enough to ensure business support.

It was the Left that demanded and obtained changes. The extreme demand for a republic was easily overridden, but the principle of 'one man, one vote' had to be embodied in the League's platform. Since the League allowed women to be members, there was strong support for the principle being 'one adult, one vote'. Deakin in the chair opposed this as likely to alienate too many, although he was a warm supporter of votes for women. In a meeting of 140, women were excluded by only one vote.[10] The Chamber of Commerce was dismayed about how much was being conceded to the Trades Hall and democracy, but decided to remain. This was the price they had to pay to gain intercolonial free trade. Only the Royal Agricultural Society withdrew.

To lure the Trades Hall Deakin also gave two new emphases to the case for federation. First, only a united Australia could reverse Queensland's decision to continue importing kanakas. Second, if wages and conditions were ever to be improved by law, it would have to be done on an Australia-wide basis. Otherwise there would be no answer to the objection that to improve wages in one colony would drive capital to another.[11] There was power in the 1891 draft to remove kanakas, but no power over wages and working conditions. Charles Kingston, the South Australian radical, had attempted to give the Commonwealth power over interstate industrial disputes. Deakin and ten other delegates voted with him against twenty-five who were opposed.[12]

In Adelaide the movement for union after the 1891 economic collapse followed the Melbourne pattern. At first the Chamber of Commerce was active, seeking a customs union or reciprocal treaties with other colonies.[13] It was of the utmost importance to the colony to keep trade flowing freely across its border with New South Wales since the one bright spot in its economy was its substantial trade with the new mines at Broken Hill. From 1893 South Australia also benefited from supplying the one colony in the country that was booming: Western Australia. South Australia now joined Tasmania as a colony for which freedom of intercolonial trade was vital. When Parkes made his move for federation in 1889, South Australian leaders were cautious, fearing that their newly established factories could not stand Victorian competition. That consideration was now totally outweighed by the advantages that intercolonial free trade would bring.

Of course the efforts of the Chamber of Commerce bore no fruit. In 1895 the Australian Natives Association organised a Federation League with support from the Chamber of Commerce and the Chamber of Manufactures. Its official launch was almost as impressive as Melbourne's: the Lieutenant-Governor, cabinet ministers, business and unions, liberals and conservatives. The president of the League was Josiah Symon, a Scots lawyer, the leader of the local bar, who began his federal career with this appointment. The secretary was Fred Stokes, who came from the Australian Natives.[14]

In free-trade Sydney the Chamber of Commerce made no attempt to take the lead on Australian union, which was much too closely associated with protectionism. Its response to depression and financial crisis was to urge that government spending should be cut to avoid the need for direct taxation.[15] Leadership in the federal cause remained with Barton.

Barton persisted with parliamentary consideration of the 1891 constitution long after the history books, including this one, declare that its moment had passed. What else was there to do? The draft constitution was in itself a huge achievement; it was now accepted that it was to be amended; let the New South Wales Parliament decide on its amendments; the other parliaments would follow; a second convention would be held and the result submitted to the people.

Before that process began, Barton declared that when the people were consulted it would be on the principle of 'one man, one vote'.[16] As minister in Dibbs's government he introduced that principle into the New South Wales electoral law in 1892. Like Deakin, he also tried to assuage Labor's hostility to federation by stressing that only the Commonwealth could deal with the kanakas in Queensland.[17] But Barton lost all credit with Labor when as Attorney-General he prosecuted the leaders of the 1892 Broken Hill strike, taking care to move the trial to Deniliquin to ensure a favourable result. The men did not stay in jail long because Dibbs's government depended on Labor support in the Assembly. Dibbs took great pleasure in releasing them in honour of the marriage of the Duke of York. Labor did not forgive Barton.

Parliamentary consideration of the constitution was inordinately slow. There was always something more important than federation to discuss. In fact the parliament never did formulate its amendments to the 1891 draft. The greatest advance came when, during the first debate in November 1892, George Reid apologised for having denounced the framers of the document as robbers of the people's liberties. He conceded that despite its faults the draft would be the basis of an acceptable constitution. He had already found occasion to praise Barton's defence of the constitution, in answer to his own attack, as the best speech he had ever read. (This might have been a subtle dig: Reid knew better than anybody that a speech that read well did not sound well.)[18]

Reid was changing his mind about free trade's chances in a federated Australia. The general trend of opinion seemed to be moving against protection. The United States, long held up as a model by protectionists, had just elected a president committed to using customs only to raise revenue. Free-traders rallied in Sydney and Melbourne to celebrate Grover Cleveland's victory, with Reid the lead speaker in Sydney and Parkes in Melbourne.[19] And protectionist Victoria had been brought low with a depression more severe than anywhere else. A questioning of its policy must follow. Its farmers, who now sold on world markets, were showing signs that they would desert protection. All around Australia farmers had turned protectionists against farmers in other colonies. In a united Australia, with the internal barriers gone, they would become free-traders against the world to keep their costs down. So Reid found signs that the five drunkards might sober up.

His new attitude was highly significant because he was now the leader of the free-trade party. When Parkes resigned the leadership, none of his ministers wanted it and Reid became leader almost by default. Parkes was enraged by the consequences of his abdication—Reid, a mountebank, leading his party, and Barton, a traitor, leading his federal movement—but this Lear had not yet lost his wits. He was scheming to create a third force of federalists, both free-traders and protectionists. To keep the allegiance of all the free-traders, Reid had to be more open on federation. He had also made another adaptation to fit him for his new responsibilities. Twelve days before he became leader, he had married a woman of 22, less than half his age.

Late in 1892 Barton began a movement to make parliament take federation more seriously. Visiting the Riverina, where border duties were a constant annoyance, he urged the formation of federal leagues. They appeared rapidly on both sides of the River Murray. Edward Wilson, a Corowa solicitor, established the first in his town and, using Barton's name, got branches started in a number of others.[20] Already Barton was personifying the cause and attracting devoted followers.

Barton planned to start a central organisation in Sydney to coordinate local efforts. The Australian Natives Association in Sydney encouraged him and offered their assistance.[21] Their most useful offering was their secretary, Edward Dowling, who thereafter worked full-time for the Federation League without pay. He was an older Native, which was unusual in Victoria but not in Sydney, a retired civil servant who worked quietly for many causes: workers' education, temperance, the promotion of Australian literature, and Aboriginal protection. He thought the Aborigines were a people of considerable intelligence who had been much underrated.[22] He was a meticulous record-keeper whose efforts allow us to know more about this League than any other.

A federation league for Sydney could not be founded in the Melbourne and Adelaide way by inviting the cooperation of all interests and community groups. In Sydney they were either hostile to federation or divided. Barton had to recruit sympathetic individuals and, making the best of his difficulties, promoted his League as a great citizens' movement. Gaining bipartisan political support was also difficult because the parties were designed for battle over the tariff, and federation on Parkes's model called for its resolution in another sphere. Reid declined to join the League because he saw it as a diversion, concocted by a minister in the protection-ist government to prevent him making free trade the issue at the next local election. Parkes also declined to join for reasons too tortuous and unprofitable to pursue since they merely hid his determination not to assist any federal movement that he did not lead.[23] Barton did manage to snare one leading free-trade politician, the merchant William McMillan, who had been Parkes's treasurer and a delegate to the 1890 Conference and the 1891 Convention. McMillan was very cautious, fearing he was going to be trapped.[24] Most of the politicians in the League were protectionists. To stop politics destroying the League, Barton stipulated that no more than two-fifths of its governing council and none of its executive could be politicians.[25]

Taking federation to the public in Sydney was still a perilous business. At the League's launch in the Town Hall there was a good crowd, mostly

Distributed at Town Hall Meeting by Socialists

BE A NATION, NOT A DEPENDENCY.

Friends of Government for the People by the People,—

A movement is on foot amongst certain leading politicians and members of the National Association to form an Australian Federation League, the objects of which shall be

"Federation UNDER THE CROWN of Great Britain and Ireland, with a Governor-General appointed by the QUEEN, at a salary of NOT LESS than £10,000 a year, who shall be Her Majesty's Representative, and who shall and may exercise such powers and functions as the Queen MAY THINK FIT TO ASSIGN HIM."—(See Draft Bill).

A Federation with many other Undemocratic Features, such as the proposed Senate, or Australian House of Lords; a Federation allowing West Australia with only 50,000 population the same representation in the Federal Parliament as New South Wales with 1,200,000 population.

The members of the South Sydney Labor Electoral League have therefore authorised the undersigned to attend the Imperial Federation Demonstration to be held in the large Town Hall this (Monday) evening, and move the following amendment to the first resolution :—

That it is expedient to advance the cause of Australian Democracy by an organisation of citizens using its best energies to establish Australian Federation on the following basis :

1. That the colonies federating shall form themselves into a Democratic Republic to be called

THE UNITED STATES OF AUSTRALIA.

2. That all laws necessary for the peace, order, and good government of the Republic shall be made by a Federal Parliament consisting of only one chamber.

3. That the Federal Laws shall provide for—

(a) One Man One Vote throughout each State.

(b) The Nationalisation of all Land.

(c) The Abolition of all Legislative Councils, and the Substitution of the Referendum.

(d) The total exclusion of all Asiatics and other aliens whose standard of living and habits of life are not equal to our own, and whose entering into competition with Australian wage-earners is a direct menace to the national welfare.

The above, we are aware, does not go as far as the more advanced democrat would wish, but it contains an expression on certain vital principles upon which all Australian wage-earners—freetrade, protectionist, single-tax, or socialist—can heartily agree. The amendment will be seconded by Mr. W. A. HOLMAN, and supported by Mr. G. BLACK, M.L.A., and others.

The suddenness with which, after a long period of lethargy, the Imperial Federation movement has been thrust upon us is our apology for not consulting other electoral leagues and democratic associations before taking the responsibility of formulating the above amendment, and in conclusion we would urge all the friends of Australian Democracy to roll up early, get well to the front, KEEP ORDER, give their speakers fair play; see also that we get a hearing; and VOTE THEM DOWN!

The presence of a large concourse of people should afford an excellent opportunity for an expression of opinion on the Railway and Maritime troubles.

W. G. HIGGS,
President South Sydney Labor Electoral League.

South Sydney Labor Electoral League Smoke Concert, Carlton Club, Albion-street, near Elizabeth-street, Tuesday Evening, July 11. Admission FREE.

"Australian Workman" Print, 97½ Bathurst-street.

The Labor Party's attempt to disrupt Barton's Federation League.

collected by the South Sydney Labor Party, which was opposed to federation under the Crown. It was a tense meeting. Barton was given a hearing only after agreeing that the Labor people could put their amendments after he had spoken. They wanted a democratic republic called the United States of Australia, with a single house of parliament, one man, one vote, and nationalisation of all land. Along with all their other difficulties, federalists now had to cope with Labor utopianism. The mayor, who was in the chair, coped with it by declaring their amendments lost, although a majority had voted for them. The League was launched. The Laborites took over and moved no confidence in the mayor.[26]

The first historian of the Federation League was impressed by the number of businessmen who joined it and by a League circular, which stressed that federation would revive commerce and restore Australia's credit rating. He suggested that the renewal of interest in federation could have been prompted by these economic concerns. It was a cautious study; the author noted the large contingent of professional men in the league who had no direct economic interest in federation and who should probably be described as idealists. He called for further research.[27] Without further research these suggestions were taken as proof of the federal movement being reinvigorated by businessmen. Now that the research has been done, these suggestions look very wan.

Note that this initiative did not come from businessmen. Their organisation, the Chamber of Commerce, did not promote it. These people were invited by Barton to join him. The League recruited its large General Council by identifying likely individuals, telling them by circular that they had been elected to the Council, and asking for a donation.[28] Unless they declined the honour, their name was added to the list. Most did not give a donation. The executive, which was the key body, had at its core a group of lawyers, who were young or in mid career, native-born, and extraordinarily talented; they included a future judge, two chief justices and a Commonwealth Solicitor-General, Robert Garran, who at 26 was the youngest and the most active.[29] The one active businessman on the executive in its first year was a building contractor.[30] It was this executive that issued the famous circular directed to leading citizens to raise money. The response was 'small'.[31]

Businessmen were more likely to give money than be active on the executive, but they were not prominent among the most generous donors. Their occupations are as follows (in declining order of amount given): lawyer (treasurer of the League); lawyer (friend of Barton); banker; lawyer (Barton); lawyer (Garran); professor of classics; manufacturer.[32] The League was severely handicapped by shortage of funds. Its income in the first year was £94, in its second £30, above which it never rose again.[33] The idea that big money in Sydney was backing this League is a joke; it would have greatly amused the League collectors, who, working on commission, could not make a go of it, even when approaching members of the League's council, most of whom were unfinancial.[34] When there were no funds, Dowling, the secretary, paid for the next batch of federalist literature out of his own pocket.[35]

The League is better thought of as a group of professional men appealing with very limited success to business for support.[36] Until the very end the majority of Sydney business was opposed to federation. If federation was designed to defeat Labor, why did business in the colony where the Labor Party was strongest take so little interest in it? The one change in the governing body of the Federation League came in its second year when a Labor MP and three former presidents of the Trades and Labour Council joined the executive, a more prominent contingent than the businessmen.[37] They were for different reasons at odds with the Labor Party but were useful in reaching its constituency.

The drive to found the League unquestionably came from the patriot politician Barton, who like Deakin did the hard work of bringing people together. At this time he was close to collapse. He was working very hard as a minister, sleeping for a few hours only, eating too much, and drinking heavily. He got the League started, stayed up all night to write its rules, had them accepted next day, and then, under doctor's orders, left on a sea voyage to Canada.[38]

Sydney, Melbourne, and Adelaide were the only capitals to form federation leagues in the mid 1890s. Their secretaries, all members of the Natives Association, kept in close touch. In all three capitals it was the nationalists, the enthusiasts for federation, who marshalled the interest groups. It was important for the success of federation that the nationalists remain in charge. As Barton warned, if the businessmen achieved their customs union first, they would lose interest in the formation of the nation.[39]

The Leagues along the Murray were the clearest instance of an economic grievance prompting support for federation. In mid 1893 they hosted a conference on federation at Corowa, inviting federalists from both colonies to attend. Garran and Dowling came from the newly formed Sydney League. From Victoria there was a large contingent of Natives, who were just starting to organise their federation league, and representatives of the radical liberals and the Labor Party. The Melbourne Chamber of Commerce sent Benjamin Cowderoy, no longer its secretary but its president. He went in high hope because here of all places, where customs houses stood at either end of the Corowa bridge, he would find support for immediate action to

Corowa remembers its great moment in a story-and-activity book for children. The court house where the Federal Conference met is top left.

remove customs barriers and establish a customs union. The bolder spirits at the conference actually thought of throwing the customs gate into the river as a surrogate for tea, but wiser heads prevailed.[40]

Cowderoy nearly wrecked the conference. There was support from the border leagues for his motion on a customs union, but, as always, talking tariffs was divisive. The Melbourne protectionists became alarmed at this move by Melbourne merchants, which must signal a desire for free trade with the rest of the world. A compromise had to be found to hold the conference together. It resolved in favour of the free interchange of Australian goods and products, which meant nothing had to be said about external tariff policy. Cowderoy returned to Melbourne in high dudgeon. Such a policy was a nonsense since the border customs houses would have to remain to check on the movement of overseas goods, which the colonies would be treating differently. He explained to his Chamber that he would have made this point at the conference but the chairman announced the compromise in a very low voice and he did not catch it.[41] Cowderoy was

80. Within a year his Chamber submitted to Melbourne's Federation League, and his long campaign to unite Australia on a 'practical' basis was at an end.

At the conference John Quick, delegate of the Bendigo Natives, hit on a new way to unite Australia. He was 41, a lawyer, who had begun working at the mines when he was 10. He had come to Australia when he was two so the Bendigo Natives had bent the rules to allow him in. The elements of his plan were not new. He proposed a new convention, elected by the people, to draw up a constitution, which would be submitted to the people for approval. The novel element, which showed a lawyer's practicality, was that the process should be embodied in a law, passed by all the parliaments, which would commit them to allowing the process to proceed and abiding by its outcome. The people would be in charge and not the politicians.

As was common, the resolutions to be submitted at the Corowa conference had been drawn up beforehand. Quick's was unscheduled. After the passing of a resolution in favour of federation, a few of the delegates were looking to do something more; to have action and not merely talk. Quick came up with his plan, which the conference adopted in a wave of euphoria.[42]

Later Quick's authorship of the plan was contested, but it is certain that he took the responsibility of publicising it.[43] After Corowa it was just one suggestion among many. Quick put it into proper legal form and presented it to the newly formed Bendigo Federation League, which, acting like a parliament, examined it clause by clause and adopted it. He next gained the endorsement of the league-in-formation in Melbourne. In January 1894 he travelled to Sydney where he presented it to the Federation League, which adopted it in modified form, and to the Leader of the Opposition, George Reid, who showed considerable interest.[44] Out of courtesy he visited the anti-federalist Premier Dibbs, who told him his scheme was years ahead of its time.

At the New South Wales election in mid 1894 Reid defeated Dibbs on a policy of repealing the new protectionist duties and establishing true free trade. One of his first acts as Premier was to contact the other premiers to get federation moving again. The cause was now in the hands of the man who had wrecked it in 1891.

7
Revival

Left at death's door by the politicians, Federation was revived by the People.
R. R. Garran, 'Memories of Federation', 2BL, January 1951

'The people, not the politicians': this became the mantra of the federalists as they took up Quick's plan for a new start in constitution-making. It was a very successful rallying cry. It pointed the way forward and explained past failure. Since the people must be in favour of federation, success would be guaranteed once the business was in their hands. The cause failed when it was in the hands of the politicians because they always have their own agenda and a great capacity for obfuscation. They were also stupid and arrogant enough to think they could create a nation without involving the people. But politicians are very thick-skinned. Among the growing chorus criticising the parliamentary approach to nationhood and invoking the people were politicians themselves. Whatever happened, they would not be left out.

Politicians in Australia did not enjoy a high standing. Democracy had widened the ranks from which they were drawn and in so doing had allowed in rogues, drunks, and the foul-mouthed. Parliaments were not gatherings of gentlemen, and their proceedings were frequently very ungentlemanly. So politicians were an easy target as unworthy nation-makers. But whatever the qualities of politicians, a higher form of democracy now seemed within reach. The 1890s—the federation decade—was the high point in Australian history of belief in the referendum and elected ministries, causes espoused by radical and democratic politicians. The referendum, regularly used, would mean the people would truly rule, and

SCENES IN THE ASSEMBLY; OR, WHAT IT MAY COME TO.
Sydney *Punch* depicts the degradation of parliament, March 1871.

a ministry elected by all parliamentarians would end fatuous and unfruitful adversarial politics and allow governments to be more representative of the people. The plan for a convention elected by the people and a constitution approved by the people was not simply a reaction against politicians; it was an affirmation of the superiority of direct democracy.

A popularly elected constitutional convention was a most un-British device. It acknowledged the sovereignty of the people whereas in Britain sovereignty formally rested with the monarch and in practice with parliament.

The idea of a *convention* was not unknown in English constitutional history. There had been two convention parliaments, the first in 1660, which summoned Charles II to the throne after the republican Commonwealth; the second in 1688–89, which declared the throne vacant after the flight of James II and set the terms for the assumption of the throne by William and Mary. They were called convention parliaments because they had not been properly summoned by a monarch. Although they made fundamental adjustments to the constitution, they were thought of as lesser or inferior parliaments, a temporary device to deal with unusual circumstances. All their measures were re-enacted by the next true parliament to ensure their legitimacy. Those backward-looking innovators, the Stuart parliamentarians, were determined not to elevate a convention over a parliament.

This use of a convention was followed by the American colonists when they too had to deal with the flight of James II. A hundred years later, when they were disputing British control, they called conventions when royalist governors either refused to summon assemblies or closed them because of their seditious talk. As in England, these bodies were first regarded as regrettable expedients. Then in the crucible of revolution they were rapidly transformed into necessary bodies; the proper expression of the people's will, self-evidently superior to a normal assembly, and the body that ought to create the constitution under which an assembly would operate. State constitutions were remade by conventions, some of them elected by all male inhabitants and referring their work to them. After the War of Independence had been won, the United States constitution was drawn up by a convention elected by the state legislatures.[1]

From the new United States, *convention* in its new meaning returned to Europe. In 1792 the French created a convention, elected by all adult males, to decide the fate of the deposed king and to frame a new constitution. Meanwhile, under the leadership of the Jacobins, it also governed France and, by its methods of terror, made *convention* synonymous with bloodshed and tyranny. But not for everyone. The summoning of a convention became the dream of British radicals. It rather than the parliament would be the true embodiment of the people's will. It would shame, confront, and control parliament and perhaps supplant it, if parliament refused to do its bidding. The long-talked-of convention finally met under Chartist auspices in 1839 and ended in fiasco when parliament remained unmoved by its entreaties.[2] In Australia the convention as radical oppositional device inspired the Land Convention of Victoria in 1857, which demanded that parliament allow poor men access to the land.

The precedents for the official federal conventions in Australia were American. During the nineteenth century British opinion about the United States and its constitution underwent a complete reversal. While democracy and republicanism were threatening the established order in Britain in the early nineteenth century, the United States constitution was suspect, more especially because radicals made so much of it. Aristocratic opinion in Britain welcomed the break-up of the American union in 1860. Canadian confederation in the 1860s was determinedly a union on British rather than American lines and directed against the United States. In the 1850s when the Australian colonies drew up constitutions for self-government no one suggested that writing a constitution was a job for a specially elected convention. The constitutions were drawn up by the existing legislatures, the legislative councils, in which a third of the members were nominated by the Governor.

In the second half of the century British admiration of the United States constitution grew. Commentators competed to praise its wisdom. Gladstone's encomium—the 'most wonderful work ever struck off at one time by the brain and purpose of man'—was well known.[3] Just as Australian constitution-making began, the English historian–politician James Bryce published his *American Commonwealth*, which became the bible of convention delegates in Australia. Bryce ranked the American constitution above every other written constitution 'for the intrinsic excellence of its scheme, its adaptation to the circumstances of the people, for the simplicity, brevity, and precision of its language, its judicious mixture of definiteness in principle with elasticity in details'.[4] He also praised the conventions still regularly called to amend the state constitutions, whose members and deliberations were far superior to those of the legislatures that created them. George Reid was well acquainted with these passages in Bryce.[5]

Service, who called the first Australian federal convention in 1883, had in mind the American precedent. He wanted the delegates to be elected by the parliaments and for them to draw up a constitution. The New South Wales leaders did not like his choice of this pretentious, un-British name.[6] Because of their objections, only ministers attended, and it produced only the very weak Federal Council. The 1891 Convention elected by the parliaments followed the United States model. To bypass the parliaments and have the people constitute a convention was a more radical proposal. It had been followed by some of the American colonies in 1776 and in France in 1792, both revolutionary situations. Authority in Australia was quite secure. The great flaw in the Quick plan was that the bypassing of parliaments required parliamentary approval before it could begin.

Barton had not been at Corowa when Quick's plan was formulated. He was voyaging on the Pacific to recover his health. When he returned after seven weeks he still intended that parliament should complete its examination of the 1891 draft. To put more pressure on it, he started a speaking campaign in Sydney and the formation of branches of the Federation League in the suburbs.

When Quick came to Sydney early in 1894 Barton and the Sydney League had to formulate a position on his scheme, which now had strong backing in Victoria. Barton did not like it; he was a conservative liberal who was not enthusiastic about increasing popular power. Under his leadership the League produced a report on the scheme, which criticised the exclusion of parliamentarians on two grounds. First, parliaments would never agree to it. Second, politicians were the experts in reconciling conflicting opinions, a skill that popularly elected delegates might well lack. Its rival plan kept the popular element but corralled it. There would be a popularly elected convention in each colony to draw up the colony's preferred mode of federation. Then politicians elected by the parliaments would gather in convention to reconcile the various proposals into a constitution, which would then be submitted to the people at referendum.[7]

The Sydney Federation League urged its plan upon the Premier, George Reid, who had called a meeting of premiers at Hobart in January 1895 to consider how to proceed on federation. Reid was respectful; he saw merits and disadvantages in the League's plan and in Quick's, but he clearly favoured Quick's. He liked the direct link, the pulse as he called it, beating between the electors and the members of the convention, which would arouse interest and enthusiasm.[8] What led Reid to embrace cheerfully the plan of a directly elected convention was his confidence that only high-profile politicians would be elected to it.[9]

'Dishing Parkes': one advantage to Reid of his embracing of federation. (*Bulletin*, 15 September 1894)

When Reid took the Quick plan to his cabinet, important changes were made. To meet the obvious objection that parliaments were being bypassed, they were given a final veto: the constitution as adopted by the people would only go to London if the parliaments resolved to send it. To ensure that only leading politicians were elected, the colonies were to vote as one electorate. Quick had provided for ten electorates. The dangers of this, as Reid saw it, were that good men would have to run against each other and local considerations would intrude. Furthermore, electors had to vote for ten candidates; there could be no plumping; that is, voting for your favourite candidate and not giving a vote to anyone else.[10]

At the Hobart premiers' conference only Kingston of South Australia was firmly for Reid's plan. He had an almost Jacobin enthusiasm for a democratically elected convention that would ignore parliament altogether. The other premiers to varying degrees had misgivings, and to meet these one further alteration was made. The convention would draft a constitution and then adjourn to allow the parliaments to suggest amendments, which the convention on reconvening would consider before adopting a final version.[11] Four premiers agreed to this modified plan. Sir John Forrest of Western Australia would have nothing to do with this pure democracy; he wanted to continue with the 1891 draft and keep the parliaments in charge. Hugh Nelson of Queensland would not bind himself to the referendum as the means of gaining acceptance.

The Federal Council was meeting at Hobart at the same time as the premiers. Its delegates came from only four colonies: Victoria, Queensland, Tasmania, and Western Australia. In this gathering Nelson made clear that he had no sympathy for the new fad of flattering the people as constitution-makers; he said he had only agreed to the election of delegates to oblige the other premiers.[12] Some of the councillors were miffed that their role as a federal body was being usurped by the premiers and their plan. A motion was proposed that federation could be advanced by the parliaments speedily considering the 1891 draft. There would then be no need for Reid's disturbing democratic mechanism. The Victorians would have none of this. Deakin told the councillors that they had had ample opportunity to examine the 1891 draft. The Victorians had founded the Council and sustained it. Now to show their support for Reid and a new beginning, they walked out of the Council and left the others to pass a useless motion on parliaments returning to the 1891 draft.

In Sydney the premiers' plan was immediately criticised by Parkes, who declared, 'It is preposterous to talk of a mob of people making a constitution for the state.' Nothing that Reid did could win his approval; he would perform any contortion to oppose him. In 1892, when the enemy was Barton and his offence the slow passage of the 1891 draft through parliament,

THE FEDERAL CHILD.
LONG-LOST MOTHER: *Gimme back my che-ild!*
THE FOSTER MOTHER: Your *child! Why, I took 'im out of the gutter, where you left 'im to starve, an' now that I've washed 'im, an' fed 'im, an' made 'im respectable like, you want to claim 'im.* (*Bulletin*, 16 February 1895)

Parkes had declared that parliaments should be bypassed and a new convention should be elected by the people.[13]

Quick's plan gave Reid the advantage of pursuing federation without disrupting his domestic program. But he would not allow the process to begin until he had carried the key element in his policy. Reid declared he would go into federation with the free-trade flag flying. The premiers had agreed that New South Wales should act first on setting the new plan into action. Reid delayed matters almost twelve months, which led federalists to think that he was trifling with the great cause. Certainly he wanted free trade for his colony more than federation.

Free trade became a radical cause in Reid's hands because he linked it with the introduction of direct taxation on land and income, which was to make up for the reduction in customs revenue. Small farmers and working people were to be exempted from the new taxes; it was the rich who were to be made to pay. This kept the Labor Party firm in its support for Reid's government. It led the Legislative Council to reject the tax by 41 votes to 4.

Now that free trade was linked with direct taxation many of the rich became converts to protectionism. Better to have everyone pay tax at the customs house than have the state touching their wealth. Reid had manoeuvred the protectionists into being the 'conservative' party, the defenders of privilege. This was untrue of the party as a whole as it included many radicals, but now they had some high-profile and not altogether welcome allies. So in New South Wales the tariff issue had assumed the opposite bearing from what it had in Victoria. There free-traders were the conservatives. Victorians were suspicious of Reid as a federalist; Victorian liberals also found it hard to recognise him as a liberal because his tariff policy was that of their enemies.

When the Council rejected his tax package, Reid launched a campaign to assert the supremacy of the people's will, such as the Victorian liberals had fought in the 1860s and 1870s. In Britain and Australia the extension of political rights to the people was the great saga of the century. Reid summoned up memories of past battles and the fervour of a renewed crusade. He insisted that the people's House, the Assembly, must control finance, which the Lords had yielded to the Commons in England. Having staked his political life to this principle in colonial politics, he would be reluctant to compromise it when he came to discuss a federal constitution.

The men in the Council blocking the people's will were nominated to their position for life by the Governor. Reid called them fossils and mummies, or, alternately, butchers bloody with the slaughter of the Assembly's measures. He could advise the Governor to create new councillors, but on this matter governors were not bound to follow their ministers' advice. To show the councillors (and the Governor) that he had the peoples' support, Reid dissolved the Assembly and went to an election, just twelve months after winning office. To frighten the Council he drew up plans for its reform. It would remain a nominated house, but the term of office would be five years rather than life; the Council could not touch the annual budget; on other money Bills it would have limited powers; ordinary Bills blocked by the Council would be put to the people for a decision by referendum.

Reid's crusade for free trade, taxing the rich, and reform of the Council was more exciting and more popular than federation. However, to Parkes and Barton, the leading federalists, Reid was diverting attention from the higher, nobler cause. The two men had recently buried their feud, after each had rehearsed his complaints against the other as a federalist and heard the other's reply.[14] They now cooperated in the election with the aim of destroying Reid and so advancing federation. Parkes left his own seat and ran directly against Reid in the King division of East Sydney. Barton campaigned for him. Barton was more active in the campaign than Parkes because just as it began the second Lady Parkes died of cancer. Barton himself was not running in the election. He was staying out of politics to recoup his finances through his law practice.

It is fruitless in Parkes's case to consider whether running against Reid served the federal cause well. His hatred of Reid had robbed him of his judgment. Barton, who did not yet hate Reid, was nevertheless convinced that he was trifling with federation and had to be opposed.[15] But it might be that, like Parkes, he did not want Reid to succeed as a federalist and claim the glory. Normally Barton—calm, devoted, high-minded—gave no indication that he wanted glory for himself. When he lost his seat at the 1894 election—to a free-trader and Reid supporter—he dropped his guard: 'I have fought the battle of immortal truth, and when the historian came to write the scroll of the victories in Australia's cause you will not find on it the name of any other candidate today, but there would be boldly inscribed upon it the name of Edmund Barton.'

As he had long been planning, Parkes had now created a Federal Party, a third force designed to gather both free-traders and protectionists. It argued that it was futile to continue the tariff dispute in colonial politics since the whole matter would have to be fought out again at the national level. But free-traders did not want to suspend the battle while the protective duties introduced by Dibbs were still in place. To them the Federal Party was a protectionist front. Parkes, the old free-trader leader, was denounced as a traitor for assisting the protectionists, and indeed, so intent was Parkes on displacing Reid that he had recently been operating openly in alliance with Dibbs.

The Federal Party attracted very few followers. Reid called it a 'knot of greedy, selfish politicians' debasing the cause of Australian union.[16] But its leader was not yet a spent force, and Parkes in his personal battle against Reid had the backing of big money, which was offered not to advance the cause of federation but to avert the direct taxation of land and income.[17]

The battle between Parkes and Reid in King division was titanic. The old sage and the usurper traded personal abuse round after round. For Parkes his case against Reid was personal. How could this uncultivated trickster who

The electoral battle of Parkes and Reid. (*Bulletin*, 20 July 1895)

employed the repartee of a backstreet larrikin hold the premiership of New South Wales, the position he had held and in which he had done so much for the country? And as for entrusting Reid with the cause of Australian union, 'we might as well expect a guinea pig to take a correct survey of the stars'.[18] Parkes spent some time honing such insults and waiting for the moment to use them. One of his campaign jibes was that if Reid had laboured as hard in public life as he had it would be impossible for 'his small brain to be accompanied by such a huge belly'.[19] But wit was a rarity in his abuse of Reid. There was mostly a tirade of wild insults and accusations climaxing with the demand that Reid be taken to a lunatic asylum.

In reply Reid was cool. There was no malice in him, and he never wanted politics to interfere with friendly personal relations. He criticised the old man more in sorrow than in anger and was prepared to praise him for his pluckiness. He had the best of it: 'He is always saying that I am perfectly mad. In one sense he is right, because if he is sane, then mad I must be.'[20]

Reid had a great victory. He defeated Parkes in his own seat, and his free-trade followers made up a majority in the Assembly without Labor support. Before reintroducing his tax measures, he softened up the Legislative Council by getting the Governor to appoint nine new members, all supporters of his measures. However, this was far from a 'swamping': the majority was still against him. But they now did agree to pass the tax measures, although Reid had to lower the exemption levels. Then the new tariff went through. Only three items were to pay duty: alcohol, tobacco, and opium, the shortest tariff schedule in the world. It did not operate immediately. Some of the existing duties were to be phased out, and in the event, a few had to be retained. The Legislative Council rejected Reid's measures to reform it, and having established free trade and direct taxation, he did not persist with them.

Parkes would not give up. Reid had shown himself a much better free-trader than he had ever been and was at the peak of his power, but Parkes wanted to be back in parliament to take the leadership of federation from him. He also desperately needed the payment that membership of parliament would bring. He was selling his books and papers to survive. In February 1896 he ran at a by-election in Sydney's eastern suburbs. There were no large backers now. On the platform he appeared with his new wife, the third Lady Parkes, a woman of 23. He was 81. On the platform he could not perform as he once did. At the 30-minute mark of his speech, he sat down for a five-minute rest. He gained only a handful of votes but, undeterred, said he would run again for the next vacancy. He died two months later. Reid visited him on his deathbed and they were reconciled. Parkes said with tears in his eyes, 'I am glad I saw him; I have misunderstood him.' On Reid's initiative, parliament established a fund for the support of the third Lady Parkes and the children of the second Lady Parkes.

Parkes had been a visionary about the nation, but his vanity would be satisfied by only the most obvious of rewards. He wanted to be first Prime Minister. He would not be the elder statesman, a role everyone was willing to grant him. He must remain at the centre of things to claim what was his due. As power slipped from him, there was no diminution of his will, which at the last became a crude, naked force butting against oblivion. He had to die before he could gain the name to which he was entitled, the father of federation.

With free trade established, Reid at last introduced to parliament the Bill to provide for the election of Convention delegates and the submission of the constitution to the people. The governments of Victoria, Tasmania, and South Australia, long waiting for this moment, followed suit. The government of Queensland was having second thoughts and delayed action. If Queensland were to attend, Nelson indicated that he wanted to renege on his agreement with the other premiers at Hobart and have parliament rather than the people elect the delegates.

In a few months over the summer of 1895–96 the Bills enshrining the premiers' agreement were passed in four colonies. The strength of opposition to the scheme was roughly in inverse proportion to the enthusiasm for federation: strongest in New South Wales; almost non-existent in Tasmania, which would agree to anything to achieve federation and intercolonial free trade. The objections were that parliaments were being bypassed, and the constitution drafted in 1891 by the best minds in the country was being abandoned in order to let the riff-raff thrown up by a popular election try their hand at constitution-making. A man would only have to stand up and say, 'I am a candidate for the federal convention and I'm in favour of the minimum wage' and he'd be elected.[21] What helped to ensure that this would not happen was the single electorate. Attempts were made in the three mainland colonies to replace it, urged chiefly so that country votes would not be swamped by urban. All these attempts were comfortably defeated.[22]

Two conservative opponents of Reid's scheme moved beyond particular objections to the broad ground that it was an attack on the British constitution. They were Sir John Downer, Leader of the Opposition in South Australia, and William McMillan, after Parkes the leading federalist free-trader in New South Wales. McMillan denied the relevance of the United States precedent. There in the 1770s and 1780s regular government had broken down and new institutions were necessary. In Australia responsible government had operated for forty years and was still in place, well tried in determining the will of the people. It was craven cowardice on the part of men who knew the difficulties of government to hand over constitution-making to the ill-informed and untrained. A single electorate was pure democracy, a defiance of the British practice that representatives should come from a particular place where representatives and electors were known to each other. To give power over constitution-making to the electors of the Assembly was to operate as if the Legislative Council did not exist. The British constitution required a review and a checking of the popular will.[23] Or, as Downer put it, the South Australian constitution divided the electorate in two; there was an Assembly electorate and a Council electorate. Reid's plan upset the constitution by treating the electorate as one.[24]

It was fitting that Reid gave the most fully developed defence of his scheme.[25] He argued that the British constitution in practice had come to accept the sovereignty of the people, for any large issue in dispute was settled by appeal to the people at a general election, which was in effect a referendum. Once the people's will was clearly established, both houses must yield to their master. Admittedly at a general election other issues intruded, but this was a blemish on the system. Those who accepted an appeal to the people should welcome the referendum, which registered the people's wish unambiguously. On the composition of a popularly elected convention, the conservatives, said Reid, were completely astray. Instead of being a body of ignoramuses, it would be far superior to existing parliaments, composed of leading politicians with an enhanced authority. (Reid's opponents entirely missed the conservative tendencies of the single electorate and of the referendum.) Although Reid criticised the federalists for being too emotional, he could be as visionary as Deakin in speaking of his project: 'Surely', he declared, 'if ever there was a competent tribunal to frame a constitution for a nation, it should be a convention chosen by the future nation itself.'[26]

Before Queen Victoria gave permission, Reid wanted to constitute the nation. Some of his critics said the body he created was illegal.[27] It was established by statute, but none of the colonial parliaments had the power to legislate for a national body. Four colonies passed laws in similar terms, establishing the Convention and determining its mode of working, and they hoped that that was good enough. The sober founding fathers might in truth have been law-breakers.

What is notable about the passage of the enabling Bills through the parliaments is how little argument was needed to support this ultra-democratic procedure. This was partly because of the new force democracy had acquired in the 1880s and 1890s. Those who had difficulty arguing against it were now reduced to mocking it as a fad. Joseph Cook, a former Labor man and now minister in Reid's government, used the language of the American revolution to defend the convention: the people who created the parliaments have the right to withdraw so much of their powers as relate to federation and place them elsewhere.[28] The other force that carried the enabling Bills through the parliaments was the desire for federation. If Reid, the Premier of that obdurate colony New South Wales and former opponent of federation, now wanted to proceed on this basis, he had to be humoured. So as these Bills embodying popular election, the referendum and one man, one vote passed through the Legislative Councils of Tasmania, Victoria, and South Australia, the members shut their eyes and thought of … Australia. Downer, after declaring that the Bill turned the South Australian constitution upside down, voted for it to secure federation.

Those who have seen federation as a reorganisation to defend capitalism against the rise of Labor have called the founding fathers 'men of property'.[29] These members of the legislative councils were the true men of property, large landed and business property. They wanted federation, or more exactly intercolonial free trade, but they were not in charge of the process. To get what they wanted they had to sanction a democratic crusade.

A federal movement of this sort was deeply troubling to the government of Queensland. The 'men of property' here composed the government. The coalition of liberals and conservatives formed by Griffith and McIlwraith in 1890 survived throughout the decade long after its founders had left the scene. The *Bulletin* called it the Griffilwraith; the Brisbane *Worker* the Boodlewraith; historians the continuous ministry. Unlike the governments in the rest of eastern Australia, it was conservative, even reactionary. The government defended plural voting and wanted to extend the principle further. The Premier, Hugh Nelson, a large squatter, thought every man who had saved a hundred pounds should have a second vote.[30] In Victoria, New South Wales, and South Australia liberal ministries operated with Labor support. In Queensland Labor was the opposition party, and the continuous ministry won elections by denouncing it as socialist and a threat to liberty and property.

When Nelson indicated that he planned to have parliament rather than the people elect delegates to the Convention, the democrats in the south criticised him and insisted that they would treat only with elected delegates. Reid and Turner, the Victorian Premier, were ready to be accommodating, but Kingston of South Australia insisted that direct democracy must be followed everywhere. He saw federation as the great democratic opportunity. If the Commonwealth were established on a thoroughly democratic basis, then democracy must be accepted in the states. He would win his battle to reform the property-based upper house of South Australia. His plan required that the new constitution establish a federal franchise, rather than have federal representatives elected according to state rules. Then one man, one vote, or perhaps one adult, one vote, would operate everywhere.[31] If the Convention took up this plan, said Nelson, the Queensland delegates would come home.[32]

In June 1896 the government introduced a Bill for members of the Assembly to elect convention delegates, but Nelson was only going through the motions to keep faith with the other premiers. He made it quite clear that he would not be disappointed if the Bill were defeated.[33] The Labor Party and a few Opposition liberals attempted to amend it to provide for direct election. They had no chance—and they complained that southern interference made their task more difficult. The occasion of the Bill's defeat was the demand by the Legislative Council that its members should be voters as well. The government piously refused to agree to this and the Bill lapsed.

Reid had delayed the calling of the new convention for a year in order to carry free trade in his own colony; he had delayed another year for Queensland to make up its mind. During that time there was not much for the people to do. Federation leagues remained in existence and kept up their educational work, but the movement had no clear focus for its activities.

Late in 1896 the Federation League at Bathurst demonstrated that the people did not merely have to await the chance to elect the official convention; it summoned its own People's Federal Convention.[34] The solid citizens of Bathurst supported the project, partly because Bathurst had aspirations to be the federal capital. They sent invitations across Australia to local government bodies, federation leagues, branches of the Australian Natives Association, trade unions, and democratic associations. Although republicans and socialists were undoubtedly part of the people, the Bathurst organisation took care that its convention was not swamped by delegates with unhelpful views on federation.[35] As it was, just enough of them turned up to give spice to the proceedings. The republican option was raised and overwhelmingly rejected.

Barton and the central Federation League in Sydney were nervous about this initiative. They did not like its claiming the word *convention* just before the official convention was to be summoned, but William Astley, its organising secretary, insisted on it. He was a radical journalist who wrote stories for the *Bulletin* on the old convict system under the name Price Warung. Barton was also afraid that delegates might bind themselves to certain propositions, which would make it harder to reach agreement at the real convention.[36] By contrast, Reid, who was the sponsor of the official convention, was happy to support this one. His government provided free railway passes to delegates.

Most of the delegates came from New South Wales, but there were enough from the other colonies to give it a national character. They spent their week going through the 1891 draft clause by clause. They accepted most of it, which assisted in the process of its rehabilitation. The chief amendments they sought were a directly elected Senate and a different scheme for financial reimbursements to the states. The debates were widely reported and had the effect of showing that ordinary people could take an intelligent interest in a federal constitution.

The convention was carried off with great éclat. Bathurst was almost in festival mood with a round of entertainments and activities being provided for the delegates. Poets sent verses in honour of the convention; a group of ladies from Bingara sent a banner; the Rev. Mr Gosman, a Congregationalist minister from Victoria, brought with him a federal hymn. The Convention adopted a specially prepared Latin motto: Foedere Fato Aequamur—By our union we are made equal to our destiny.

The last day was given over to speeches from prominent people, among them Reid and Barton. Bathurst's coup was to secure as key-note speaker Cardinal Moran, Catholic Archbishop of Sydney. He had only recently come out as a federalist, a development that the Sydney federalists had seized on and publicised widely.[37] Hitherto it had only been Protestant clergy who were supporters. He gave a powerful address that breathed a national and ecumenical spirit. As leader of the Irish clan, he was very reassuring about the imperial connection, declaring that Australia must stay loyal to the mother country and that as a republic it could enjoy no more liberty than it did at present. He appeared to nurture no grievance about the position of Catholics in colonial society. He praised its civil equality and opportunities open to all. To secure Australian union, he urged Catholics to work hand in hand with their Protestant fellow citizens. The audience loudly applauded, and the Anglican Dean of Bathurst proposed a vote of thanks. Just for a moment it looked as if Catholics and Protestants could unite in the national cause.

Reid used the occasion to show that he had been right to trust the people: 'This convention without the prestige of high government rank has created and will create infinitely more practical feeling in favour of union than its brilliant predecessor.' He announced that he was going to Queensland to see if he could secure its participation in the convention. Barton was a little wary of this move, fearing that it might further delay the calling of the convention. The delegates welcomed it. They had sent a message to the Queensland Government urging it to attend.

Reid very much wanted Queensland to be part of the federation. He saw it as similar to New South Wales, a large territory with ample resources, a land of great potential, and if for the moment following a protectionist policy, more easily won from it than the other colonies.[38] Furthermore, without Queensland, New South Wales would be located at the edge of the

'My dear Nelson, the labour party practically holds the keys of the position, and our business, clearly, is to conciliate them.'
Reid (left) instructing Premier Nelson during the Brisbane River cruise. (*Brisbane Worker*, 19 December 1896)

federation; with Queensland, New South Wales would be central and hence better able to claim the capital.

In December 1896 Reid travelled to Brisbane.[39] It was a difficult assignment. Part of Queensland's misgivings about federation was fear of southern interference, and he was an interfering southerner. But he was the most interesting politician in the country—everyone wanted to see him—and he was superb in this situation, not at all the missionary; he was genial, casual, frank, and in addition, of course, flattering of his hosts' colony. He fixed up a deal with the ministers that two Legislative Councillors should be included in the Queensland delegation. Nelson then gave him the opportunity to speak to the parliament by inviting all members on a picnic cruise down the river and across to St Helena in Moreton Bay.

Reid's speech at the picnic was very well received, although ominously there were great cheers at his mentioning the alternative route to union of the Federal Council. Reid told the members how much he wanted Queensland in the union and that the selection of their delegates was their business. They were entirely within their rights to disregard the premiers' agreement at the Hobart conference. He did not care and he hoped no one else cared—this was a warning to Kingston—how they chose their delegates. So the champion of direct election in the south sang a different tune in the north. This pragmatism was not to secure a united Australia so much as a free-trade Australia.[40]

It was close to Christmas, and if the deal were to pass the parliament there would have to be no determined opposition. On the cruise down the river Reid tried to persuade the Labor men not to press the case for direct election again. They were promised two of the ten delegates. Reid thought he had been successful, but the ministers' soundings found otherwise and so they did not persist. There was simply no will to push the issue. Reid was alarmed at the lack of interest in federation in Queensland. There was even less than he imagined—Nelson pretended to Reid that he was keen about federation and that it was only his colleagues who were not.

When Reid returned to Sydney he said he could not now abandon the Convention on which New South Wales had given the lead, but if he had known the lack of interest in Queensland, he would not have embarked on his federation project. If Queensland would not join a full union, then the Federal Council mechanism might have to be used instead.[41] With some misgiving, then, Reid finalised arrangements for the Convention election. The people in three colonies, New South Wales, Victoria, and Tasmania, were to vote on the same day, 4 March 1897, and South Australia two days later. More than two years had passed since the plan to include them had been agreed.

The Western Australia delegates to the Convention would be elected by parliament. To this Kingston raised no objection.[42] Forrest had after all not supported the Hobart agreement. South Australia wanted Western Australia in the union to safeguard its trade with that colony, and it wanted Western Australia to be at the Convention to make the balance three small colonies to two large.

8
Convention

Because they live among us, and we know
The unheroic detail of their days,
Since they and we move in familiar ways,
We scant the greatness of the deed they do.

They weld an empire, not in old world wise
'Mid crash of war and clamour of armed men
But in calm conclave, where each citizen
May speak his share of truth with fearless eyes.

Contemporary Review, October 1891

Conservative critics of the plan to allow the people to elect delegates to write a constitution denounced it as 'pure democracy'. Pure it turned out to be. At the Convention elections there was no free beer, no rowdy meetings, no dirty tricks, no free cabs to take electors to the poll—and not much interest. Considerably fewer people voted than at a normal election. Only in New South Wales did more than half the electors participate. The lowest turn-out was in Tasmania where only a quarter of the electors voted.[1]

Since the electorate was the whole colony, the intense campaigning of a normal election—house-to-house canvassing and meetings in every neighbourhood—was impossible. Nor across this arena could the usual inducements of free beer and free cabs be employed. The typical campaign was a city meeting and a couple of country meetings, which would be well reported in the newspapers, with perhaps some newspaper advertising as well. As Reid predicted, only public men of established reputation were elected. All but one of the delegates was or had been a politician. In three colonies—New South Wales, South Australia, and Tasmania—leading men from both sides of politics were elected. This was also the result of the parliamentary election of the West Australian delegates, who were less able and less committed to federation than the rest.

In Victoria the elections turned into a fully fledged party contest between liberals and conservatives. This was the work of the *Age*. It chose

'THE REFERENDUM' AT WORK.
David Syme, editor of the *Age*, controls the Convention election in Victoria. (*Melbourne Punch*, 11 March 1897)

its liberal ten and campaigned hard for them. Having taken the precaution of including in its list two conservatives who had the saving grace of being protectionists, the *Age* managed to have all ten of its candidates returned,[2] which was a terrifying demonstration of its power. David Syme, its editor, was only lukewarm at best about federation. He would not look favourably on any constitutional settlement that did not guarantee protection as national policy and include his hobby-horse of the referendum as a means of solving deadlocks between the two Houses.

In New South Wales the federal cause benefited enormously by being removed from normal politics. The local battle over free trade and protection, which had always disrupted federal deliberations, was more or less laid aside. This was Parkes's truce, which he managed to impose to achieve the writing of a constitution in 1891 and which had eluded him thereafter. Six free-traders and four protectionists were elected. They were all federalists, although one, William Lyne, was opposed to equal representation in the Senate. He was a large-framed, dogged, country politician who had succeeded Dibbs as leader of the protectionist party.

Voters in New South Wales had a real choice. The patriots, calling themselves prudent federalists, campaigned on a platform hostile to federation. They would support cooperation between the colonies, but not much more than the existing arrangements under the Federal Council. The central body could have funds, but only by payments from the state governments; there was to be no central power to tax and no power to interfere with tariff policy.

The patriot leader, Louis Heydon, a lawyer who had served in old John Robertson's last ministry, opened his campaign with an illustrated lecture. The illustrations were maps showing how under federation the colony would be carved up by its neighbours. Victoria was the chief of these brigands. It was turning on 'federal gush' and 'brotherly love' now that it was aware that it was falling behind the mother colony.

Heydon was aware of the emotional appeal of federation. He answered it by boosting New South Wales as a future nation with Sydney as one of the great cities of the world. If her sons wanted more than that, let them remember that they belonged to the British Empire, something much grander than an Australian federation, which on present plans would not include the whole continent.[3]

The Labor Party put forward candidates who supported a federation but one that would be run on unitary lines. Their allocation of powers between state and federal governments was of the usual sort. They were very definite that control of working conditions and public health must remain with the states. However, the central government was to consist of

'GENTLEMEN, HERE YOU PERCEIVE A BALL! I NOW TAKE THIS CONE INTO MY HAND;—I PLACE IT OVER THE BALL, AND—HEY, PRESTO!—ON RAISING IT AGAIN, THE BALL WILL HAVE DISAPPEARED!'

Federation as a Victorian plot.

a single house of parliament elected according to population. There were to be no states house and no concession of any sort to the smaller states. If they did not like these terms, federation should be abandoned.

The patriots and the Labor Party were both well represented in the New South Wales Parliament, but their federation platforms were decisively rejected by the electors at large. They would have their chance again when the constitution was put to the people.

The Labor Party very foolishly ran a full slate of ten candidates. The appearance of wanting to capture the whole delegation told heavily against it. The prevailing mood was to have a high-quality delegation representative of all parties. In South Australia the Labor Party ran four candidates, and even this was considered a touch ambitious.[4] None was elected. In Victoria, where the Labor Party was more a radical wing of the liberals, only one Labor candidate was run. William Trenwith, a bootmaker, was included in the *Age*'s ten and was returned. Compared with its numbers in the colonial parliaments, Labor was certainly underrepresented at the Convention. But Labor's suspicions about federation were in the forefront of the delegates' minds since they knew their handiwork was to be referred to the electorate at large.

Overall more liberals and radicals than conservatives were elected. At the 1891 Convention the balance had been the other way. The liberals would not be a united group. Whatever other views they might have, all delegates were representatives of their colonies. A liberal from South Australia or Tasmania would likely have a different view of a federal constitution from a Victorian liberal. All the delegates elected from the small states were in favour of a strong Senate with equal representation of the states.

The federalists did not allow themselves to be disheartened by the low turn-out at the polls.[5] They could see with everyone else why such an election was less engaging. The contests were not local and personal nor were the benefits as obvious as roads, bridges, railways, and government jobs, the usual political rewards. The ruling assumption of political campaigners was that there was a huge disinclination to vote, a problem that modern Australia has solved by making voting compulsory. In the absence of the usual inducements, the turn-out was not discreditable. Unquestionably the federal movement had gained in consequence and authority by having the direct endorsement of the people. Federalists could no longer be mocked for pursuing a fad.

A hundred years after this election Australians voted again to elect dele-gates to a constitutional convention. The voting for the republican convention in 1997 was voluntary, but the electors did not have to go to a polling booth: voting was by post. The response rate was 47 per cent.

What was positively encouraging to federalists was the discrimination shown by the voters. This might have been a consequence of the low turn-out since it was more likely that the well-informed and the committed voted. In Victoria John Quick was returned second, after Turner the Premier and ahead of Deakin, because of his contribution to the federal cause; he was not otherwise notable. In New South Wales James Walker secured election because he had made a name for himself as an expert on federal finance. He was a bank director and the one non-politician among the delegates.

Barton, the federal leader and at the time out of politics, headed the poll in the mother colony, pushing George Reid, the Premier, into second place. When asked whether he was miffed, Reid with characteristic frankness said he was. His explanation was that after being Premier for three years he had made numerous enemies.[6] Still Barton was well enough known as a protectionist and imprisoner of strikers, yet he did well in free-trade Sydney and in Labor electorates. He was rewarded for his devotion to the cause. He gained the support of almost a hundred thousand voters, which made him an awesome figure in an age when electorates had only a few thousand voters and premiers received their endorsement from the parliament rather than the electorate at large.

The elections were notable because for the first time a Catholic cardinal and a woman ran for public office. Cardinal Moran, the austere Irish Archbishop of Sydney, and Catherine Helen Spence, the dumpy Scots social reformer from Adelaide, were not so much out of place in this election. Clergymen and women had been natural and welcome allies to a cause as sacred and pure as federation.

The Cardinal had enhanced his reputation as a significant federal figure by his appearance at the Bathurst People's Convention. Now he was hoping to use his national reputation to advance the Catholic position, about which he was far from content. His vision was of a strong, self-reliant nation guided by the Catholic Church—and Protestantism in ruins. Although he had hidden his contempt for Protestantism at Bathurst, on other occasions he was perfectly explicit.[7] So when he announced his candidature for the Convention, Protestants rallied to defeat him. But it was not necessary to think that Moran was a 'sworn soldier and servant of a foreign power'—the pope—to regret his candidature. The sectarian conflict would not go away, and Moran had broken one of the rules for controlling it: that clergymen, who were the most bitter partisans, should not hold or seek public office.

Moran had hoped to confound the bigoted Protestants; instead he inflamed them. The Orangemen ran a totally Protestant ticket to keep him out. A caucus of more than two hundred Protestant clergy, showing more intelligence and restraint, decided to choose a ticket of the ten men, apart from Moran, who were most likely to succeed. By increasing their vote, they would defeat the Cardinal. The ticket included one Catholic, Barton's friend O'Connor, and the leader of the Labor Party, McGowen.[8] They were good prophets. Only McGowen of their ten failed to be elected. Moran came fourteenth in a field of fifty. Of the colonies that elected delegates to the Convention, New South Wales had been the most lukewarm over federation, yet it registered the highest turn-out partly because of the Protestant interest in defeating the Cardinal.

The movement of federation into practical politics coincided with the arrival of women in public life. In the social history of Tenterfield, Parkes's federation speech in 1889 is most notable as the first time women sat down with men at a public banquet.[9] In the federation campaigns that followed, places were regularly reserved for ladies at meetings. A large contingent of ladies was present when Barton opened his campaign for the Convention. At Reid's meeting the chairman addressed the company as 'Gentlemen' and was met with the cry 'Ladies!'—which he ignored.[10] By their presence here—a sort of half-way house to the rowdy meetings of ordinary elections—women strengthened their claim to the vote, the campaign for which was in full swing in the 1890s. Its first success was in South Australia, where women gained the right to vote and to sit in parliament in 1894. They voted for the first time at a general election in 1896, and in March 1897 they voted for the delegates to the constitutional Convention.

Long before women agitated for the vote, Catherine Helen Spence had a secure place in public life as an expert on child welfare and an advocate of effective voting, what we now call proportional representation.[11] At first she was not an enthusiast about votes for women since she believed the vote was a poor thing if it was not an effective vote. She stood for the Convention not to advance women's rights but to ensure that the nation began its life with proportional representation.

At her campaign meetings, Spence demonstrated the advantage of proportional representation by conducting mock elections for the Convention on her model and according to the official rules, under which the elector had to cast ten votes and the ten candidates with the highest number of votes were elected. Of course Spence was right about the significance of the voting scheme. If the Convention elections had been conducted like a modern Senate poll, in New South Wales the Labor Party, the Patriots, and the Cardinal would have won seats. Reid quite deliberately organised the voting system to avoid this outcome. He did not want different groups or localities each to have its own representative; he wanted only those representatives who could gather general support.

Spence gathered only enough support to come twenty-second in a field of thirty-three. She might have done better if she had not run on the single issue of the voting system and if doubts had not been cast on her eligibility to sit in the Convention. But if the 7,383 people who gave her a vote had given her their first preference under a system of proportional representation, she would have gained a seat.

Although only South Australian women had the vote, women everywhere had the ancient right of petitioning. If women's organisations could persuade the Convention to adopt votes for women, a great victory would be won and the states would have to fall into line.

The largest women's organisation was the Woman's Christian Temperance Union, which campaigned against alcohol and for giving women the vote so that their moral influence would reform men and society at large. A resolution from their national body in favour of equal political rights for the sexes was waiting for the Convention when it assembled.

The first formal petition received by the Convention came from the Womanhood Suffrage League of New South Wales. The signatures were headed by Maybanke Wolstenholme, president, and Rose Scott, secretary. These two women had very different experiences of life and of men. Rose Scott was a great beauty who turned down all offers of marriage. She was very close to her cousin David Mitchell, the book collector, and was disappointed that he did not want to marry her. Having enjoyed an intellectual companionship with him, she was not going to be a mere decorative wife to anyone else. She had an independent income and in Sydney conducted a salon where politicians, journalists, and reformers met.[12]

Maybanke Selfe married Edmund Wolstenholme when she was 22. She was probably already pregnant, and in eleven years she bore seven children, of whom four died in infancy. Her husband was a handsome no-hoper. After the passage in 1879 of the Married Women's Property Act, her brother gave her a good-sized house that could be her own. She took in boarders and later established a school to support herself and her children. Her husband left in 1885. When reform of the divorce laws was carried in 1892, she divorced him for desertion. *Woman's Voice*, the journal she ran from 1894, talked frankly about sexual matters and supported planned motherhood; that is, contraception.[13]

The women of the Suffrage League put these arguments to the men of the Convention in support of their demand for the vote:

> Women of the various colonies are taxpayers under their respective Governments, and will be taxpayers under any Federal Government which may be established.
>
> Women are patriotic, and law-abiding citizens, taking an equal part in the religious and moral development of the people, and doing more than half of the educational, charitable, and philanthropic work of society as at present constituted.
>
> In view of the facts and considerations above mentioned, we are justified in appealing to your honorable Convention to so frame the Federal Constitution as to give the women of all colonies a voice in choosing the representatives

Rose Scott.

of the Federal Parliament, so that United Australia may become a true democracy resting upon the will of the whole and not half of the people.

The opening session of the Convention was to be held in Adelaide, which represented the first victory of the small states over the large. Kingston, the South Australian Premier, persuaded Tasmania and Western Australia to support an Adelaide meeting and so outgunned New South Wales and Victoria. Their delegates would have preferred not to meet in

Maybanke Wolstenholme.

the 'city of churches'. On this matter true federal principles prevailed: each colony had one vote no matter what its population.

The New South Wales delegates left Sydney by train without any ceremony. At Albury on the border, where there was much more enthusiasm for federation, the mayor was on the platform to read an address of good wishes. The Tasmanian delegates sailed from Launceston, where there was a crowd on the wharf to bid them farewell. In Melbourne the mayor gave a civic reception for the New South Wales, Tasmanian, and Victorian delegates.

They left together for Adelaide on the express train. Stations on the way were decorated, and crowds gathered on the platforms. At the refreshment rooms at Ballarat station there was another civic reception—but this gesture was part of Ballarat's campaign to be the federal capital.[14]

At an informal meeting before the Convention opened, the delegates decided to act for the moment as if Griffith's draft did not exist. Barton was strong on the need to keep the promise that there was to be a fresh start. Reid, who had criticised that draft unmercifully, thought this was a waste of time. He wanted to make the necessary amendments and be off. However, as soon as the delegates divided into committees to start detailed planning, the 1891 draft was the foundation of their deliberations, and it was a modified version of this draft, not a new creation, that the Convention then considered in detail.

Kingston as host premier became, according to custom, the president of the Convention, much to the chagrin of his conservative opponents. With able candidates they had done well at the election, much better than in local politics: liberals and conservatives each returned five members.

The conservatives hated Kingston not so much because he was a radical as because he was a fiery, savage, ungentlemanly radical.[15] He outlived the scandals that should have destroyed him. His admission to the bar was challenged by a young man who claimed that Kingston had seduced his sister. Having been admitted, Kingston punched up the brother and married the sister. While Attorney-General, he was cited as co-respondent in a divorce case. While Premier he challenged Richard Baker, the leader of the conservatives, to a duel. Baker sent the police to the meeting spot, and the Premier was bound over to keep the peace. Baker never spoke to him again except on official business. At the Convention they had a lot to do with each other because Baker was chairman of committees, to whom Kingston passed his authority when the delegates were examining the draft constitution in detail.

By common consent Barton became leader of the Convention. No one could match his claims. He was leader of the federal movement in the mother colony, a position that had just received resounding popular endorsement. He was an able lawyer, although not the best in the Convention, which he recognised. His temper was conciliatory, and as a conservative liberal he could consider the views of most delegates without distaste.

Barton combined the roles that Parkes and Griffith had performed in 1891. He introduced and led debate on the principles that should underlie the constitution, as Parkes had done. Like Griffith, he chaired the constitution and the drafting committee and was responsible for steering the

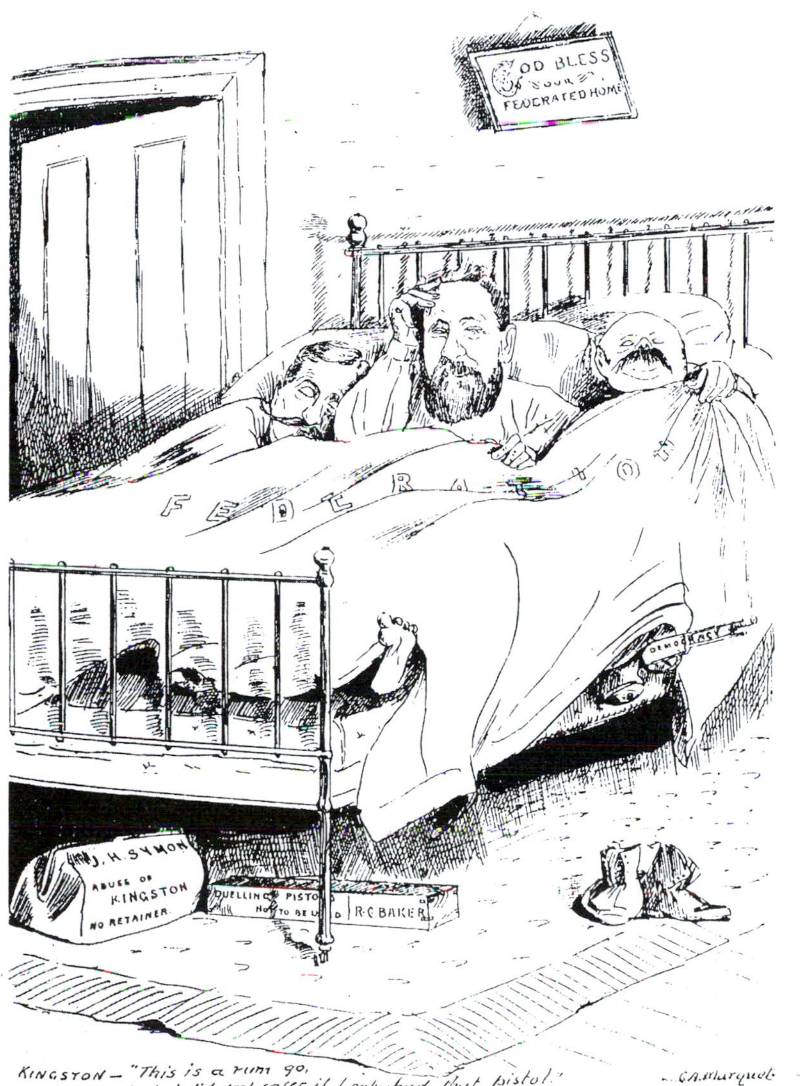

Federation produced strange bedfellows in South Australia: Kingston (centre) with his conservative opponents, Baker and Symon. (*Quiz*, 12 May 1898)

draft through the Convention. This was the great labour of Barton's life. Week after week, he alone of the delegates always had to be in the chamber, always alert. As suggested amendments tumbled forth, he had to know which to reject out of hand, which to take seriously, which to postpone for further consideration. For any proposal that looked like gaining support, he had to ensure that it was embodied in clear, concise, and elegant words. If he misread the sense of the Convention, he would be told soon enough, but without his leadership, its deliberations would have been even more confused and protracted. When the other delegates were asleep, when Downer and O'Connor, his two colleagues on the drafting committee, had gone to bed, he worked on, refining the drafts to be put again to the Convention in the morning. Beside him as secretary was young Robert Garran, whom he had recruited to the Federation League in Sydney. Being first prime minister was easy work compared to this. It was here that Barton gained the authority to assume that job. He was, says Deakin, loved by most and respected by all.

According to the plan, the first session of the Convention was to prepare a constitution and then adjourn to allow the parliaments to consider it. The delegates spent six weeks in Adelaide in the autumn of 1897. They did write a constitution, but not everything had been resolved. They could not take any longer because the premiers were leaving for London to attend Queen Victoria's jubilee celebrations. They reassembled in Sydney in the spring when they had the responses of their parliaments. They went through the constitution again from the beginning and after three weeks had reached clause 52 in a document of 121 clauses. The Convention then had to adjourn because the Victorians went home to fight an election. It reassembled in Melbourne in January 1898 in searing summer heat. This time they would have to finish. It took them eight weeks, sitting regularly into the night and sometimes until three or four in the morning. Having reached the end of the document, they recommitted it four times for further consideration. Eight weeks of talk was not enough to prevent a rush at the end. On the last day, 400 drafting changes, not all of them insignificant, went through on the nod.

This was a very different style of constitution-making from that of 1891. The Convention of that year sat only once, for five weeks. Griffith took the sense of the opening discussion and the committee decisions and produced a constitution that gained general acceptance. The Convention, sitting from 11 a.m. until 6 p.m., took only six days to adopt it. It was recommitted only once on the second last day when Griffith passed through six drafting amendments. The document had Griffith's authority and its own freshness to support it. The delegates were half startled that a constitution for an Australian union had been brought into existence. They approved it virtually in the form in which it left Griffith's hands.

By the time of the second convention, Griffith's constitution had been subject to detailed scrutiny. The delegates arrived having very definite (and

The Convention in session in Melbourne: Kingston as president, Baker as chairman of committees in front of him, Barton as leader sitting at the table on the president's right.

different) views of what had to be omitted, what added, and possible interpretations that had to be squashed. These views, moreover, carried the authority of the electors who sent them. So divisions were more pronounced and compromises more difficult to achieve. Some differences could not be reconciled and would remain as long as the Convention sat. In the last days in Melbourne, the delegates, fagged by the heat and late sittings, had finally to make binding decisions on contentious issues to which they had returned again and again.

No danger spurred the Convention to rapid decision. None of the powers to be conferred on the Federal Parliament was needed immediately. At the time of the financial collapse, federation had briefly looked like the best means of restoring the confidence of British investors, but that moment had passed. The colonial governments had reformed themselves and regained the confidence of the markets, and were now borrowing again at very low interest rates.[16] The argument was still put, as it had been before the crisis, that a united Australia could borrow at even better rates and could favourably convert the old colonial debts, but this was just one argument among many. The panic had passed. Federal control of borrowing was an advantage, not a necessity.

Intercolonial free trade was the great economic benefit to be gained from federation, but the need to secure it had lessened since New South Wales had opened its borders under Reid's free-trade policy. The other colonies were now in an ideal situation. They still protected their own industries but had free access to the largest market in Australia.

The Convention was no more commanded from within than without. No single intelligence directed its deliberations. Barton's role was very different from Griffith's. He was in charge of the amending of Griffith's plan; he was not defending the integrity of his own work. He needed a draftsman's skills, but his work was as much political as legal. He had to ensure that everyone was heard, that the differences among the delegates did not lead to rupture, and that the Convention took no decision that would endanger the chance of acceptance in any of the colonies.

The discipline that constrained them was the shared desire for union and the recognition that compromise was necessary. This was the common theme of the opening speeches in Adelaide. By the judgment of the people in the gallery, Deakin's speech was the most eloquent. When he finished they broke into applause for which they were mildly rebuked by Convention president Kingston. These were his closing words:

> The Constitution we seek to prepare is worthy of any and every personal sacrifice, for it is no ordinary measure, and must exercise no short-lived

> influence, since it preludes the advent of a nation. Awed as I feel by the fact that we come from, that we speak to, and that we act for a great constituency, awed as I feel in the presence of those who sent us here, I am more awed by the thought of the constituency which is not visible, but which awaits the results of our labors—we are trustees for posterity for the unborn millions, unknown and unnumbered—whose aspirations we may help them to fulfil and whose destinies we may assist to determine.[17]

It was typical of Deakin that he spoke not of compromise but of 'personal sacrifice'. Earlier in his speech he said he would rather that his tongue should be 'withered at its roots' than that any words of his should chill or give offence and impede their great purpose. Deakin had prepared himself for the Convention with prayer: 'Infinite Spirit of Unity Order & Harmony, be present with us in our gathering of representatives, fitting us our words & work & aims utterly & absolutely to Thy divine will for the best results to Thy people here & elsewhere, to all Thy peoples everywhere & to the coming of Thy Kingdom.'[18] Although he could speak so well, he determined not to speak too often. He would allow others to have the limelight and devote himself to smoothing the way behind the scenes.

The opening speech in which the delegates took most interest was that of Reid, the man who had wrecked the work of the first convention and who had arranged this one. Did he genuinely want federation now? The conclusion of his speech was less elaborate and less polished than Deakin's, but who could quarrel with this conception of their task and his commitment to it?

> Whilst I have expressed freely and fearlessly my opinions, I will not have the slightest hesitation to go as far as reason and justice will allow to meet the various difficulties which may be suggested by other members of the Convention, for it really is, after all, in the courtesy of our intercourse, in the kindliness of our differences, in the breadth and liberality of our views, in our perfect readiness to yield to superior argument, and above all in our indomitable resolve to crown this movement with success, that the full significance and grandeur of this Convention will reveal itself.
>
> We, I hope, will faithfully discharge the trust committed to us. I hope we will truly voice the patriotism and brotherly instincts of the Australasian people. I hope that, since they have called us to this task, we will be enabled to fashion a fabric of national government which shall be strong enough to withstand the shocks of time, which shall be elastic enough to overtake the mightiest possibilities of this grand new world of ours, and which will be just enough to do no wrong to any man.[19]

Deakin on Reid

The most conspicuous figure of the Convention, its official author and in matters of moment its leader, was the Premier of New South Wales, physically as remarkable as his predecessor Parkes, but without his dignity, and even more formidable in discussion because less self-respecting. Even caricature has been unable to travesty his extraordinary appearance, his immense, unwieldy, jelly-like stomach, always threatening to break his waist-band, his little legs apparently bowed under its weight to the verge of their endurance, his thick neck rising behind his ears rounding to his many-folded chin. His protuberant blue eyes were expressionless until roused or half hidden in cunning, [and] a blond complexion and infantile breadth of baldness gave him an air of insolent juvenility. He walked with a staggering roll like that of a sailor, helping himself as he went by resting on the backs of chairs as if he were reminiscent of some far-off arboreal ancestor. To a superficial eye his obesity was either repellant or else amusing. A heavy German moustache concealed a mouth of considerable size from which there emanated a high, reedy voice rising to a shriek or sinking to a fawning, purring, persuasive orotund with a nasal tinge. To a more careful inspection he disclosed a splendid dome-like head, high and broad and indicative of intellectual power, a gleaming eye which betokened a natural gift of humour and an alertness that not even his habit of dropping asleep at all times and places in the most ungraceful attitudes and in the most impolite manner could defeat. He never slept in a public gathering more than a moment or two, being quickly awakened by his own snore. He would sleep during the dealing of cards for a game of whist and during the play too if there was any pause, but he never forgot the state of the game or made a revoke. In the Assembly or in a train he indulged with the same facility both of sleeping and waking if necessary with an appropriate retort upon his tongue …

He cared nothing for the heights of outlook or depths of insight, discarding all decorum of deliverance, finish of style or grace of expression, aiming always at the level of the man of the street and reaching it by jest, logic, appeal, rant or ruthless abuse as appeared most effective. He always was effective for he possessed a really marvellous political instinct, a readiness and adaptability, a quickness of repartee and a rolling surge of *ad captandum* arguments which were simply irresistible. He knew the average man better than he knew himself for he was the average man in every respect except in his amazing platform powers, political astuteness and the intensity of his determination to carve out and keep the first place for himself in New South Wales and in Australia if possible—but in New South Wales at all events until sure of the other by any means and at any cost.

Deakin, *The Federal Story*, pp. 62–4.

To the modern taste Reid's speech might seem more genuine than Deakin's. The speeches are a revealing contrast. Whereas Deakin's faults were hypothetical—his tongue was to be withered *if* he had given offence—Reid named his: he had been 'too positive and pugnacious' in expressing his views. He again praised the work of the men of 1891, which he had formerly criticised so severely.[20]

At Adelaide it was Reid's convention. At the opening banquet he took pride in the quality of the delegates who had vindicated his willingness to trust the people with their election. Indeed, they were an outstanding group, the pick of the local parliaments, and, in the absence of the demagogues, drunks, and the roads-and-bridges members, they constituted a deliberative assembly of which any nation could be proud. They spoke well and were courteous and conciliatory. Reid, who had been the doubtful quantity, helped to set this tone. When he left Adelaide two days early, Deakin, Barton, Kingston, Turner, and Braddon praised him, and the Convention adjourned so that he could be afforded an official farewell at the railway station.[21]

At Melbourne eleven months later when the constitution had been settled, his relations with his Convention colleagues were very different.

9
Constitution

Federation in cold blood is a mighty difficult matter.

A. C. Onslow to J. Symon, 30 March 1897

The constitution was shaped in Adelaide in secret committee meetings of the Convention. When it appeared for debate before the whole Convention, it was clear that the liberals had had a great victory. Griffith's 1891 draft had been democratised.

In 1891 the Senate, as was still the case in the United States, was to be elected by the state parliaments. It was now to be directly elected by the people. The voters were to be the same as for the House of Representatives. The requirement that a senator had to be older than 30 was dropped. The Senate was still to be a states house, with each state having equal representation, but there was little left to give it the character of a conservative house of review. At the end of the Adelaide session its conservative elements were that senators were to be elected for six years, that the Senate could not be dissolved, and that the Senate electorates were to be the whole state. Since these electorates had returned convention delegates of such high quality, the system was to be continued.

An upper house elected on a democratic franchise was almost a contradiction in terms. Dobson, a conservative delegate from Tasmania, was flabbergasted at this proposal being carried through the Convention without resistance. He asked for the constitutional experts to cite one precedent for such a house. He appealed directly to Barton for some justification. Barton said he was too tired. After this little flurry, Dobson gave up.[1] Only in private did he suggest that Senate voters might have to be owners and occupiers of property or be qualified by education.[2]

Dobson was left a lone protester because the conservatives knew that to make a determined stand against democracy would endanger the federal cause, still viewed with great suspicion by Labor and the radicals. The more intelligent conservatives had also realised that it would be easier to preserve the powers of the Senate if it had a democratic electorate. Admittedly this was a dangerous precedent when they were still defending upper houses elected by property-holders, but this risk had to be borne.[3]

The 1891 draft had followed the federal principle that state law should determine who had the right to vote for the Commonwealth Parliament. Since then Kingston had led the case that the nation had the right to define itself. The constitution should establish a federal franchise—and it should include all men and women. The Convention was not ready to go so far. Probably a majority were in favour of female franchise, but to force it on the states, when only one so far had adopted it, would endanger federation. Kingston's principle that there should be a federal franchise was accepted, but it was to be determined by the Federal Parliament, not laid down in the constitution. For the first election the voters would be those who had the vote for the colonial assemblies, which would include all adult men (except in Tasmania) and in South Australia women as well.

The South Australians were quick to see a danger. What if the Federal Parliament set a common franchise that excluded women? South Australian women would vote at the first election and then be rejected. So the Convention agreed that when the Federal Parliament set the franchise it could not exclude anyone who already had the vote. That would virtually oblige the parliament to enfranchise all women, since it could hardly leave South Australian women with the vote and exclude the rest.

In 1891 the constitution was to be amended in the American way with changes being endorsed by specially elected state conventions. Now the people were to vote directly on proposals by referendum. A majority of people and a majority of states would have to approve an amendment for it to succeed.

The democratising of the constitution was symbolised by a change to its preamble. Now it was to read that 'the people' rather than 'the colonies' had agreed to union. 'We, the people …' were the famous opening words of the American constitution, but the Australian founders were defining the people more broadly and involving them more intimately than the Americans had. It was fitting that this change to the preamble was proposed by John Quick, the chief promoter, if not the author, of Australia's distinctive style in constitution-making. Quick also wanted the preamble to acknowledge God. The Convention at first rejected this. It took a flood of petitions before the Convention at its Melbourne session set aside its own preference for a strict separation of church and state and allowed God in.

Responsible government was now established by the stipulation that ministers had to be members of parliament. Griffith had wanted to leave open the possibility that some new form of executive would develop in a federal system with houses of almost equal strength. That option was now closed. The federal system, borrowed from the United States, was to be worked on the principles of Westminster. However, the words of the constitution did not fully provide for responsible government. They did not stipulate that ministers had to have the support of the lower House and that the Governor-General had to act on their advice. Barton, like Griffith in 1891, said these were conventions that could not be made law. The words of the constitution said: 'the executive power of the Commonwealth is vested in the Queen and is exercisable by the Governor-General as the Queen's representative.'

There was some interest from the small states in exploring alternatives to a Westminster executive. That body would sit in the House of Representatives where two-thirds of the members would come from the large states. The nightmare for the small states was a government made up entirely of ministers from New South Wales and Victoria. Baker proposed that the ministry be elected, three from the Representatives and three from the Senate. Kingston wanted ministers from the Representatives to be able to speak in the Senate and vice versa. These and other modifications were swiftly set aside and not pursued. Whatever the fears of the small states, their attachment to the system they knew was very strong.

All these amendments were clean, quick, and decisive. Many of the others, painfully assembled over the three sessions, were not so much changes to Griffith's document as a worrying at it. Where Griffith had made bold and terse provisions, the Convention now elaborated, fussed, and fudged. This was the result of its open, consultative process and the determination of the delegates to protect the interests of their colony. But it has to be said about the work of the delegates to the 1897–98 Convention that Griffith's document remained a document; theirs was adopted as the constitution of the Commonwealth of Australia.

For elaboration, consider the provision for postmen, soldiers, and customs officers transferred from the states to the Commonwealth. Griffith said simply that their existing rights would be preserved. Re-examination and consultation revealed this provision as inadequate. What of their accruing rights, which they did not hold now but would acquire by further service? What of the officers whom the Commonwealth might decline to employ, even if their departments were being transferred? And what of officers whom the Commonwealth might want to hire, even if their departments were not being transferred? And who should pay the pensions of transferred officers: the states or the Commonwealth? Or should each pay according to the time the officer spent in its service? Griffith's one line became twenty-two. Barton was happy to spend time getting this right because he wanted no injustice done. And of course all these officers would be voting on this constitution.[4]

Modern readers of the constitution look for a stirring preamble or a bill of rights and are disappointed. They miss its distinctive feature. No constitution has given so much attention to pension rights of postmen.

For fussiness, consider the case of the Perth Post Office. It was located in a government building that it did not fully occupy. On looking at the Adelaide draft, the West Australians feared the Commonwealth might claim the whole building. So a new subsection was added that made different arrangements for buildings 'used but not exclusively used' by a transferred department.[5] The provision was no different from what the two governments would have reached if the constitution had been silent on the matter.

For fudging consider the case of special railway rates. Griffith's draft said simply that the Federal Parliament could annul state laws and regulations that interfered with freedom of interstate trade. New South Wales, fearing the worst, saw this as giving Victoria the chance to annul the special rates by which the New South Wales railways were luring Riverina trade to Sydney. If that happened, the trade would revert to Melbourne, which was much closer, and New South Wales would be paying off railways on which there was no traffic. The New South Wales delegates insisted that they must be able to keep their special rates; if there was to be any interference, it must be by an expert commission and not by the parliament, which could well be a hostile cabal under Victorian leadership. Victoria, on the other hand, expected that a federation that promised interstate free trade must protect its right to the Riverina trade, which Sydney had diverted from its natural channels. The constitution gave the Victorians the principle of free trade, but they were disappointed with the way New South Wales had hedged it around. This is pure fudge, vintage Melbourne, March 1898:

> 102. The Parliament may by any law with respect to trade and commerce forbid, as to railways, any preference or discrimination by any State, or by any authority constituted under a State, if such preference or discrimination is undue or unreasonable, or unjust to any State; due regard being had

> to the financial responsibilities incurred by any state in connexion with the construction and maintenance of its railways. But no preference or discrimination shall, within the meaning of this section, be taken to be undue and unreasonable, or unjust to any State, unless so adjudged by the Inter-State Commission.

These words were produced after five days of debate. The issue of the rivers was settled in the same way after a debate of two weeks. South Australia was here pitted against New South Wales and not poorly matched. It had the ablest delegation and, of course, numbers equal to the rest. Split between liberals and conservatives, with several members not speaking to each other, the South Australians were nevertheless a powerful machine in defence of their province. One of its hopes was that the paddle-steamer trade on the Murray river system would revive and that Goolwa at the river mouth would become the New Orleans of the south. Meanwhile, New South Wales had nurtured hopes of damming the Darling and turning the desert into a garden. Since river water was often in short supply, there might not be enough to water the land and float the boats.

The 1891 draft had given the Commonwealth power to control river navigation. If that power remained, the New South Wales delegates insisted that it must be offset by the right to irrigate. They finally secured this

The paddle-steamer *Bourke*, built at Milang near the Murray mouth, pictured at Wilcannia on the Darling. The South Australians wanted constitutional protection for river navigation.

guarantee, a right not often noticed by those looking for rights in the constitution. A state and its people had 'the right … to the use of waters of rivers for conservation and irrigation'. But then the clever South Australians inserted 'reasonable' before 'use' and Reid and co. could not get it out again. What was reasonable? The courts would have to decide, but New South Wales counted this amendment as a loss.

Apart from their implications for railway rates and irrigation, very little time was spent debating the powers of the Federal Parliament. As in 1891, everyone agreed that they should be strictly limited. No one in Australia thought the Federal Parliament had to be clothed with the powers to create the nation. The federalists said the nation already existed. The colonies were not a diverse group or foreigners to each other. Federation was a matter of breaking down artificial barriers. The nation was to be revealed, not constructed.

The barriers were the customs houses. Their removal was the central symbolic act of federation, and when making constitutional provision for it, the delegates, including even the sharpest lawyers, were for once tempted into grandiloquent language. They declared in section 92 that trade between the states 'shall be absolutely free'. Having declared much more than they intended, they left the way open to the High Court to use this section to limit the powers they had given to the Commonwealth over commerce, banking, and corporations.[6]

In Canada the central government had been made strong, holding all powers not specifically given to the provinces; necessarily so since the central government had to weld very disparate provinces together. In Australia an intercolonial railway system existed ten years before federation; in Canada the central government had to create it. The Australian founding fathers quickly rejected the Canadian model. But even in the United States, whose model the Australians chose to follow, there was the power to provide for 'the general welfare' in addition to the specific powers allotted to the central government. The Australians did not copy this power.

Except for Western Australia, which seemed unlikely to join the federation, the Australian colonies were already well integrated economically and socially. It might be thought that such a grouping would seek or accept a strong central government. The opposite was the case. The two new powers given to the Commonwealth in 1897–98 are the exceptions that prove the rule.

From the time of the 1891 Convention Kingston argued that the Commonwealth should have power over interstate industrial disputes. At the 1897–98 Convention he was powerfully supported by the Victorian Henry Higgins, a highly principled, uncompromising radical, a newcomer to politics who owed his Convention position to Syme's support. Kingston and Higgins appeared to have an unanswerable case in the great intercolonial strikes of 1890 and 1891, which were notable because they were intercolonial. Capital was federated; labour was federated; only a federal government could deal with their disputes.[7] Yet they were constantly rebuffed, even by those quite sympathetic to a government role in industrial relations. It simply seemed like a state responsibility or at odds with the minimal role being envisaged for the Commonwealth. At the last minute in Melbourne the power over interstate industrial disputes was given to the Commonwealth because the West Australians, for reasons not altogether clear, gave it their support.[8]

Another South Australian, James Howe, a former farmer and policeman, was even more persistent in pressing the case for a Commonwealth power to grant old-age pensions. The core of his argument was that working men in Australia were always on the move. No colony had yet established pensions, although they were under discussion. Howe feared that if states gave pensions they would be reluctant to include recent arrivals

Employers protected by police drive their own wool to Circular Quay in Sydney during the Maritime Strike. Did this intercolonial strike justify a Commonwealth power over industrial relations? (*Sydney Mail*, 27 September 1890)

from across the borders. Here was another very strong case that most delegates found totally unpersuasive. Supporters of pensions, including the Labor man Trenwith, thought that they had a better chance of getting pensions established in the states.

A special factor at the last came to Howe's aid. Delegates feared that if they kept voting against a federal power over pensions, people would think they were opposed to pensions, which would give a handle to the enemies of federation.[9] So the opposition melted away, and Howe's motion was carried. The same consideration meant that God was included at the last although most delegates were still opposed. To oppose pensions was risky; to oppose God was suicide.

When the Labor Party came to power in the Commonwealth it could not implement its program to control the economy and reshape society because the constitution blocked its way. This was the foundation of the belief that Labor's enemies had created a weak federal government with that purpose in mind. Some time ago, the great scholar of the constitution, John La Nauze, exploded this view.[10] Labor was opposed to federation but not because the central government's powers were limited. Labor disliked the composition and powers of the Senate, and it feared a seemingly powerful Governor-General. Trenwith's attitudes on pensions was typical. Labor saw its best hope in controlling the colonial parliaments.

Although the founders wanted a limited central government, they could not help making it rich. It would take over a very substantial customs revenue from the states and so have more funds than it needed.[11] Obviously it would have to return its surplus revenue to the states or they would go bankrupt. The Convention went through contortions over its financial scheme. The Parkes formula of leaving the Federal Parliament to set the tariff solved one problem but created another. No one knew what the new tariff would be, how much it would collect, and how much, after the Commonwealth had met its needs, would be available to distribute to the states. The settling of the finances—the most business-like issue at the convention—was protracted and chaotic because the delegates were proceeding in such an unbusiness-like way. They needed to know how the customs union would work, but they were forming a nation instead.

The other problem of financial planning was that the states differed in the extent to which they relied on customs duties for revenue, which made it difficult to find a fair redistribution formula. In free-trade New South Wales the reliance had been slight. Its fear was that under the Commonwealth it would pay higher duties, which would then be funnelled to the other states where the reliance had been heavy. New South Wales would pay the cost of federation!

On this matter all premiers and treasurers were eagle-eyed, but there was a shared commitment to getting it right. Colonies could visit some defeats on their rivals and hope they would still join the federation, but if a premier were to leave the Convention to tell his people that federation meant a depleted treasury and more local taxation, then the cause was lost. A fair solution could not be simple. The delegates began by agreeing that the 1891 solution was totally unsatisfactory and, then after trying several others, returned to it as the least bad option. It was agreed that the formula would not solve the special problems of Western Australia, which relied very heavily on customs duties. Deakin organised a deal under which Western Australia could continue to collect duties on interstate trade for five years after federation.

But the problem remained of ensuring that the Commonwealth would not gorge itself on the surplus and leave little or nothing to be distributed to the states. The colonial treasurers were looking for a Commonwealth guarantee of their solvency. In whatever form this proposal came forward, Reid opposed it. If the Commonwealth were bound to raise a certain amount by customs to distribute to the states, that could well close off the option of the Commonwealth following a free-trade policy. To stave off this danger Reid had to throw his weight around. At Melbourne, one scheme was passed on a Monday morning when he was absent because the train from Sydney was late. He had it rescinded by the following day.[12]

However, since all the other premiers wanted a guarantee, they were going to win in the end. It was almost at the end, after midnight on the last Friday of the Melbourne session, when the delegates passed a proposal from Sir Edward Braddon, Premier of Tasmania, that the Commonwealth return to the states three-quarters of the customs revenue it raised. Reid was resigned; of all the schemes, this was the least objectionable since it did not commit the Commonwealth to raise a set amount. Barton was more alarmed and attempted unsuccessfully to limit the operation of the clause to five years. He was a protectionist himself and so not concerned at the Commonwealth raising a large sum through customs, but he knew that the free-traders of New South Wales would be hostile to this clause, which they soon christened the Braddon Blot.

It was widely recognised that having the states rely on the Commonwealth for funds broke the central tenet of federalism: that each government should be independent in its own sphere.[13] Largesse, begging, and haggling should not characterise the relationship between the two levels of government. The easy solution to the problem of a rich Commonwealth was to give it more to do. It could then spend all the customs revenue; the states would receive nothing from the Commonwealth, but they would have fewer responsibilities.

It happened that the combined interest payments on the colonies' debt roughly equalled the estimates of Commonwealth customs revenue (about which no one could be sure since the tariff was not yet set). The benefit of the Commonwealth taking over the debts and borrowing more advantageously was part of the standard argument for federation. That the Commonwealth should have this option was included in the 1891 and 1897 drafts. If the Commonwealth was definitely given this responsibility, then this benefit would be immediately secured and the financial problem solved.

Bold plans had little chance at this Convention, which had to take serious note even of misgivings and displease the fewest people. Reid did not want Commonwealth financial responsibilities expanded, thinking again that greater responsibilities might compel a high tariff. Some colonies had borrowed more per head than others, so a takeover of debts would deliver unequal benefits to the states. Imprudent states would be saved from their folly at others' expense! The seemingly most compelling argument against an immediate takeover was that it would make a present to the holders of colonial debt. They would draw their interest as before, but they would gain the greater security of a national backing of their loan. Better to use the attractiveness of greater security to convert the old loans to a lower rate of interest as opportunity offered. (This argument incidentally shows that the delegates felt no need to reassure and placate the London money market.)

The proponents of an immediate takeover replied that of course the Commonwealth treasurer would choose his moment, but 'shall take over' lost out to 'may take over'.[14] The Commonwealth did not take over the

The *Bulletin* (28 November 1896) jokes about a coat of arms for the new nation, but in the end the pooling of the debt was not immediately provided for in the constitution.

debts until thirty years later, during which time disputes over Commonwealth–state financial relations were almost continuous.

James Walker, the only delegate from business, was to the forefront in arguing for a takeover of the debt. He was also the chief advocate of a Commonwealth takeover of the railways. As a director of the Bank of New South Wales and the AMP, which operated in all the colonies, he had a national outlook, and his private interests were also spread around the continent.[15] He argued that interstate free trade would be only half realised if the state rail systems were determined to stop traffic in their territory flowing over a border. (The debate on railway rates showed this fear to be well founded.) To run the railways as a national system there would have to be a national controlling body, which would quickly abolish the breaks of gauge, remove local politics from railway construction and operation, and run the lines on business principles.

There had been a chance that the debts would be taken over by the new Commonwealth; there was never a chance that the railways would. These colonial politicians did not want to take the politics out of the railways. They touched the business and social concerns of every community and were integral to land settlement—all of which pointed to state rather than federal control. New lines still had to be built to open up the country—and how could that happen if strict accounting was applied? And should the suburban trains be taken over—and the trams? The most the Convention would do was to give the Commonwealth the option to take over railways and build new lines if the states consented. After a hundred years the break of gauge has been fixed, but there is still not a single body controlling the national rail network.

James Walker was an unusual businessman. If the ordinary businessman took any interest in federation it was to secure intercolonial free trade, which he would be equally happy to acquire through a customs union. Walker saw in union other economic advantages that depended on a stronger national government. He was a member of the Sydney Federation League and its third largest financial backer. His views were shared by another bank director, Reginald Black, and the merchant A. W. Meeks, who sat with him on the board of AMP. They were also members of the League but not so supportive.[16] They formed the core of a Sydney group that argued the case for national control of borrowing and the railways before the Convention met. They gave papers to the Economic Association and the Bankers Institute and debated the issue in their journals. They had the support of the influential financial journalist Robert Nash of the *Daily Telegraph*.[17] Walker took their proposals to the People's Convention at Bathurst, which adopted them.

It is at first surprising to find this group in free-trade Sydney. Reid as the defender of free trade did not want to increase the responsibilities of the federal government for fear that his own state would end up paying for them. This business group was less defensive. Federal control of the debt and the railways would deliver greater efficiency and real savings in the cost of government, which was a better form of protection for New South Wales.

Because the founding politicians were broadly middle class, they are sometimes assumed to be the agents of the business class. In founding a nation rather than a customs union they did more than the average businessman wanted; in not making the central government a controlling force in economic affairs they disappointed the Sydney financial group. If these financial experts had been in control there would have been a stronger national government—something that would have given Labor much more opportunity when they came to control it.

The central constitutional problem that preoccupied the delegates from beginning to end was the relationship between the two houses of parliament.[18] The United States model of two houses, one representing the people and the other the states, had been adopted in 1891 and accepted since by everyone except the Labor Party of New South Wales. The small states wanted the Senate to be a strong house because in it they were to have equal representation with the large states. But a strong upper house might paralyse the operation of the ministry, which was to be formed in the lower house. This problem had been dealt with in 1891 by prohibiting the Senate from making amendments to the budget and taxation measures. It was allowed to make suggestions—or to reject them outright, an extreme act likely to be used only very rarely. This limitation on the Senate's power was a concession of the small states to the large and to the principles of responsible government, which most favoured. It was passed comfortably, although there were four small-state delegations and two large. Three out of the seven delegates from South Australia, Queensland, and Tasmania supported it. Even Western Australia supplied one vote.[19]

In 1897 positions were more entrenched. The absence of Queensland reduced the small-state delegation to three, but if they voted solidly they could defeat New South Wales and Victoria. At first in Adelaide the Senate's powers were expanded: only on the budget was it to be confined to making suggestions and not amendments. On taxation measures, its powers were to be equal with those of the Representatives. The delegates from large states declared that if this provision stood, if the lower house did not control taxation, then they could not support federation.

George Reid led the push to reinstate the compromise of 1891 in full. Having asserted in his own parliament the right of the lower house to control taxation, he was not going to abandon it in the federation. He was a committed democrat, but on this issue he talked of the rights of taxpayers. If the small states were prepared to make equal contributions to the treasury, the Senate should have full power over finance. If two-thirds of the tax was to be raised in the two large states, then those taxpayers must be in charge through the House of Representatives.

Sir John Forrest of Western Australia was not daunted. 'We have a majority,' he boasted. He wanted the matter settled quickly so he could go home early. But there were small-state men keener on federation than he was. Two delegates from South Australia—Kingston and Glynn—and three from Tasmania—Henry, Brown, and Lewis—voted with the large states to give them a victory of one. It was a close-run thing. The large states were not bluffing. Had this vote gone the other way, federation would have been finished. Deakin was very active behind the scenes in persuading the Tasmanians to desert the 'small-state' position and went out of his way to praise the five men who had saved the cause.

That did not settle the issue of Senate power. A strong upper house seemed at odds with democratic principles—at least to the liberals and democrats from the large colonies. Most liberals and democrats from the small colonies saw nothing odd in it. They argued that this upper house was not a conservative body like those in the colonies. The principle of federation was that the states as well as the people had to consent to a law, and since in this case the states' house was to be directly elected by the people, what could be said against it?

Two things. The states were hugely unequal in population: why should the three-quarters of a million people in South Australia, Tasmania, and Western Australia control the Senate and hold a nation of three million to ransom? And a federation did not require that the states as such consent to federal law. The federal principle lay in the distribution of responsibilities between central and state governments. The protection for the small states—as of the large—was that the Commonwealth could act only on specific matters and that the states had power over everything else.

This alternative view of the federal principle was advanced by three clever Victorian delegates, all lawyers: Deakin, Higgins, and Isaac Isaacs, who was something of an outsider at the Convention because he was a Jew and because he paraded his learning at tedious length. These three tried to persuade the small-state men that they were not thinking clearly about how national politics would work. The divisions would not be between small states and large: parties would operate, and the division would be between conservative and progressive forces. The liberal and democrat delegates from the small colonies should combine with those from the large to ensure that in this battle the people's house should not be frustrated by the Senate.

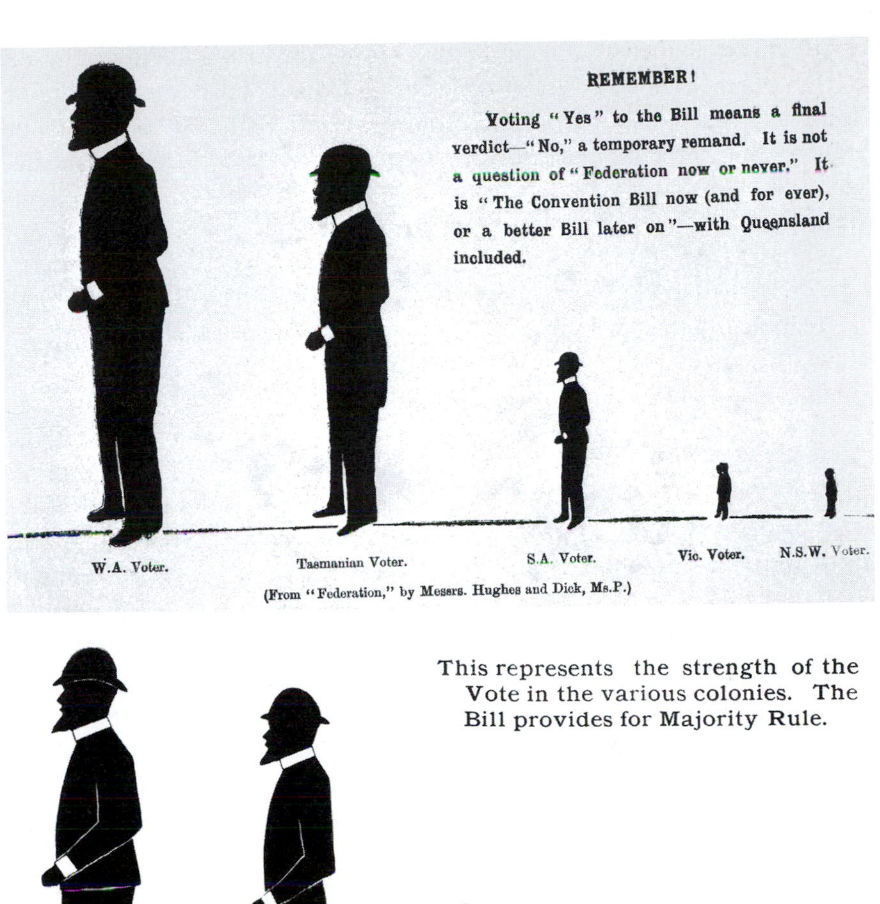
REMEMBER!
Voting "Yes" to the Bill means a final verdict—"No," a temporary remand. It is not a question of "Federation now or never." It is "The Convention Bill now (and for ever), or a better Bill later on"—with Queensland included.
W.A. Voter.
Tasmanian Voter.
S.A. Voter.
Vic. Voter.
N.S.W. Voter.
(From "Federation," by Messrs. Hughes and Dick, Ms.P.)
This represents the strength of the Vote in the various colonies. The Bill provides for Majority Rule.
N.S.W. Vote. 31 Members.
Victorian Vote. 28 Members.
S.A. Vote. 13 Members.
Tas. Vote. 11 Members.
W.A. Vote 11 Members.

Two views of representation in the Federal Parliament: the relative influence of Senate voters in the different states (above); the states' share of the representation in both Houses (below).

Their sophistication and eloquence were in vain. The small-states delegates thought that the interests of their states could well be threatened by the federation. What they felt, but could not say, was that their self-esteem required a strong Senate in which they would count as equals.

Higgins went further and attacked the provision of equal representation in the Senate. This was the principle of the United States constitution, he conceded, but it had been extracted from the large states by a terrible threat: some of the small states said they would return to their British allegiance if it was not granted. Neither in the Canadian nor German federations formed since the US had this principle been followed. It was not essential to federation.

Higgins had the support of William Lyne, the Leader of the protectionist Opposition in New South Wales, who could not match Higgins's sophistication but was quite definite that for no purpose could the great wealth and population of his colony be counted as equal to the others.

At the Adelaide session Higgins attracted only four votes against equal representation. The draft constitution was then considered by all parliaments. In New South Wales equal representation was overwhelmingly rejected by both houses. Members were scathing about giving equality to the minuscule populations of Tasmania and Western Australia. The very idea of Tasmania as a state was a joke: it was no more than a parish; let it be amalgamated with Victoria and run by a mayor. If Tasmania and Western Australia insisted on equal representation, the others should federate without them. They would not be missed and would soon beg to be admitted.[20]

Encouraged by such strong support from the mother colony, Higgins tried again when the Convention reassembled in Sydney—in the very chamber where the pretensions of the small colonies had been mocked. He received no more support. The other delegates from the large colonies were ready to accept equal representation, even against their inclinations, in order to secure the adhesion of the small colonies who would not federate without it. In return, they wanted to include a new provision in the constitution so that in the case of deadlock between the two houses the popular will would finally prevail. For Reid, this was the test of whether he could accept the constitution.

They pursued this cause through the three sessions, gradually wearing down their opponents. In Adelaide the assumption formed that something would be done about deadlocks. In Sydney it was agreed that the whole Senate could be dissolved if it persisted in defying the Representatives, which meant the loss of one of its few surviving conservative characteristics. In Melbourne a fully worked scheme had to be agreed on. If there was a deadlock, which house should be dissolved first and sent to the people, the Representatives or the Senate? They resolved finally that the houses should be dissolved together. If the two houses could not agree after the election, how was the issue to be resolved? The Victorians made a tremendous effort to secure settlement by national referendum, the pet scheme of the *Age*. But the small states would not consider a national referendum; if there was a referendum a majority of states as well as a majority of the electors would be required for a verdict. The alternative was a joint sitting of the two houses. Here the small states insisted that decision by simple majority was unacceptable; a special majority of three-fifths would be required. Whichever way they turned, the liberals and democrats from the large colonies could not establish straightforward majority rule as the ultimate controller of the Commonwealth. The Convention's decision was that ultimately power would lie with a three-fifths majority at a joint sitting.

During these discussions Reid lost his temper. He reported that delegates were constantly saying to him: 'Now, Mr Reid, it all depends on you. If you fight the battle of this Bill, all will be well.' But how could he advocate a measure in which the people were not the final arbiters? He declared, 'The whole spirit of the Constitution is being deformed and twisted in such a way that no man who has any sort of belief in democratic government could possibly support it; and this is the last straw.' 'Oh, oh,' said Sir John Forrest. Reid turned on him: 'I speak as one having some knowledge and experience of Australia. My honourable friend happens to represent some very successful goldfields at one extremity of the continent.' Those who complained of this rudeness were served with abuse as well. Barton adjourned for an early dinner.[21] After dinner those who did not want the people to rule continued to complain of Reid's outburst. Braddon of Tasmania regretted that the man who had called the Convention together was now striking a blow against federation.[22] Reid was not to be stopped. Later in the evening he clashed with Sir John Downer, the man who had slipped in 'reasonable' at the end of the debate on rivers:

Downer: I dare say my right honourable friend has many things in his career to regret.
Reid: I have not to regret meeting you.
Downer: And I have never regretted meeting my right honourable friend, but I have regretted many things that I have heard him say.
Reid: I regret that I cannot return the compliment, because I have never heard you say anything.
Downer: Well, I am not going to be rude: I am going to be civil.[23]

Reid was a practised hand at dealing with interjections. But he was now not on the verandah of a Sydney pub or in those scarcely more salubrious environs, the New South Wales Parliament.

Deakin reported that by the end of the Convention Reid was the most unpopular man in it.[24] He blamed him for not making clear what his minimum requirements were. Reid had made this perfectly clear. The Convention was simply refusing his demands. What was he to do? Walk out? That was scarcely possible given the standing that the Convention, his Convention, had acquired. He was trapped. His response was to be rude to those who would not give him a constitution he could cheerfully support. And then he left early and so missed the formal adoption of the constitution, the mutual congratulations, and the declarations to fight for the constitution's adoption. This time there was no official farewell.

The democratising of the constitution could go only so far when the small colonies had equal representation at the Convention and when their support was taken to be essential for federation. Why was it essential? The hard men in New South Wales did not accept that it was. The material benefits of federation would not be much lessened by the absence of Tasmania and Western Australia. Heydon, the leader of the New South Wales patriots, was amazed at the unique phenomenon of citizens being willing to make large sacrifices out of *loyalty to a continent*.[25] Indeed a smaller federation might have been created, although the rivalry between New South Wales and Victoria was a barrier to the union beginning with their fusion. They were each looking for allies among the other colonies. It happened, however, that the men keenest about federation were least concerned about its material benefits and most inspired by the noble vision of a complete Australian union. Barton and Deakin were the last people to practise *realpolitik* in their relations with the smaller colonies. Their notion of federation as brotherhood and the establishing of a higher life absolutely forbade it.

Reid was closer to being a hard man. He had shown by his attitude to the 1891 draft that he would not accept any constitution. He was supreme in New South Wales, a colony reluctant about federation and essential to its success. He was in a good position to drive a hard bargain. Yet he was captured by the federal ideal in aim and method. He revived the federal process by organising a convention of the same sort as 1891 in which delegates in equal numbers from the several colonies deliberated openly on a constitution to which they hoped all could assent. He had created a body that did not reflect the relative importance of New South Wales to the federal project. The weight of New South Wales would finally tell, but Reid himself would suffer because he was not enough of a hard man.

It is as well to be reminded of these fundamentals of the federal movement for, in following the affairs of the Convention closely, it is easy to form the opinion that there was not much national sentiment abroad. The historians who see federation as a business deal are at their most persuasive when they point to delegates belying their nationalist protestations by fighting desperately for their own colony's interests.[26] But it is putting too demanding a test on national feeling to require that all other attachments and interests yield to it. And it is misleading to characterise a conference only by the matter and manner of its disputes. We must also consider what the delegates are conferring about. Why are they being drawn into these arguments? To gain the economic advantage of intercolonial free trade? Certainly, that was highly valued and properly so by politicians who had a care for the prosperity of their societies. But they were creating a nation, not a customs union, and since it was to be a nation it had to include all the Australian people and gain their willing consent. This nationalist commitment was not overridden by the delegates' concern to protect colonial interests; in the absence of any other compulsion, it was the force that kept them together.

10
No–Yes

We intend to mete out justice to George Reid—the most faithless imposter that ever wore the cap and bells in Australian political life.

B.R. Wise to J. Symon, 5 June 1898

Some were rather absurdly shocked at the idea that 'bargaining' should enter into so noble a national cause.

George Reid, *Reminiscences*, p. 181

On the breaking up of the Convention, the prospects for federation looked bleak. The premiers of the two large colonies were refusing to endorse the Constitution Bill. Turner said he would take two weeks to look at all the figures again and then declare a position. Reid was saying nothing. The *Daily Telegraph*, which supported Reid's free-trade government, and the *Age*, which sustained Turner's protectionist government, were both opposed to the Bill. Neither liked the financial arrangements and the absence of majority rule. They were also united in fearing the likely tariff policy of the new Commonwealth: the *Telegraph* thought it would be strongly protectionist; the *Age* that it would not be protectionist enough.

Reid and the Victorians left the Convention much more dissatisfied than the delegations from the small colonies. New South Wales had secured the right to only 'reasonable' use of its water and had been forced into giving some guarantee for the finances of the other colonies. Victoria's hopes for the Riverina trade had been blighted by a commission that was to give 'due consideration' to the money New South Wales had spent in getting its railways to the border. The liberals and democrats of both colonies had failed to secure unencumbered majority rule. Of course no delegation achieved all it wanted. The concession of the small colonies on the Senate was made early. The string of defeats for the larger colonies came in a rush at the end.

The delegations from Tasmania and South Australia—liberals and conservatives; government and opposition—went home united in their support for the Bill. This unanimity fed suspicions in the larger colonies that too much had been given away to the small. Forrest of Western Australia adopted a wait-and-see attitude. He would not face up to the difficulties of putting the case for federation in his colony until the Bill had actually been adopted in the east.

In Tasmania and South Australia there was some opposition to the Bill. In Adelaide the No case was put by an alliance of manufacturers fearful of Victorian competition and the Labor Party upset at the Bill's undemocratic features.[1] The *Mercury* in Hobart led the case that the financial arrangements would not save Tasmania from bankruptcy.[2] It was because of his concern for Tasmania's finances that Andrew Inglis Clark, the republican founding father, would not endorse the Bill. It was a surprising position for a man who had been so passionate for the cause. Instead of standing for the Convention in 1897 he had kept to a longstanding arrangement to revisit the United States.

South Australia and Tasmania both stood to benefit greatly from intercolonial free trade. A federation which gave that and equal representation in a strong Senate could not be spurned. 'We'll never get such good terms again' was a powerful Yes slogan.[3]

It was commonly thought that Victoria was equally keen to secure intercolonial free trade in order to obtain new markets for its manufactures. This greatly annoyed the *Age*, which claimed that Victorians had been defeated at the Convention because everyone assumed that Victoria would accept any federation. That was not the *Age*'s position. There would be no point in federation if the Commonwealth Government followed a free-trade policy and wiped out Melbourne's factories. Syme had never accepted Parkes's strategy of letting the first Commonwealth Parliament settle the tariff. Even as the Convention dispersed, he was insisting that a tariff be written into the constitution. He was also upset at the failure of the Bill to incorporate his scheme of the referendum as a solution to deadlocks. According to Deakin, his deepest concern was that he would never exercise in the Commonwealth the influence he had wielded in Victoria.[4]

It would be hard for the Victorian ministry to carry federation with the *Age* opposed to it. Governments in those days had no way of reaching the whole electorate except through newspapers. Liberal governments in Victoria had long accepted that they could not govern against the *Age*. In this case the two leading ministers were not disposed to make a fight of it. Turner was a cautious contriver of economies and balanced budgets; he had no emotional commitment to federation. Isaacs the Attorney-General was a nationalist, but he had failed to have the national principle that the people should rule inserted in a constitution that remained resolutely federal. No one had brought more learning or more attention to the constitution than Isaacs, but he was always the outside critic. It was not his Bill.

Against the ministry and the *Age* stood the Australian Natives Association. For them federation was more than trade, finance, and the referendum. Deakin, who had declared for the Bill at the close of the Convention, was ready to lead them.[5] The Victorian Assembly now included a number of members who were Natives. They were young and able and, being liberal, were supporters of Turner's government. Deakin met with them, and they resolved to act together to save the Bill. They told Turner that if he failed to support the Bill they would go into opposition and take as many as they could with them. That put a new factor into Turner's figuring.

It happened that the Natives were holding their annual conference at Bendigo just as the Convention was completing its labours. Bendigo was one of the strongholds of the Association, the home town of John Quick, from which he had launched the campaign for a popularly elected convention. The delegates met in the hall owned by the local Association. Their most important business became the consideration of the Constitution Bill.

The Natives were earnest young men, responsible citizens of Victoria, and mostly liberal. They had to take seriously all the liberal and Victorian objections to the Bill. They were not going to be mere enthusiasts. They proceeded to debate the Bill. Against the claim that it was undemocratic stood numerous democratic elements: one man, one vote; an upper house elected by the people and dissolvable if it defied the Representatives; payment for members of both houses. Against the claim that Victoria would suffer financially, it was argued that it had the resources to cope perfectly well. When the motion to accept the Bill was put, there was a roar of Ayes, and members leapt to their feet yelling and cheering and waving handkerchiefs. The pretence was over. They were going to do what they had always intended: devote themselves to carrying this Bill and so establish the nation of which their association had dreamed for twenty years.[6]

There were three moments in federal history when a group of people were transported by the idea of Australian union. This was not a matter of audiences responding with enthusiasm to federalist oratory. There were innumerable cases of that. These manifestations had no such crude prompt. The first was when Parkes rose to speak at the Federal Conference banquet in Melbourne in 1890. The second was at Corowa Court House when Quick produced his plan for a people's convention. The Natives Association conference in Bendigo was the third. Their journal described it as being like the 'new baptism' when the disciples of Jesus were filled with the holy spirit.

The editorial staff at the *Age* had feared that the Natives would react in this way. Before Deakin left for Bendigo they called him in to persuade him that he should moderate their enthusiasm. Deakin had begun his career as a protégé of Syme. At the first Convention he had followed Syme's line in seeking some guarantee for Victorian manufactures after federation. Now he most deliberately defied him.

Deakin was not present when the Natives decided to support the Bill. He arrived later as one of the speakers invited to address the conference banquet. Isaacs was also invited and spoke in answer to the toast of 'the ministry'. He urged caution and further consideration of the Bill. He was heckled, and Purves, an ex-president of the Natives, shouted at him: 'Are you in favour of the Bill?'

Deakin spoke late in the proceedings and briefly. He declared unequivocally for the Bill and told the Natives that this was the moment of crisis for the federal ideal that they had so long nurtured; no matter what the opposition they must devote themselves to consummating the union. He gave their own determination new fire, and he was received rapturously.[7] This speech came to be thought of as his best and the most influential, the one that turned the tide in favour of the Bill in Victoria. It did not do that. The news from Bendigo that day was not Deakin's speech but the conference resolution. Deakin in his speech paid tribute to that decision: 'Never have I felt more proud of my fellow Australians than when I learnt that the Conference had this day pledged itself to support the Bill.'[8]

At first the Natives wanted to downplay the influence of the speech, to make clear that they had not supported the Bill under the influence of drink and Deakin's oratory. But it was a very good speech, and they were proud of it. They became its guardians. Deakin had spoken without text or notes so at first the only record was the newspaper reports. When a good transcript taken by an experienced shorthand writer was offered to the ANA board, they paid three guineas to acquire it.[9] They set it as one of the items to be performed in their elocutionary competitions. And so the passionate declaration for the Bill by one man came to stand for what the Natives had done at Bendigo.

The Natives were well organised to realise the national ideal. They had branches throughout the colony, real operating branches, as they had to be for the management of their health insurance scheme. The Federation League organised by the Natives in 1894 was moribund. They reactivated it and staffed it with their own people. At the local level the Natives ran the campaign in their own name or were the backbone of Federation

Deakin's Speech to Australian Natives Association

Bendigo March 1898

MEMBERS OF THE ANA—We have heard much tonight of politicians and a good deal from them. We have also heard something of the Federal Convention and addresses from some of my fellow-members; but it is in neither capacity that I propose to speak, because I recognise that the united Australia yet to be can only come to be with the consent of and by the efforts of the Australian-born. I propose to speak to Australians simply as an Australian.

You are entitled to reckon among the greatest of all your achievements the Federal Convention just closing. The idea of such a Convention may be said to have sprung up among you, and it is by your efforts that it must be brought to fruition. One-half of the representatives constituting that Convention are Australian-born. The President of the Convention, the Leader of the Convention, the Chairman of Committees and the whole of the drafting committee are Australians. It remains for their fellow-countrymen to secure the adoption of their work.

We should find no difficulty in apprehending the somewhat dubious mood of many of our critics. A federal constitution is the last and final product of political intellect and constructive ingenuity; it represents the highest development of the possibilities of self-government among peoples scattered over a large area. To frame such a constitution is a great task for any body of men. Yet I venture to submit that among all the federal constitutions of the world you will look in vain for one as broad in its popular base, as liberal in its working principles, as generous in its aim, as this measure. So far as I am concerned, that suffices me. Like my friends, I would have secured something still nearer to my own ideals. But for the present, as we must choose, let us gladly accept it ...

At a time like the present this association cannot forget its watchword—Federation—or its character, which has never been provincial. It has never been a Victorian, but always an Australian Association. Its hour has now come. Still, recognising the quarter from which attacks have already begun, and other quarters from which they are threatening, we must admit that the prospects of union are gloomier now in Victoria than for years past. The number actually against us is probably greater than ever; the timorous and passive will be induced to fall away; the forces against us are arrayed under capable chiefs. But few as we may be, and weak by comparison, it will be the greater glory, whether we succeed or fail ...

This cause dignifies every one of its servants and all efforts that are made in its behalf. The contest in which you are about to engage is one in which it is a privilege to be enrolled. It lifts your labours to the loftiest political levels, where they may be inspired with the purest patriotic passion for national life and being. Remember the stirring appeal of the young poet of genius, so recently lost to us in Bendigo, and whose grave is not yet green in your midst. His dying lips warned us of our present need and future duty, and pointed us to the true Australian goal—

Our country's garment
With hands unfilial we have basely rent,
With petty variance our souls are spent,
And ancient kinship under foot is trod:
O let us rise,—united,—penitent,—
And be one people,—mighty, serving God!

Deakin, *The Federal Story*, pp. 177–9.

Leagues.[10] Soon after the Bendigo conference the press was carrying reports of Natives Association branches springing into action.[11] There would be a good campaign organisation, and in Deakin it would have a formidable leader. Would Turner and the *Age* oppose this movement or join it?

A few days after the Bendigo Conference the *Age* conceded that from a liberal point of view there was nothing to complain of in the Bill. It covered its retreat with a dig at its conservative rival, the *Argus*. That paper was a champion of the Bill; so did this mean, asked the *Age*, that it had abandoned its defence of plural voting and a restricted franchise for the upper house, since neither found a place in the Commonwealth Bill? Like Kingston in South Australia, the *Age* seized the opportunity of using the federal constitution as weapon for reform of the state constitution. But it was still not whole-hearted about the Bill.[12]

It was four weeks after the end of the Convention before Turner spoke. With Deakin on the platform he endorsed the Bill and urged a Yes vote. He had looked to Deakin for help with his speech. Could he supply arguments to show that farmers would benefit from federation? He wanted to show that everyone would benefit, but the evidence on the farmers seemed to point in the other direction. Once the Premier had declared that Victoria would benefit from federation the *Age* quite uncharacteristically accepted that the matter was settled and dropped its own arguments. But it was only a few days before the poll on 3 June that the paper finally gave its endorsement to the Bill and urged a Yes vote. The editorial had, at Syme's invitation, been drafted by Deakin.

Federal sentiment had always been strong in Victoria. But No campaigns are very easy to run. A No-case led by the *Age* and Turner would not have been against federation but against this proposal for it. Deakin and the Natives scared them off by showing how much enthusiasm they could summon up for the Bill as it stood.

The Bill still had its opponents. There was a question over the farmers. The external tariff of the new nation was still uncertain, but there was no doubt that Victoria's stock tax would disappear and so allow easier access to Victoria of cattle and sheep from New South Wales and Queensland. The disaster certain to follow the abandonment of the stock tax was the centre-piece of the campaign in the country against the Bill. Allan McLean, a minister in Turner's government, resigned his post to lead it. With a cascade of figures he showed that federation would reduce the value of rural property.[13]

In Melbourne the No case was led by Higgins, the only Victorian delegate to the Convention who opposed the Bill. Deakin had tried hard to persuade this man of principle to settle for second best. He had agreed at Deakin's request not to declare his position immediately after the Convention when his defeats were fresh in his mind, but to think about the Bill for a month. It made no difference. His views had not changed, and he could not compromise. The Bill was undemocratic because of equal representation in the Senate, hard to amend, and enshrined provincialism rather than providing for a united nation.[14] In this he had the support of most of the Labor Party and its weekly paper, the *Tocsin*.[15] Trenwith, the one Labor delegate to the Convention, was a powerful advocate in support of the Bill.

Is the Federal Constitution Democratic?

This Constitution is not only the most democratic of any existing Federal Constitution, whether we compare it with that of Switzerland, Canada, the United States or Germany, but it is infinitely more democratic than the Constitution of any Australian Colony. It contains almost every democratic principle for which the Democrats of Australia have been striving for the last forty years.

In no less than eight important points it is in advance of the present Victorian Constitution:

1. Abolition of plural voting for both Houses.
2. No property qualification for electors of the Senate.
3. No property qualification for members of the Senate.
4. Payment of members of the Senate.
5. Power to dissolve the Senate.
6. A remedy for deadlocks in the Federal Parliament.
7. All Federal Ministers must sit in the Federal Parliament (save for a maximum period of three months). In Victoria, not more than four Ministers need be members of Parliament.
8. Every adult person who has now or who acquires at any time in the future a vote for the Assembly in Victoria or any other State, shall thereby have a vote for both Houses of the Federal Parliament.

With such political machinery, the Democrats of South Australia, Victoria, and New South Wales can command majorities in both Houses, and secure in the first Federal Parliament the passage of further democratic measures.

J. Haase, Printer, 17 Swanston St., Melbourne

Persuading democrats in Victoria that they could vote for the Bill (even with equal representation in the Senate).

As before, the fate of the federal proposal would be determined in New South Wales. The man with the most influence on what attitude that colony would adopt was its premier. Federalists constantly puzzled over Reid. Was he a true federalist or an opportunist? Would he go straight or wriggle? To the question of whether he was a federalist Reid would have given the politician's answer: it depends—on what the proposal is and how it bears on other issues and concerns. As zealots for their cause, federalists could not countenance calculation; they demanded devotion. They would not allow that a true federalist could favour federation but not the proposal currently under discussion. They could never understand Reid.

Bernhard Wise, a free-trade federalist who had fallen out with Reid, wrote a book on the federal movement in which the monster Reid is the central character. To Wise Reid was an enigma; he predicted that historians would have great difficulty with Reid since he was hard enough to understand at the time.[16] The historian is at a disadvantage because Reid kept none of his letters and papers. His *Reminiscences* reveal very little—except a man who was strangely disengaged from the politics he practised so skilfully. In politics he mocked himself, admitted mistakes, and cracked jokes. He was the fat man in history. His enemies saw him as a clown or a mountebank. This did not mean he had no fixed beliefs. He believed strongly in free trade. He could see the advantages of federation but without having the personal need for it that drove the federalists. They were right in recognising that he was not one of their own.

At the last session of the Convention Barton had offered to make a great sacrifice to induce Reid to go straight and so make federation safe. If Reid would support the Bill, he would renounce his own claims to be first Prime Minister and back Reid for the job. Reid replied that he could not commit himself because too many of his own free-trade party were opposed to the Bill.[17] Of course he remained Premier only while he had the support of his party. Deakin, who loathed Reid, listed as one of his offences his desire to remain Premier of New South Wales. He was looking to him to back federation no matter what the consequences.[18] One other Premier of New South Wales and leader of the free-trade party had done that: Sir Henry Parkes. Reid would have had Parkes's fate well in mind since he himself had been Parkes's destroyer. In a colony where there was so much opposition to federation, it was by no means clear that a Premier's endorsement could carry it.

When Reid had to make up his mind on the Bill, it was opposed by two-thirds of the parliamentarians, which included a clear majority in his party and all the Labor Party.[19] Lyne, the Leader of the Opposition, was certain to oppose since he had gone into the Convention an opponent of equal representation in the Senate and champion of New South Wales interests. The free-trade *Daily Telegraph* was gearing up for a ferocious No campaign. The protectionist *Australian Star* was also opposed. Of the main Sydney papers only the *Sydney Morning Herald* was in favour.

On 28 March 1898, two weeks after the conclusion of the Convention, Reid broke his silence on the Bill.[20] Five thousand people packed into the Sydney Town Hall to hear him; they occupied every seat and stood in the aisles and passageways. Reid said he would speak not as a partisan or an advocate, but as a judge. He went right through the Bill, acknowledging its good features and pointing out its drawbacks. Supporters of the Bill cheered some passages, opponents others. No one knew how he was to end. He was speaking without notes, giving a clear exposition of a constitution in his customary slangy style. Everyone in the vast crowd could hear him; their attention did not waver.

After two hours he came to the summing up. 'With all the criticisms I have levelled at this Bill, with all the fears I have for the future, I feel I cannot become a deserter from the cause of federation.' A loud cheer went up, but Reid did not want great enthusiasm. This was a political speech like no other. He returned to his balancing act.

'I cannot take up this Bill with enthusiasm. I see serious blots in it which have put a severe strain upon me … after all, great as a nation's worth is, great as an Australian union is, in this day of humanity, in a continent free as this is, we ought to have, I admit, a more democratic constitution.' That gave the opponents of the Bill something to cheer.

He came for a second time to his conclusion. 'Now, I say to you, having pointed out my mind, and having shown you the dark places as well as the light places of this constitution, I hope every man in this country, without coercion from me, without any interference from me, will judge for himself.' So was it to be a pure balancing act? No. He had one more thing to say. 'I consider my duty to Australia demands me to record a vote in favour of the Bill.'

The cheering and yelling lasted for two or three minutes. This was truly an occasion. Only here, at this moment, was his declaration applauded. These words, the greatest speech in his life, came to dog him. The antis were the first to be disappointed; if he saw so much to criticise how could he vote for the Bill? The pros soon joined them, for his criticisms, being recorded in full in every newspaper, acquired a weight that overwhelmed his declaration to vote for the Bill.

Most of the free-trade party had been expecting a firm recommendation from the Premier against the Bill. Immediately after the speech there was a movement to displace Reid from the leadership. Reid thwarted this by cancelling a projected meeting of parliament, saying that it would distract voters from a calm consideration of the Bill. The *Daily Telegraph* excommunicated Reid: he was no longer a free-trader or a democrat.[21]

For a time the federalists claimed Reid as a supporter since he was going to vote for the Bill. They could not do that after he spoke again. At three country centres, Goulburn, Bathurst, and Newcastle, he repeated his Sydney performance but each time the criticisms of the Bill became more severe. Barton now regarded him as a traitor who had broken an undertaking that he made at the end of the Convention. When Barton had asked him whether he would support the Bill, he had said that there was much in it he did not like but that he would not oppose it. Barton saw the Sydney speech as being in line with that assurance. But now he felt he had been duped at the Sydney Town Hall. All along Reid had intended to defeat the Bill.[22]

Reid's explanation for his later speeches was that he was annoyed at Barton and the federalists being so fulsome in their praise of the Bill whose defects they had criticised in the Convention. He needed to restore the balance.[23] As his criticisms became more severe his intention to vote Yes seemed more perverse. Reid's explanation of that declaration was that a recommendation from him to vote No would have killed federation. He wanted 'to give the Bill a show'.[24]

Reid would have been fairly safe in opposing the Bill outright. In accounting for his behaviour his enemies always assumed he was a man of great cunning. He did not need to be very clever to predict that his position on the Bill would disappoint both sides. If he did give an ambiguous message because he could not desert federation, his was one the great sacrifices for the cause. He had been a successful reforming Premier, determined and courageous. But on federation he had given a speech that was dubbed Yes–No and he himself was shadowed thereafter by the reputation of being a trickster; he was Yes–No Reid. Typically he made jokes about this. When accused of being Yes–No he replied indignantly, 'That is a baseless lie; the exact opposite of the truth—I was no–yes.'[25]

Apart from making these four speeches at decent intervals, Reid spent the referendum campaign governing New South Wales. Barton, abandoning his law practice, threw himself into the fight for Yes with a punishing speaking program that took him around the colony. He was the person whom all supporters of Yes wanted to hear. He had come to embody the federal ideal, and thousands were personally devoted to him.

The Yes and No forces in New South Wales were evenly matched. Supporting No were most of Sydney business, the Labor Party, and the New South Wales patriots.[26] It was an odd assortment, quite incapable, as the Yes side said, of agreeing on a constitution if this proposal should fail. Yes had some business support, the enthusiasm of the young professionals, and a strong constituency in the countryside, particularly the border territories. The Noes had the easy task of frightening the electors.

Reid kills federation while his Attorney-General and leading anti-federalist Jack Want prepares a grave for the infant and Barton watches over the fence. (*Bulletin* cartoon by Hop, 9 July 1898)

Federation meant the free port of Sydney at a standstill, New South Wales taxed to the hilt to benefit its neighbours, and the nation in thrall to the senators from the small states. Against the complexities and restraints of federalism, the Noes shouted for British liberty and majority rule.

The Yes side attempted to kill the scares constantly set running by the Noes and then talked up the benefits of federation and the grand destiny

Federation as the enemy of democratic principles: a view of the referendum outcome in New South Wales.

that awaited a united people. The nationalist appeal was undoubtedly strong, so much so that the Noes could not present themselves as opposed to federation, as many had been until now. They said they were opposed only to this Bill. Campaigning for No was a great engine for making federation an unassailable good.

The Womanhood Suffrage League, like many Sydney organisations, was split on federation. Maybanke Wolstenholme was stirred by the prospect of union bringing a higher national life, and she believed women had a good chance of getting the vote in the Commonwealth. She organised the Women's Federal League. Rose Scott believed New South Wales would suffer under federation and was suspicious of men creating for themselves a new realm that was to have control of marriage and divorce. She regularly spoke at No meetings.[27]

The Yes case not only had to win a majority; it also had to secure at least 80,000 votes. The figure was originally 50,000. Parliament raised it after the Sydney session of the Convention ignored its criticisms of the Bill. The plan was to make the figure even higher. Reid organised 80,000 as a compromise. Once he was identified as a federal traitor, this deed was added to the indictment.

On polling night the Yes vote trailed at first, then led No narrowly, and at eight o'clock, three hours after the polls closed, the board outside the *Herald*'s office posted Yes at 80,284. A mighty cheer went up from the crowd in the street. It alerted the leading federalists, who were wining and dining in an upper room at a hotel over the way. Barton's friends grabbed their leader and chaired him around the room. The crowd below called for him. He spoke a few words from the window, the federal flag was hung out, and the celebrations began. They lasted for twenty minutes until the *Herald* announced it had made an error. The 80,000 had not been reached and was not going to be. The No supporters outside the hotel now had their moment. 'You're a bit previous, Toby.' 'Take in that flag.' The street celebrations continued outside the office of the *Daily Telegraph*, which during the campaign had ceased to be a newspaper and had become a propaganda sheet for No. It did not get the figures wrong.[28]

The final figures in New South Wales were 71,595 Yes to 66,228 No, or a 52 per cent Yes vote. In the other three colonies the Bill was carried easily, 67 per cent voting Yes in South Australia, 81 per cent in Tasmania, and 82 per cent in Victoria.[29] These colonies would not federate on their own. The shortfall in the New South Wales Yes vote meant that the federal movement had failed for the second time.

For twenty glorious minutes the New South Wales federalists thought they had won. This partly explains why they so badly misread the political situation after the poll. They were furious at being robbed, and their first thought was to have the 80,000 requirement revoked, which would then make the Yes votes victorious. They were also determined to remove the traitor Reid from the premiership. So Barton planned to form a federal party of free-traders and protectionists that would contest the next election, due very soon, on the demand that the Bill be accepted. The old reforming cry—'The Bill, the whole Bill and nothing but the Bill'—would work its magic again. The federalists would defeat Reid, Barton would become Premier, the 80,000 requirement would be revoked—and federation achieved.

Reid too was immediately thinking of the election. The morning after the poll he sent to the other premiers telegrams that coolly began, 'I could not cordially support the Bill ... but I should be sorry to see all our labours brought to a standstill.' He suggested a conference of premiers to amend the Bill to make it more acceptable to New South Wales. He would then obtain the people's endorsement of the amendments at the forthcoming election.[30]

Barton was immediately in difficulties. It would be unpopular to oppose the Premier's attempts to seek better terms. He must ensure that the other colonies treated Reid as a pariah with whom they would have no dealings. Then New South Wales would turn to him. The official correspondence between Reid and the premiers was shadowed by the sometimes frantic correspondence between Barton and the premiers in which they discussed how Reid's invitation was to be handled.[31]

Braddon of Tasmania and Kingston of South Australia needed no prompting from Barton. They flatly refused to reopen discussion on a Bill that had received majorities in all colonies. However, Deakin, who was advising Turner, did not agree with the tactics of his friend Barton. He thought Reid would use a refusal by the other colonies to negotiate to strengthen his position in New South Wales and that Barton was not certain to beat him at the general election.[32] The best way forward was to support Reid in office and for the federalists to keep the pressure on him until federation was achieved. Deakin, who despised Reid as much as Barton did, recognised that he was asking a great sacrifice from his friend—to allow the traitor to do the good deed rather than the honest man. Barton could not come at it. He thought Reid must be destroyed.

Nevertheless, Turner, under Deakin's advice, agreed to a conference. Barton was in a panic. If there was a conference it must be short, all wrapped up before the elections, and Reid must be told he would get nothing. The two small colonies maintained their refusal to talk, which was set down as arrogance in New South Wales. So Barton switched course and suggested to Braddon and Kingston that they should at least meet Reid. They refused. Turner would not proceed without them, and so the conference plan lapsed. Deakin was right. Reid's position as champion of New South Wales strengthened. He reversed the order of proceedings. He would put his amendments first to the people; if they were accepted the premiers would have to talk.

Barton had taken a great risk in attempting to undermine Reid's negotiations. If Reid was a traitor to federation, Barton was a traitor to New South Wales. He knew the danger and, in case Reid had a spy in the telegraph office, he sent telegrams to Deakin in code. One of Reid's ministers did accuse him of undermining the Premier. Barton did not fudge or shuffle; he replied with the big lie: 'I took no steps of any kind, by suggestion, by persuasion, or otherwise to interfere with the success of Mr Reid's negotiations; and the answer of each Premier as it came was as much news to me as to anyone else.'[33] The leader of the noble cause had what it takes.

Less than two weeks after the poll, Barton realised that he could not beat Reid at the election if he were advocating the Bill and Reid the Bill with amendments. Too many people had voted Yes with misgivings who were pleased at the prospect of a better Bill. Barton began to back and fill.[34] He would support amendments—but not as many as Reid and not in his belligerent, take-it-or-leave-it style. The amendments the two men agreed on were the abolition of the Braddon Blot, a simple majority rather than a three-fifths vote at a joint sitting, and the capital in New South Wales. The Bill had left the location of the capital to be determined by parliament.

1540/11/81

For	Write
Reid	Higgins
Want	Dobson
Kingston	McSharry
Barton	Walker
Braddon	Boma
Forrest	Eden
O'Connor	Ashton
Turner	Holder
Deakin	Leake
Commonwealth Bill	Budget
Convention	Court
General Election	Litigation
N.S.W. Parliament	Syndicate
Victorian Parliament	Aviary
Bounties	Cartoons
Sugar Beet	Salt
Wineries	Wool
Amendments	Hooks
Referendum	Argument

Barton sends Deakin code words for their telegrams so that Reid could not spy on them.

New South Wales claimed it not only as the oldest and most populous colony but also as the one that would have to make the greatest sacrifice for federation.

Braddon and Kingston were furious privately with Barton for deserting the Bill. In public they still had to support him in preference to Reid. Turner and Deakin minded much less the prospect of amendment, because a constitution that reduced the power of the small states would better please Victoria.

Reid had great fun with Barton as a prospective wheeler-dealer. The man who had said the Bill was perfect was going to get a better Bill! The man who wanted to treat the other colonies gently was going to extract concessions from them! He was the candidate of the other colonies! Barton replied that Reid's stand-over tactics would endanger federation in which he had never believed and which he had wrecked several times over. Reid was happy not to have Barton's consistency. Barton was a supporter of federation at any price. He had supported the 1891 constitution until it had been superseded by the much-improved version of 1898; he had said the 1898 constitution was the best in the world until he agreed to its amendment. Reid would give his whole-hearted support to federation when there was a constitution that was good for New South Wales and worthy of Australian democracy.

Who will uphold the people's will
And in those smaller States instil
Need for a better, fairer Bill?
Our Georgie!

Whose brief is for each other State?
Whose last word is 'Negotiate'
And thus leave Sydney to its fate?
Why Toby's![35]

Hostility to the other colonies and pride in New South Wales were the forces Reid exploited to carry the mother colony into union under his leadership. Barton thought it very unfederal not to treat the people of other colonies as brothers.

At last in July 1898 there was an election over federation, the first in the long history of the movement. The battle for federation was actually over before the election began because both sides proclaimed themselves federal and were competing over means and leaders. Since the referendum, politicians had been converting to federation in droves. To their surprise the people had voted Yes. Some forty members (in a House of 125) who had recommended a No vote were defied by their constituents.[36] This was the great service the referendum performed for the cause in New South Wales: it gave the people their own voice.

The party divide of free trade and protection still existed. Reid's free-trade party became the Liberal and Federal Party. Barton organised the National Federal Party, which included free-traders and protectionists who were federalists willing to follow him. But to beat Reid they had to combine with the protectionist party, whose members held very diverse views on federation and the Bill. Lyne, their leader, had opposed the Bill outright.

Now in combination with Barton he was denouncing Reid as an unworthy federal leader! At the constituency level this opportunistic alliance to destroy Reid caused great heartache. Local federation leagues were told they had to support candidates who had campaigned against the Bill.[37]

Barton wanted the issue of the election to be federal leadership and for the tariff to be forgotten. He promised not to disturb Reid's free-trade policy for the life of the parliament. Lyne would promise only until federation had been settled. The tariff could not help being an issue if only because voters for years had defined themselves in relation to it. Federation could disturb but not obliterate those allegiances. This was also the first election since Reid had introduced land and income taxes to cover the fall in customs revenue. There were many disgruntled taxpayers eager to vote for the protectionists. This factor had more to do with the election outcome than federal leadership. Reid lost many seats but just held on with a majority of three or four. He was now absolutely reliant on the Labor Party for survival.

Barton did not gain a seat at the election. Boldly he took on Reid in his own constituency, as Parkes had done at the previous election. Twice Reid had been targeted for destruction by federalists—and again he survived. But Barton's honourable defeat gave heart to federalists everywhere after the disappointment of the referendum. It was a noble deed by 'Australia's noblest son', as Barton's followers began to call him.[38] Deakin congratulated him on fighting 'so chivalrously and so devotedly'. His congratulations were perhaps more heartfelt than they would have been if Barton and his party had won. Deakin believed Reid would be much more dangerous in opposition.[39]

During the election Barton and Reid thoroughly traduced each other and competed to be the better federalist: I created the Convention, boasted Reid; I worked there all through the night, replied Barton. At the declaration of the poll they shook hands and talked of their old friendship, which had begun when they were young men. Reid was genuine in not wanting political differences to damage personal relations. Barton was going through the motions. He had long lost respect for Reid.[40]

Everyone expected that Barton would soon be in parliament. Someone would resign a safe seat in his favour. No one did. One man who had promised to resign was dissuaded by Lyne, who did not want to be overshadowed in the House by Barton.[41] After six weeks Frank Clarke, the member for Hastings-Macleay, did the noble thing. This electorate was a dairying and sugar district on the north coast, a fairly safe seat for the protectionists. Barton would have little trouble winning it. But then Reid took extraordinary measures to defeat him. He ran a very good candidate against him, a former minister of agriculture, and went himself to campaign on his behalf. His minister of works also visited the electorate to

The *Daily Telegraph* presents Barton as a mugger, supported by O'Connor and Wise, robbing Reid of office (election edition, July 1898).

make clear that there would be fewer roads and bridges from the government if the farmers voted for Barton.[42]

Public works were of course of prime significance for the electorate. Barton with his national responsibilities would not have time to chase around departments for grants for culverts, so the former member announced he would do this work for him. Reid pounced on this: Barton was getting someone else 'to hump the swag'. Barton wanted to be in parliament not to serve this electorate, not for the sake of federation, which was safe in his (Reid's) hands, but for his own glory.[43]

Reid's standing with federalists sank to a new low. This was not killing federation by cunning; this was an open, vindictive attack on the federal leader, the chosen of New South Wales and of the Convention, whose rightful place was in the parliament to oversee the completion of the great movement. Reid had a plain answer to this hyperbole. Barton, although not himself a member of parliament, had been admitted to the Opposition party room to advise on tactics designed to defeat his government. He had every reason to treat him as an opponent.[44]

The *Bulletin* presents Barton as an avenging angel driving Reid and Want out of Paradise (30 July 1898).

Federalists around Australia followed the battle in Hastings-Macleay believing the fate of their cause hung on the outcome. For them it was a clear conflict between the forces of good and evil. For the townspeople of Kempsey and the farmers along the Macleay the matter was not so simple. Would they accept Australia's noblest son, who was silent on the tariff but known to be a protectionist, or vote for a free-trader and get more roads and 'practical federation' from Reid? They decided for Barton. Deakin reported 'universal rejoicing' in Melbourne.[45]

On entering parliament Barton took over from Lyne as Opposition Leader in a closely divided House. He attempted to displace Reid, but the Labor Party always saved the Premier.[46] It was not enthusiastic about federation, but Reid was much more willing to talk about a democratic federation than Barton. On domestic reform some party members were becoming impatient with Reid, but Barton would give them less and he had not been forgiven for jailing the Broken Hill strikers.

During the general election Reid had been insulting and belligerent towards the other colonies. Having won it, he became much more conciliatory. The requests for amendments that he passed through the parliament were not outrageous. The other premiers agreed to meet him. He now had a forum with which he was comfortable. Although he had created the Convention, he chafed at its methods. He had wanted less talk and more getting down to business.[47] Now a small group of men meeting in secret would settle the constitution. When he first proposed a conference after the referendum, he considered that the premiers' amendments would need no further endorsement. Kingston and Turner quickly disabused him of that notion. Whatever was decided would have to be approved by the people in the federating colonies, which would put limits on what Reid could demand.

All the premiers were present: the four from the colonies that had voted on the Bill—New South Wales, Victoria, South Australia, and Tasmania—and the two from the reluctant colonies of Western Australia and Queensland. Reid got his way on his key demands with some modifications. The Braddon Blot—requiring the Commonwealth to give three-quarters of its customs revenue to the states—was not abolished altogether but limited to ten years. The capital was to be in New South Wales but at least a hundred miles from Sydney, and until it was built the parliament would meet in Melbourne. The boundaries of states were protected further by the people as well as the parliament having to approve changes. However, Reid failed to persuade Kingston to drop the word *reasonable*, which qualified the right of New South Wales to use water from the Murray–Darling for irrigation.

These were matters that particularly concerned New South Wales. On his more principled demand for a more democratic constitution, Reid was also successful. For a joint sitting of the houses, the three-fifths voting requirement was dropped in favour of an absolute majority. On the amendment of the constitution, either House could now put a proposal to the people, in order to allay the fear that the undemocratic Senate would block all attempts to reform it. This measure was promoted by the Labor Party in New South Wales, which Reid was pleased to assist.

A seemingly innocuous amendment provided that the Commonwealth could grant money to the states on terms and conditions it saw fit. This was to assist the finances of any state whose loss of customs duties was not made good by the agreed financial formula. The small states gained this reassurance as their reward for giving Reid what he wanted. When the Commonwealth became supreme in finance this section (number 96) enabled it to exercise authority over matters that the constitution had left to the states, such as roads, health, and education—and in all the states, small and large.

At the end of the conference Reid announced that he would urge a Yes vote at the second referendum. There was still plenty of opposition to federation from free-trade Sydney and the New South Wales patriots, which was honed into spine-chilling slogans by the *Daily Telegraph*. The opponents claimed that the amended Bill was in essence the same and in one respect distinctly worse: Sydney was not to be the capital. The Legislative Council refused to allow the amended Bill to be put to the people. To overcome this opposition, Reid had to persuade the Governor to appoint twelve new councillors. To the dismay of Sydney's elite, he transformed four Labor men into Legislative Councillors. The skill and determination that Reid had used to establish free trade and direct taxation were now devoted to the carrying of federation.

Reid and Barton campaigned together for Yes. Lyne, reverting to type, campaigned for No. The Labor Party was still opposed, but there were now two Labor dissenters—Sleath and Ferguson from Broken Hill—who played an important part in the Yes campaign. The battle was still hard fought. Barton and Reid had trouble getting a hearing at their opening Town Hall meeting. The dissenters kept up a chant consisting of two words: Yes–No. One man stood up in the middle of the hall, climbed on his chair, slowly turned his coat inside out, and then pointed to Reid.[48]

The Yes vote increased a few percentage points on the 1898 figure. As it had done in 1898, the founding city of the nation refused to vote Yes, but the result was now very close: No scored 50.2 per cent in Sydney. In the country Yes scored 60 per cent, which gave Yes 56 per cent overall. There was no requirement of a minimum vote, but with a heavier poll the Yes vote easily exceeded the minimum set in 1898. In the other colonies the Yes vote increased despite the fact that the Bill had been amended against the interests of the small states. Tasmania and South Australia were keener on federation than New South Wales, and they needed the mother colony more than it needed them. The Convention, with its equal representation and formal mode, had masked this difference. After the failure of the first referendum, Reid had exploited the difference to get his way. In South

Australia the Yes vote was 79 per cent, in Tasmania 94 per cent, and in Victoria 94 per cent.

Immediately on the carriage of federation, Barton resigned as Leader of the Opposition in favour of Lyne. Labor was ready to accept Lyne as Premier and he to offer them more than Reid. To the protectionist–Labor alliance was added those free-traders who wanted to punish Reid for carrying federation. The pretext for Reid's overthrow was trifling: an unauthorised payment to an MP for a report on old age pensions. Once Reid was assured that his own integrity was not being impugned he cheerfully accepted that his reward for carrying New South Wales into the union was to be dismissed from the further conduct of its affairs. He bore no ill will to his attackers—except to Barton. He believed Barton had attacked him personally.[49] The hostility between the two was now mutual. Reid did not hate Barton as an opponent; in ordinary politics he could defeat him. He was riled by the special aura Barton had acquired.[50] Barton hated Reid because he had trifled with the noble cause; Reid hated Barton because the cause had made him noble.

By resigning as Leader of the Opposition Barton ensured that when the federation was inaugurated Reid would not be Premier of New South Wales. The holder of that office was assumed to have the strongest claim to be first Prime Minister. Reid and Barton both wanted that honour. Free-traders and protectionists both wanted their man to form the first government and give their cause the advantage of incumbency. The competition was now very open. Neither of the strongest contenders had any official position. Lyne, who held the key official position, had assured Barton that he had no designs on the top job.[51]

11
Continental

During my tenure of the Colonial Office, a gentleman attached to the French Government called upon me. He asked me how much of Australia was claimed as the dominion of Great Britain. I answered 'The whole'.

Lord John Russell[1]

For the first time in the world's history, there will be a nation for a continent, and a continent for a nation.

Edmund Barton[2]

Federalists believed that the island continent was the natural boundary of the new nation. They were a long way from achieving that goal when the second referendum was held in mid 1899. Only four colonies—New South Wales, Victoria, South Australia, and Tasmania—had voted to form the Commonwealth of Australia. Setting Tasmania aside (which federalists did in their tropes, although not in their plans), three colonies out of five on the continent had joined, and the two that had refused—Queensland and Western Australia—were the largest in land area.

There are smaller islands than Australia that are not politically united. The physical boundaries of the continent seemed a natural national boundary only because the British had thought continentally long before there were Australian nationalists.

For a time Australia had been bisected by an international boundary. When the British settled at Sydney they claimed only the eastern half of the continent under the name New South Wales. The Dutch were presumed to have a good claim to the western half, which bore the name 'New Holland'. While this land boundary survived, the only people who crossed it were the Aborigines. It gave no more trouble to them than longitude 135 degrees East along which it ran.

The Dutch were not interested in colonising the lands they had discovered, of which all reports were unpromising, and their days as a great power were over. It was the French who took an interest in the south land.

To forestall them the British dotted settlements around the coast: inside Port Phillip in 1803, at Hobart in 1803 and near Launceston in 1804, in northern Australia in 1824, and in the west at King George Sound in 1826 and Perth in 1829. With the settlement at Perth the British laid claim to the whole continent. It already carried the name 'Australia'. Matthew Flinders, the first man to sail around it, had recommended the name, albeit only in a footnote to his *Voyage to Terra Australis* published in 1814. Governor Macquarie, ruling a settlement that did not extend more than 200 kilometres from Sydney, liked the name and began to use it in his official correspondence. It passed into common usage and was used by the Colonial Office in 1829 to christen Britain's new colony of Western Australia.

Once the continent had been claimed by the British, the boundaries that did divide Australia were, as the federalists claimed, artificial because there were people of British stock on each side of them. They thought of themselves as British and were strongly attached to their particular colonies, but they also bore the name of the continent. The immigrant settlers were called and knew themselves to be Australian colonists. The native-born in every colony thought of themselves as Australians. On this commonality the nation could be built.

However, there were significant differences in the political and social development of the Australian colonies. Long before they showed a reluctance over federation in the 1890s, Western Australia and Queensland were thought of as the problematic candidates for an Australian nation.

Western Australia was poor and backward, and had very few ties with the settlements on the other side of the continent. When the eastern colonies achieved self-government in the 1850s the population of Western Australia was 10,000, much too small to be freed from British tutelage. It remained a Crown colony. Around 1850 the eastern colonists showed their determination to be a free people by resisting the resumption of convict transportation. Western Australia was so desperate to climb out of poverty that it begged the British Government to supply it with convicts.

Some of the convicts moved east when their time was up. This was a minor annoyance, but the very presence of convicts in the west was a reproach to the east. It kept alive the association of Australia with convictism, which the eastern colonists were desperate to put behind them. In the 1860s they mounted a strong campaign, led from Victoria, to persuade Britain to abolish transportation. The *Argus* in Melbourne sent a reporter to the west to do an exposé on the degradation brought by convicts.[3] When the colonial governments threatened to stop subsidising the mail steamer that called at Albany, the British Government gave way, and transportation ended in 1868.

Western Australia obtained self-government in 1890. Its population was still very small, only 48,000, a third of Tasmania's. At the last minute there was a hitch because some parliamentarians in Britain were reluctant to give this tiny population concentrated in the south-west control over a third of the continent. There were suggestions that the colony be divided and self-government given only to the south. The governments and parliaments in the eastern colonies pressed Britain to agree to the west's demands. If Western Australia remained a Crown colony or if a new Crown colony were formed in the north, there would not be self-governing colonies covering the whole continent to unite in an Australian federation. Still worse, a northern colony might be worked by coolie labour and threaten the White Australia policy, which had just been put in place by coordinated action against the Chinese.[4] The danger passed. After a parliamentary inquiry at Westminster, the new parliament at Perth was given control over the whole colony.

The eastern colonies had assisted the west to become like themselves; whether the west would consent to join the east was another matter. Western Australia relied heavily on goods imported from the east, on which it collected tariffs, but sent almost nothing in the opposite direction. The establishment of interstate free trade would benefit eastern suppliers and give the west no compensating advantage. Its farmers would struggle against competition from South Australia and Victoria. There would be no hope of establishing local manufacturing. The loss of customs revenue to the Commonwealth would be particularly damaging. Western Australia collected nearly all its revenue from this source and a high proportion from intercolonial trade. None of the financial schemes in contemplation would give it adequate compensation. Federation would require the imposition of new, direct taxes, and how could federation be sold if that were the consequence?

Economically, federation appeared to be a disaster. It would bring the advantage of the east protecting the west against invasion—a concern in a huge, sparsely settled territory—but in the absence of a railway across the Nullarbor, Commonwealth troops could not give ready assistance.

It is surprising, then, that such a devoted West Australian as Sir John Forrest gave any support to federation. He became Premier on the inauguration of self-government in 1890 and held office throughout the decade. Among the founding fathers his career was unique. He was a native-born Australian who had worked in the British imperial service. For twenty-five years he had been a government surveyor in the Crown colony of Western Australia, rising to the position of Surveyor-General. He had the instincts of an imperial federationist. His strongest feeling about Australia was that it should be united to advance the consolidation of the British Empire and the giving of assistance to the 'dear old mother country' to which the colonists owed so much.[5] He was not clever or a visionary, but a good-hearted, bluff fellow who knew where his duty lay.

Forrest's dilemma was that his duty to assist in the union of the Australian colonies conflicted with the interests of the colony he led. The dilemma was most acute because his personal connections and closest political supporters were the old pastoral and farming families who were most opposed to federation. He was not born into this group—he was the son of a miller—but he had married into it. Margaret Hamersley, a cultivated independent woman, gave Forrest the added distinction of having a wife who was an accomplished political hostess.

In 1893, the third year of Forrest's premiership, the gold rush to Kalgoorlie began. While the east was suffering from economic collapse and drought the west boomed. In the east politics was concerned with retrenchment and new taxation; in the west Forrest borrowed heavily and built railways, ports, and water supplies. He kept control of the parliament by giving every electorate some of this largesse and by recruiting critics into his ministry. But he used his power wisely. He was an enlightened despot rescuing his country from backwardness and ensuring that social division did not breed social strife. So he supported manhood suffrage and payment of members, established a state bank to lend to farmers, and rewrote the labour and employment laws to benefit working people. All this brought West Australian practice into line with the east.

Most of the gold-diggers came from the east. They were more Australian in outlook than the old settlers and much more interested in federation. The removal of tariffs on their food and supplies from the east would lower their cost of living. They resented the old settlers for taxing their food, and they attacked Forrest for not providing them with enough local services and giving them insufficient representation in parliament. Poor Forrest! In principle he was a supporter of federation; in practice the keenest supporters of federation were his political enemies.

Federalists in the south-east of the continent were more concerned about Queensland than Western Australia. If Western Australia did not join now, it would join later. If Queensland did not join now, it might evolve into something different and threatening.

Along its northern coast, Queensland had developed a plantation economy where sugar was cultivated by black labour from the Pacific islands. There had been two responses to this social anomaly from the rest of Australia: either to press for the end of black labour or to accept that Queensland could not be part of an Australian union.[6] God's purpose for Australia was not completely plain. The island continent suggested unity, but since a third of the continent had been placed in the tropics, it might be too diverse for union. Climate was held to have a determining influence on national character and race. The debate on whether white men could work in the tropics was not yet over. In 1898 the Premier of Queensland declared that there was no federation that embraced tropical and temperate zones.[7]

The problem looked to be solved when Griffith's liberal government announced in 1885 that recruitment of black labour must cease after 1890. But the response of the northern planters was to back the creation of a separate colony in north Queensland. Black labour would then be protected by a planters' government.

Separation from Brisbane had long been an issue in Queensland politics.[8] The capital of this huge colony, located in its south-eastern corner, could not command the whole territory. The settlers in the centre and the north looked to their own coastal ports—Rockhampton and Townsville—whose ties were more with Sydney than with Brisbane. From these ports railways were built directly inland so that the rail system was not focused on the capital. Queensland was the most decentralised colony in Australia. Still, the settlers in the centre and the north complained that too much of their taxes were spent in the capital. This complaint was heard all round the continent. In Queensland an obvious solution was at hand: there should be three Queenslands and not one.

Griffith opposed separation, but like other Queensland premiers he could not ignore it. Just before he went to Sydney in 1891 to write an Australian constitution, he drafted a federal constitution for Queensland. It divided the colony in three and then reunited it. There was to be a Queensland House of Representatives and a Queensland Senate. The measure was defeated in the upper house.

In 1892 Griffith, now in coalition with his former opponents, changed his mind on black labour and allowed recruiting to continue. This was to be an interim measure until the plantations were replaced by small-scale farms, which would employ white labour rather than black. The southern colonies were alarmed at the change and formally protested. Griffith told them to mind their own business. Parkes replied that it was the business of all Australia to ensure that within the nation there was no degraded caste.[9] Since the colonies had blocked Chinese immigration in the 1880s, black labour in Queensland was now the touchstone of the White Australia policy. Deakin and Barton had attempted to win Labor support for federation by arguing that only a united Australia could bring Queensland to heel. The chief reason why the conservative Queensland Government dragged its feet over federation was that it feared a democratic Commonwealth that would be used to destroy the sugar industry.[10]

WHY QUEENSLAND HOLDS FEDERATION IN ABEYANCE.
'Queenslanders are not likely to make stupid sacrifices for the benefit of selfish politicians and merchants elsewhere in Australia, when Queensland with tropical conditions would be at the mercy of communities inexperienced in, and unsympathetic with, her peculiar interests.' (*Courier*)
The Queensland cabinet waited on by kanakas; Premier Nelson is seated, centre (*Brisbane Worker*, 21 November 1896).

Once the Queensland Government became a defender of black labour, the planters had no need to press for separation. In the 1890s it also became clear that if there were a separate north Queensland, the planters would not control it. The region that had the most distinctive economy in

Australia also contained those typical Australian settlements: goldfields. The inland miners, mostly from Victoria, were a unifying force in Queensland as they were in Western Australia. At Charters Towers in the 1870s they supported the Australian Natives Association, in the 1880s trade unions and republican clubs, and in the 1890s the Labor Party. After the 1896 election a majority of the seats in north Queensland was held by the Labor Party, which was implacably opposed to black labour.

Separation was a dead issue in the north. It continued strong in the centre, where Rockhampton was angling to be a capital city under the leadership of George Curtis, a real estate agent who owned a good deal of the town. The Central Queensland Separation League had in the usual way shifted its agitation from Brisbane to London. If the Queensland Parliament would not surrender its authority, it lay within the power of the British Government to make it.

In 1896 the Secretary of State found a new way of stalling on the Queensland demands for separation. He suggested that separation and new states could be dealt with by the new federal government. That sounded well, but Rockhampton knew better. If the new constitution followed the 1891 draft, separation would be harder, not easier. The draft provided that new states could be formed only if the parliament currently controlling their territory gave permission. Rockhampton would still be in Brisbane's power and with no appeal to Westminster. This was directly contrary to Parkes's intention when he called the federal Convention. He envisaged the central government developing remote areas and creating new states. He thought the present boundaries of Queensland and Western Australia must be treated as temporary. But all this had to be abandoned because the New South Wales delegates feared that if the Commonwealth had an independent power over state boundaries it would be used to dismember New South Wales.

The attitude of Queenslanders to federation was complex. It was attractive to the north and centre because they would be united economically with the rest of Australia, with which they did more business than Brisbane. Miners could obtain food and supplies more cheaply when Brisbane's tariffs were removed; pastoralists could send cattle into Victoria without paying a stock tax; planters would have a national market for their sugar. However, the planters feared that the Commonwealth would rob them of their labour force, and Rockhampton feared it would lose the chance to be a capital. In Brisbane and the south-east, where most of the population lived, federation was seen more as an economic threat. Farmers and manufacturers feared southern competition; Brisbane merchants feared that Sydney would increase its hold over Queensland trade and make their city even more a branch-office town. The Labor Party was divided, suspicious in the south and supportive in the north.

There was no organised group advocating federation. In 1896 the Australian Natives in Victoria sent missionaries northwards to stir up Queensland with not much success.[11] In not sending delegates to the Convention of 1897–98, the Queensland Government did not disappoint many of its citizens.

However, the Queensland Government did not want the rest of Australia to federate and leave it isolated. Just before the 1897 Convention assembled, it made a concerted effort to establish an attractive alternative to full federation. It proposed at the Federal Council meeting in January 1897 that the Council be elected by the people. To argue its case it put up the bright young man of the continuous ministry, Thomas Byrnes, born in Australia to poor Irish parents, educated in the law on scholarships and Attorney-General at 33. He was good enough to match Deakin against whom he was pitted in this debate.

Byrnes depicted the Council as protecting the equality and independence of the colonies; the constitution as drafted in 1891 gave too much power to the central government and too much scope to those southerners who would make north Queensland a desert if they could. Australia as yet had no need of a federal government. The Council could grow and develop in the British tradition to meet needs as they arose. The Victorians had put this argument to Parkes when he wanted to bypass the Council and establish a nation; now Deakin argued that loose confederations never worked and never evolved into full union.[12]

Four colonies were represented on the Council. The Queensland delegates were supported by the West Australians, led by Forrest, who said it was very hard to tell people to enter a federation under which they would be losers.[13] The attraction to him of expanding the Federal Council was that he would not have to give up his customs revenue. The delegates from Victoria and Tasmania voted against Byrnes's motion. The voting being equal, the motion was lost. If the Convention failed, as the governments of Queensland and Western Australia hoped, the Federal Council would still be there, but not with the authority of being elected by the people.

Forrest did take a delegation to the Convention, elected by the parliament rather than the people. He had two aims: to ensure that any constitution agreed on protected the small states and that federation be delayed. Pursuing the first aim could well secure the second. The West Australians intended to vote in a block against the compromise on the Senate's money powers. Barton made a pointed reference to this in his speech pleading with the delegates to restore the compromise. Why, he said, should Western Australia be allowed to imperil federation, which its leader declared it was unlikely to join? The speech did not change any Western Australian vote, but it did help Barton pick up one extra vote (from McMillan, a New South Wales conservative) and give him a bare majority.

The Convention recognised that Western Australia faced a particularly acute problem with its finances and was ready to adopt special measures to assist. Forrest was very ambivalent about this. He would have much preferred a general guarantee for state finances. Although he was eloquent over the difficulties federation posed for the west, he did not like his colony—the one prosperous colony, the one with enormous potential—being treated as if it were a basket case. Perhaps he would have preferred to have been left with his grievance. It was only reluctantly that he agreed to accept the deal fixed by Deakin: for five years after federation Western Australia could continue to levy duties on goods imported from the other states, the duties reducing by a fifth every year.[14]

The Queensland Government pretended to make an effort to send delegates to the Convention even after it convened. They were to arrive in time for the second session in Sydney, then for the final session in Melbourne; they never materialised. There was a ritual sameness about these attempts. When the government proposed to send delegates elected by the parliament, Thomas Glassey, the Labor leader, successfully moved they be elected by the people. When the government proposed they be elected by the people, Curtis, the Rockhampton champion, successfully moved they be elected by the people of the three regions. Having been rebuffed, the government then abandoned their attempt. Glassey and Curtis prevailed because voting with them were members opposed to federation or fearful of the current proposal—as was the government itself. In the absence of Nelson in Britain, the government was led for much of 1897 by Horace Tozer, who privately damned the new constitution as 'the Federated Social Democracy scheme evolved by Kingston, Reid and co.'[15]

Although Queensland was not formally represented at the Convention, its rival leaders showed up as lobbyists. Nelson and Tozer wanted the Convention to give express permission in the Constitution for black labour to be used in Queensland down to some fixed line, say latitude 26 degrees South (just below Bundaberg). This scheme received little mention in the formal debates because, of course, it was dynamite.[16] To have agreed to it—even to have discussed it—would have destroyed the Bill's chances with the working class in the south. On the other hand, Glassey,

Queensland offers to join the Convention.—An unpleasant preliminary.
The *Bulletin* regarded the abandonment of black labour as a pre-condition of Queensland's entry into the federation. (*Bulletin,* 3 April 1897)

the Labor leader, failed to persuade the Convention to insert a provision banning black labour.[17] That would have destroyed the Bill's chances in Queensland, although it might have united Labor behind it.

Curtis of Rockhampton wanted the Convention to amend its draft to allow the subdivision of Queensland without the Queensland Parliament having to give permission. This proposal was debated by the Convention. Barton was not unsympathetic but extremely cautious. He was aware of the simple facts that most people in Queensland lived in the south and were opposed to separation. To give Curtis what he wanted might damage the Bill's chances if it were ever put to the Queensland voters. He postponed a decision until he had telegraphed Nelson for his opinion. Nelson predictably did not want separation made easier, and so it was settled.[18]

Queensland's formal absence was most frustrating to its only federalist of any stature, Samuel Griffith. He wanted Queensland to be part of the union, and he did not like being a spectator to the rewriting of his draft. By his own contrivance he was now Chief Justice and so somewhat constrained in his political activities. However, he was regularly consulted on the drafting and wrote a pamphlet on the Adelaide version, which the Queensland Government published. When belatedly in 1898 a Federation League was formed in Brisbane he became its president.[19]

As the Queensland Government pretended to be organising delegates to the Convention, the Convention pretended to be eager to welcome them.[20] The small-states men did want them there. They wrote to Griffith complaining of the compromise on the Senate's money powers and looked forward to overturning it when Queensland arrived. Deakin wrote to Griffith to warn him that the large colonies were not bluffing and that without the compromise they would not federate.[21] Had Queensland been present, there would have been four small colonies to two large. The compromise would have been very much more difficult to reach, and the Convention might well have failed to agree on a constitution.

This Convention took a much more hard-headed approach than that of 1891 on the admission of laggard colonies. The 1891 draft listed the colonies that might form the Commonwealth and offered them all the same status as states no matter when they were admitted. Now equal representation in the Senate was to be given only to the foundation states; laggard colonies were to be given such representation as the parliament chose. The small-states men argued that equal representation was a fundamental principle of the constitution and should be given to all member states. The large-states men regarded equal representation as a political concession, not to be extended more than necessary. What if Queensland should divide itself in three states and each part qualify for equal representation? Then the larger states would have even less hold over the Senate, and the constitution would be even more undemocratic. The large-states men prevailed on this issue because there was also a feeling that colonies not ready to bear the risks and costs of forming the union should not be able to enter later and claim the full privileges of membership.[22]

Join now—or else ... This approach would finally concentrate the minds of the governments of Queensland and Western Australia. Forrest labelled it coercion.[23] Leading a colony with a very small population, he would give up two guarantees if he did not join at the beginning: equal representation in the Senate and at least five members in the House of Representatives.

'UP TO HIS NECK IN IT.'
Scandals over the Queensland National Bank severely damaged the standing of the continuous ministry. (*Bulletin*, 4 December 1897)

When the four south-eastern colonies voted Yes in mid 1898—although in New South Wales not in sufficient numbers—it seemed that a federation of some sort would occur. But a hundred things could still go wrong. There would be delay. The moment of crisis had not yet come for the two laggard governments. Forrest, facing strong opposition in his cabinet and parliament, made no attempt to put the Bill to the people. The government of Queensland was now led by Thomas Byrnes, the youngest man in the cabinet. He was the last, best hope of the continuous ministry, which had been disgraced and discredited early in the year when its corrupt dealings with the Queensland National Bank had been revealed and the bank had to be propped up for a second time. The Premier, Nelson, had taken refuge in the nominated Legislative Council with the paid position of president. Tozer, his deputy, had gone to London as Agent-General. Byrnes was the cleanskin. Native-born, clever, handsome, much was expected of him. He seemed a different breed from the old gang, and he looked as if he would turn away from their reactionary stances. But on federation he was quite determined that Queensland should not join, at least for the present. The sugar industry could not be put at risk.

Then in September 1898, after only five months in office, Byrnes died. Robert Philp, the strongest minister left in this debilitated team, was a supporter of federation. But he was from Townsville in the north and a former partner in Burns Philp, the great shipping and trading company based in Sydney. He recognised that he could not carry Brisbane and the south into union. He backed James Dickson for the premiership on condition that he support federation.[24] Dickson was a Brisbane merchant, English-born, gentlemanly and uninspiring, and previously no enthusiast for federation, the cause he now took up. To his mind the strongest reasons for supporting it were that Queensland could not risk isolation and the loss of original state status, nor the opprobrium of obstructing the consolidation of the British Empire in this quarter of the globe. Like Forrest, his patriotism was more imperial than national.[25]

When Reid planned his premiers conference to revise the Commonwealth Bill, he wanted Queensland to be represented, although it had not been at the Convention. The absence of Queensland had been one cause of his lack of enthusiasm for the 1898 Bill. Dickson accepted Reid's invitation, as did Forrest, so the premiers of six colonies revised the Bill on which four had voted.

At the conference, Dickson's first request was that another Convention be held so that Queensland could participate. That was very quickly rejected. He then asked for a five-year concession on tariffs, as had been granted to Western Australia. That too was rejected. Forrest was now asking for a ten-year exemption.[26] Interstate free trade would unravel if these concessions were made. All Queensland was given was the right to divide the colony into three for the first Senate election. But the cause of separation in Queensland was damaged more than helped by the premiers because they made approval by the state's people as well as its parliament a precondition of separation. Forrest received nothing from his fellow premiers on the grounds that Western Australia's case had been considered at the Convention where it had been represented.

In May 1899 Dickson called a special session of parliament to endorse the putting of the constitution to the people, which would only occur if the second referendum was carried in New South Wales. There was still plenty of opposition to federation, and the usual games began. Labor was divided on federation but united on the need for a franchise free of tough residential requirements. It demanded that all white men in Queensland be allowed to vote on the constitution. This manoeuvre might have again led to the defeat of the federal cause had not one Labor man, W. G. Higgs, and the leader of the independent liberals, James Drake, come to the government's support.[27] Higgs and Drake both went on to become federal ministers. To defy his party in the cause of federation represented a huge shift in Higgs's views. In 1893, as president of the South Sydney Labor League, he had set the Sydney Town Hall in turmoil when Barton was launching his Federation League.

The acceptance of federation by the continuous ministry represented an abandonment of key aspects of its domestic policy. As Dickson confessed, he had opposed one man, one vote but now, yielding to the 'voice of Australia', he was accepting it in the federal constitution and in the referendum on its acceptance. He had defended black labour, but now he was ready to let the Commonwealth Parliament decide its fate.[28] The noble cause of union provided an escape route for this enfeebled government and gave it a new purpose.[29] Instead of attacking southern interference, Dickson appeared on Brisbane platforms with Barton and Deakin and basked in the reflected glory. Queensland had realigned itself to the south-eastern colonies before the voting on the constitution took place.

The campaign in Queensland before the referendum on 2 September differed from those in the south-east. There the argument was whether a union should be formed and whether the terms were acceptable. Queenslanders knew that a union of three million people was going to be operating to the south and that its constitution was settled. The question for them was whether to join it. There was less idealism and more hard-headedness in this campaign. A new ideal was proclaimed by the No campaigners: 'Queensland for Queenslanders'—for they had to argue that the northern colony was strong enough to defy the south and live on its own, an ideal not yet dead.

The Yes vote was overwhelming in the north and centre, except at Rockhampton, which rightly saw the federal constitution as freezing the boundaries of the continent. Other separationists persuaded themselves that they would be no worse off under this constitution, since appeals to London to overrule the Queensland Parliament had got nowhere.[30] In the north the appeal to Labor was that the federal government would end black labour on the sugar plantations, but that argument could not be put too strongly because the planters were persuading themselves that the Federal Parliament would act justly towards Queensland and that men of common sense would not destroy a whole industry.[31] This shows how keen they were to gain access to a national market and have it protect them against the sugar of low-wage countries and the heavily subsidised beet sugar from Europe. The risk they took in voting Yes was not too great because most assumed that in time the industry would move to white labour.

In the south the Yes campaigners took each industry and farm crop by turn and argued that it would not be damaged by federation, but this tactic did not turn around the long-held hostility of this region. The south voted 61 per cent No and Brisbane 64 per cent No. The overall result in Queensland was a narrow victory for Yes (55 per cent). The north and centre did have this victory over the south: they forced it into the Commonwealth—with the penalty that there was to be one Queensland and not three.

Western Australia now stood alone. Forrest did not put the Bill to the people. After the second referendum in New South Wales, he submitted it to a select committee of both Houses. The committee stipulated four conditions under which federation would be acceptable:

1 The tariff concession granted by the Convention should not require Western Australia to reduce its tariff by 20 per cent every year. For the whole five years it should be able to maintain its tariff in full.
2 The Inter-State Commission, the body that was to police interstate free trade, was not to interfere in Western Australia during the five-year exemption period.
3 The Commonwealth should be given explicit power to construct a railway to the west; as the Bill stood, the states through which it would pass would need to give agreement.
4 Western Australia should be able to subdivide the state for Senate elections, as Queensland was to be permitted to do.

Forrest persuaded the Assembly to put two proposals to the people: the Convention Bill and the Bill as amended by the select committee. He hoped that only the amended Bill would win acceptance whereupon the

The monster petition to the Queen from the Western Australian goldfields requesting separation and federation with the Commonwealth.

other colonies would have to agree to the amendments to secure Western Australia for the union. But the Legislative Council would not agree to both Bills being put to the people, or either of them separately. Nothing was to be put to the people.

There was a small group of federalists in the parliament who championed the Convention Bill. In the Legislative Council they had voted with the out-and-out opponents of federation to ensure that the amended Bill alone was not put to the people. In the Assembly the federalists were led by George Leake, who had the hapless task of being Opposition Leader, and Walter James, a lively young lawyer who sat on the cross benches. Both had been part of the Western Australian delegation to the Convention. They were also the leaders of the newly formed Federation League in Perth.

The political muscle of the federalists came from the goldfields. When the Legislative Council refused to let the people vote on any federation proposal, a representative congress of the eastern goldfields voted for separation from Western Australia and incorporation into the Australian union. Collection of signatures began on a monster petition to the Queen requesting separation. This was a well-organised and well-resourced movement, supported by local business and the press, and with a mass following—the only occasion when a whole community was organised to demand federation.

Forrest ignored it. He now hoped to pressure the Legislative Council into accepting the amended Bill by securing the prior agreement of the other colonies to the changes. He wrote to the premiers and leading federalists, he addressed an open letter to the press of Australia, and he travelled

Forrest, the wild man of the west, addresses the premiers (from left), Turner, Kingston, Reid, and Braddon. (Cartoon from the South Australian *Critic*, February 1900)

east to put his case in person.[32] Leake wrote ahead to his federalist friends urging that Forrest be given nothing. He had to act circumspectly for a premier pursuing a better deal for his colony was a difficult beast to tackle, as Barton had found in his encounters with Reid.[33]

Forrest's pitch to the east was that nothing in his requests affected the principles of the constitution; the tariff concessions would last only five years, a blink in the life of a nation; and the whole labour of federation would be spoiled if Western Australia were omitted. There was a lot of sympathy for him. The difficulty he faced was that federalists were reluctant to reopen discussion on the Bill no matter what the merits of the case. In part they feared the anti-federalists' power to make mischief, but more importantly they thought no one had the power to tamper with a Bill that had been accepted by the people of five colonies. Carrying the authority of the sovereign people, the Bill had become a sacred text. And certainly there was not to be another round of referendums to please Sir John Forrest.

Among the governments, Queensland's was the most supportive, which is to say that Griffith was. From September 1899 he was acting Governor, able to impress his own views on ministers inexperienced in federal affairs and to broadcast them through official channels. In the last phase of the federal movement, he became a significant player again. He refused to accept the Bill as sacred.[34] He himself could see a number of flaws in it, which he hoped would be corrected by the imperial parliament before it was ratified. Griffith was upset at what the 1897–98 draftsmen had done to some of his work, and now had his revenge.

The government most firmly opposed to Forrest was South Australia's. Kingston was immovable, having both a principled and a self-interested motive. Of all the premiers he was most committed to an open, democratic process of constitution-making and most opposed to any bypassing of it. His colony also relied most heavily on trade with the west and stood to lose most if Western Australia could persist in taxing goods from other colonies. At the Convention the South Australian delegates had voted in a block against the tariff concession to Western Australia. They were determined to give it no more. Kingston offered advice and encouragement to the Separationists on the goldfields and was able to tell them that Forrest, along with the other premiers at their Melbourne meeting, had promised to put the revised Bill to the people.[35] Josiah Symon took on Griffith in the press for not showing proper respect for the Constitution Bill as adopted by the people.[36]

To the great puzzlement of Forrest, Barton and Deakin refused to help him. He challenged Barton directly: 'Are you the great federationist going to spoil your own work?'[37] Their position is at first surprising. Barton had given the movement the slogan 'A nation for a continent'. Both men had always scotched plans for ignoring the small colonies and starting federation with the large. Like the other federalists, they did not want to reopen discussion on the Bill but, more than that, they felt Forrest had broken faith with the federal movement. They had faced difficulties and taken risks; they had urged a Yes vote for a constitution that was not their ideal. Why should Forrest complain because the going was hard? Deakin was quite bitter at Forrest and the West Australians for voting solidly the small-state line at the Convention, which had made the Bill much harder to sell in the large colonies, and then coming back and asking for more.[38] So the federal leaders were impervious when Forrest listed all the difficulties he faced: the press, his own following, the Legislative Council. They thought he should put his authority on the line and go for the Bill. Forrest did not want to attempt that because he believed the Bill's critics were correct. He was using them to bargain for better terms.

Barton and Deakin would not have taken such a hard line had they not believed there was a majority for the Bill among the people of Western Australia.[39] Forrest believed that too. He was afraid not of the Bill's failure at the polls but of its success. The newcomers who had rescued his colony from obscurity cared nothing for it and were waiting to vote Yes to spite him. To drive Forrest to put the Bill to the people, Deakin worked on two fronts. He offered funds and advice to James and stiffened up the premiers to ensure Forrest received nothing.[40]

Forrest was still campaigning when Joseph Chamberlain, the Secretary of State for Colonies, requested a delegation to go to London to discuss the Bill before it was put to the imperial parliament. Federalists were alarmed: Britain was not treating the adoption of their Bill as a formality. The premiers met to choose the delegation and gave them instructions to work for the adoption of the Bill without amendment. Forrest would now find it even harder to have the Bill altered for Western Australia's benefit. His last hope was that Chamberlain would alter the Bill for him, although he knew he would not act without referring the matter back to Australia.

There were five men in the delegation, one from each of the federating colonies: Barton, Deakin, Kingston, Dickson and, for Tasmania, former Premier Sir Philip Fysh, who was already in London as its Agent-General. Deakin travelled first on his own. When the mail steamer carrying Barton, Kingston, and Dickson called at Albany, Forrest was there to meet them. He had made the long train journey down from Perth to put his case yet again. It was a distressing experience. A friend of Forrest had made his house available for the meeting, and there, in the friend's presence, Barton

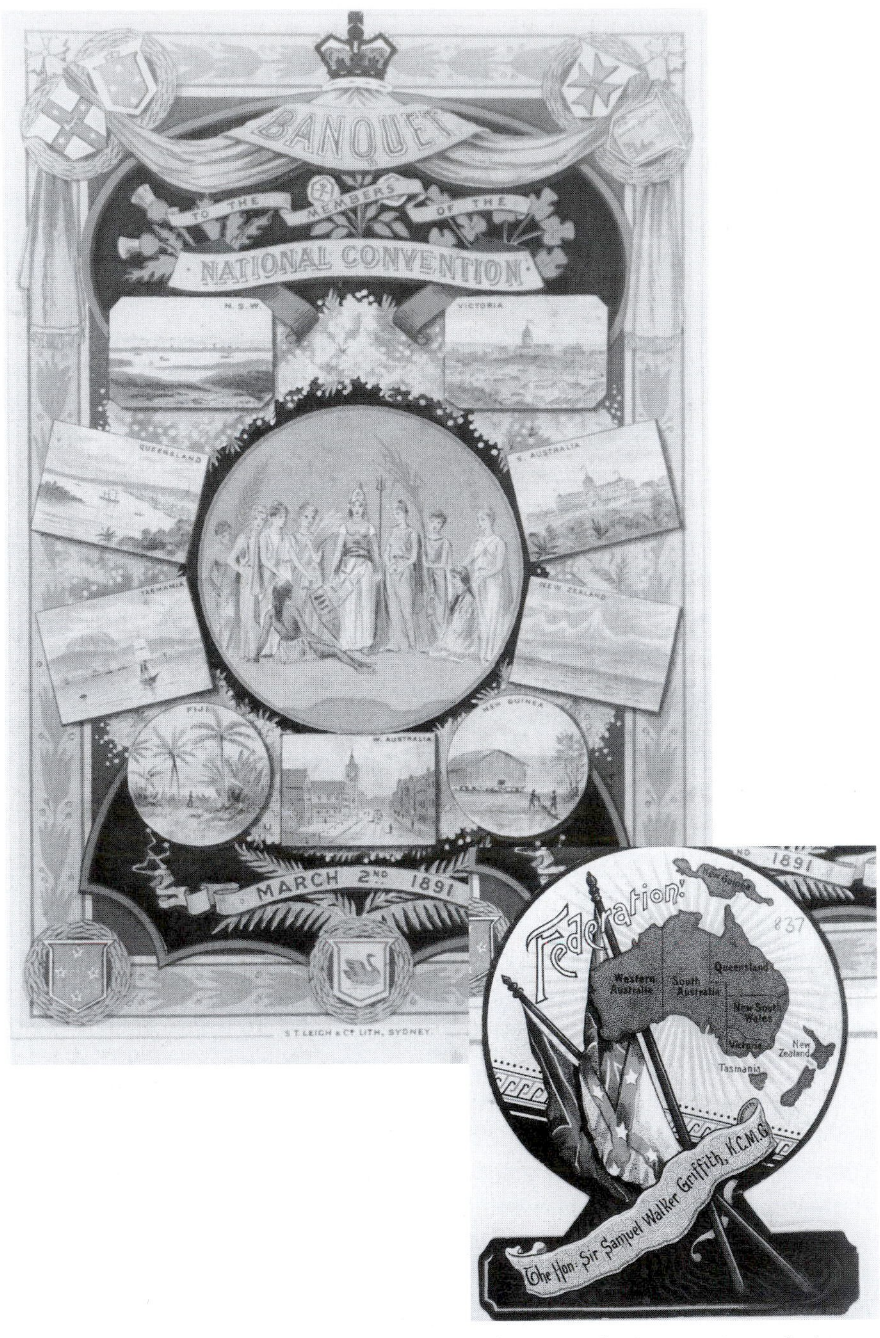

The menu (left) at the 1891 Convention banquet depicts an Australasian union with New Guinea, Fiji, and New Zealand included. On the place-markers (right) New Zealand is brought close to Australia.

told Forrest that if he were an honest politician he would have put the Bill to the people. And after this rudeness, Barton called him 'my dear old friend' and 'dear old chap'![41]

Representatives of the Separation League had also come to Albany to see the delegation. To prevent their meeting, Forrest went out in the pilot launch to collect the delegates and kept them under his wing all day.[42] But after the delegates had returned to the boat in the evening, they met the Separationists, with whose views on Forrest and federation Barton and Kingston were in full accord. The Separationists already had an agent acting for them in England. Forrest was also sending a delegate to argue against them and the delegates of the uniting colonies who would be insisting the Bill could not be altered. Whether the Australian union at its foundation would embrace the continent was to be settled in London.

After a long period in which it had taken very little interest in federation, the New Zealand government also wanted to take part in these deliberations. If New Zealand joined the Commonwealth, the continental trope would have to be dropped. There was no immediate chance of that, but its government did want to preserve the right to join at any time as an original state.

New Zealand had participated in the first movement to federation at the Sydney Convention in 1883 when the preoccupation was to resist the advance of Germany and France in the Pacific. Since these powers threatened the British people and possessions of the south seas, Australia's five colonies, Tasmania, New Zealand, and Fiji deliberated on how to check them. New Zealand sent delegates to the Convention of 1891 but not to that of 1897–98. The movement still officially kept the name 'Australasian' so that New Zealand was not forgotten, although strictly the term was also necessary to embrace Tasmania.

Why New Zealand lost interest in federation has been hotly debated, more by New Zealanders than by Australians.[43] Sir John Hall, a New Zealand delegate to the 1890 Melbourne Conference, said the 1,200 miles of the Tasman Sea were 1,200 reasons why New Zealand should not join. As was pointed out at the time, this was a poor argument since the sea *linked* all seven colonies of Australasia, carrying most of the intercolonial trade in goods and people. Steam ships ran faster and more regularly between Sydney and Auckland than between Sydney and Perth.

In the last two decades of the nineteenth century eastern Australia and New Zealand were economically and socially integrated.[44] Large numbers of people seeking work moved both ways across the Tasman. Banks and insurance companies operated on both sides of it. The organisations of churches, trade unions, and professional men spanned it. Australian newspapers circulated widely in New Zealand: the *Australasian* from

Melbourne in the south island, the *Sydney Mail* in the north island, and the *Bulletin* in both. This network of connections was much denser across the Tasman than the Nullarbor.

One New Zealand historian, taking his cue from the economic interpretation of federation in Australia, argued that New Zealand was less interested in federation because it traded less with the Australian colonies than they did among themselves. Unfortunately he misinterpreted the Australian figures.[45] New Zealand's trade with Australia was significant, quite significant enough to make its Prime Minister, Richard Seddon, interested in a reciprocal trade treaty before, after, and at the time of federation.[46] It was the fear of losing access to the Australian market that led to the last-minute revival of the federal cause in New Zealand in 1899.[47]

Prime Minister Seddon appointed a royal commission on federation. It found that there was a minor economic advantage in federation but that it was outweighed by all the disadvantages, the chief of which was the loss of independence.[48] The commissioners considered all the well-known arguments for federation. Some did not apply with the same force to New Zealand simply because it was not part of the continent (a common army, for example), but in these hands all arguments became lame because they were not knitted together and fired by a sense that union was destiny. The notion that a higher and wider life would be provided by union, a regular part of the Australian case for federation, frankly puzzled Seddon's commissioners. Although there are only hints of this attitude in the royal commission, many New Zealanders thought Australians an inferior people stained by convict origins with whom association would be damaging.[49]

The fundamental reason why there was so little interest in federation was that New Zealanders did not think of themselves as Australians.[50] It is revealing to see what happens to the federal equation when that element is omitted from it. If federation was merely a business deal, if it was a natural evolution of deepening relations of neighbouring communities, if it was an association of British people, then New Zealand should have been part of it or showed a lot more interest in it.

It was partly by contemplating Australian union that New Zealanders realised they had a separate destiny. Prime Minister Seddon responded to the imminent arrival of the Commonwealth by renewing the attempt to acquire Samoa, Fiji, and Tonga and make his country the head of an island dominion in the Pacific. But he wanted to keep his options open. He instructed his Agent-General in London to be at the Colonial Office when the Australian constitution was finally settled.

12
Empire

Whatever is good for Australia is good for the whole British Empire.
Joseph Chamberlain, House of Commons, 14 May 1900

The Colonial Office in London had long been in favour of Australian federation. It would immediately make life easier in the Colonial Office to have one government to deal with rather than six, and Australian federation was a necessary step towards the closer integration of the British Empire. The problem for the Colonial Office was that the Australians seemed bent on planning a nation that would move away from the empire rather than towards it. This was the conclusion the Colonial Office drew when it examined the draft constitution drawn up in Adelaide. That document claimed power for the nation over external relations, shipping, and defence, with no acknowledgment of British paramountcy in these spheres, and severely limited the right of appeal from Australian courts to the Privy Council in London.

The civil servants who regretfully noted these tendencies to independence were not at all optimistic about reversing them. The Australians were known to be touchy and cantankerous. If the Colonial Office made objections there would be a fight that the Office would eventually lose, leaving a legacy of bitterness. Better not to make the attempt.

Avoiding a fight was not the style of their political boss, Joseph Chamberlain. He was the most daring and resourceful minister ever to have charge of the Colonial Office, which he transformed from a sideshow into the central drama of the British Government. He told the British people that their survival as a great power depended on what happened in his department. Britain was being overtaken by Germany and the United States; unless Britain's colonial possessions were strengthened, reordered, and integrated, Britain was done. Since Australian federation was connected to that momentous issue, Chamberlain was perfectly ready to take on the Australians. What constitution they developed for the governing of Australia was their business; how a new Australian government related to the empire was his.

It is often said that Chamberlain's vigour as a minister was owing to his having been a businessman, an unusual background then for a British statesman.[1] But he was also highly unusual among the Birmingham manufacturers of wood screws. Coming to his uncle's small business when he was 18, he made it into a huge undertaking by buying up all the small screw-making businesses in Birmingham and aggressively marketing Chamberlain-Nettlefold screws, produced by the latest machinery. At the Colonial Office he became a takeover merchant and super salesman for the empire, so his business career had been a good training, but he had been bright and creative before he reached Birmingham. Perhaps he acquired his steeliness there.

He entered politics in Birmingham as an advanced Liberal, embarrassing his party by his radical proposals but commanding its attention. He moved rapidly from being a reforming mayor of Birmingham into Gladstone's cabinet. In 1886 he left the government and the party because he opposed Gladstone's new policy of Home Rule for Ireland. He became leader of the breakaway group of Liberal Unionists, which moved into cooperation with the Conservatives. As a Liberal Unionist he became Colonial Secretary in 1895 in a coalition government led by the Conservative, Lord Salisbury.

It was easy for Australians to admire the man who was determined to frustrate them. He was a self-made man, dynamic and modern. He was an enthusiast for the British Empire, which they much preferred to the indifference shown by many Liberals, and he was a social progressive, unlike most Conservatives. Serving under a Conservative prime minister, Chamberlain had not abandoned his plans for social reform. He was the antithesis of the stuffy, Tory aristocrat.

One of Chamberlain's greatest admirers was Rudyard Kipling, the literary star of the age. The poet and the politician were both working for a new form of empire. Kipling was a poet of the empire, but of the empire as opposed to England. He was scathing about the indifference and contempt of many people in England towards the colonies. 'And what should they know of England who only England know?'[2] It was a long time before Kipling, who was born in India, could live contentedly in England. His first stories and poems were about India, but after visiting Canada, New Zealand, Australia, and South Africa, he widened his scope to include the lands of British settlement overseas.[3]

No one has written with more poignancy of the desire of these settlers to be noticed and accepted by the metropolis. These lines are spoken by the native-born in 'The Song of the Sons':

Count, are we feeble or few?
Hear, is our speech so rude?
Look, are we poor in the land?
Judge, are we men of the Blood?

He brought the colonies to the notice of England by writing poems that were panoramas of their different forms of life. For those who were completely ignorant, his first task was to identify and name. Here is the Australian section of 'The Flowers', the fruit of his visit to Lorne, Melbourne's holiday place in the Otways on the south-west coast of Victoria:[4]

Buy my hot-wood clematis,
Buy a frond o' fern
Gathered where the Erskine leaps
Down the road to Lorne—
Buy my Christmas creeper
And I'll say where you were born! ...
Through the great South Otway gums
  sings the great South Main—
Take the flower and turn the hour,
  and kiss your love again!

He was in Australia only briefly, but he was a good listener and picked up the local talk and experience. So the words 'Never-never country' appeared in 'The Explorer' and 'thin, tin, crackling roofs' in 'The Native Born'.

In 'The Houses: A Song of the Dominions' Kipling conveyed in his simple ballad form the same message as Chamberlain: the parts of the empire must come together for mutual protection:

For my house and thy house no help shall we find
Save thy house and my house—kin cleaving to kind;
If my house be taken, thine tumbleth anon.
If thy house be forfeit, mine followeth soon.

Chamberlain's first great success was the staging of the Queen's jubilee celebrations in 1897 as a pageant of empire. He invited all the colonial premiers. The Adelaide session of the Convention had to be curtailed to enable them to attend. They were honoured and feted; all who would receive knighthoods were given them, and they were all made Privy Councillors, which carried the title 'Right Honourable'. Colonial troops also came from every quarter of the empire to be part of the great procession that was to escort the Queen to give thanks at St Paul's. The colonial troops were objects of great fascination: crowds gathered around them in the streets, tram conductors allowed them to ride free, military experts admired their splendid physique and horsemanship.[5]

Chamberlain (seated) with the colonial premiers at the jubilee: Reid to his left with Forrest behind him; Turner and Kingston are directly behind Chamberlain; Braddon is on Turner's right; Nelson on Kingston's.

As the plans for the great anniversary were unfolded, Australians, reading their newspapers on the other side of the globe, witnessed their premiers and troops being moved closer to the centre of the festivities.[6] The colonial troops were to escort the premiers in the procession. Then 'by special desire of the Queen' (for which read Chamberlain), they were to be drawn up when they reached St Paul's so that they could all see the Queen. Then it was announced that some of the Australian troops were to form a special detachment as the Queen's bodyguard and to ride immediately before her carriage. The premiers on arriving at St Paul's were not to remain in their carriages; they were to join the great ministers of state in formally receiving the Queen on the steps of the cathedral.

All this was very satisfying. And on the day itself the newspapers could produce even more consoling news: the cheers for the colonial troops were second only to those for the Queen; there were cries of 'Coo-ee' and 'Good old Australia' from the crowds; the premiers were called to by name and cheered separately with the wildest enthusiasm. Australia was known in the streets of London.

All this information reached the Australian newspapers through the cable service. Chamberlain knew the importance of instant information in binding the empire. Before the Queen left for St Paul's, he arranged for her to push a button in Buckingham Palace and send a message of greeting to all the empire: 'FROM MY HEART I THANK MY BELOVED PEOPLE. MAY GOD BLESS THEM.'[7] Kipling wrote a poem, 'The Deep Sea Cables', which concluded with a Chamberlain moral: 'Hush! Men talk today o'er the waste of ultimate slime,/And a new Word runs between: whispering, "Let us be one!" '

Although Chamberlain had made a great fuss of the premiers, they gave him very little when they gathered in formal conference as the festivities continued. They turned down imperial federation and an imperial council; they did agree to take home and consider proposals to give some preference to British trade. Nearly all the premiers were content with relationships as they were. Only Braddon of Tasmania and Seddon of New Zealand were willing to consider more formal ties. All the conference agreed to was that there should be regular conferences. Chamberlain seized on this as a breakthrough, the first step to a unified empire, an ideal that he would continue to pursue.

An imperial council had been what Parkes had requested of Salisbury eight years before. He had wanted it as a way of halting separatist tendencies in the colonies on the assumption that if ties were not strengthened they would weaken and break. There was no occasion now for an Australian premier to entertain these fears. Enthusiasm for the empire had grown. The independent nationalists had disappeared, and republicanism survived only on the fringes of political life. The *Bulletin,* its most powerful advocate, had abandoned the cause in 1891 and in 1894 accepted federation under the Crown.

Of all the premiers, Chamberlain was most impressed by Reid. He was as firm in rejecting new constitutional arrangements as the rest, but he took a wider view. He could see the problem of the empire from Britain's perspective: the colonies benefited enormously from the Royal Navy and open access to the British market, and they gave very little in return. Although he liked none of Chamberlain's present plans, Reid said he would keep an open mind. Chamberlain saw him as the only premier ready to run risks for imperial unity. To Reid, therefore, he passed a list of the Colonial Office's objections to the Commonwealth Bill in the hope that he would quietly be able to effect some changes.[8]

Reid took his commission seriously. Without revealing their source, he had a number of the Colonial Office amendments made without any fuss. Once there was almost a slip-up. When he was urging the curtailment of the powers over shipping, he ran into objections. He insisted that if the change was not made the Bill would run into trouble in London. 'Have you been talking with Joe?' called one delegate. No, said Reid, lying; he had merely collected all the relevant information on his recent trip to London. On this matter Reid had to settle for less than the Colonial Office wanted.[9]

Reid passed the Colonial Office amendments to Barton, who made the members of the drafting committee privy to them. Still the secret did not get out. In their rewording of the draft, the committee took account of the Colonial Office suggestions, and many minor changes were made. Many were also rejected as fussy and misguided. Barton complained that the English law experts did not know the difference between a constitution and ordinary legislation, which is all they worked on.

Since the delegates accepted that Australia was to be a nation within the empire, much of what the Colonial Office wanted was uncontroversial. Some of the wording claimed more than they wanted to insist on, which was the legacy of Griffith's bold drafting. Neither Reid nor Barton was abandoning earlier views in putting these amendments. When they disagreed with the amendments they simply ignored them. On Privy Council appeals, which is what the Colonial Office cared most about, neither was any use to the Office. They both supported limiting appeals.

The Convention had to revisit the appeal question because it was bombarded by petitions in favour of retaining appeals. Petitions came from banks, insurance companies, accountants, and chambers of commerce and manufactures. This was the most decisive intervention of businessmen in the whole federal process. (Had they been in charge of the process—as is often alleged—they would not have been reduced to petitioning.) Their chief claim was that British investors would lose confidence in Australia (always a good card to play) unless they had the ultimate protection of appeal to a British court. Their own chief worry was probably that this new democratic Commonwealth might be anti-business. It would be as well to have the fail-safe of appeal to a British court if social experimentation in

Australia got out of hand. The emotional appeal of their case came from the accusation that the Convention was breaking an imperial link and denying British subjects their hallowed right of appeal to the monarch against injustice.

In the Convention the stoutest defender of limitations on appeals was Josiah Symon, who was chairman of the judicial committee. He was leader of the bar in Adelaide, highly ambitious, and frustrated by the longevity of the judges on the South Australian bench. He hoped under the Commonwealth to be a judge of the High Court, which he wanted to be a court of final appeal and not a mere conduit to London.[10]

Symon could very readily demonstrate the hollowness of the emotional case for Privy Council appeals.[11] All subjects did not have a right to carry their lawsuits to the Queen. Cases involving more than £500 could be appealed to the Privy Council, which was, true enough, the Queen's court—as were all the other courts and as the High Court would be. And far from being hallowed, the Privy Council had acquired the supervision of colonial law only in 1833. But Symon could make little headway in the wake of the jubilee. The appeal of Queen and empire was very strong; the Privy Council had come to symbolise them no matter what Symon said. The nationalist claims that Australia should be self-sufficient in its legal affairs and that the ability of Australian judges was being impugned by the insistence on appeals to the Privy Council aroused little passion except from the lawyers, and among them only the elite.

During the final sittings in Melbourne, the Convention changed its mind and allowed all private cases to go on appeal to the Privy Council. But the nationalist lawyers were determined to save something of their declaration of independence. They now insisted that the interpretation of the constitution itself remain in Australian hands, unless the interests of some other part of the empire were involved. There were good grounds for the claim: since Australians had drawn up the constitution, they were best placed to interpret it, and certainly better equipped than the British, who had little experience of federalism. The oddity is that in the Adelaide draft constitutional cases were the ones that could go to the Privy Council, whereas the private ones were to remain in Australia. The switch is explained partly by the delegates' growing pride in their handiwork, but more by their determination, after yielding on the private cases, to have something that the British could not touch. Of course private companies and individuals could be parties to constitutional cases, so the demand that all cases must be able to go to the Privy Council would not go away.

The final sitting of the Convention coincided with the fourth and fifth test matches in the Ashes series. England had won the first test and

Which is the burning question? 1. The interest in Federation. 2. The interest in Cricket.

Melbourne *Punch* gauges the interest in federation and cricket. (7 February 1895)

Australia the next two. Here the contest between England and Australia was played out very differently. The sports-mad Australians wanted to see England beaten. There was huge interest in the cricket, much greater than in the doings of the Convention. The newspapers chided Australians over their sense of priorities, but they reflected and encouraged it by printing more on the cricket than on the constitution.

There were cricket fans among the Convention delegates. Parliament House, where the Convention met, and the Melbourne Cricket Ground, where the fourth test was being played, were only a mile apart. If the afternoon debates finished at five o'clock, members could go across to the oval to see the final hour of play. A few members went when debates were in progress.

The cricket and the debates were conducted in searing heat. Smoke from bushfires penetrated Parliament House and lay over the cricket ground. The Englishmen complained that it interfered with their batting, one of them declaring that it was an odd country that would set itself alight to win a cricket match.

At first it looked as if England would win. Australia, having won the toss, batted and collapsed to be only 58 runs for six wickets. Then Clem Hill, the South Australian left-hander, still only 20, saved his country from humiliation by remaining at the crease for the rest of the day and scoring a magnificent 182. His innings still stands in the record book: highest score for a player younger than 21, the biggest partnership for the seventh wicket. This great day was a Saturday so the Convention delegates could be present. Australia won the match and the fifth test in Sydney three weeks later. The English captain Stoddart complained about Australian barracking and was declared a poor loser.[12]

This four-one victory over England marked the beginning of Australian supremacy in the game. It had been a long struggle for the colonies to reach this point. At first Australian sides had fielded twenty-two or fifteen men against the English eleven. When an Australian eleven beat an English eleven, Australians could be more confident of their future: the convicts and the heat had not sapped their strength; they were the equal of the old stock. And then they became better than the English. What joy it was to trounce the English since it was their game and it was they who regarded the colonials as inferiors. It was in this arena that Australians most clearly showed their defiance of the mother country. If Australian cricketers were better than the English, who cared whether Australian judges were up to the mark?[13]

Cricket was more exciting than constitution-making, but war was more exciting than both.[14] The last phase of the federation movement was overshadowed by news of the growing tension in South Africa and then of the Boer War itself, which began in October 1899. Chamberlain was the architect of the war, which he regarded not as a diversion from his project of uniting the empire but as a new way to its realisation.

Chamberlain had followed a perilous course in bringing the empire to war. He knew his prime minister did not want war; he feared that the British people would not support a war. He told them both he was hoping for a peaceful solution, but meanwhile he kept increasing the pressure on the Boer republics, determined one way or another to make them part of a British South Africa. The peaceful way was for the Transvaal to agree to grant political and legal rights to the new settlers, the uitlanders, who were working the gold mines on the Rand. Most of them were British, and they greatly outnumbered the Boer farmers. The Boers were naturally reluctant to pass control of their state to foreigners, but if they resisted too much, Chamberlain would have grounds for war.

To help stiffen the resolve of the British parliament and people, Chamberlain summoned support from the empire. In July 1899 he asked the governments of Canada, New South Wales, and Victoria to make a 'spontaneous' offer of troops to serve in South Africa if war should come.[15] They all refused. Reid and Turner were both concerned at the expense. Reid thought the British did not need help to deal with two tiny republics and, being reliant on the support of the Labor Party, he was reluctant to commit his colony to an imperial adventure. The memory of the Sudan fiasco in 1885 was still fresh. The troops themselves, regulars and militia, were keen to be involved. Both premiers reported that they could serve if Britain called for volunteers.

Chamberlain was disappointed: he wanted spontaneous offers from governments. He did receive such an offer from Dickson in Queensland, who had not officially been asked. Dickson did not have to worry about Labor's attitude since Labor was the opposition, and he might be more pleased than otherwise if it were to oppose his offer. He was also about to launch his campaign for a Yes vote in Queensland's belated federal referendum. To his mind the two causes were closely allied. Both were ways of strengthening the empire.

When Chamberlain next had to justify himself to parliament, he declared the issue was not whether uitlanders were to vote after a seven-year or a five-year residence (the current state of the negotiations), but whether Great Britain was to be the dominant power in South Africa. He said everyone understood this—except the Liberals on the opposition benches. The empire understood it. He then listed the colonies from which offers of troops had come: Victoria, New South Wales, Queensland, Canada, West Africa, and the Malay States.[16]

At this stage among the Australian colonies only the Queensland offer was a government offer, but it had the effect of putting pressure on the other governments to follow suit. By the time war broke out, all Australian governments had offered to send troops. The commandants of the Australian armies had planned for a united Australian contingent, but the War Office did not want this. Australian troops were needed for a political purpose. They were not to advance the war effort; indeed it was feared they might hinder it. They were to come in small detachments of 125 men and be distributed among British units.[17]

There was some misgiving about the sending of troops. Labor men, a few radical liberals, and the *Bulletin* were the outright opponents. Echoing the arguments of British opponents of the war, they denounced it as an act of bullying, unworthy of Britons, and prompted by the rapacious capitalists of the Rand. But there was much less opposition to the war in Australia than in Britain. Once Britain was committed, the earlier circumspect attitude of the governments disappeared. The predominant feeling was that the colonies had to support Britain, no matter what the rights and wrongs of the war. Dependent on the empire, they wanted it strong and, anxious for approval, they were delighted to serve. The contingents marched down to the ships through huge cheering crowds.

The Boer farmers took the offensive, and in one week in December 1899 they inflicted a series of humiliating defeats on British troops. On the continent Britain's enemies were jubilant. Now the empire was in real danger—it had to be rescued from defeat and ridicule. The British race had to stand together. Opposition to the war lessened and in Australia almost disappeared. Chamberlain was initially under attack for these disasters, but he emerged triumphant by unveiling to the House of Commons the new empire that the war had created:

> Our colonies, repelled in the past by indifference and apathy, have responded to the sympathy which has recently been shown to them. A sense of common interest, of common duty, an assurance of mutual support and pride in the great edifice in which they are all members, have combined to consolidate and establish the unity of the empire … you are the trustees, not merely of a Kingdom, but of a federation, which may not, indeed, be distinctly outlined, but which exists already in spirit.[18]

The War Office now called for more Australian troops, not for show but to help win the war. The Australian horsemen had shown they were a match for the mounted Boer farmers. Special contingents of bushmen were raised—squatter's sons, shearers, stockmen, boundary riders—who had not been trained as soldiers but who could ride, shoot, and look after themselves.

In the 1890s Paterson and Lawson had made the bushman the subject of their poems and stories, but although their works were enormously popular, bushmen did not immediately become widely accepted as a national symbol.[19] The trade union contribution to the federal procession on 1 January 1901 included mounted bushmen, but they rode behind a figure representing Australia who was, as tradition dictated, a young woman dressed in pure white. However, a bushman serving Queen and

Australia as a virginal young woman in white, on the trade union float, Sydney, 1 January 1901, surrounded by the male figures who would later stand for the nation: shearers behind and gold-digger on the float.

country was by that act a national figure. The Boer War did much to advance his status.

Paterson was commissioned by the *Sydney Morning Herald* as its war correspondent in South Africa. This was the first time his writings appeared in that highly respectable paper. All his poems had appeared in the raffish, radical *Bulletin*. His despatches brought good news of the Australian troops. They fought well, although they were not as well disciplined as the English, and were superb as scouts and scavengers. When the Bushmen contingents arrived English commanders competed to get hold of them.[20]

Kipling gave a similar verdict. In 'The Parting of the Columns' he wrote of the colonial troops generally: 'You had no special call to come, and so you doubled out,/And learned us how to camp and cook an' steal a horse and scout.' He described Australians through the eyes of an Indian in a short story, 'A Sahibs' War': 'They said on all occasions, "No fee-ah", which in our tongue means *Durro Mut* (Do not be afraid), so we called them the *Durro Muts*. Dark, tall men, most excellent horsemen, hot and angry, waging war *as* war, and drinking tea as a sandhill drinks water.'

Paterson and Kipling first met in South Africa.[21] Paterson was a great admirer of Kipling, whose elevation of the common man as the one who did the real work of the empire gave Paterson a warrant for writing of the ordinary bushman.[22] Paterson's work, however, is free of the social condescension that still marked Kipling's. One of Paterson's war poems has a distinctly Kiplingesque theme. It describes General French's column as it marched to the relief of Kimberley:[23]

His column was five thousand strong—all mounted men and guns;
There met beneath the world-wide flag, the world-wide Empire's sons;
They came to prove to all the earth that kinship conquers space,
And those who fight the British Isles must fight the British race!
From far New Zealand's flax and fern, from cold Canadian snows,
From Queensland plains, where hot as fire the summer sunshine glows;
And in the front the Lancers rode that New South Wales had sent:
With easy stride across the plain their long lean Walers went.
Unknown, untried, those squadrons were, but proudly out they drew
Beside the English regiments that fought at Waterloo
From every coast, from every clime, they met in proud array
To go with French to Kimberley to drive the Boers away.

This poem was published in the *Sydney Morning Herald*. The *Bulletin* would not have wanted it.

A new national figure: Boer War soldiers receive medals from the Duke of York, Melbourne, May 1901.

The war was still to be won when the Australian federal delegates arrived in London to shepherd their constitution through the imperial parliament. The town was abuzz with the feats of the colonial troops, which was one bright spot in the story of bungling and inefficiency by the British military. When the British Empire League held a banquet to welcome the delegates, its other purpose was to honour the colonial troops. No more illustrious company could have been gathered. The Prince of Wales proposed the loyal toast. Lord Salisbury, the Prime Minister, proposed the health of the colonial contingents. Chamberlain gave the toast to the delegates. The Prince was the most fulsome about the troops—magnificent, he called them, well disciplined and notable for their dash and courage. *The Times* next day said he might have gone further and held them up as a model for Britain to follow, but perhaps that was not politic in the presence of the commander-in-chief.

Some things in the speeches jarred on the Australian delegates. Salisbury said that he was surprised—pleasantly surprised—that Australians, not directly affected by the war, were so willing to serve in it. Barton in his speech of reply said the troops were only doing their duty. This surprise of the English was disturbing: it suggested that they did not regard Australia as being as much a part of the empire as England. But on the other hand Barton also dissented from the suggestion in Chamberlain's speech that an Imperial Council should be formed to bind the empire more firmly together.

These were merely differences in emphasis, and they did not disturb the pleasure the company took in contemplating British and colonial troops fighting together and the imminent formation of the Australian nation. There was no dissent from Chamberlain's view that no man could put a limit to Australia's greatness and that it would play 'a great and increasing part in the history of the British race'.[24]

In their negotiations over the constitution Chamberlain and the delegates were at loggerheads. Ignoring the advice of his department, Chamberlain insisted that further changes be made. The delegates insisted that the constitution, having been approved by the Australian people, could be altered only by them. Chamberlain would not accept that a referendum was a vote on every last detail, nor that the Australian people expected that the British parliament, responsible for the whole empire, should be a mere registry office for Australian decrees. Nevertheless he dropped all his objections except to the limitation on appeals to the Privy Council.

The Australians pointed out that they had allowed constitutional cases that affected other parts of the empire to go on appeal to the Privy Council. Their right to self-government required that they be allowed to settle all other constitutional cases within Australia. But these, said Chamberlain, could involve British interests in Australia. The interests of British investors, with which the delegates were constantly regaled, concerned Chamberlain only as much as the grievances of the uitlanders: as a means of advancing his plans for a new empire. The empire already had a unified system of law maintained through Privy Council appeals; he was not going to let the Australians dismantle that while he was working for a more integrated empire.[25]

To make the unified legal system more attractive, Chamberlain promised to create a new single court of appeal for the whole empire. At present only colonial appeals went to the Privy Council; British appeals went to the House of Lords. Judges from the colonies would be appointed to this new court, their salaries would be paid by Britain, and they would be made life peers. For the first time there would be an imperial institution staffed from and responsible for both Britain and the colonies.

This was a very attractive proposal to the two Australians most likely to be appointed to such a court: Samuel Way, Chief Justice of South Australia, and Samuel Griffith, Chief Justice of Queensland. They had both secretly told Chamberlain that he could safely ignore the dogma of the sacred Bill and amend it to retain Privy Council appeals. Way was already a member of the judicial committee of the Privy Council as a result of a very limited scheme to make that body more representative of the whole empire. Way had taken his seat, heard some cases, and then come home again since no salary was provided to support him in London.[26] A salary and a peerage would lure him back without a doubt. A new unified court of appeal, which would reward its judges in this way, also exactly fitted Griffith's notion of the empire and his own aspirations.[27] He was criticised for changing his views on appeals, but in 1891 that very judicious man had opposed appeals going to the Privy Council *as it was presently constituted*.[28]

Since the delegates refused to negotiate, Chamberlain appealed to their principals, the premiers. By cable he put to them the case for retaining appeals and the plans for the new court. He also instructed the Australian governors to report the views of the chief justices and press on his proposals so that he could undermine the delegates' claim that they represented a people committed to every word of the constitution. Already in London he had some success. Dickson, the Queensland delegate, had switched sides and given his support to Chamberlain, telling him that there had never been in the colonies 'a more enthusiastic desire to be bound up in the unity of the great British Empire'.[29] When next the delegates met, Kingston refused to do business until Dickson left the room.[30]

Chamberlain also had to deal with the requests from Western Australia and New Zealand that the constitution be altered. Parker, the Western Australia delegate, wanted his colony to be able to keep its tariff on interstate goods for five years without having to reduce it year by year. Forrest had abandoned all his other demands. The railway issue had been fixed by South Australia's indication that it would give its assent to the Commonwealth building a line to the west. William Pember Reeves, the Agent-General for New Zealand, requested that his colony be allowed to use the High Court, cooperate in defence and, most importantly, retain the right, for (say) seven years, to enter as an original state.

Chamberlain invited them to put their case before the delegates of the federating colonies. The delegates were totally opposed on the usual grounds that the constitution could not now be altered and that the two colonies had ample opportunity to put their case in Australia. Kingston was positively belligerent, cross-examining Parker and Reeves as if they were hostile witnesses. He was pushing Parker to concede that the people of Western Australia would vote Yes to the present Bill if given a chance. That was useful information for Chamberlain, who was very keen to have the great work of federation completed by the inclusion of Western Australia. His first response, however, was to urge the delegates to accept Forrest's request. He was also very sympathetic to the New Zealand case, especially since New Zealand had been so willing to send troops to his war.

But the delegates refused to bend, so Chamberlain remitted these questions too to the premiers, making clear, however, that since they were exclusively the colonies' business, he would not press his own views.[31]

The premiers of the five federating colonies met in Melbourne in late April 1900. They stayed together for three days while they and the delegates in London argued back and forth by cable over their response. Their people meanwhile were preoccupied with the war and the fate of Ladysmith and Mafeking, still besieged by the enemy. The war, in uniting the empire, was the delegates' enemy. As Deakin conceded, the limitation on appeals had never been popular; during the war it seemed indecent and disloyal to break an imperial tie.[32] As the governors were reporting to Chamberlain, nearly all the newspapers were in favour of accepting his position on appeals. There was no movement to support the delegates. Only the Natives Association raised a faint voice in favour of the constitution as it stood.[33]

The premiers were able to give a clear decision on the request of Western Australia and New Zealand. Two colonies, Queensland and Tasmania, favoured acceptance; the other three were against. On the Privy Council, Lyne of New South Wales reported to Barton that they were equally divided. Dividing five equally is awkward arithmetic, which indicates probably that Lyne himself had doubts about limiting appeals; Queensland and Tasmania were definitely for Chamberlain. The premiers composed a very mixed message. They urged Chamberlain to accept the declared wish of the people but conceded the right of the imperial parliament to amend the Bill. The new court would 'doubtless' be attractive to the Australian people. If the choice were between amendment in Britain and delay, delay was worse.

This reply was sent to Barton in draft form. He asked the premiers to modify it. Change 'doubtless' to 'perhaps', and drop 'delay worse than amendment'. They could not agree to this request. The message went to Chamberlain in the original form. To limit the damage, Barton then asked for a clarifying statement. He pleaded with them—'we should not be deserted'. They were.[34]

Chamberlain was true to his word about the two claimant colonies. Having been rebuffed by the premiers, he immediately switched tack on Western Australia and urged Forrest to put the Bill to the people. If Forrest did so and it was accepted, Chamberlain would arrange for Western Australia still to be treated as an original state. Forrest did not resent this request; he was eager to cooperate with imperial authority and grateful to Chamberlain for trying his best for him.[35]

It is sometimes said that Chamberlain threatened Forrest that he would grant separation to the goldfields if he did not comply. This does not appear to be true.[36] Chamberlain had refused to see the goldfields representatives.

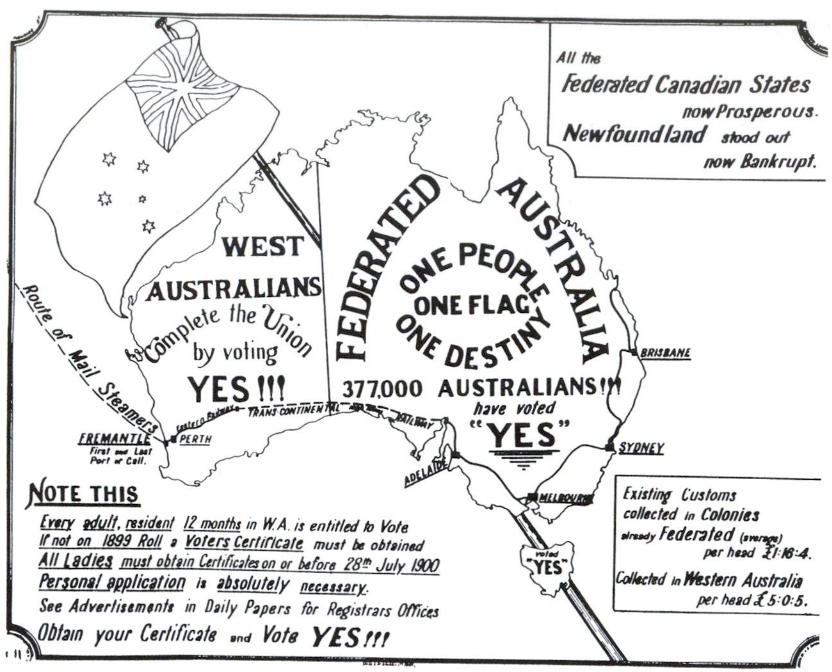

The referendum in Western Australia: the appeal not to be left behind.

Still he was eager to receive their petition, and when the Agent-General of Western Australia tackled him about his attitude to separation, he refused to comment.[37] Chamberlain was the master of the veiled threat, and maybe these words in his message to Forrest, through the Governor, were a threat to any who needed it: 'Your Ministers will also, of course, take into consideration effect of agitation of the Federalist party, especially on goldfields, if Western Australia does not enter as an original State.'[38]

Having done all he could for his colony, Forrest put his immense prestige behind the case for union. He persuaded the parliament to hold a referendum on the Bill. It knew that no better terms could be had and that the West would lose original-state status if it refused. The result of the voting was as the hard-headed federalists had predicted: a comfortable win for Yes (69 per cent). The goldfields were almost unanimous, but even without them federation would have been carried. Perth voted Yes. The old farming areas were very strongly No, even more strongly than the farming areas near Brisbane. These were Forrest's constituency, and, like Reid, he was disowned by part of his own following for taking the colony into the union.[39]

Meanwhile in London the Privy Council issue was being settled. Rebuffed in Australia, the delegates set out to win over English opinion.

They were the celebrities of the London season, and at whatever dinner or banquet they attended they put the case for Australia controlling its own constitution. Deakin had good connections with the Liberal Opposition, which promised its support, and with the great Liberal newspaper, the *Manchester Guardian*, which backed the delegates.[40] Newspaper opinion was more evenly divided in Britain than in Australia.[41]

In *The Times* Kingston published scathing attacks on the Australian chief justices, who had all come out in support of Chamberlain.[42] He was particularly vicious against Way and Griffith, accusing them of betraying their country in the hope of fat salaries and peerages on the new appeal court. Deakin had urged him in vain not to make these personal attacks. In Australia they were maintained with equal venom by Symon, who joined his erstwhile enemy Kingston in this vendetta. There was an almost revolutionary recklessness about Symon's behaviour: the leader of the bar libelling the bench; the conservative cooperating with the arch radical and proclaiming the sovereignty of the people to protect the Bill. He would do anything, it seemed, to ensure that the new high court was not overseen from London. It is the clearest example of how a colonial professional can become a fervent nationalist. Professional pride and status worked in the opposite direction in the case of Way, Griffith, and the other judges. They were desperate to keep appeals to London open to avoid a High Court composed of Symon, Kingston, and Barton being the final arbiter of their judgments.[43]

Chamberlain, boosted by Australian support, now brought negotiations to a close. He bluntly told the delegates he would make his amendments and that further discussion was useless. Barton was so flabbergasted he forgot to announce that the delegates would immediately go home, the course they had agreed to follow if their Bill were tampered with. Kingston spoke next, almost inarticulate with rage, and only after sitting down did he utter the walk-out threat.[44] Going home would not have been wise; the delegates would have been transferring to an arena in which they had less support rather than more.

Chamberlain introduced the Bill to the House of Commons without the clause limiting appeals. The Liberal leader, Henry Campbell-Bannerman, immediately called his omission 'an open rebuff to the Australian people'. It was this opposition that prompted Chamberlain to back down.[45] He could win a battle in the House, but perhaps he did not want a party dispute to sully the great achievement of Australian federation. If he was ready for battle, some of his cabinet colleagues might not have been.[46] That evening at a small private dinner he and the delegates began discussing a compromise. Since their clause had disappeared, there was no longer any point in the delegates' refusing to discuss change.

The compromise was that constitutional cases involving only Commonwealth and state governments would be settled finally in Australia; constitutional cases where private interests were involved could go on appeal to London. Further, the Australian parliament would be able to pass laws limiting appeals, but any such law would require the assent of the Queen. For Chamberlain the compromise meant that any case relating to the empire or its people could go to London; for the delegates it left them with some business that was exclusively Australian. Having achieved this much, Chamberlain postponed and then did not pursue the plan for the new appeal court, which had served its purpose of undermining the Australian attempt at judicial independence.

War and blood as the unifying force of the British Empire: a commemorative federation plate showing (at top) Hopetoun, the first Governor-General, and Parkes; the Duke and Duchess of York (left and right); Australian and imperial troops (centre); and a message from Chamberlain (below).

It took several days to settle the wording of the compromise. Deakin describes what happened when the delegates were left alone after the final meeting: 'they seized each other's hands and danced hand in hand in a ring around the centre of the room.' It was a rather childish victory dance. What were they celebrating? Not the victory of Australia over Britain. More the success of four Australians in getting something out of the mighty Chamberlain—and that was an Australian victory of sorts. The delegates went home to a heroes' welcome, in which those who had publicly opposed them on Privy Council appeals joined.[47]

Three weeks before he became Prime Minister Barton reflected on his English experiences when he lectured in Sydney on 'The Unity of Empire'.[48] His thinking was very close to that of Chamberlain, from whom he quoted extensively. He bore no grudge against Chamberlain; on the contrary he praised him for dealing so fairly with the colonies and the delegates.[49] With Chamberlain, he saw the federation of Australia as part of the larger project of empire unity. Unlike Chamberlain, he did not think unity required formal ties. The bonds were kinship, war, and the recognition of the principle of full self-government: what Barton had contended for in England. He confidently declared that equality of citizenship and respect within the empire had been established. The inferiority of colonial status had passed. It was more than that. He reached for a formulation that would completely allay colonial doubts: 'In the United Kingdom from the highest statesman to the lowest citizen there was for Australians in the Commonwealth but one great voice of welcome and one great heart of love.'

This had been Barton's first visit to England. Feted everywhere, he had no experience of the contempt and condescension met by Australian visitors, even of the highest standing, before and since. In London he corresponded with the editor of the *Academy*, who was running a competition to find a word to replace *colonist*, which Barton too was eager to bury. The winner was *Englander*.[50] *Colonist* and *Colonial*, with their implication of inferiority, would survive for a long time yet.

Barton framed his lecture with the first and last verses of Kipling's poem, 'The Sea-Wife':

> *There dwells a wife by the Northern gate,*
> *And a wealthy wife is she;*
> *She breeds a breed of roving men*
> *And casts them over the sea.*

After their roving, whether they have succeeded or failed, they come home again.

Home, they come home from all the ports,
The living and the dead;
The good wife's sons come home again
For her blessing on their head!

The trajectory of the nation was no longer a line of escape from the old world but a circle returning to it.

New returning to old was the theme of 'The Young Queen', the poem Kipling wrote to honour the inauguration of the Commonwealth. It was published first in the London *Times*, where he placed poems about grand themes and great occasions in the life of the empire, looking for no payment and acting the part of the unofficial poet laureate. When copies of *The Times* reached Perth the poem was telegraphed to the east and run prominently in the daily papers.[51] The work was completely different from the local federation poems, which were heavy with piety and abstract nouns.

Kipling's work was a simple ballad with two characters: the Old Queen and the Young Queen, Britannia and Australia. The Young Queen comes to the court of the Old Queen to be crowned. What was arresting in this conception was that Australia is not Britannia's daughter but her equal; she is a queen too. When she arrives in the Old Queen's court, the Old Queen at first refuses to crown her:

How can I crown thee further? I know whose standard flies
Where the clean surge takes the Leeuwin or the coral barriers rise.
Blood of our foes on thy bridle, and speech of our friends in thy mouth—
How can I crown thee further, O Queen of the Sovereign South?

The Old Queen relents because the Young Queen urgently requests to be crowned by her hands.

Kipling's second innovation was the creation of a new female image of Australia, no longer a virginal girl but a young warrior sexually attractive in a different way. This is the first verse:

Her hand was still on her sword-hilt, the spur was still on her heel,
She had not cast her harness of grey, war-dinted steel;
High on her red-splashed charger, beautiful, bold, and browned,
Bright-eyed out of the battle, the Young Queen rode to be crowned.

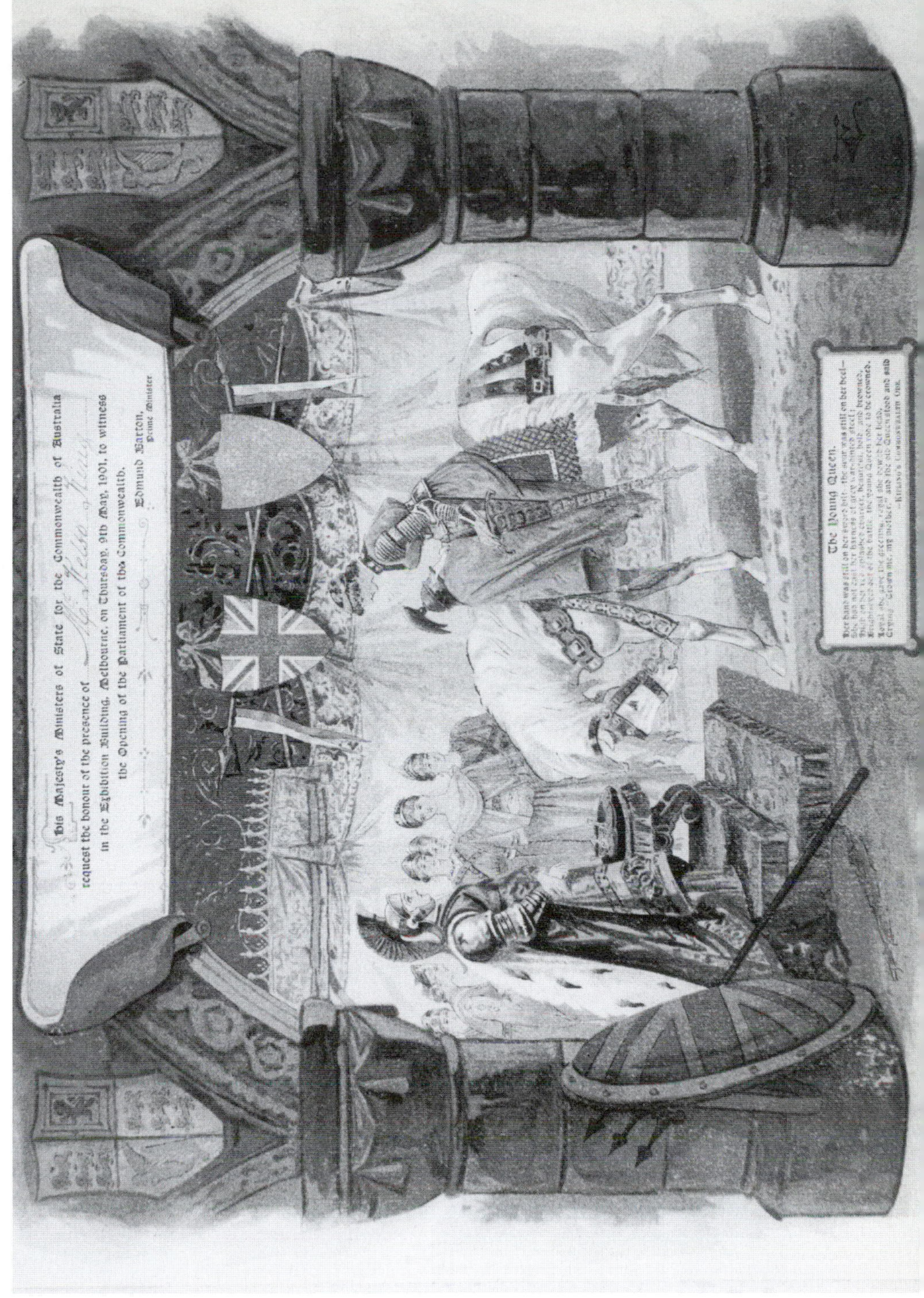

The invitation to the opening of the first Federal Parliament: the Old and Young Queens with the opening lines of Kipling's ode.

THE PRIME MINISTER CHRISTENS THE BABY.
Barton baptises the nation with blood: a *Bulletin* view (11 January 1902).

This became a highly acceptable image. Representations of the Young Queen decorated the Exchange in Sydney on 1 January 1901 and Parliament House in Melbourne in May. The image and the first verse of the poem were on the official invitations to the inauguration of the Federal Parliament.

The war became part of all the talk on the nation's birthday. The readiness with which blood and sacrifice were embraced reveals that patriots had not fully persuaded themselves of the sufficiency of the themes of peace and purity with which perforce they had previously to work. Those themes married well with the belief in progress and Australia as a new dispensation, but there was no escaping that other nations defined themselves by battles and heroic death. Australia could now be one of them, but the test that placed her in this rank had been performed not in defence of Australia but in the service of the British Empire. Uniting British people and strengthening the empire had always been part of the appeal of federation; by the time of its consummation, they were central to its rationale. The other meaning of federation—as a step towards full independence—had receded. The slogan Parkes had coined in 1891 had been open: 'One

People, One Destiny'. By 1901 it had been added to and closed: 'One Queen, One People, One Destiny'; or 'One People, One Destiny, One Flag'; or 'One People, One Empire, One Destiny'.[52]

The *Bulletin*, opposed to the war, produced a female image of Australia very different from Kipling's. These verses are from 'Red-Handed' by 'R':[53]

We had a dream—it seems but yesterday—
That dream is dashed—to direst darkness hurled,
For where our Commonwealth, a virgin lay,
A Wanton fronts the world.
Think what we lost—the forward March of Man,
The ranks of Progress positioned us a place,
Not last, not last, but foremost in the van
With sun illumined face.

The Young Queen had an easy victory over the Wanton. And as for the virgin, she went into a decline.[54]

The federalists had claimed that the new nation would end the inferiority of colonial status and raise Australia in the world's respect. It was to do so. But for Australians within the empire there were other, more immediate and more satisfying ways to these ends: to beat the English at cricket and to produce good soldiers for the empire's wars. Being a citizen of this new nation did not become a key element in Australian identity; those for whom citizenship was important were more likely to identify as British citizens of the empire.

All this was as it was meant to be, according to Brunton Stephens, the doyen of the poets of union. His 1877 poem began: 'She is not yet', and it asked: 'How long "not yet"?' In his 1901 poem, 'Fulfilment', the answer was plain: Australia had been made to wait for the fiery ordeal of war 'that tries the claim to nationhood'. And in 1877 he had misread her destiny, which was more than her own union:

O People of the onward will,
Unit of Union greater still
Than that today hath made you great,
Your true Fulfilment waiteth there,
Embraced within the larger fate
Of Empire ye are born to share.

13
Ways and Means

> Never before have a group of self-governing, practically independent communities, without external pressure or foreign complications of any kind, deliberately chosen of their own free will to put aside their provincial jealousies and come together as one people, from a simple intellectual and sentimental conviction of the folly of disunion and the advantages of nationhood.
>
> Quick and Garran, *The Annotated Constitution of the Australian Commonwealth*, p. 225

In December 1900, just a week before the Commonwealth was inaugurated, a huge volume dealing with its constitution arrived in the bookshops. Its authors were John Quick and Robert Garran, and its title *The Annotated Constitution of the Australian Commonwealth.* The book goes through the constitution section by section, word by word, explaining why these words were chosen, what they mean, and how courts might interpret them. No other Australian reference book has been so influential. It sits on the desk of every High Court judge and every constitutional lawyer. For a long time the High Court would not allow the debates at the conventions to be cited in argument over the constitution, but it always allowed references to Quick and Garran.

The authors were well qualified for their task. They were lawyers, of course, and had been closely involved with the federal movement. They met first at the Corowa conference in 1893 when Quick, aged 41, was delegate from the Bendigo Natives Association and Garran, aged 26, represented the newly formed Federation League in Sydney. They were together again at the Convention of 1897–98, which was called according to the plan formulated at Corowa. Quick was a delegate from Victoria and Garran the secretary of the drafting committee. Garran had gone to the convention as Reid's secretary, but Reid had generously passed him over to Barton.

Quick and Garran also wrote a history of the movement in which they had been activists. They placed it in their book before the exposition of the constitution. It too has been very influential and will not be eclipsed by this book or any other written to mark the hundredth anniversary of federation. It is a comprehensive chronicle and, like the rest of the book, a work of reference, sympathetic as you would expect to the federalists, but sober and measured—except in one place. After the authors have recorded the votes at the second referendum in 1899, they break into a hymn of praise to the Australian people who without threat or coercion freely decided to be a nation. They hail them as a people of 'high political capacity', an accolade that no one else has ever thought to give them.

The people are the heroes of the history. Like other federalists, Quick and Garran divided the federation movement into two. Before 1893 it was a politicians' movement, and it failed. After 1893 it became a people's movement, and it succeeded. The turning point came at Corowa, when Quick introduced his resolution for a popularly elected convention and the referendum.

Can we accept this explanation of success? Not really.[1]

The process of involving the people as electors of the Convention and judges of the constitution was certainly unique, but the politicians were involved in federation as much after 1893 as before. The new federal leagues in Sydney and Melbourne were brought together by the politicians Barton and Deakin. Premier Reid persuaded the other premiers to take up Quick's plan at their conference in Hobart in 1895. Since there was a remarkable stability in the colonial governments in the second half of the 1890s, the same group of premiers amended the constitution early in 1899 after the failure of the first referendum in New South Wales. They constituted in effect a committee of management for the whole federal project. They were all members of the 1897–98 Convention, which, although billed as a people's body, was composed almost exclusively of politicians.

Federation was a magnificent political achievement of the politicians, and in particular of Reid. He led the colony crucial to success, which was divided on the issue, and in a divided colony he led the free-trade party, which was more suspicious of union than the protectionists. He reassured his party by establishing free trade before he moved on federation; he then stayed in office long enough to carry federation against considerable opposition from his party.

If the politicians remained important after 1893, it is also true that the people were not excluded before 1893. If we are looking for a federal movement controlled by the politicians in which the people were kept at arm's length, we will not find it in Australia. Something like this did occur in Canada, the one British precedent for a colonial federation.

The delegates who deliberated on Canadian union in the mid 1860s were appointed by the parliaments of the various colonies. They did not draw up a constitution; they agreed on the principles of union, which were then carried to London to be put into legislative form. The delegates met in secret. The press was excluded. There were no briefings for the press, and no leaks to the press. Even after the conferences were over, details of what had been agreed were slow to emerge.

Only in one colony were the proposals put to the people at election. Those in charge of the process were desperate to avoid any such scrutiny of their work. They worked in haste so that everything would be sown up before the various parliaments had to be dissolved. The opponents of union demanded that the issue be put to the people, but they were easily rebuffed. To suggest that the people must be consulted was republican, the sort of demand that would be made in the United States, the enemy over the border.

The maritime colonies were very reluctant to join Canada. The British Government wanted them to join, and it instructed its governors to see that they did. They achieved this by much more than warning and advising ministries. Unpopular ministries were kept in office by governors so long as they would support union.[2]

One of the historians of Canadian union describes Confederation as being imposed on British North America 'by ingenuity, luck, courage and sheer force'.[3] By contrast, the Australian movement from 1889 onwards was open, sought popular support, and acknowledged that federation would not be achieved without it.

The movement to write a federal constitution began with an appeal to the people. When Parkes made his call for a constitutional convention late in 1889, he was told by the other premiers to arrange for New South Wales to join the Federal Council. He responded, as he told the Governor of New South Wales, by appealing from the politicians to the people. The Victorian politicians were incensed at what their Governor called Parkes 'platforming' about the faults of the Federal Council.[4] But finally they could not resist it, and they agreed to meet Parkes to consider whether a convention should be summoned.

The delegates to the 1890 federation conference were aware that the press had been excluded from constitutional deliberations in both Canada and the United States. At previous intercolonial gatherings in Australia the press had been excluded. On this occasion the delegates deliberately chose the opposite course. They took their lead from Parkes, who argued that federation more directly interested the inhabitants of all the colonies than any other issue. So the thirteen delegates were surrounded by a press corps of more than fifty, coming from every colony and including representatives of the overseas cable services. The telegraph operators at the Melbourne Post Office sent out 50,000 words each day and 70,000 on the final day. The newspapers ran columns of reports on the debates. As the *Daily Telegraph* put it, the papers were the great sounding boards of the conference, making the debates audible to the whole of Australia and giving a new spaciousness to Australian politics.[5]

When delegates met to draw up a constitution in 1891, they again decided to let the press in, as they did in 1897. Arguments against doing so were put. Delegates might oppose a particular measure in the Convention and then, having lost or compromised, they would still want to advocate a Yes vote for the Bill when it was before the electors. If their speeches in the convention were public knowledge, this would give an easy handle to opponents. Barton faced this problem in urging a Yes vote in New South Wales in 1898. He was forcibly reminded that he was supporting provisions he had opposed in the Convention. But this consideration could not prevail against the great educational advantage of publicity.

Newspapers had a very high circulation in Australia by world standards, and in the 1890s federation was their staple long-running story. It was a national story: in each colony the papers reported what was happening to the federal cause in the others. In New South Wales, where the struggle was most intense and most significant, the papers carried in full the key speeches of Parkes, Barton, and Reid. Reid's Yes–No speech took up five closely packed columns in the *Sydney Morning Herald* and amounted to more than 10,000 words. There were thirty-five reporters, working in relays, at the Town Hall to record his words. Before he reached his dramatic conclusion, the first part of the speech had already been set in type, not only in Sydney but also, courtesy of the telegraph, around the country.[6]

The Convention of 1891, elected by the parliaments, planned to send its constitution for the approval of the people. The delegates explicitly rejected approval by the parliaments. They did not want the parliaments even to discuss their Bill for fear that it would unravel before it reached the people. How popular approval was to be obtained was not defined. The old New Zealand radical Sir George Grey proposed that the colonies must hold a referendum, but this was defeated. Griffith in Queensland and Clark in Tasmania drew up Bills to provide for ratification by popularly elected conventions, but neither was proceeded with while the outcome in New South Wales was awaited.[7] In the New South Wales Parliament George Reid, later champion of the popular course, complained that the Convention had downgraded the parliaments in expecting that they were

Fifty delegates at the Federal Convention, Adelaide, 1897.

Thirty-three press representatives at the Federal Convention, Adelaide, 1897.

to be mere messengers, carrying the constitution to the people.[8] He led the opposition that killed the Bill.

A people can be involved in politics as no more than voting fodder, giving judgments when asked. Or they can be active citizens, informing themselves, debating issues, and creating public opinion. Between the failure of the 1891 constitution and the assembling of the Convention of 1897, two unofficial gatherings on federation were held: the Corowa conference of 1893 and the Bathurst Convention of 1896. From Corowa came the plan for a new start, and the Bathurst Convention indicated the capacity of ordinary people outside formal and official channels to discuss a federal constitution. But citizens had been actively concerned with federation before 1893, which was meant to mark the origins of popular involvement in federation. The 1890 Conference on federation in Melbourne was preceded by an unofficial conference, which debated the same issues in the same city, organised by the Australian Natives Association and attended by delegates from all over the country. Over a long period before 1890 the Natives Association had done much to place and keep federation on the political agenda. In Sydney in 1889 it organised the Town Hall meeting that brought Parkes and Barton together to outline the new strategy to achieve federation.[9]

The Natives were one of many voluntary associations—the Mechanics Institutes, the Schools of Arts, and the literary and debating societies—that were concerned with adult education, public speaking, and self-help. When Parkes or Barton wanted publicity for a speech or debates on federation, they arranged for copies to go to every school of arts.[10] These bodies heard lectures and conducted their own debates on federation.[11] In 1889 before Parkes made his move, the Hobart Debating Society was considering whether imperial federation or independence was better for Australia. In June 1891, an intercolonial debating competition took the constitution written by the first convention as one of its subjects. Before the 1898 referendum the Bathurst School of Arts, recognising that federation was the 'most momentous issue ever placed before the people', resolved to give both sides free use of their hall except for the cost of gas lighting and the door-keeper.[12]

In Adelaide the literary and debating societies sent delegates to a model parliament, which met weekly and mimicked the real parliament in the issues debated and in its procedure. There was a ministry, an opposition leader, backbenchers, and on special occasions a Governor, who might be a real politician, often a former member. In the 1880s and 1890s no subject received more attention than federation. The model parliament deb-

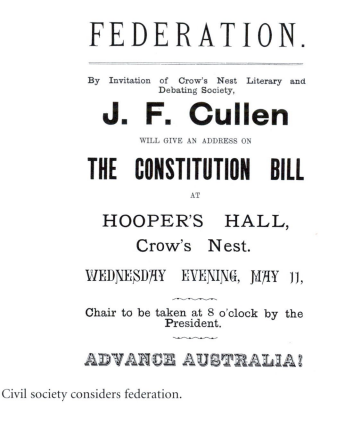

FEDERATION.

By Invitation of Crow's Nest Literary and Debating Society,

J. F. Cullen

WILL GIVE AN ADDRESS ON

THE CONSTITUTION BILL

AT

HOOPER'S HALL,
Crow's Nest.

WEDNESDAY EVENING, MAY 11,

Chair to be taken at 8 o'clock by the President.

ADVANCE AUSTRALIA!

Civil society considers federation.

ated every stage of its progress. In 1885 it was considering whether the colony should join the Federal Council and in 1897 the merits of the new Commonwealth Bill.[13]

During the campaign for the election of delegates to the 1897 Convention, a young men's church group at Redfern in Sydney organised a conference to discuss federal issues. Young men under 30 were invited from other churches, debating clubs, and friendly societies. More than two hundred attended. They threw out a chairman who had been chosen for them because he was older than 30 and installed Robert Garran, the young lawyer and stalwart of the Federation League. Over three nights they debated the principles of a federal constitution, and Reid and Barton made guest appearances.[14]

This was an impressive involvement of civil society in the great question, but the young intellectuals of the federal movement wanted something more: a public debate on federalism as sophisticated as had occurred in the United States. They had in mind the *Federalist Papers* produced during America's constitution-making in which three of the founding fathers gave a profound philosophical defence of the new constitution to promote its acceptance in the state of New York.

In 1890 Bernhard Wise, educated at Oxford and well read in political philosophy, proposed to launch an Australian *Federalist* with the support of the Natives Association. He wanted a forum in which the questions involved in federation could be explored in greater depth than in the newspapers.[15] Nothing came of this plan. In 1894 the young lawyers in Sydney's Federation League did launch such a journal, a monthly magazine called *The Commonwealth*. At first it maintained a high quality and took a general interest in Australian culture as well as federation. It reviewed *Seven Little Australians* and carried an article by Arthur Streeton on Australian art.[16] On federation Garran contributed a learned piece on the position of the state governors in an Australian union and debated with Andrew Clark whether federal principles allowed for the setting of a national franchise.[17] But sales were poor and quality declined. It lasted only ten months, complaining that too many young men were more interested in sport than public affairs and that rich men, unlike their counterparts in the United States, were unwilling to support patriotic causes like *The Commonwealth*.[18]

Australia did not have much need of a *Federalist*. The fundamental thinking about federalism had already been done by the Americans. Australia's constitutional debate was more concerned with marrying different elements taken from elsewhere: federalism from the United States, responsible government from Westminster, the joint sitting from Norway, the referendum from Switzerland. The typical federation publication was a guide to the federal constitutions of the world. There were difficult matters to be determined, more of detail than principle, and the daily press did carry quite long and learned articles on these questions. The monthly journal, *Review of Reviews*, was strongly federalist and regularly published articles on the prospects and progress of the movement. The greater need was the education of ordinary citizens in the operations of a federal constitution.

In Victoria in 1895 the poet William Gay attempted to raise the level of debate by producing a book of essays by leading federalists. He attracted a very distinguished stable of contributors, but his book did not sell well. Instead of giving him some income, he had to sell 'the last things I had left to sell—my books' to pay the printer.[19] The collection is notable for a despairing piece by Deakin on the people's lack of interest in federation. The movement was then at a low point. Reid had obtained the agreement of the premiers to the Quick plan, but nothing was being done while Reid pressed on with his domestic program. All Deakin could hope for was that the devoted federalists would remain in the field ready to take advantage of opportunities as they eventuated. He thought it would require a very favourable conjunction of the planets to achieve federation.

Gay's own contribution was a gentle riposte to Deakin's from the idealist perspective, which they shared. The people's indifference should not surprise or dishearten. 'Every reform first appears as an idea in the mind of individuals … Progress is the result of a gradual communication to the many of the ideals of the few.' And this is not the arbitrary imposition of the will of the few on the many but a working out of Reason, which is the same in all and is gradually shaping human affairs to its own form.[20]

The federalists generally were insisting that once the people were involved in federation, the cause would be won. Here from the idealists was a more realistic account of 'the people'. Mostly they were not interested in or enthusiastic about federation. The informed and committed citizens were a thin layer on a mass of ignorance and indifference. The editor of *The Commonwealth* also acknowledged the lack of enthusiasm but was more hopeful: there was a deeply rooted national sentiment in favour of union, and 'if the people do not clamour, they are none the less ready, and will welcome federation when it comes'.[21]

Part of the case for a popularly elected convention and the referendum did acknowledge the widespread lack of interest. The people would become enthused, it was said, as they were given the opportunity to be involved. The opponents of the plan to involve the people argued that the people were too ignorant for constitution-making, but mostly they were concerned that the people would elect inappropriate delegates to the Convention.

As it turned out, the Convention did not introduce a new element into public life. Reid was confident that leading politicians would be elected, and he was proved right. The claim that the people were to be involved had given the federal movement a fresh start and a democratic air, but the politicians were still in charge. After the Convention had concluded its labours, a real change did come. The people were asked to pass judgment on a constitution of 128 clauses. This was truly testing their political capacity. Deakin was aware of how great this challenge was because he had read in Bryce that the American constitution would not have been carried had it been put directly to the people.[22] The editor of *Review of Reviews* wondered whether it might not have been better to ask the people an in-principle question first and then come to the detail.[23] *The Commonwealth* had earlier warned that in Switzerland the referendum was a 'deadly engine': the slightest blemish in a proposal was used as an excuse to demolish the whole.[24]

This unprecedented experiment in direct democracy has fortunately left behind a unique collection of records. Edward Dowling, the secretary of the Central Federation League in Sydney, kept everything. The Dowling Papers in the National Library hold the letters sent to his office from more than a hundred branches of the League in New South Wales. They report on the progress of the Yes campaign in their area and detail the assistance they need. For the second referendum of 1899 there are complete records of who gave money to the Yes campaign and how it was spent. These documents are our *Federalist Papers*. They are highly revealing about what was distinctive in our constitution-making, which was not profound thought on the nature of federalism but the direct approval of the constitution by the people. The issues explored here are not whether a strong national goverment is a threat to liberty, but whether hotel balconies are better for meetings than halls; not whether a republic can operate over a large area, but how to operate on the minds of ordinary people in a referendum campaign.

In every part of New South Wales the little knot of people who constituted themselves as a local federation league confronted plenty of apathy and ignorance. They tried to convert No supporters, but they were preoccupied as much with would-be Yes supporters who had to be prodded into voting. Voting was then voluntary. Enrolment had been voluntary as well, but since 1893 the police had been made responsible for putting people's names on the roll. The 'electoral right', which the police issued, had to be taken by the voter to the poll. If you moved districts or lost your right, you had to secure a new one. Making sure voters had their 'rights' was part of the business of the federation branch. The Junee branch was pleased to discover that the drovers were not only keen on federation but also carried their 'rights' with them.[25]

no monies 5/1/94

Copy of Resolutions, passed at a Meeting held in Mulwala, on Saturday, the 11 March, 1893. for the purpose of forming a local Branch of the Australian Federation League.

(1.)

Proposed by Mr Robert McGeoch and seconded by Mr Bernard Bott,–

"That a Branch of the Australian Feder-" "ation League be formed at Mulwala to be" "called the Mulwala Branch of the " "Australian Federation League".

(Carried unanimously)

(2.)

Proposed by Mr Arthur Camplin and seconded by Mr William Sloane Jun,–

"That all persons above the age" "of sixteen years be eligible for member-" "ship and that the enrollment fee be" "the sum of 2/6. for such members."

(Carried unanimously.)

(3.)

Proposed by Mr E. H. Street, and seconded by Mr Archibald McKenzie,–

" That a Committee, consisting of the following Members be forthwith appointed to conduct the affairs of the Branch and arrange for further meetings, to be added to, if required.

Messrs, James Sloane, William Sloane Jun. Lonsdale, Jeremiah Dunn, E.J. Laurence, E.H. Street, A.D. Cowan, Arthur Camplin,

Branches of the Federation League abided by the formal rules: resolutions passed at the first meeting at Mulwala, 1893.

How far would a man walk or ride to cast a vote, not for a local candidate promising local benefits but for a constitution? The drought made it hard for farmers to get into town to vote since there was no feed for their horse, unless they were to pay for it. Federation branches tried to make it easier to vote by getting more polling booths opened. At Lucknow the government saved money by placing the polling station at the schoolhouse, which was out of town, rather than hiring the Miners Hall in the town. H.W. Newman, the league secretary, thought it was essential to have the vote in the town: 'There are a lot of fellows absolutely indifferent and do not know nor want to know anything about Federation who will vote for the Bill just to oblige if the Hall can be used, but who will not climb the School Hill for me or anyone else.'[26]

At Laurel Hill in the Alps, H. Jeffrey Joyce feared that if it snowed on polling day or before, few would make the five-mile journey to Cherry Hill. When he was told that it was too late to open a polling station at Laurel Hill, he replied: 'For myself I shall be 84 years of age tomorrow and if the weather is very bad it is doubtful whether I will go but I will try to induce as many as I can to go and record their votes for federation. We have three days snow in this month already.'[27]

The newspapers were full of federation, and in New South Wales, as in the other colonies, every elector had been sent a copy of the Bill. But not everyone read the papers or what was sent to them. A few could not read.[28] In the country especially, the Yes case had to be heard and seen; it had to be performed. There had to be a meeting at which a speaker would outline the case. The time had to be chosen carefully, not Saturday night, which was pay day and late shopping, and not to clash with other functions—discussion of the constitution could not win an audience against *HMS Pinafore*, Scottish bagpipes, or a hospital concert; preferably a day when the farmers were already in town for court or a show. The speaker had to be eminent. Everyone wanted the stars, Barton or Wise. To send a second-rater was an insult to the town, especially if the No side had sent one of their best.

At the meeting the No side would put up their local leaders to ask questions of the speaker. If these opinion-leaders could be bested, then a great victory was won.[29] If the meeting could carry a vote in favour of the Bill, it concluded very satisfactorily. Staving off hostile amendments and counter-demonstrations was the work of good organisation. If the No campaign had produced an effective speaker, the word would go out to headquarters: this man must be answered. Speakers were set the task of following a particular speaker around the country. Their case had to be answered not so much to change opinion but so that supporters would have the confidence to go on believing what they believed before.

Everyone believed that nothing was as effective as a personal canvas of the electorate; that is, house-to-house visiting, putting the case, ensuring that people were on the roll. Good organisers kept lists of likely supporters so they could be checked off on polling day and stragglers rounded up.[30] This was one of the tasks performed by the Women's Federal League, which was organised in Sydney by Maybanke Wolstenholme, past president of the Womanhood Suffrage League. Women did not have the vote, but they could persuade men to vote and incidentally by these activities persuade men that women were worthy of the vote.[31]

The campaign for Australian nationhood was run on a shoe-string budget. If federation was to benefit the big-money men, very few of them were prepared to spend big money to achieve it.[32] In 1898 the Yes case in New South Wales had £1,330 to spend.[33] This was not a large sum. A rich man running for parliament might spend as much in one electorate.[34] In Victoria the Yes case reported that it spent no more than one man might spend getting into parliament.[35] In 1899 in New South Wales the bagmen did better and raised £2,180.[36] Sydney business was mainly hostile to federation. Of the twenty-five large donations in 1899 (£25–£100), only half came from this source. The other half came from pastoralists in the country and Victorians with interests in New South Wales, chiefly Riverina property.[37] The federalists were denounced during the campaign for betraying New South Wales with Victorian gold,[38] but just how much Victorian money was accepted remained a secret. Dowling had a formula for hiding its extent. He said very little was contributed other than by 'citizens and taxpayers of New South Wales'.[39] Of course the Victorian donors paid tax in New South Wales.

Nearly all these donors stood to benefit from intercolonial free trade. James Fairfax, the owner of the *Sydney Morning Herald*, was a more purely patriotic donor. James Dalton, an Orange pastoralist, was also a patriot. He was a poor Irishman who had made good and supported Irish causes. When the Redmond brothers, the Home rule advocates, visited the colony they were denied a hall in Orange and spoke in a shop. To avoid such embargoes in future Dalton paid for the building of the Australian Hall.

This central fund was spent on advertisements, literature—dodgers, handbills, a campaign newspaper—and on the expenses of speakers who went to the country. Only a very small portion was spent on drink for electors and supporters.[40] These were very dry campaigns. Two members of the Natives Association door-knocking in a working-class area encountered a jovial little man who said, 'A vote is it? Right you are, my hearties. Who's puttin' up? Is he good enough for a drink?' They told him Australia was 'puttin' up' and there was no drink. He knew this already and was only having them on.[41]

Local branches had to meet all local expenses: hire of hall, lighting for hall, advertisements and handbills for meetings, a bellman to call the meeting around the streets. In an ordinary election these expenses were borne by the candidate, who would also pay for canvassing or entertain those who worked for him. The central fund covered the costs of Sydney meetings. Maybanke Wolstenholme turned down an offer of funds from the Federation League. Her Women's Federal League covered its own costs and made a contribution to the central campaign fund.[42] In Victoria local expenses were frequently met by the Natives Association. At Geelong the Natives contributed ten guineas and the Chamber of Commerce two.[43]

Fewer people turned out to vote at the referendum than usually did at an ordinary election. This fact has been used to show that there was no widespread enthusiasm for federation. Those who worked to get people to the polls knew this well enough. It is their enthusiasm for federation that has so far gone unremarked. The federal cause was carried by these active citizens who gave their money and time. In the Dowling Papers we can identify their leaders in the country towns: solicitors and newspaper editors were most prominent, the local professionals who had no direct economic interest in federation but were able to respond to its wider vision and write letters to headquarters. Other names appear. If ever we seek to honour these founding fathers, the roll could read like this:[44]

- T.S. Davies, the stationmaster at Trangie, who, with the school-master, constituted the federal league and canvassed house to house for 'the noble cause'
- the manager of Gunbar station at Gunbar, who kept men on his payroll for two weeks before the poll 'solely to have their votes and who took all his men 8 or 12 miles to vote, polling 22 votes for the Bill'
- John Kendall on the Manning River, who interjected at a No meeting and at its conclusion successfully called for cheers for federation
- the Rev. Lionel Nye of the vicarage, Hillgrove, who read up on federation and put in a word for it on his pastoral visits
- T.G. Sloane of Young, 'who has taken a large strip of country and, a bushman talking to bushmen, will do a lot of good'
- Robert Ross, who led the West Maitland branch, which consisted of seven paying members, none of them moneyed men, and three working men
- George Walton, who for two months sang the 'New Federation Ode' in hotels and business houses in Sydney and Newcastle—and then asked for payment.

Overall the Yes campaign had the harder task. It had to explain a document that embodied a totally foreign system of government. The standard Yes speech was an exposition of the constitution and usually ran for well over an hour. Two hours was not uncommon. On two occasions Barton spoke for three hours and at places not previously known for their interest in constitutional law: Hay and Bourke.[45] After ten years of public debate very basic information still had to be supplied, such as the survival of state parliaments and with them the local member to look after roads and bridges.[46]

The No case declared that it was in favour of federation but raised objections to this plan and ran with scares or 'bogeys', as they were called. The most damaging was the cost of federation. Cost was an admitted difficulty. There were so many unknowns that the calculations of experts differed widely. It was easy for the No side to pluck a large figure and run with it. Federation was to cost 22s 6d per head annually; to which the Yes side replied that it would cost no more than a dog licence. Among the bogeys proper were that you wouldn't be able to let your horse drink from a river without asking the Interstate Commission (since all the water had to flow to South Australia) and (for the Irish) that federation was depriving the colony of Home Rule.[47]

It was impossible to lay the bogeys. One campaign worker declared you could chop a bogey to pieces and still 'it would kick'.[48] Barton was disoriented by this novel situation. The lies were exposed, and the usual consequence did not follow: they were not withdrawn; they were simply repeated.[49] The 'usual consequence' operated when there was an audience following a debate; with a substantial part of the audience unengaged and ill-informed, the No case could feed off ignorance and apathy. 'If you are unsure Vote No.'

The maestro of this business was the *Daily Telegraph*. It abandoned all distinction between news and views. The scares and bogeys were disguised as paragraphs among the news items and blazoned as slogans in huge capitals running right down the page. It was so daring, so outrageous that the federalists could not help admire it, although they were witnessing the overthrow of one of the central tenets of the age: that the press was an engine of enlightenment. The *Daily Telegraph* mailed a copy of its special referendum edition to every elector in the colony. The cost was not very large because newspapers were carried free in New South Wales, something that might well be lost under federation.

To this the Yes side made only a feeble response. It mailed copies of the special edition of the *Sydney Morning Herald* to every elector. But the *Herald* was far too sober to match the *Telegraph*'s catchy sloganeering.[50]

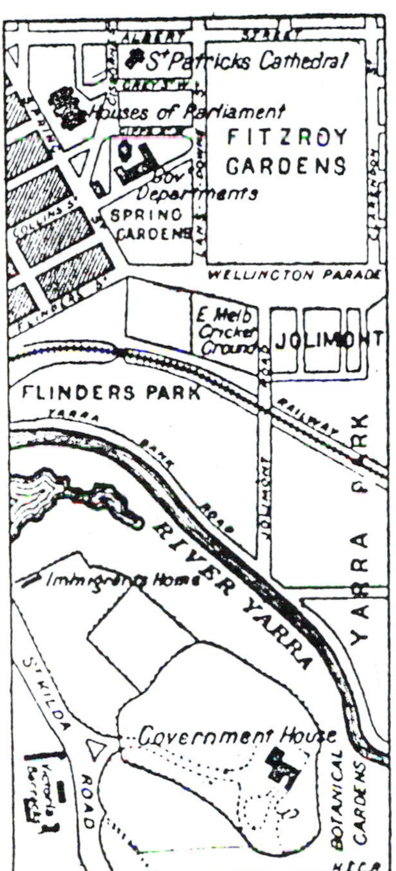

A *Daily Telegraph* scare: how the federal capital could be carved out of Melbourne.

The Yes side also distributed free copies of its own campaign newspaper, to which they had given the honoured name *The Federalist*. It probably was more immediately influential than the American original, which went over the heads of the New York electors and their delegates to the ratifying Convention.[51] The Australian *Federalist* included advice on farming methods and a serial story. Garran and other smart young lawyers wrote for it, but they too could not match the *Daily Telegraph*. They might well have been able to produce as good a No case. Like other advocates of Yes, they were obliged to explain and were put on the defensive.

The Yes case nevertheless won—in New South Wales narrowly and very comfortably in the other three colonies that voted in the first round. Think of it! A No campaign failed when it had 128 clauses to find fault with. Yes

HE WAR INDEMNITY.

AYMENT OF ARREARS.

N, Wednesday Night.—The Porte ed to pay over to Russia the ar- the indemnity incurred in connec- f the Russo-Turkish war. nt of £300,000 is to be paid at once and the balance in three annual in- s.

GLAND AND CHINA.

Y OF THE WEI-HAI-WEI.

FORTIFICATIONS WEAK.

N, Wednesday Night.—Surveys ve been made of the harbor of Wei show that there is a greater of deep water than was expected. ortifications are weaker than they erally believed to be.

ANISH FINANCES.

RUN ON THE BANKS.

VERNMENT BUYING SILVER.

N, Thursday.—A run on the Span- s, occasioned by the change of coin, is causing the Government up silver largely, and to prohibit

ITALIAN CABINET.

CONSTRUCTION COMPLETED.

N, Thursday.—The Marquis di as completed the reconstruction of an Ministry, changes having been ted by the death of Admiral Brin, of Marine, and by the differ- ating between the Marquis Venosta, for Foreign Affairs, and Signor li, President of the Chamber of , in connection with the recent riots

w members of the Cabinet are as

r and Minister of the Interior, the di Rudini.

r for Foreign Affairs, Signor Ca-

r for War, General Asinari di San

r for Marine, Admiral N. Canovaro, manded the Italian squadron until stationed in Cretan waters.

BOTTOMLEY COMPANIES.

V.A. AND N.Z. MARKET TRUST. APPROVED.

EME OF RECONSTRUCTION.

ON, Thursday.—At the recent meet- d to consider the position of the ustralian and New Zealand Market Mr. Horatio Bottomley explained trust was in need of £250,000, and a scheme of reconstruction on the an assessment of from 3s to 4s per

cheme of reconstruction, as drawn committee chiefly composed of lead- kbrokers, has been unanimously ap- y the shareholders of the trust.

CE HENRY OF ORLEANS.

PER NILE EXPEDITION ABANDONED.

ON, Wednesday Afternoon.—Prince of Orleans has abandoned the expe- r the Upper Nile which he proposed me ago.

UOR PROHIBITION IN CANADA.

OSED GENERAL PLEBISCITE.

ON, Wednesday Night.—The Cana- arliament has been asked to vote dollars to cover the expense of tak- ebiscite throughout the Dominion on ation of prohibition of the liquor

NERAL CABLE NEWS

IF YOU ARE IN FAVOR OF THE BILL STRIKE OUT THE ABOVE WORD "NO."

IF YOU ARE AGAINST THE BILL STRIKE OUT THE WORD "YES."

THE MOMENTOUS THIRD.

THE BILL SHOULD DIE TO-NIGHT.

KILLED BY AN OUTRAGED DEMOCRACY.

BE ON THE SIDE OF SAFETY, AND VOTE "NO."

BE JUST BEFORE BEING GENEROUS.

FEDERATING IN HASTE MEANS REPENTING AT LEISURE.

IF STILL IN DOUBT STRIKE OUT "YES."

IT IS THE SAFE THING TO DO.

VOTE FOR THE BILL, AND THE STEP IS IRRETRACEABLE.

THE BILL LAYS THE AXE AT THE ROOT OF DEMOCRACY.

DEFEAT IT, AND REJECT A DANGEROUS CONSTITUTION.

THE BILL SPELLS CALAMITY TO THIS COLONY,

AND IMPOSES ON NEW SOUTH WALES THE BURDEN OF THE SMALL STATES.

DELAY WILL GIVE A BETTER FEDERATION.

A CONVENTION BILL SHOULD NOT RECOGNISE CLASS INTERESTS OR STATE DOMINATION.

THE BILL TAXES EVERY MAN, WOMAN AND CHILD £1 2s 6d A YEAR EXTRA.

IT REDUCES THE VALUE OF WAGES.

IT MEANS A MILLION AND A HALF MORE CUSTOMS DUTIES.

EVERY AUSTRALIAN SHOULD VOTE "NO."

EVERY DEMOCRAT SHOULD VOTE "NO."

EVERY BELIEVER IN EQUAL RIGHTS SHOULD VOTE "NO."

EVERY MAN WHO LOVES HIS COUNTRY SHOULD VOTE "NO."

EVERY GENUINE FEDERALIST SHOULD VOTE "NO."

DON'T BE MISLED BY MERE SENTIMENT.

DON'T BE BEGUILED BY BANDS AND BUNTING.

DELAY WILL ENSURE A REAL AND COMPLETE UNION.

POINTS TO NOTE BEFORE VOTING.

Referendum Day has at last arrived. To-day the Convention Bill goes to the electors for judgment.

The vote is being taken also in Victoria and Tasmania. To-morrow it will be taken in South Australia. In West Australia the bill has first to be considered by the Parliament. Sir John Forrest has promised to take steps for referring it afterwards to the electors.

THE OTHER COLONIES.

Possibly it may be known to-night what fat has overtaken the bill in New South Wales an Victoria. Naturally, with the advantages tha Victoria will derive under the scheme, the vot there will be in its favor. This is the genera impression. The effective vote in the south i 50,000, so that the Conventionists have not th difficulty in securing the statutory majority tha they will have in this colony.

There has been some opposition to the mea sure in Tasmania, and some also in South Aus tralia. It is unlikely to prove a serious bloc to the adoption of the bill. In Tasmania the ob jections to the bill are based on the financia clauses. In South Australia they are mainl against the powers of the Senate, which are con sidered to be insufficient. South Australia want not only equal representation but absolutely co ordinate control over legislation.

DEMONSTRATIONS AND "THE DEAD MARCH."

The two principal events last night were th magnificent demonstration against the bill in th Town-hall, and a much smaller and a rathe apathetic meeting addressed by Mr. Barton in th New Masonic-hall. The Town-hall gatherin served to confirm the belief that in the metro polis the bill will be defeated by positively a overwhelming majority.

As a spurt to the bill cause the Federal Asso ciation arranged a "demonstration" in the street last night. It was a depressing affair, rendere even more melancholy by the rain. Four prank ing horses drew the Conventional drag throug part of the city. There were bill men on boar and banners, and colors. But the populace wa unresponsive. Some newsboys chased the vehi cle a few hundred yards. But their interes quickly evaporated. With their spirits dashe by the rain and their hearts battered with th prospects of defeat the processionists made thei way into King-street. In front of this office, an immediately facing the display boards that ar to exhibit the vote bulletins to-night, the ban played the "Dead March in Saul." Another ban may play it to-night!

DISPLAYING THE RETURNS.

The usual complete arrangements have bee made by "The Daily Telegraph" office for pos ing the detailed returns immediately on the arrival. There will be not only the totals, b the voting in each district, and a barometer i indicate the relative position of the pro and an bill parties.

TAXATION VERSUS SENTIMENT.

The father of a family of eleven writes thus o the subject of taxation under this bill:—"I a the sole family breadwinner and taxpayer. Sou authorities inform me that my extra taxation f Federation will be £1 2s 6d per head per yea in my case a yearly total of £12 7s 6d, or a tot for the bookkeeping period of five years of £61 1 6d. Billites assert that in this period the su of £57 5s will be returned, not direct to me, fro whom it has been taken, but to the Treasur My position, then, is that, for the prospecti benefits of the present bill, I must certainly p £61 17s 6d in extra direct taxation for whatev possible indirect benefits that follow Federati on the present lines. Is there a parent in Ne South Wales who has to labor hard and long f himself and family, often scarcely able to kee the wolf from the door, who is prepared to suff direct monetary loss for a sentimental and vagu ly possible gain? If not, then the striking fro his ballot paper to-day of the word "Yes" is sacred duty. It will further prove to chatterin charlatans and windy-worded orators that sent ment alone does not butter the bread of the stru gling worker, even though it be the Federatio creamery brand of '98."

CLUES TO THE RESULT.

At the harbor excursion given yesterday by th Ministers for Agriculture and Public Works, honor of Mr. Taverner (Victorian Minister f Agriculture), the topic of general conversati was naturally Federation. One enthusiast member of the party took the trouble to cou heads, for and against the Convention Bill. E cepting the three or four Victorian representativ present, he found that everyone else intend voting "No" at the polls to-day. On hearing th result, Mr. Smith remarked, "That's a very goo indication of public feeling on the question."

An employee of a leading firm of wholesa softgoods merchants canvassed his fellow-em ployees as to how they intended voting for th Federal Enabling Bill. The following was th result:—Employees canvassed, 49; against th bill, 26; for the bill 15; undecided, 3; neglect to obtain their rights, 5.

All branches of the civil service, including th railways, will give heavy votes against the bill.

THINGS TO REMEMBER.

Do not jump at a bad bargain. You can easi get better terms if you only hold off for a whil

The *Daily Telegraph* on the morning of the referendum.

had two forces working for it: the economic benefit that would flow from intercolonial free trade, and national sentiment, both of which could sway voters without their knowing the details of the constitution. Yes campaigners interwove these economic and nationalist appeals in their speeches, although usually not as crudely as the Tasmanian campaigner who is reputed to have said:

> Gentlemen, if you vote for the Bill you will found a great and glorious nation under the bright Southern Cross, and meat will be cheaper; and you will live to see the Australian race dominate the Southern seas, and you will have a market for both potatoes and apples; and your sons shall reap the grand heritage of nationhood, and if Sir William Lyne does come back to power in Sydney he can never do you one pennyworth of harm.[52]

The economic interpretation of federation claims that people voted at the referendum according to whether the economy of their district was likely to gain or lose under intercolonial free trade.[53] For instance, border districts in New South Wales voted Yes to improve their access to Melbourne, Adelaide, and Brisbane, which were closer to them than Sydney, whereas manufacturing districts in Adelaide voted No for fear of competition from Melbourne factories. This factor was clearly a very strong influence—it has been used earlier in this book to explain responses to federation—but it does not fully explain the vote. What is striking in the four south-eastern colonies is that although many areas voted very strongly Yes, the No vote was never overwhelming. There were 265 electorates in these four colonies. In 1898 in 105 of them the Yes vote exceeded 75 per cent. In only one electorate did the No vote exceed 75 per cent—and then only narrowly: in the Hawkesbury electorate in New South Wales 76 per cent voted No.[54]

This voting pattern suggests that there was a solid base for the Yes vote that could be swollen when there was a clear economic gain from federation, and which could be cut back when danger threatened, but not so that it became insignificant. No Victorian town was more threatened by federation than Maffra, the centre of the beet-sugar industry, which would disappear if sugar from New South Wales and Queensland had free access to the Victorian market. Maffra was much less enthusiastic for federation than Victoria generally, but still in 1898 it recorded a Yes vote—78 votes to 77.[55]

Yes gained its base vote because federation itself was generally seen as a good thing, even if the details of the constitution were in dispute. The good might be the making of a nation and a central government or the economic good of a colony. In Tasmania, Victoria, and South Australia there was a broad consensus that intercolonial free trade would bring great benefits.

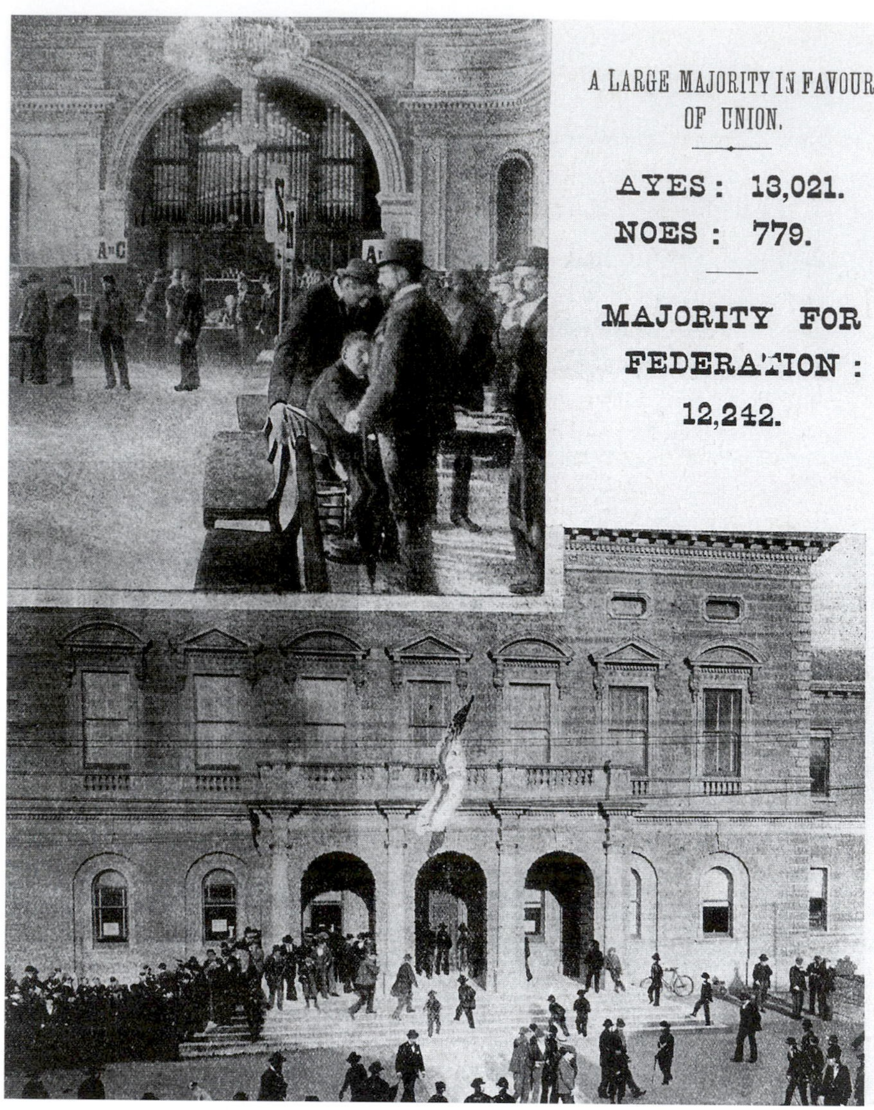

A record of the Tasmanian vote: the overwhelming Yes vote, and a rare picture of the voting taking place in Hobart Town Hall (*Tasmanian Mail*, 5 August 1899).

In the laggard colonies of Queensland and Western Australia the voting was more polarised: strong Yes areas and strong No areas. There had been no campaign for federation in these colonies until the last minute, and both were so internally divided that there were plans for the creation of new states. Local concerns could produce an extreme vote either way.

A nationalist crusade: a torch-light procession at Summerhill, a Sydney suburb. (*Sydney Mail*, 11 June 1898)

The No case had economic scares in its armoury to put against the benefits of intercolonial free trade. Tasmania would be bankrupt, New South Wales taxpayers would be milked, Victorian farms would fall in value. But it had no answer to national sentiment, which it identified as its chief enemy.[56] As the campaign proceeded the Yes side relied more heavily on sentiment. Its meetings became nationalist rallies with patriotic airs, flags and bunting, banners and badges, young men spouting poetry, and the singing of federation songs. In Hobart the Federation League decided to stop debating the *Mercury* on the effects of federation on Tasmania's finances and to call in the bands and the poetry readers instead. In Melbourne a federal choir was formed to perform at meetings. The centrepiece of Barton's final rally in a packed Sydney Town Hall was the unfurling of the federal flag made by the ladies of the federal movement.[57]

At his first campaign meeting George Turner, the staid Premier of Victoria, gave a cautious endorsement of the Bill based on Treasury figures. At his final

The federation flag about to be unveiled in the Sydney Town Hall to join the Stars and Stripes and a British ensign. (*Town and Country Journal*, 11 June 1898)

meeting he called on Miss Fanny Lyndhurst for an encore of 'United We Will Be' and led the audience in the singing of the chorus.[58]

'Tis the Land we love! the Grand New Land!
the Home of the Frank and Free!
Then Hurrah! Hurrah! for Australia, united soon to be!
For peace, not Strife, the Call goes forth,
from East to West, from South to North,
United we will be!

The standard themes of federation poetry were now being rendered as campaign songs. Here are the four verses of 'United We Will Be' as sung by Fanny Lyndhurst to wild enthusiasm in the town halls of Melbourne and its suburbs:

We're a land that claims no blood-stained roll
of war on land and sea,
But its name shines fair on History's scroll
as the Home of the Frank and Free!
Its sons have proved, through fire and flood,
Brave, Steadfast, Staunch and True;

Right worthy they of their British blood
and the Land of the Kangaroo.

We've a land that laughs in sunshine strong,
and ripples with harvest corn
That has never felt a tyrant's thong,
nor suffered a despot's scorn!
We hold our own! We rule our own!
shoulder to shoulder stand
For Right and Might, by Britain's Throne,
and the dear old Motherland!

We've a land that gleams with treasures vast
of gold and silver store;
But we proudly deem our wealth is cast
in our sons and daughters more.
But though our Austral Land is one,
and one our tongue and lore,
We're barred apart, though one in heart,
by the curse of the Customs' door.

Say! shall Australians stand apart beneath
the Austral Cross
And let dividing rancours start the feuds of
Strife and Loss?
It cannot be! it shall not be! divided we
must fall!
United shall Australia be, For Strength,
and Peace, and all!

The No campaign mocked these displays and issued solemn warnings against allowing sentiment to override reason. The Melbourne Labor paper, the *Tocsin*, edited by Bernard O'Dowd, made a sustained attack on sentiment.[59] It described the Australian Natives as empty-headed clowns ready to saddle Australia with an undemocratic constitution so long as they obtained some sort of federation. Knowing the power of the word *federation*, O'Dowd rendered it 'fetteration'. He published anti-sentimental verse:

They daze us with 'Our Destiny',
With blare of 'War' and 'Fame':
To part us, shriek out 'Unity'
And drug us with a Name.

Norman and Lionel Lindsay in the *Tocsin* (2 June 1898) depict Deakin leading the circus of federal sentimentalists.

Some federalists responded to this criticism of sentiment by pointing out that the case for federation could be rendered in perfectly rational form.[60] And it was. Here is the final appeal of Kingston and his Treasurer, Frederick Holder, to the electors of South Australia in 1898: 'We favour Federation in the interests of Australian National Life; for the sake of unity and fraternity, and for the strength and safety which they beget; and for the sake also of the progress and prosperity, peace and concord, which history tells us Federation alone can secure.'[61] When the *Review of Reviews* asked a hundred opinion leaders why they supported federation they received high-minded statements like this, not at all jingoistic.[62] But the people who offered them had some attachment, which was more than rational, to the ideal of Australia. Scratch the rational case for union, and you find the sentiment underneath.

Some federalists were happy to acknowledge sentiment. They replied to their critics that sentiment was the underpinning of most things that are worthwhile and that the basis of a nation is sentiment.[63] The *Federalist* printed the best defence: 'The opponents of the Bill are continually decrying sentiment. They say it is not a matter of sentiment, but of practical business. And yet it is sentiment alone which makes Federation possible. Without the feeling and desire for unity, spread throughout the land, no number of Conventions, no series of carefully drafted constitutions can bring about Federation.'[64]

Federations have been brought about without national sentiment. Dangers within and without have compelled unity. In Australia's case, where there was no pressing need for federation, national sentiment was the precondition of union. Parkes appealed to it in 1889 to launch the movement; those who crafted and fought for the constitution were inspired by it; and at the referendums that brought success it was the one thing that the No bogeys could not touch.

Whether citizens waving flags and singing patriotic songs were showing a capacity to be guardians of a federal constitution is another question.

Afterwards

14
Beginning

They come, they come! their banners stream on every wind that blows,
And Federation's holy name in every fold disclose.
Now halt! O standard bearer! and face the risen sun—
Australia's first great festival, its joyance hath begun.

Marion Miller, 'Australia's Cherished Dream'[1]

The contest to control the Commonwealth began before its official inauguration on 1 January 1901. In the previous October George Reid launched the first national election campaign. He told huge audiences in the Adelaide and Melbourne town halls that the new nation must not hobble itself with the outmoded doctrine of protection.

In supporting federation Reid had taken an enormous risk. Could he win national support for free trade when five out of the six colonies were protectionist? Some of his supporters always thought he had no chance. A few took their revenge by helping to vote him out of office in September 1899. In New South Wales he was now Leader of the Opposition to the protectionist government of William Lyne.

Reid's meetings in Melbourne and Adelaide were a great success. Here where free trade was thought wicked, reactionary, or irrelevant came this democratic advocate of the cause with his rollicking wit and home-spun talk. Is it not time, he asked, to take these overgrown babies, the infant industries, from the generous bosom of the state? They are not sucking for nothing. In fact they are pocketing benefits conferred by the state and paying low wages to their workers. They put up prices to the consumer and do not create more jobs. When he was challenged to name a nation that had grown great without protection, he asked what family had ever grown old without getting measles! Australia as a new nation should not repeat the mistakes of the past. In Melbourne he answered the *Age*'s blast against him point by point and dubbed it *Past Ages*. When 'the whole world was open to the whole world', a new age of progress and humanity would dawn.[2]

Barton, who was widely expected to be chosen as first Prime Minister, did not attempt to match Reid. He accepted invitations to speak but made a virtue of not campaigning for the job. He said an all-out battle over free trade and protection would damage the nation, which needed a moderate, common-sense tariff, an even-handed government, and the right people in charge. He depicted Reid's free-trade campaign as an invitation to the rabid opponents of federation in free-trade Sydney to play havoc with the new Commonwealth.[3]

Barton held no official position. He had resigned as Leader of the Opposition in the New South Wales Assembly to allow Lyne to supplant Reid. He had resigned his seat in parliament when he went to London as head of the federal delegation. On his return Lyne showed who was boss by querying Barton's claim for expenses. Barton was still in debt as a result of having abandoned his law practice to campaign for federation. His federalist friends around Australia helped out by contributing to a fund from which payments were made to his wife.[4] They hoped that under the Commonwealth he could soon gain the security of a judgeship.

The officials at the Colonial Office, assuming that Barton would be first Prime Minister, sent him copies of the official documents that would establish the Commonwealth.[5] Still Barton would not assume that the prime ministership was his. Only with Deakin's prodding did he begin to make plans for the first cabinet. Since Barton was in a difficult situation and could make no firm offers, it was easier for Deakin to do the soundings. He was very conscious of all the work that had to be done to establish a whole new system of government. Having created the union, they now had to ensure that it had a smooth and successful launch.[6]

There were seven ministerial posts, and as good federalists they wanted as far as possible to have every state represented in the cabinet. From New South Wales there would be Barton himself and his friend O'Connor; from Victoria Deakin and Turner, who after a short interval had returned to the premiership. Forrest would represent the West; he still counted Deakin and Barton as friends, although they had refused to help him achieve better terms for his colony. Deakin had some trouble persuading Barton to accept Kingston from South Australia. The three of them had become very close campaigning for the constitution in London, but Kingston's fiery radicalism worried Barton.

Queensland was a problem. Knowing all the legal work that had to be done, Deakin wanted the best talent in the country: Griffith. He was interested, but immediately, as was his wont, made stipulations about rewards and advancement. He could not give up his salary as Chief Justice unless the Queensland Parliament agreed to pay him the pension due on his retirement, and he expected to proceed from the cabinet to be first Chief Justice of the High Court. This was too much for Barton. He would not begin the Commonwealth 'with bargains about offices'. Others had made sacrifices for the cause. Why should Griffith assume that he must be 'provided for'? But if they did not take Griffith, they would have to accept Dickson, who had betrayed them in London.

Deakin and Barton were doing their own sparring. Deakin was a much stronger protectionist than his friend. The *Age* and the Victorian protectionists were terrified that the first Commonwealth tariff would remove the high duties that protected Melbourne's factories. They were as committed to their doctrine as Reid was to his. Deakin reported to Barton that the Victorian liberals had adopted a policy that the Commonwealth tariff should be modelled on the Victorian 'subject to Australian interests and conditions'. Barton was appalled. To name Victoria as a model would be suicidal in New South Wales. He reminded Deakin that their own agreed formula was that the tariff be designed to raise revenue without injury to any existing, substantial industry.[7]

By the agreement of the premiers the Commonwealth was to be inaugurated in Sydney. This meant that the celebrations would occur in a city that had twice refused to endorse the constitution and that the celebrations would be controlled by Sir William Lyne, who had at both referendums campaigned for No. Lyne planned on a lavish scale. The celebrations would last more than a week. On 1 January there would be a grand procession through the city to Centennial Park on its outskirts, where the inauguration would occur.

Once the colony had voted Yes to the Bill, Lyne had declared that he would be loyal to the Commonwealth, although preserving his right to press immediately for the constitution to be amended in a democratic direction. He found it easier to be loyal to the Commonwealth once he had taken charge of its launching, a responsibility he did not seek to share.[8] For the moment Lyne and Sydney owned the Commonwealth.

Soon Melbourne would be home to the Commonwealth Parliament. The provision that it should meet there until a capital was provided in New South Wales aroused suspicions in Sydney. Would Melbourne ever give up its prize? So that there would be no delay in choosing a capital, Lyne appointed his own royal commission in November 1899 to inspect and make recommendations on sites.[9]

Lyne did not accept that the presence of the parliament made Melbourne the capital. He persuaded the premiers to agree that the Governor-General would have residences in both Melbourne and Sydney and would travel to the other capitals. He encouraged the present Governor of New South Wales to take leave so that Government House would be available for the Governor-General's use. Meanwhile the chief justice served as Lieutenant-Governor.[10]

If the Governor-General had to maintain two houses and entertain at both, the salary provided in the constitution would be inadequate. Chamberlain suggested that until the Federal Parliament provided an entertainment allowance, the parliaments of New South Wales and Victoria should do so. Lyne secured the agreement of his parliament. The Victorian Parliament refused.[11]

None of this did Lyne's reputation any damage in Sydney. Dogged and unexciting, he turned out to be an effective administrator and capable Premier. In alliance with the Labor Party he led a progressive, reforming government. It was nominally a protectionist government, but since the Commonwealth was shortly to assume responsibility for customs, Lyne did not disturb Reid's free-trade tariff, to the great relief of the Sydney merchants. When Lyne took office he assured Barton he had no interest in the prime ministership. Now he had changed his mind.[12]

Around Australia Barton was thought to be the only possible Prime Minister. Sydney did not share this view. Whatever his national reputation, Barton was known locally as a protectionist with very little administrative experience. Indeed his national reputation told against him. Reid's complaint had always been that he was sensitive to the needs and wishes of every colony except his own. In the Sydney papers the rival claims of the three candidates were debated with Reid and Lyne being strongly pushed.[13] If the test were service to the federal cause, Reid had as good a claim as Barton. If the test were administrative competence, Lyne was much better than Barton.

Reid was bitter about Barton's reputation as the pre-eminent federal leader. He felt that he had done much more of the real work for the cause, but he knew he could not win the prime ministership for himself by arguments about past service. Instead he backed Lyne for the job. This would bring him several benefits. First, Barton would be deprived of the honour. Second, since Lyne was a stronger protectionist than Barton, the fiscal issue, on which he wanted to fight the election, would be starker. Finally, Lyne would be easier to beat than Barton. His argument for Lyne was that the Governor-General could not possibly know and judge the intricacies of federal politics. He needed to act impartially, and the formula of commissioning the Premier of the senior colony allowed him to do so.[14]

Lyne undermining Barton with the new Governor-General; Reid (left) looks on, puzzled; the premiers of the other states behind.

It was certainly difficult for a Governor-General to know how to act before there were federal elections and a Federal Parliament. He needed ministers to put the federal machinery into operation, but no politician yet had any official standing in the federation. The man called on to solve this problem was John Adrian Louis Hope, seventh Earl of Hopetoun, appointed first Governor-General of the Commonwealth on 13 July 1900. The Colonial Office officials told him before he sailed that Barton seemed the natural choice but left him a free hand.

Hopetoun was typical of the new breed of governors chosen in the 1880s and 1890s when Britain was taking her colonies more seriously. Not career administrators but bright young men of the aristocracy, they brought a new style and flair to the office. Hopetoun had been in Australia before as Governor of Victoria from 1889 to 1895. Only 29 when he was appointed, he was a great success. He entertained lavishly, which pleased the Government House set, and his easy-going manners and generosity endeared him to ordinary people. That he should want to return to Australia was flattering to the country, and his appointment as Governor-General was genuinely welcomed.

On the voyage to Australia he caught typhoid fever in India and was still weak when he landed in Sydney on 15 December, only two weeks before the Commonwealth was to begin. Those who think he made a mistake in not choosing Barton as Prime Minister cite his illness in extenuation. Kingston wrote to Deakin that Hopetoun could scarcely acquaint himself with Australian sentiment when 'his whole time must have been occupied in attending to his bowels'.[15]

Hopetoun did not have to be in the pink to see the problem of appointing Barton: Reid was opposed to it. He had a long meeting with Reid at Government House on 18 December. The two men knew each other. Hopetoun was a friend of the Reid family in Scotland, and he and Reid had had lunch together in London at the time of the Queen's jubilee.[16] We do not know what Reid said to Hopetoun in support of Lyne. He could scarcely have failed to point out that he was a contender against Barton for the leadership of the Commonwealth and that His Excellency would be acting improperly in choosing between them. On the same day Hopetoun saw the Chief Justice of New South Wales, who probably also recommended Lyne. Reid's advice would have been more influential since he was not subject to a code of silence if it were ignored.[17] Barton studiously avoided calling at Government House.

The oddity—if not the risk—in choosing Lyne was that he had opposed the constitution he was being called on to inaugurate. Hopetoun did not know him in this oppositional mode. He knew him as the planner of the large-scale Commonwealth celebrations about to commence. Lyne was consulting him about the final details. For the Governor-General's arrival Lyne had put on a great show. A special pavilion had been built at Farm Cove, where Hopetoun landed. On the ceiling in gold were the names of four great federalists, all from New South Wales: Parkes, Barton, Reid—and Lyne.[18]

After much consideration, Hopetoun asked Lyne to form a government, but he put a special condition on him. Since the circumstances were so unusual, the Governor-General would not accept any ministry Lyne assembled. It must contain 'nothing but first class men from each of the

The landing pavilion built by Sir William Lyne in which he welcomed the Governor-General.

colonies, and that above all Victoria should have her proper share both in quality and quantity'. He was not so sick that he had forgotten the central rivalry of Australian life. If commissioning Lyne was a risk, this was the fail-safe mechanism. The commissioning itself reduced the risk. As Prime Minister-elect, looking for followers, Lyne announced he would not be pressing for amendments to the constitution, nor for a high tariff.[19]

The commissioning of Lyne has acquired the name 'the Hopetoun Blunder'. Generally this was not how it was described at the time. Hopetoun exaggerated only slightly when he reported to London that his decision was generally endorsed with only one paper, the Melbourne *Argus*, hostile.[20] The press and public men around the country were certainly surprised, but they were very reluctant to criticise the Governor-General and were eager to find excuses for his deed: that he was acting on orders from the Colonial Office or that choosing the Premier of the senior colony was a rule since it had been followed in Canada. (In fact Macdonald, when commissioned as Canada's first Prime Minister, had ceased to be Premier of the senior colony; he was appointed on the ground that he had led the federal delegation to England—which in Australia pointed to Barton.)

More positively it was recognised that the Governor-General had followed a constitutional course in being blind to rival claims in the federal sphere. The *Daily Telegraph* in Brisbane put Hopetoun's dilemma succinctly: the Prime Minister had to be from New South Wales; it couldn't be Barton because of Reid; it couldn't be Reid because of Barton; Lyne was the only person left.[21]

In Sydney the decision was accepted by all political parties: protectionist, free trade, and Labor. Reid issued a strong statement in support of the Governor-General. The Premier of the colony to be Prime Minister with the indulgence of the Leader of the Opposition: this was a hard act to criticise. Hopetoun's decision against Barton has been described as influenced too much by Sydney opinion, but Sydney was for the moment the capital, and the Governor-General must have been pleased at how well his decision was received in a city through whose streets he was shortly to ride in an open carriage.

'Blunder' was Deakin's word. 'Who could have believed that Hopetoun would make such a blunder,' he wrote in reply to Barton's news, which came as a telegram. 'It is Lyne. I have declined to join him.'[22] Deakin was sickened at this climax to the federal story. The Commonwealth to which he and Barton had devoted themselves was being passed over for implementation to an anti-federalist second-rater who had cut a pitiful figure at the Convention. He would have felt as bad if it had been handed over to Reid, that free-trade trickster. He had no sense of Hopetoun's constitutional difficulties. The Commonwealth should be in the hands of the true believers.

Deakin immediately resolved that he would in no circumstances join a Lyne cabinet. He would rather leave politics. He then set about securing undertakings from Turner and Kingston, the most senior protectionists in their colonies, that they would not serve. In Sydney O'Connor had joined Barton in refusing a post under Lyne. If all these refusals held, Lyne could not assemble a viable protectionist cabinet.

But Lyne was a convinced protectionist, and Victorian protectionists and the *Age* were desperate to protect Victorian industry in the new regime. From Turner and his circle and from the *Age* Deakin started to hear the case for cooperating with Lyne. He was in possession—a great windfall for protectionism; protectionists would have to support his government so better to do so from within than without; to hold out would divide protectionist ranks and make it easier for Reid and free trade to gain the ascendancy, which would mean ruin to Victoria.

Deakin wrote telling Barton of this pressure, angry at himself, hating the transfer of the pressure to his friend. Next morning the *Age* came out strongly in support of a Lyne protectionist government. Syme did not limit his argument to constitutional propriety: 'the Governor-General has a perfect right to assume that the protectionist party is the strongest at this moment in New South Wales and the sister states.'

Deakin felt the game was up. Turner would not be able to resist this pressure, and once Lyne had Turner, others would follow. At seven in the morning he wrote to Barton an agonising letter, a tumble of news and argument until he tied it down with numbers:

> Now to your position.
> 1. You object to Lyne as I do because he has been and is an Anti-Federalist. But Hopetoun has waived that—and we cannot persist in it to the public prejudice. That would be personal.
> 2. He treated you scandalously. That too is personal and must only affect personal relations. It cannot and must not govern public action.
> 3. He ought to give way. He ought, but you cannot get a silk purse out of a sow's ear. Personal again.
> 4. You cannot work with him. He would be in a Cabinet which would be yours and not his and every man in it zealous for your honour. His would be the painful position.
> 5. You can command your own terms. They ought to be leadership—but after today's 'Age' it would be wiser to join him even if he retains the nominal supremacy—you being joint head and controlling all the selection of colleagues. You would then have the reality of power and he the shadow. You would do your work as you planned it and your colleagues would permit no interference with it. What you would sacrifice would be just personal resentment and just personal claims. I do not think either the starting of the Union or the policy to be adopted in its first parliament ought to be lost to us even for these ... I think you ought to join ... Your own judgment and conscience must decide. Australia will suffer if you refuse to crucify yourself.
>
> Yours ever,
> Alfred Deakin

What a satisfying conclusion! Not merely sacrifice but a crucifixion! Deakin had always wanted a cause that would require martyrs, and now he had it. If Barton would make this sacrifice he would join him in it. They would serve under Lyne together. However, Barton had no intention of falling in with this scenario. He might talk of sacrifice, boasted about it sometimes, but he did not agonise as Deakin constantly did over personal desire and public duty. He was not looking for the grand gesture. He had a sense of what was due to him and what he should not be asked to bear; more an old-fashioned sense of a gentleman's honour. He simply would not serve under Lyne, although he was persuaded to agree that if Lyne gave up his attempt in his favour, he would include Lyne in his cabinet.

On the day Deakin sent his sacrifice letter he received by telegram Barton's response to his first letter outlining the case for joining Lyne: 'Will include him but not serve under him.' Next day at Syme's house Deakin turned from would-be martyr to political operator, a transition to which he was accustomed. Syme had summoned him because he had been commissioned by Lyne to put offers of cabinet posts to Deakin and Turner. Lyne hoped that offers from this source could not be refused.

For the second time in the federal story Deakin took Syme on. He declined Lyne's offer and managed to persuade Syme to tell Lyne that he (Syme) would only support a cabinet that contained Barton. Deakin was putting a condition on Lyne that he knew he could not achieve—'will include him but not serve under him'—unless Barton was persuaded by the sacrifice letter. The Syme–Lyne axis had been fractured.

Lyne lived up to his reputation for stubbornness. When he could not break through Barton and the ring of his supporters, he offered Syme the right to nominate any two Victorians to the cabinet in return for Syme's support. Syme replied that the cabinet had to include Turner. That was the end of this deal for Turner would not serve if Deakin wouldn't. Lyne offered Griffith a post with the right to the chief justiceship, but Griffith, realising that Lyne was finished, replied that he would talk about the matter in Sydney. On Christmas Eve at 10 p.m. Lyne resigned his commission and advised that Barton be sent for.

Barton chose a cabinet close to what he and Deakin had planned, except that the inclusion of Lyne meant that O'Connor became an honorary minister without salary. The others, when they remembered, paid O'Connor a portion of their salary. Dickson, not Griffith, was the Queensland minister. Barton, Kingston, and Deakin did not have to put up with him for long because he died on 10 January. The cabinet met for the first time on a launch in Sydney Harbour on 30 December, and the names were sent to the Governor-General that afternoon. They were sworn in at Centennial Park two days later.

The failure of Lyne, and Barton's rapid assembling of a strong ministry, suggests that the Governor-General had indeed blundered. But Barton taking office from a Governor-General acting on formal advice from Lyne was very different from his doing so by vice-regal fiat. Hopetoun would truly have blundered if he had appointed Barton and Reid had openly criticised him and gone to the election as the people's champion against the vice-regal nominee.[23]

In the inauguration day procession in Sydney Barton received some cheers, Reid many more, and the Governor-General the most. If the

Governor-General had chosen Barton first the response might well have been different: boos for Barton, cheers for Reid, and who knows what for the Governor-General?

The blunder was Reid's. The resolute refusals Lyne met amplified the message that Barton was the only true leader. Barton came to the office with a greatly enhanced prestige, not a vice-regal nominee but the man the Governor-General was obliged to accept. In supporting Lyne, Reid had not been unaware of the possibility that he might fail. In that case, he said, the Governor-General would have to turn from protectionism to free trade (and to him) because protectionism could not be given two chances of fastening itself on Australia.[24] That was whistling in the wind. He himself urged Lyne's appointment on the ground that he was Premier of the mother colony. The Governor-General did indeed give protectionists two chances but by following what he called the 'constitutional course' of allowing the Premier of the senior colony to be Prime Minister or advise him on who should be.[25]

Barton launched his election campaign soon after the celebrations were over, on 17 January. He had the advantage of incumbency without the disadvantage of a previous record. He had a full ministerial team and presented a wide-ranging policy. Reid had no shadow cabinet and was running solely on the tariff issue. Barton said the tariff was really a non-issue. Any government had to use the tariff to raise funds for the Commonwealth and to distribute the surplus to the states. Free trade was not an option. And in his eyes destruction of existing industries was not an option. So the policy was not protection but 'revenue without destruction'. Even Reid, Barton pointed out, had reneged on pure free trade when the abandonment of the sugar duties would have destroyed the north coast farmers in New South Wales. He himself was not going to celebrate Australian nationality 'to the tune of the pattering of the poor feet of people driven out of employment'.[26]

Reid had to concede that pure free trade was not an option, but he fought hard to keep the fiscal issue alive. If Barton did not want to make the tariff an issue, why had he chosen a cabinet of protectionists? Once protection in any form gained a hold on national life, it would be very difficult to tear it out.[27] His policy was to raise money by tariffs for revenue only. He did give new life to free trade as a possible national policy and found a new constituency for it among the farmers in the 'protectionist' states. With all his handicaps, he did extremely well. In the House of Representatives protectionists won thirty-two seats and free-traders twenty-seven; in the Senate Reid had a win: seventeen free-traders to eleven protectionists.

The Labor Party was the third force in the parliament, having secured sixteen places in the House and eight in the Senate. It could determine who should rule. Labor was divided on the fiscal issue on which it allowed its members a free vote. The Labor members supported Barton's government because he had included in his policy White Australia, industrial arbitration, and old age pensions, which featured prominently in their platform. This alliance between protectionists and the Labor Party provided the foundation legislation of the Commonwealth and lasted with one short interval until November 1908. Barton remained as Prime Minister until 1903 when he retired in Deakin's favour and went to the High Court.[28]

The Commonwealth was a much more active government than anyone had envisaged, not at all the inexpensive housekeeper envisaged in much of the debate over federation. The predictions about its operations had been made by reference to its powers. If the states kept control of such vital matters as public works, land development, education, and living conditions, indeed of everything not specifically granted to the Commonwealth, then the newcomer seemed destined for a limited role.

The actual operation of the Commonwealth was determined by the desires of those who ran it. In 1901 the leading politicians of the colonies and the major political groupings transferred their attention to the Commonwealth, and the progressive liberal agenda of the colonies became the Commonwealth agenda. Much of this agenda could not be directly pursued through the use of Commonwealth powers, so it was pursued indirectly or deviously. This was most apparent in the Labor Party, which had opposed the creation of the Commonwealth. When Labor entered its parliament it made no adjustment to its central concern, which was to improve the wages and conditions of the workers, a purpose that very few had envisaged for the Federal Government.

Even in what seemed like house-keeping matters, wages and conditions could be addressed. The Act establishing the Commonwealth civil service set a fair minimum working wage, the same for men and women. The Act establishing the post office prohibited mail steamers contracted to the Commonwealth from employing coloured labour, which was always paid lower wages than white.

The first substantial legislation passed by the new parliament was the Immigration Restriction Act, which enshrined the White Australia policy. There was almost no opposition to it. The government's battle was to obtain agreement to excluding people by dictation test rather than by racial categories, to which Chamberlain on behalf of the multiracial empire objected.

There was no pressing need for the legislation since the colonies had adequate defence against Asian immigration. The government's immediate purpose in giving it prominence was to win votes at the election and attract Labor support in parliament. But this policy more than any other had come to express the social ideals of those who had dreamt of a united Australia and hence was a fitting foundation for it. The 'inferior' races were to be excluded to preserve Australian society as pristine, harmonious, and progressive.

Much bolder action in pursuit of a white Australia was the government's decision to provide immediately for the gradual elimination of the kanakas in Queensland. Recruitment was to cease, and the remaining kanakas to be deported in 1906. Philp, the Queensland Premier, and the planters were furious—so this was their reward for supporting federa-

Barton defies the kanaka interest and cleans up Queensland. (*Bulletin*, 19 October 1901)

tion!—but the majority of the state's federal representatives supported the policy. Labor had done very well in Queensland's first federal elections.

Black labour had been an issue in Queensland politics for twenty years. Without federation the forces against it in Queensland would probably have prevailed, but only after a long struggle. The anger at the Commonwealth's decision shows that for all the recognition among the planters that the old system would eventually have to go, they did not want to yield when it came to the point. But they had no chance of countering the new instrument for the voice of Australia, the Commonwealth, which ensured a quick and decisive end to an economic and social system that flouted Australian ideals.

The Commonwealth was closely involved in the restructuring of the sugar industry. It kept out foreign competition by a tariff. It encouraged the transition to white labour by imposing an excise on locally grown sugar. The excise was to be remitted on sugar produced by white labour. Barton thought the use of the excise power for this purpose was unconstitutional. In 1903 the scheme was changed to the payment of a bounty to white-grown sugar, and from 1905 the bounty went only to those farmers who paid the going rate of wages, a matter in which a Commonwealth minister had to interest himself. When some of the kanakas protested at their deportation, the government allowed those who had strong attachments to Australia to remain, but they were no longer permitted to work in the sugar industry.

A harmonious Australia was also the aim of the Commonwealth's most distinctive legislation, the establishment of compulsory arbitration in industrial disputes. The large-scale bitter strikes of the 1890s mocked the poets' claim that Australia was free of old-world strife. Progressive liberals looked to arbitration as the means by which the state would force workers and their employers to resolve their disputes peacefully. Some of the colonies already had schemes. Kingston in South Australia in 1890 had been the first to propose legislation. As one of the chief advocates at the conventions of giving the Commonwealth power over interstate disputes, it was fitting that he draw up the Commonwealth law.

There were disputes about how far the Commonwealth Act should reach. Deakin actually introduced the legislation because Kingston had resigned when Barton's cabinet refused to include seamen. When the Labor Party carried an amendment to include railway workers employed by the states, the government dropped the Bill. When he was Prime Minister, Deakin reintroduced it. Labor again carried its amendment, whereupon Deakin and his government resigned. The experience of governing briefly on its own without a majority taught Labor that it was better off for the moment supporting Deakin and the protectionists. A short-lived government led by Reid finally passed the Arbitration Act with railway workers included. Then Deakin and Labor came together again. The High Court declared that the inclusion of state workers in Commonwealth arbitration was unconstitutional.

The High Court's policing did not prevent the unions from transforming the Commonwealth Arbitration court, which was meant to deal with interstate disputes, into a body for regulating wages and conditions for whole industries, nation-wide. The court's defining moment came when Justice Higgins had to declare what 'fair and reasonable' wages were. He said they must meet 'the normal needs of an average employee regarded as a human being in a civilised country', an Australian act of defiance against the dictates of the market and an assertion that the country was to remain a true new world.

The constitution of the Commonwealth was claimed with some justice as the most democratic in the world (so long as equal representation in the Senate is overlooked). However, the framers had stopped short of giving all women the vote. In 1902 the first parliament established a national franchise, and since the women of South Australia and Western Australia could not be deprived of their votes, the vote was given to all men and women. Barton had been an opponent of votes for women. He yielded to his colleagues on this matter, but insisted that women should not be eligible to sit in parliament. This part of his policy speech was cheered by an all-male audience, women having been excluded from the meeting.[29] But he yielded again to his colleagues, and women were allowed to be candidates. Vida Goldstein ran for the Senate in 1903.

The government intended that Aboriginal men and women, as British subjects, should qualify for the vote. Some members objected, especially those from Western Australia and Queensland, where there were many Aborigines and the state government had deprived them of the vote. Labor members were also worried that in the outback states employers would control the votes of the Aborigines. The government gave way. At a time when a white Australia was the national ideal, uniformity for Commonwealth elections was reached by levelling down rather than up. The Aborigines lost the vote as women gained it.[30]

The establishment of a democratic Commonwealth gave added force to the democratic cause in the states. This process began in 1895–96 when the colonial parliaments agreed that at the elections for the Convention and at the referendum, the principle of one man, one vote should apply. That put the advocates of plural voting on the defensive, just as the advocates of a male electorate were undermined by the introduction of votes for women

Australia as world leader in granting women's suffrage: a banner used in suffrage demonstrations in England.

at the Commonwealth level. Both practices quickly disappeared from the states. Western Australia was the last to abolish plural voting in 1907, and Victoria the last to introduce votes for women in 1908.[31]

However, Kingston's hope that a democratic Commonwealth would be a completely transforming force was not realised. In the states the legislative councils elected by property-holders remained. Kingston had used the weapon of the referendum against the South Australian chamber. On the same day in 1899 when the electors voted on the Commonwealth Bill, they supported the introduction of household suffrage for the Council. The Council was unmoved. Kingston vowed he would not leave South Australia for Commonwealth politics until he had reformed it. In 1900 Holder, his successor, introduced a Bill for a democratically elected convention to rewrite the state's constitution. The new constitution would come into force without having to be returned to parliament for the Council's approval. There was no hope of the Council passing the Convention Bill, and Holder abandoned the attempt. The Assembly resolved to free Kingston from his pledge.[32] Property-holding as a qualification for voting did not disappear in South Australia until 1974.

The longest debate in the first Commonwealth Parliament was over the tariff, which was contested closely item by item, with Kingston the minister in charge. The Labor members were free of their caucus control, and the effect of their votes was sometimes to help the government protect industries and sometimes to help the free-traders protect consumers. Reid made great play of the government taxing bushmen's tents and the mangles used by poor washerwomen.[33] In the Senate the free-traders proper and the Labor free-traders constituted a majority. The tariff ended up less protective and less likely to raise revenue than the government had planned.

Neither New South Wales nor Victoria would have agreed to this compromise tariff if it had been proposed as the tariff of a customs union. But as Parkes had planned, the nation was formed first and the customs union second, with the authority of the nation being used to resolve the intractable customs dispute. On the day the new tariff was introduced into the Commonwealth Parliament, Tuesday, 8 October 1901, late in the afternoon, interstate free trade was established.[34]

The tariff became decidedly protectionist only in 1908 in Deakin's second government when he was ruling again with Labor support. Deakin persuaded all the Labor men to support protection by insisting that industries receiving protection must pay fair and reasonable wages. Deakin's 'new protection', as it was called, was a stroke of genius. It secured Labor support for protection and disarmed Reid's criticism of protection as benefiting only employers.

The device used to link protection and wages was the Commonwealth power to levy excise. Manufactured goods protected by tariff were to be liable to an excise of the same amount. The excise would be remitted to those manufacturers who paid fair and reasonable wages. The High Court upset the scheme by ruling that the excise power could not be perverted into a power over wages. Undeterred, Deakin and the Labor Party committed themselves to finding a constitutional defence for new protection. This never eventuated, but the rulings of the Commonwealth Arbitration Court and the equivalent state bodies did protect wages in manufacturing without the explicit connection between tariffs and wages. Labor's support for protection held, and protection became a settled national policy.

Although given limited powers in the constitution, the Commonwealth's acquisition of customs duties made it wealthy at the states' expense. How to deal with this surplus had been a central dilemma at the conventions. The states seemed to have acquired a satisfactory solution with the requirement that the Commonwealth distribute no less than three-quarters of its customs revenue to the states, but when Reid objected to the so-called Braddon blot its operation was limited to ten years. Deakin was one of the first to realise how the states would be placed after ten years. In 1902 he wrote that they would be 'legally free, but financially bound to the chariot wheels of the central Government'.[35] Even before the ten years were up, Deakin found a way to short-change the states. To finance old age pensions, he channelled part of the Commonwealth's surplus into a special trust fund and so made it unavailable for distribution to the states. The High Court upheld him.

The High Court plainly played a key role in the Commonwealth's affairs. It came into operation in 1903. Deakin as Attorney-General had asked Griffith to draft the legislation that was to establish it. He was full of praise for his work, but suggested that the clauses dealing with salaries and pensions be put at the end to make them as 'fire-proof' as possible.[36] The parliamentarians still noticed them. The number of judges was cut from five to three and the pensions abolished. Even without the pension, Griffith agreed to be Chief Justice, once Deakin had responded to his concerns over travel allowance and precedence ('the Chief Justice comes next after Prime Minister and Privy Councillors'). There were objections to Griffith in the cabinet, probably on the grounds that no state judge should be put on the federal court, and that he had played a devious part over Privy Council appeals when the constitution was in London. Deakin had to threaten resignation before cabinet accepted him.

With the reduction in the number of judges, Deakin could not offer a place to the Tasmanian Andrew Clark, whose draft Griffith had worked from in 1891. About Clark's qualifications there was no doubt. Deakin had earlier sounded him out and found he was interested; he was very bitter about being passed over. The other two places went to O'Connor, who had led for the government in the Senate, and to whom Barton was committed, and to Barton himself. The Prime Minister was briefly tempted to claim the chief justiceship, but he had always acknowledged that Griffith was his superior in law. Still, not all former prime ministers would be happy to take second place. Barton now had the security of a large salary and much less demanding work. He was worried about whether it would be possible to make Griffith laugh.

The first High Court as depicted by Low: (from left) Barton, Griffith, O'Connor.

As Prime Minister, Barton is not known for any particular achievement; he was continuously successful in keeping together a cabinet of heavyweights, all of whom had more ministerial experience than he had, and for giving a judicious and honourable face to the new government. A Commonwealth Government was bound to create resentments in the states as their territory was invaded; an active Commonwealth Government needed to provide all the reassurance that Barton could supply.[37]

The High Court, composed of three men who had worked so closely on writing the constitution, was committed to preserving its federal principle. That is, the Commonwealth and the states must be supreme in their spheres and not interfere with each other. Hence their ruling that the Commonwealth Arbitration Court could not set wages and conditions for railway workers employed by the states. The principle worked both ways. The court's first major constitutional decision was that the Tasmanian Government could not make a post office worker pay a tax on his salary because the salary came from the Commonwealth.

In 1906 the parliament agreed that the High Court should be increased to five judges. Deakin made very different appointments this time: Henry Higgins (who was also to head the Arbitration Court) and Isaac Isaacs. Both men had been at the 1897–98 Convention where they were best known as critics of the work of the founding fathers. They had wanted a strong national government instead of a cautious federalism. For a long time the two new judges were usually in a minority on the court. The Commonwealth's attempt to link tariff and wages was rejected three votes to two.

The politics of the early Commonwealth were complicated because there were three parties, and after the second election in 1903 they were of roughly equal strength. Deakin likened it to playing cricket with three elevens in the field. He said that somehow the three had to be reduced to two. An understanding between Labor and his protectionists was his preferred solution. He found it easy to work with the Labor leadership in parliament, although he was alarmed by the Labor machine outside.

As it became obvious that protection could not be undone, Reid and his following changed from being free-traders to a party warning about the dangers of an expanding state. This was directed at Labor and its ally, Deakin. Reid himself had worked with Labor in New South Wales and had expanded the role of the state but, accepting the logic of the political situation, he turned himself into a crusader against socialism.

Forrest and some others of Deakin's following were worried about Labor's growing strength. They urged Deakin to break his alliance with them and create a grand anti-Labor coalition. That is what the Labor machine wanted. It was suspicious of alliances and was working for the day when Labor would govern alone. Deakin could never work with Reid nor adopt the view that the state was a dangerous force. Although aware of the threat from Labor, he would cooperate with them while he could do useful work. At the third election in 1906 he campaigned against both anti-socialism and the Labor Party, had his following reduced to the smallest of the three groupings—and yet continued to rule.

His following was now composed chiefly of Victorians, a number of them like himself members or former members of the Australian Natives Association. It was from Deakin and this group that the early Commonwealth received its firmest impress. They wanted to develop a strong manufacturing sector and pride in local production and skill; to have the state ensure decent living conditions for all; and to see Australia shrugging off colonial status and becoming a self-reliant nation in the empire. Their views on the economy remained settled policy until the 1970s when the message preached by George Reid found an audience again.

Deakin did not dare face the 1910 election alone. He finally agreed to join the erstwhile free-traders, although he did not have to join Reid because he was to be the Commonwealth's first High Commissioner in London. Deakin became the leader of this new grouping, which called itself the Liberal Party, and for one parliamentary term was Prime Minister with its support. Labor denounced him for his treachery in deserting them, but they were going through the motions. William Lyne, who had been an effective minister under both Barton and Deakin, did genuinely feel that Deakin had betrayed him. When Deakin first addressed the House in his new position Lyne yelled from his corner: 'Judas! Judas! Judas!' He might have been so angry because with the fusion of the parties he had lost his chance to succeed Deakin as leader of the protectionists and perhaps become Prime Minister.[38]

Labor won the 1910 election with majorities in both Houses. The foundation years had passed. The Commonwealth was now controlled by a party that had opposed its formation. Labor's own success belied its claim that the Commonwealth was to be an undemocratic arena controlled by conservatives and reactionaries. It already knew that, as far as its purposes were concerned, the fault in the Commonwealth was not what Labor had claimed in the 1890s but its limited powers over wages, working conditions, and the economy. In 1911 it put to the people an amendment proposal to give the Commonwealth power in these areas. Deakin made his last great political effort in the No campaign. The amendment was comfortably defeated with only one state, Western Australia, voting Yes.

A few months before this campaign Deakin heard a voice speaking to him early one morning: 'Finish your job and turn in.' Before he went to breakfast he had filled seven pages analysing the source of this message and what it meant. He agonised over it for two weeks. He decided that the message was his higher self addressing his lower self and that the 'job' must be to protect the federation by defeating Labor's amendment proposals. But when they were defeated the instruction to quit did not return. He stayed on as Liberal leader, conscious that his great mental powers were slipping rapidly away. He now needed notes when he spoke and had to follow them closely. He hid his decline so well that he had trouble persuading his party in January 1913 that he must resign. Before he was 60 his mind had gone.[39]

In 1913 Labor brought forward its amendments again. They did much better: a close defeat nationally and success in three states: Queensland, South Australia, and Western Australia. The party never came so close again to creating the sort of constitution it wanted. Nearly all its proposals (and those of others) to expand Commonwealth power have been defeated.

Commonwealth power has expanded but chiefly by the High Court's interpretation of the constitution. The court's foundation years lasted until Griffith's retirement in 1919 and Barton's death the following year. In 1920 it was composed of Isaacs and Higgins and three judges appointed by a Labor man, Billy Hughes. It considered again whether the Arbitration Court could deal with employees of a state instrumentality. It overturned the doctrine of the founding judges and decided that the engineers employed in a state sawmill in Western Australia could be covered by a federal award.

Isaacs wrote the leading judgment in the *Engineers* case, which declared that the full meaning had to be given to the powers conferred on the Commonwealth without concern for the imagined principles of a federal constitution. If the engineers were involved in an interstate dispute, they could go to the Commonwealth court even if they were employees of a state. To give a literal interpretation of the document appears sensible and cautious; in fact it has subverted the intentions of the founders.

Section 96 read literally is lethal for the states. Inserted at the last minute to reassure states worried about their finances, it allows the Commonwealth to make grants to the states on any terms and conditions. In 1926 the court held that the Commonwealth can make grants and stipulate how they will be spent in areas reserved by the constitution to the states, such as roads, education, and health. This power has grown as the Commonwealth became supreme in revenue-gathering. The court helped that process in 1942 by allowing the Commonwealth to make grants to the states out of its income tax on condition that the states abandon their right to tax income.

In 1983 the Commonwealth's power over external affairs was interpreted in the same literal way. If the power covers all external affairs, then as the objects of international concern expand, the Commonwealth's powers expand. It can control state affairs on any matter on which it has signed an international treaty.

There is a strange mismatch between a people refusing to vote extra powers to the Commonwealth and acquiescing in the expansion of the Commonwealth powers at the hands of judges. It parallels the mismatch between a group of communities closely integrated socially and economically creating a weak national government.

Since the colonies had no pressing need to federate and the process of union was open and consensual, existing interests and attachments had to be accommodated rather than overridden. There was no need to override them since the uniformities and bonds of nationhood already existed. A weak central government immediately expanded its power by devious means, which was quietly accepted because social uniformity existed to support central direction and control. In the first decade of the Commonwealth one of its agencies controlled the routine of workplaces across the continent. There were and are still interests and attachments hostile to central power, and these are mobilised to defeat any formal moves to increase it. These defeats are not followed by a retreat of central power but by its expansion by new back-door means. The machinery of the state governments does not contract; rather it is penetrated and duplicated by the Commonwealth.

The result is an ever-more complicated system of government for a remarkably uniform society. This is the paradox of the sentimental nation.

15
Forgetting

Now Mudgee planned to celebrate the Federal Jubilee
But the only thought most people had was to do it with a spree.
Yes—fun and games appealed to them as having most relation
To the objects of the gala—the birthday of a nation.

G.H.B., Mudgee, 1951[1]

At the time of its inauguration the Commonwealth had its myth: 'Ours is not the federation of fear, but the wise, solemn rational federation of a free people.' These words appeared in one of the guidebooks to the celebrations, which also explained why the latest nation should be proud of its achievement of uniting without coercion from within or without: 'Such a federation as ours has only become possible through the advance of intelligence and the development of a higher system of morality than the world ever saw before.'[2]

This was a foundation myth with more truth to it than most. It was widely known and accepted. It appeared in the commemorative supplements in the newspapers as well as in the history by Quick and Garran, in the guidebooks as well as the formal speeches. The *Advertiser* in Adelaide adapted President Lincoln's words and put the myth in the form of an epigram: 'The Commonwealth has come from the people by the people to the people.'[3]

The myth died—and with it all knowledge of federation. All the people, events, and places that federalists declared would be historic never became so. The names of the convention delegates, the electoral battles of Barton against Reid, the landing place of the first Governor-General and the site of his swearing-in, the name of the first Prime Minister—all are forgotten. Parkes alone, to the great annoyance of the historians, is remembered.

The process of forgetting federation can be traced in the celebrations of its success.

The dove of peace as symbol of the new nation: a suggested design.

Sydney, January 1901

William Lyne, the Premier of New South Wales, had two thoughts that guided him in preparing the celebrations in Sydney: first, that the most exciting thing about the new nation was its membership of the British Empire; and second, that the whole community should be involved and have a good time. He did not think that the celebrations should honour those who had created the nation. If such a thought had occurred to him, he would quickly have suppressed it since he would then have had to exclude himself. At both referendums he had advocated a No vote. But that fact does not explain his approach. His preferences were widely shared and were evident in other celebrations, large and small, around the nation. All Australia admired the show he put on in Sydney.

When new regimes are established by force or against determined resistance, their ceremonies are both instructive and coercive: 'This is what is to prevail and you'd better believe it.' Anyone who does not participate runs the risk of being branded—depending on the regime—a traitor, an aristocrat, a bourgeois, or an enemy of the people. The Australian federation was established by the democratic vote of its people. By the discipline of democracy, its opponents accepted this decision since they could not quarrel with the will of the majority. The Commonwealth ceremonies did not have to justify the Commonwealth. The desire that everyone be included meant that the history of its making had to be overlooked, particularly in Sydney, where the city had been almost evenly divided on the issue.

The procession on 1 January included civic, educational, and religious leaders and representatives of the leading community organisations, the friendly societies, and the trade unions. These were brought together according to a well-tried formula. Among them were supporters and opponents of federation. The leader of the No campaign paraded as the Chancellor of the University of Sydney in his robes of office. The foot soldiers of that campaign appeared as trade unionists marching behind the Eight Hours banner.

Those who had been devoted to the federal ideal had to honour themselves privately. The Federation League prepared a commemorative certificate, which it distributed to its supporters and campaign workers.[4] A plan to write a history of the federal movement was abandoned because it would reopen divisions. The secretary, Edward Dowling, put together a book of documents—all the annual reports of the League—and lodged copies in libraries.[5] Later his carefully preserved letters and papers went to the Commonwealth Parliamentary Library, the forerunner of the National Library.

Only one federalist received anything like public homage: Sir Henry Parkes, who was conveniently dead. His image and his federal slogans appeared in the decorations and on the memorabilia. The procession passed under a banner that declared him to be the father of federation.

Parkes gets his reward; further down Bridge Street is one of his slogans, 'One Destiny'.

This pre-eminent position was willingly given to Parkes by the federalists, including Barton and Reid, who some historians think had the right to challenge it. Barton in particular was punctilious in acknowledging Parkes when the federal movement scored its successes.[6] The New South Wales Parliament provided special funds for the rehabilitation of Parkes's grave and for honouring it on 1 January.[7] Parkes as father of federation was a myth of a different sort, the heroic individual. Parkes himself had opposed the moves to include the people as electors of Convention delegates and judges of the constitution.

Lyne was personally in charge of the celebrations, but they took shape in a very open way. The government appointed individual citizens and representatives of organisations to take charge of different aspects of the celebrations—procession, music, theatre, athletics, cycling, regatta, and so on—and they in turn appointed one delegate to the Organising Committee, which had oversight of the whole. This committee was a huge body and was often bypassed in decision-making, but more attention was given to democratic symbolism in the organisation of the celebrations than in the messages they conveyed.[8]

Outside this official structure, there was a citizens committee appointed by a public meeting at the Town Hall. Initially worried that the mayor and council were being overlooked, it took charge of the decorations, entertainment of visitors, and gifts to the poor, raising its own funds to do so. This committee managed to do what was thought impossible in a British community: get all the property-holders in a street to decorate their buildings harmoniously.[9]

The arches, which were a feature of the decorations on the procession route, had diverse origins. The government paid for some. The citizens committee designed and paid for the Commonwealth or Citizens Arch. Those associated with the coal, wool, and wheat trades put up the arches celebrating these products with some government assistance. The ethnic communities put up their arches, assisted by their consuls.[10] The presence of German, French, and American arches and an Italian float in the procession might seem odd in what was a very British celebration, but it was the boast of Britons that they gave equal protection of their laws to foreigners, and a celebration that sought community involvement welcomed their participation. At Kalgoorlie the chief float in the procession was a Japanese warship. In Melbourne in May the most suspect group of foreigners, the Chinese, were allowed to erect an arch and hold a Chinese procession.[11]

The Commonwealth or Citizens Arch was the only place where there was a public display of the history of the federation movement. This was an arch in the classical style similar to the triumphal arches of Rome, which

The Citizens' or Commonwealth Arch with history scenes, federal slogans, busts of federalists, and (within the arch) names of Convention delegates.

Napoleon had copied in the Arc de Triomphe in Paris. On its two faces, paintings, bas-reliefs, and medallions depicted the grand story of the dawn of civilisation in Australia, the rise of commerce, and the development of government. This was the context for federation, which was represented by the names of the delegates to the 1891 and 1897 conventions (on the inside of the arch), scenes of the first Convention and of the first Federal Parliament, epigrams from leading federalists, and busts of Parkes, Barton, Reid—and Lyne.[12]

Lyne's inclusive approach to the celebrations was fully exploited by the churches. If their desire to turn the inauguration into a religious ceremony had been put to the Convention or any of the colonial parliaments, it would have been rejected. But for the moment policy for the Commonwealth was determined by Lyne's response to those who trooped into his office. He agreed that the Anglican primate, who had the support of the other Protestant churches, would offer prayers. Choirs would sing 'O God our help in ages past' before the inauguration and afterwards the Te Deum, a Federal Anthem, the Hallelujah chorus, and 'God Save the Queen'.

Patrick Moran, the Catholic Cardinal, then claimed the right to offer his own prayer and to take precedence in the procession over the Anglican primate. When Lyne refused these requests, Moran declared that he could not participate. Some of the other Protestant leaders were upset about where they were placed in the procession. Disputatious churchmen were in and out of the Premier's office until 10 p.m. on 31 December. Next morning the Cardinal, surrounded by clergy and a choir of school children, watched the procession from the steps of his cathedral.[13] The episode made it perfectly clear why politicians usually chose to keep the churches at arm's length.

Lyne was not alone in thinking of the procession as an imitation of the Queen's jubilee procession, but he was responsible for securing the key element to make it so. He asked Chamberlain to send a thousand British and Indian troops from a number of regiments. Chamberlain was keen on the idea, but the Chancellor of the Exchequer baulked at the cost. He said it was one thing to bring together representatives of all the military forces of the empire at the capital of the empire for the Queen's jubilee; it was quite another to do so at Sydney. Chamberlain persuaded him by promising that no troops would be sent with the Duke of York when he went to open the first Federal Parliament in Melbourne.[14]

To the imperial troops were added troops from all the federating colonies, some of them veterans of the Boer War. The troops followed the civilian participants, and behind the troops came the Governor-General. This strong military element was unusual in local public processions. But it was not such a big step to regard the demonstration of the military might of the empire at the jubilee as a proper model for the celebration of a nation within that empire, especially when Australian troops were fighting for the empire in South Africa. That it was completely at odds with the peaceful theme in the story of Australian union went unremarked.

The imperial troops were the stars of the procession. Only the Governor-General attracted more cheers. They looked magnificent in their brightly

Imperial splendour: the Life Guards having just passed through the German Arch.

coloured uniforms: the Queen's Own Hussars in tall busbies, the Imperial Life Guards in shining breastplates, the Indians in their turbans. There never was such a gay parade up Oxford Street until the Mardi Gras. These troops had a glorious and lengthy history. The newspapers gave full accounts of each regiment represented and the battles they had fought. A doggerel epic on the celebrations caught the significance of their presence: 'The Flower of British Valour thus we see,/Are come to grace our opening pageantry,/And vouch our Commonwealth of high degree.'[15]

Some Labor members objected to the militarism of the celebrations, not because they wanted to celebrate the peaceful union of the colonies, but because militarism was always evil. Lyne brushed them off.[16] Securing the imperial troops was a great personal coup for him. However, the support of Labor members was crucial to Lyne's survival, which allowed them to have some influence over the parade. Billy Hughes suggested to Lyne that, in addition to the usual trades, the trade union section should include working men from the outback. Lyne agreed, and Hughes organised the appearance of mounted shearers from the Australian Workers Union who, as he said, symbolised the real Australia.[17] They did not arouse much interest. There were grumblings that the whole trade union section was too long. People were anxious to see the troops.[18]

Even without the troops, the celebrations would have had a strong imperial flavour. Federation under the Crown was not a mere formality. The signing of the constitution into law by the Queen, the issue by the Queen of the proclamation announcing when it would come into force, the appointment by her of the first Governor-General, his Australian landfall, and his assumption of office—all these were regarded as important events that gave imperial force and authority to the union.

The Queen gave her approval to the constitution at Windsor. She did not actually sign the Constitution Bill; she gave written authority to three members of the House of Lords—Hopetoun was one of them—to sign the Bill in the Lords on her behalf. Barton asked the Queen whether she would allow him to take to Australia the desk on which this document lay when she signed it and the inkstand and pen with which she performed the deed. For months previously he had been proclaiming the doctrine of the sovereignty of the Australian people to save the constitution from amendment. However, when it came to memorials, Barton thought not of the people but of royal approval.

The Queen agreed to his request, and Barton assured her the objects would be treasured possessions in Australia. He cabled the good news to the premiers. There was great interest in Australia. The Australian press in London received permission to see and photograph the relics before they left. In Sydney Barton sent them to the Art Gallery where they were put on display. The table was used for the signing of the official documents at the inauguration. Today, table, pen, and inkwell are displayed, to the puzzlement of visitors, in Parliament House, Canberra.[19]

The Queen's proclamation setting the date for union was also a sacred object. It was reproduced in the federation supplements of some of the newspapers, and a parchment copy was given to every school child in New South Wales.[20] Quick and Garran, having dedicated their book to the People of Australia, included a facsimile of the proclamation as a frontispiece. Holder, the Premier of South Australia, thought the date of the Queen's proclamation could be the day on which Australians celebrated federation.[21]

In himself the first Governor-General signified the union of Australia and its connection to the Queen. By late December 1900 Hopetoun had become a cult figure in Sydney. His photo was on programs, guidebooks, menus, and official invitations. His colours of blue and gold were used to decorate streets and the tails of dogs; they were interwoven as laces on boots and corsets; they could be eaten as cake icing and ice-creams.[22] A man totally unconnected with the federation movement was the person most often represented as its success was celebrated. Hopetoun saw the anomaly himself. When his carriage passed near the Town Hall on 1 January a man in the crowd called for

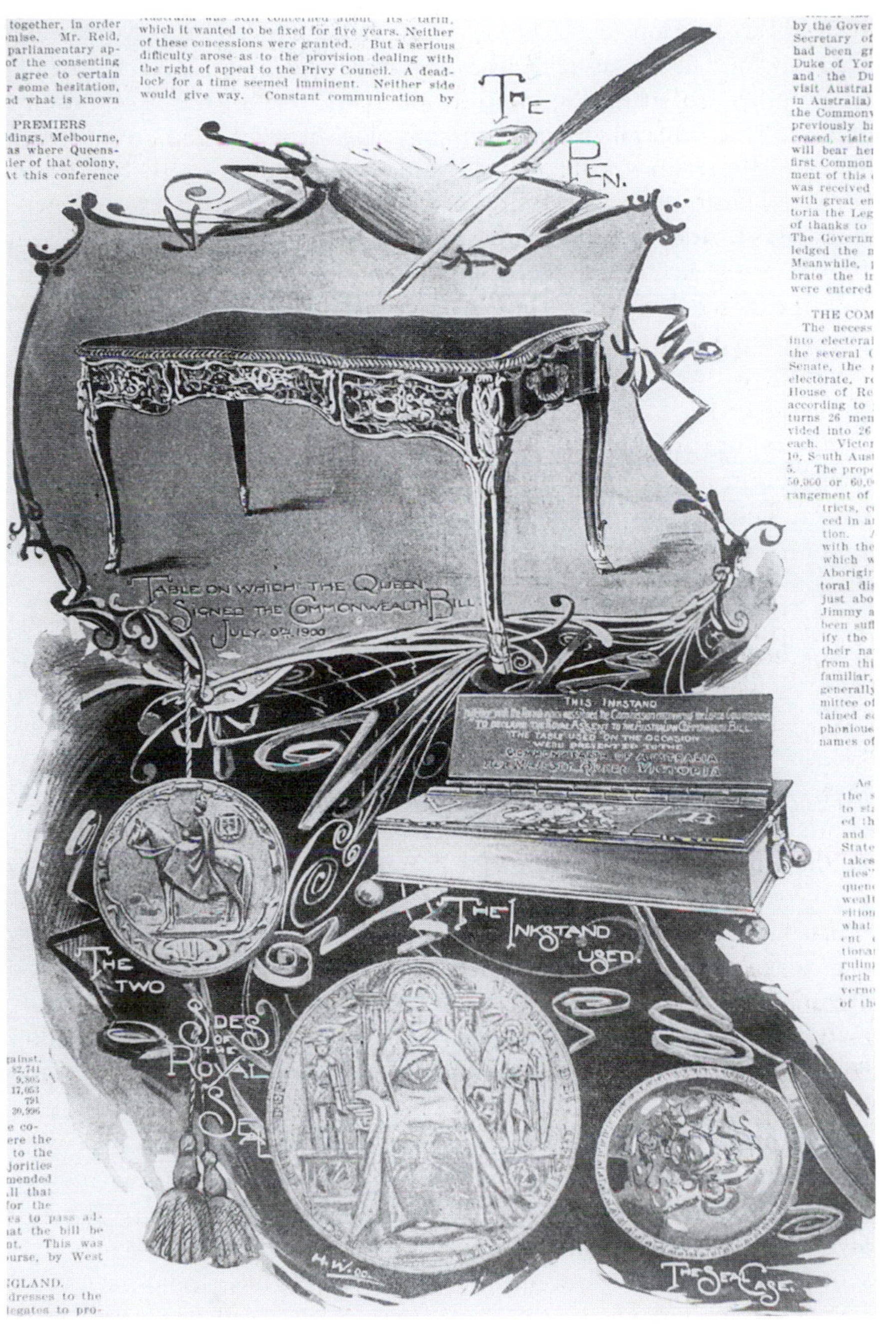

The royal relics of nation-making: the table, pen, inkstand, and seal used by the Queen to authorise assent to the Commonwealth Bill (*Town and Country Journal*, 5 January 1901).

three cheers for Hopetoun. The Governor-General called back: 'Not for me, old man, but one for Australia.' The crowd then did cheer for Australia.[23]

No other vice-regal person has been treated in this way. The circumstances were unusual: it was the beginning of a new era, and until 1 January Hopetoun was the only official of the Commonwealth. But he was playing a customary role. Governors of the colonies were powerful symbolic figures; they had official duties as agents of the Colonial Office, but they also represented the monarch by playing the social and ceremonial role of a monarch. Their periods of office were akin to reigns. They arrived and departed with great ceremony with crowds gathering in the streets to cheer them.[24] On the arrival of a new governor, every church, organisation, and association presented a formal address of welcome attesting their loyalty to him and the Queen. At Government House a governor was the centre of an imitation court society. Colonial democracy was carried on within these monarchical forms. The new Commonwealth, boasting that its authority came from the people, was continuing them. Hopetoun had been receiving loyal addresses at Government House.

The leaders of the new democracy were prepared to conform to the usages of court society in what they wore on formal occasions. The correct dress for a minister of the Crown was the Windsor uniform of close-fitting silk breeches, silk stockings, and jacket with gold buttons and braid. On 1 January Forrest, Dickson, and Kingston wore the Windsor uniform for their swearing-in. Barton, Deakin, Lyne, and Turner wore morning dress.[25] In Melbourne, when the Duke of York was present, Barton and Turner donned the Windsor uniform. Deakin was less conspicuous in trousers.[26]

The swearing-in of the Governor-General, not of his ministers, was the official event that would inaugurate the Commonwealth. There had been a great debate as to where this event should take place. Everyone was agreed on a procession, but where should it deliver its principals? The early favourites were historic or civic locations: at Dawes Point where Phillip had his flag pole; at Circular Quay, the cradle of the colony; or at Queen's Square, which took its name from a statue of Queen Victoria. The square was an open space at the south end of Macquarie Street framed by St James Church and the old Convict Barracks, both the work of Greenway, Macquarie's convict architect. Being close to Parliament House, it was a favourite meeting place for protesters.

Lyne was worried about all these locations. Stands would have to be built, but they would have no hope of accommodating all who would want to see the event. Stands were also an expense and potentially dangerous. Lyne took up the suggestion that the event be staged at Centennial Park on the edge of the city so that everyone who wanted could see it. Within the

Crowd swallowed by the park: the inauguration taking place, 1 January 1901.

park there was a natural amphitheatre, which could accommodate a hundred thousand people or more. Here Lyne departed from his model. At the jubilee the thanksgiving service had been held in St Paul's churchyard with stands for invited guests.[27]

It was not so much an amphitheatre as a broad stretch of level ground with low rises on either side. In the middle of the level ground was erected the portable, temporary, plaster pavilion in which the ceremony was to take place. Whatever the event's chances of becoming historic, there was no hope for the building. On the level ground surrounding the pavilion were chairs for the VIPs. The people would gather on the slopes.

Well over a hundred thousand people did come, perhaps two hundred thousand.[28] The pavilion was open-sided so they could see at least something, that human figures were moving. But they could not hear. The citizens were sightseers; many treated it as a picnic to which was added a distant sight of a nation being born. They had a better chance of hearing the choirs of children and adults. The choirs were large, but there was a stiff breeze blowing so not everyone would have heard them.[29]

Reports differ on how closely the crowd followed the events in the pavilion. Some say that the people close by cheered at the right moments and

The press get the best view: their enclosure is immediately to the left of the pavilion; the stand for the movie camera is to the right.

that the cheers were taken up around the park. For the key moment when the Governor-General had taken the oath there was the prompt of guns firing and the flag being unfurled on top of the pavilion. But of this moment the *Bulletin* said: 'Suddenly guns boomed, grey smoke rolled in clouds across the park, there was a meagre cheer, and Australia was born.' This comment came from a not unsympathetic reporter, the writer of the Women's Column. She summed up the effect of Lyne's well-intentioned choice of location: 'Bands played. Voices sang. But the great park swallowed it all up, and left an impression of vastness which the pageantry and thronging thousands only intensified.'[30]

John Norton's *Truth* gave a scurrilous account of the proceedings. Under the headlines 'Triumph of Tinsel Tawdriness' and 'Listless Apathy', it declared that there was not a single spontaneous cheer at the park. The crowd was 'curious, orderly, apathetic'. The school children cheered when ordered. The pressmen cheered to encourage others to do so, which, if true, would not be the last time they staged an event before reporting on it.[31] It is well to be reminded of their presence. They had the best seats, closer to the pavilion than anyone else. The Governor-General came to the opening of the pavilion facing their enclosure to read the telegram from the Queen.[32] If they heard, their readers, who were much more numerous than the crowd in the park, would hear. They used the unhearing crowd to make the event significant to the readers of newspapers: 'It was a sight of a century; it was a sight worthy of an epoch.'[33] And when the readers looked at the photos in the illustrated supplements the crowd was spectacle.

The papers could reproduce all that was said in the pavilion. Most of them did not bother. The great majority of the words shouted into the vastness of the park came from official documents: the Proclamation, the Letters Patent of the Governor-General, the Commission of the Governor-General—great dollops of imperial legalese.

In the evening there was a banquet at the Town Hall. This was a well-established civic event in the usual location. It was an occasion for speech-making. Parkes had produced his most memorable speeches at banquets, the 'crimson thread of kinship' at Melbourne and 'One People, One Destiny' in Sydney. Here, before the leading men of all the Commowealth's states, there was the opportunity to proclaim the significance of the day. It had been a long day, and too many of the guests became drunk. They refused to listen to the speeches. They went on talking to each other and calling the waiters to fill their glasses so that the speakers could not make themselves heard. The great hubbub continued when Griffith gave the toast of the evening to the Commonwealth. The chairman twice pleaded for silence. Barton pleaded for silence. All to no avail. When Barton spoke

Queensland Aborigines brought to Sydney for the inauguration (above) and performing as resisters to Cook's landing (below).

in reply he berated the diners for refusing to listen to such a distinguished man and made no attempt at a great oratorical performance himself.[34]

Meanwhile the first cycling races were being held at the Sydney Cricket Ground. The rest of the week was given over to sports and entertainments and a military review. There was one historical re-enactment: of the landing of Captain Cook at Botany Bay. The great navigator had not wandered off course in becoming part of the federation celebrations. His landfall was seen as the first stage in the story of progress, as federation was the most recent. His landing was the foundation scene on the Citizens Arch. It was also a feature of the decorations at No. 2 Fire Station, George Street.[35]

The Aborigines who performed at Botany Bay were shipped down from Queensland. They played their part well, advancing down the slope to menace Cook and his party, looking, according to the *Herald*'s report, 'exceedingly weird and barbaric'. After the landing there was a tableau with speaking parts for Cook, Banks, and Solander, Tupia (a native of Tahiti), and Australia (a nymph) and walk-on parts for Sailors, Marines, and Aborigines. At the luncheon for invited guests the Minister of Native Affairs from New Zealand struck a discordant note when he expressed the hope that some day the Aborigines would be treated as well as the Maoris.[36]

Before, during, and after the celebrations there was much discussion about a permanent memorial. Among scores of suggestions for columns, monuments, statues, and useful institutions, one made an attempt to capture the myth of the nation's democratic origins. This was a plan for a seven-sided obelisk showing the numbers who voted Yes and No in the six states and for Australia overall.[37] Planning advanced furthest to rebuild the Commonwealth Arch in stone with a stronger federation theme: a history of the movement and portraits of twenty leading members of the Convention—an attempt at individual heroes rather than an honouring of the people.[38]

The most grandiose proposal was for a huge statue of 'Australia Facing the Dawn' with explorers depicted around the base. It was to be placed on an island in the harbour and be Australia's equivalent to the Statue of Liberty. This was the brainchild of E.W. O'Sullivan, the Minister of Works in Lyne's government. Because of his penchant for borrowing, the *Bulletin* dubbed him Owe Sullivan. To ensure that the cost of this project would be shared, he took leading men from other states to the site during the celebrations and received an endorsement from them.[39] Cost was an issue. The New South Wales Government had hugely overspent the budgeted allocation for the celebrations. A federal monument should be a federal responsibility, and surely, opined the *Sydney Morning Herald*, there would be no provincial jealousies at its being located in Sydney![40] None of these plans came to anything. The chair in which Hopetoun rested during the ceremony in the pavilion was preserved and is now in the Mitchell Library. The memorials that were built honoured the soldiers of the Boer War.

There was in 1901 a very new medium for capturing and recording events: film. With official support from Lyne, the Salvation Army, the only production house in the country, filmed the procession and the ceremony at the park. They shot from five locations, a much bigger operation than anything yet attempted. Every camera in Sydney and several from Melbourne were requisitioned. The film was developed at the Salvation Army headquarters in Melbourne and premiered in Sydney on 19 January at a J.C. Williamson pantomime. Running for an exceptionally long thirty minutes, it was extremely popular and in Melbourne was the first film to be shown in two theatres simultaneously. Banjo Paterson acquired distribution rights for Queensland and showed it in conjunction with his lectures on the Boer War.[41] To preserve the film for posterity, a negative and positive print were placed in tin boxes and their lids soldered on. This trapped the gases that destroy early film.[42]

Since federation was a peaceful process the premiers of the six colonies had the opportunity to determine when exactly the historic moment of union would occur. They made this decision in mid 1900 with the pattern of public holidays very much in mind.

The formalities had yet to be completed in Britain, and the election that was to follow the inauguration had to fall at a suitable time of the year. This pointed to January as a convenient month in which there were already two public holidays, New Year's Day and Foundation Day on the 26th. The majority of the premiers chose the 1st, which had the attraction for a new nation of being the first day of a new century.

McLean of Victoria, lobbied by the Australian Natives, pushed for the 26th. The Natives had been responsible for making the 26th a national holiday, and they better than anyone else knew the difficulties of persuading all Australia to take seriously the anniversary of a convict settlement in Sydney. There had been an earlier attempt to give the 26th more significance when the writs for the election of the 1897 Convention were issued on that date.

Holder of South Australia wanted to avoid existing holidays, especially summer holidays, when everyone would be too busy with sport and recreation to take any notice of the anniversary of federation. The Commonwealth should have its own day for 'the cultivation and expression of a national Australian sentiment'. He failed to budge his colleagues. Forrest thought there were quite enough foundation holidays already: Western Australia honoured Australia on the 26th and itself on 1 June. He offered a rather confused argument in reply to Holder: '1 January would do very well as it is always a day of sport and enjoyment which would be always associated with the inauguration of Federation.'[43] There was never any confusion about the honouring of the day. The term 'Commonwealth Day' was used for it only once—in 1901; thereafter it was New Year's Day on which sport scored highly and federation not at all.

The new holiday in the calendar, although only a half holiday for children, was Empire Day. It was held on 24 May, Queen Victoria's birthday, and was first honoured around the empire in 1905. The state schools, but not the Catholic, took it very seriously. Before children went off to their sport and recreation, they were well drilled in the splendour of the empire and its high moral purpose. No one thought it necessary to teach them about the creation of the Commonwealth. Australian history of any sort could be only a subsidiary theme to the history and present drama of the empire.[44]

Melbourne, May 1901

Melbourne was different. It had always been keen on federation and voted for it almost unanimously. It was the headquarters of the Australian Natives Association, which had believed in federation most passionately. But Melbourne in May 1901 went wild over a duke and duchess. For months the preoccupation of the town was with the royal visit, during which one of the events was to be the opening of the first Federal Parliament.

The premiers in 1897 and the federal delegates in 1900 had had informal talks with Chamberlain over the royal and vice-regal possibilities for the Commonwealth. There was no possibility of a royal Governor-General. A royal to open the parliament was a possibility, but the Queen was not keen. The heir to the throne was an old man, and he now had only one son, the Duke of York. The Queen finally agreed that her grandson could go, but not on an extensive visit. The colonies had been pressing for him, but Chamberlain arranged for the visit to come as a 'spontaneous' gesture from the Queen.[45] Who knows whether the Melbourne *Argus* was deceived or was itself deceiving when it wrote, 'It was Queen Victoria's thought that her grandson should open parliament.'[46]

Then the Queen died only a few weeks after the Commonwealth began, and it seemed that the royal visit would be cancelled. The new King, Edward VII, was very definitely opposed to his son going. Lord Salisbury, the Prime Minister, tried to change his mind and failed. Arthur Balfour, Salisbury's nephew and leader of his government in the House of Commons, then penned a letter that did persuade the King. The announcement that the visit would take place contained a double deception: the King wanted the visit because the Queen had wanted it.

Balfour's letter to the King read:

> Surely it is in the highest interests of the State that he should visually, and so to speak corporeally, associate his family with the final act which brings the new community into being; so that in the eyes of all who see it the chief actor in the ceremony, its central figure, should be the King's heir, and that in the history of this great event the Monarchy of Britain and the Commonwealth of Australia should be inseparably united.[47]

Balfour's reputation as philosopher–statesman is well deserved. This is exactly what happened. The *Bulletin* saw it happening and wished it were otherwise:

> Among the ceremonies which attended the union of a continent and the beginning of a nation there moved a thin, undersized man who has never done anything save be born, and grow up, and get married, and exist by breathing regularly, and be the son of his father who did the same things. And in the public eye he was, apparently, about three-fourths of the pageant. The men who made the Commonwealth were eclipsed for the time by the man who made nothing of any importance.[48]

A few days before the Duke and Duchess of York arrived a memorial to Victorians who had voted at the 1899 referendum was unveiled in a small ceremony at Parliament House. The memorial is to all who voted, since with a secret ballot the identity of those who voted Yes could not be discovered. In Victoria it mattered little since the Yes vote was 94 per cent.

The funds for the memorial came, indirectly, from BHP. In its first year the company's books had been kept by William Knox. It was a part-time job for which he was paid £75 a year. In 1888 he was offered a full-time job at the princely salary of £1500 a year and became in effect the chief executive of the company. At the first Commonwealth elections he was returned to the House of Representatives. He paid for the whole cost of the memorial, but its dedication reads:

In recognition of the noble work accomplished by
The Australian Natives Association
and
The Municipal Association of Victoria
in promoting the federation of the Australian colonies

Knox was a member of both organisations. As president of the shire of Malvern, an outer Melbourne suburb, he had convened a federation conference of Victorian local government bodies in August 1894 and an Australia-wide conference in November.

His memorial is a noble failure. He chose to express popular involvement by having all the voters' names recorded, but it was hard for anyone then to think of a public monument carrying thousands of names of ordinary people. Instead he had the names inscribed by hand in ten massive volumes, running alphabetically from 'Aanenson, Bernt, 102 Dow Street, Port Melbourne, Labourer', to 'Zwicker, Leo, Downshire Road, Elsternwick, Importer'. Two extra blank volumes were provided for the signatures of the voters.

The memorial to Victorians who voted at the 1899 referendum, Parliament House, Melbourne.

The memorial has the appearance of a multivolumed encyclopedia. To consult it you stand at a waist-high sloping desk, open the glass doors of a book case above it, and with two hands remove one of the volumes. The desk and book case, a single unit, was provided by Knox; it is beautifully made in polished blackwood.

It is certainly an interactive memorial, but it is not immediately arresting and it is not public. Only one citizen at a time can consult it or discover its purpose. As a set of books, readily damaged, it was housed in the library of Parliament House. At its unveiling this Parliament House was the nation's; in 1927 it reverted to being Victoria's. The memorial is now located in the lobby of the Legislative Council, an area not traversed by tour parties. It serves a historical purpose rather different from what Knox intended. In the form of microfilm, it is much consulted elsewhere by those tracing their family history.[49]

There are only a few pages of signatures in volume 11. The board of directors of the Australian Natives Association signed together. They might have done so when they gathered a few days after the unveiling to welcome office-holders of their association from other states who had come for the opening of the parliament. There were a few speeches and toasts. Quick said that in generations to come their work for Australia and the empire would be regarded with pride and envy. For the present it was enough to secure seats at the opening, but no special place in the ceremonies.[50]

The Duke and Duchess of York had the briefest of encounters with the history of federation. At a very crowded reception at Parliament House they moved quickly from Queen's Hall to the garden. As they passed through the library, Quick presented the Duke with a handsomely bound copy of Quick and Garran. The Duke was heard to say that its preparation must have involved an immense amount of labour.[51] While they were in the library, the Duke, the Duchess, and Lord and Lady Hopetoun signed the flyleaf of the volume that was to carry the signatures of those who voted at the referendum.

The ceremonial opening of the parliament took place in the Exhibition Building, which consists of three wings that meet under a central dome; it is designed to hold exhibits rather than an audience. Before the Commonwealth was inaugurated, the Victorian Government chose this site and for the same reason as Lyne chose Centennial Park: it wanted to accommodate the maximum number of people.[52] The result was the same as in the park: a large crowd who could hear nothing and for whom the principals were no more than 'tiny marionettes'.

The disappointed reporter on this occasion was W.H. Fitchett, who could never be thought to be unsympathetic; he was the author of the bestseller *Deeds that Won the Empire,* headmaster of Methodist Ladies College and editor of the reputable monthly, *Review of Reviews*. For him this deed lacked cohesion and dramatic power. A great building shaped like an amphitheatre or an opera house would have been preferable; as it was half the audience was invisible to the other half.

At the beginning of the ceremony there was an awkward pause while the members of the House of Representatives were summoned. True to parliamentary tradition, the Exhibition Building was cast as the upper house, the only one to which the royal power had access. The Representatives had met in an annex, the new home of the Victorian Parliament. They came eventually not in an orderly procession but 'in a sort of disintegrated crowd'. The master of ceremonies here, as in the Sydney pavilion, was Edwin Blackmore, clerk of the South Australian Parliament and of the Convention. He was renowned for the power of his voice, but it 'scarcely caused a vibration' where Fitchett was sitting. The Governor-General's voice carried better. He read the prayer to avoid the trouble that had occurred in Sydney. At the end of the prayer Fitchett thought the audience could have recited the Lord's Prayer. What an effect if 12,000 people had been so joined together! But the opportunity was missed.[53]

Those who could hear heard the Proclamation summoning parliament, prayers, the King's Commission to the Duke for the Opening of Parliament, the Duke's speech opening the parliament, a telegram from the King, and the members swearing allegiance to the King. In his speech the Duke conveyed the King's earnest prayer that the new union would still further promote 'the welfare and advancement of his subjects in Australia, and the strengthening and consolidation of his empire'.

Fitchett conceded that the gathering on the dais was impressive: royalty, the state governors, judges, naval and military officers. It excited a man who had a strong visual sense, the artist Tom Roberts. Amid the pressure for seats, he had wangled a ticket—he painted portraits of society ladies as well as bush scenes. He could not find a seat, or not one that was worth having, and so he climbed up on some rails in the eastern gallery to get a good view. It was only two weeks later that he was commissioned to paint what he saw. He then painted from memory and photographs an impressionistic sketch of the sort that had surprised and outraged the Melbourne art world a decade earlier. The final work would have to be very different. The leading figures on the dais and the parliamentarians in front of them had to be recognisable; for each of these he was to get an extra guinea to add to the fee of 1,000 guineas.

The painting took two years to complete. Roberts treated it very seriously. He had all the VIPs sit for him, and he measured and weighed them,

Tom Roberts at work on what he called 'the Big Picture', taking care to make all the notables recognisable.

except Forrest, who refused to get on to the scales. Roberts' painter friend, Arthur Streeton, thought he was taking it too seriously, and some critics have seen the painting as a diversion from his true work. But Roberts was always interested in capturing the life of the nation. With the scene in the Exhibition Building, he was continuing the work he had done in shearing sheds. Shearing stood for the economic and social life of the people. At the Exhibition there was royalty, the governors of the states, the members of parliament representing democracy, and the people. 'That's the Empire and they all meet under one roof. And that's what I'm painting.'[54]

The commission came from a private company that enjoyed official support. It would make money by selling prints. The original was to be presented to the Commonwealth. When the Commonwealth received the painting, it gave it to the King. Its present owner is the Queen, who lends it to the Commonwealth. It hangs in an unsuitable location in Parliament House.

The Queen's table came from Windsor Castle. Roberts' painting went to Buckingham Palace. Australia understood itself in relation to the empire, and it sought registration of its deeds from the heart of the empire. It is hard sometimes to detect the nation in the empire. It was there: in the desire to possess full self-government and the status of nationhood, to be white and socially progressive, to be more self-reliant within the empire rather than being absorbed into it—and to have Australian symbols.

In 1901 the government held a competition for the design of an Australian flag. Five people shared the prize for the flag we have today. There was no stipulation that the Union Jack be part of the design, but it was almost self-evident that it should be. Most entries used the Union Jack and the Southern Cross. The flag was not to fly alone; it could be flown with the official national flag, which was the Union Jack. Five days after the opening of parliament the Duchess returned to the Exhibition Building to push a button that sent a telegraphic signal to schools around the nation so that simultaneously they raised the Union Jack.[55]

Canberra

The national capital in a memorial to federation in a double sense. It had to come into existence because neither Sydney nor Melbourne was happy with a union in which its rival became the capital. It is also the place where the Commonwealth can express itself.

While Sydney was discussing memorials to federation in January 1901 arguments over the site of the capital city were in full swing. In Melbourne in May 1901 a congress of engineers, architects, and surveyors was debating what form the capital should take.[56] A forward-looking nation would make its own best memorial in its capital city. Town planning then was a socially progressive art: its disciples believed that the blights of city living could be removed by proper planning and that a new form of society could be created in the City Beautiful.

In 1901 people thought that the capital would be taking shape in a few years time. The argument over the site lasted for nine years. Walter Burley Griffin won the competition for the city's design in 1912. The minister in charge then had his department cannibalise his and other entries to produce a cheaper plan. With a change of government in 1913, the Griffin plan was reinstated and the designer put in charge of it.

Like other entrants in the competition, Griffin assumed the national capital would be a place for monuments. On Kurrajong Hill he planned not the parliament house but a Capitol, a monumental building to be 'the sentimental and spiritual head' of the nation. This was his rather vague response to the suggestion in the brief that there be a 'state house' with a large hall for ceremonial occasions and a home for the national archives. The Capitol was the anchor for Griffin's land axis, which would run in a broad avenue down the hill across the water axis (the lake) and up to the foot of Mount Ainslie. On the land axis below the Capitol would be parliament house. At the other end of the axis would be what he called a casino, a place for restaurants and entertainment. Behind would be 'a formal semi-circle of commemorative structures' with paths leading up Mount Ainslie.[57]

The first structure built on the land axis was the base of the Commencement Column, which was located just down the hill from the proposed Capitol. It was in place when Lady Denman, the wife of the Governor-General, named Canberra on 12 March 1913. The Column was never built; it was to have represented the states, the Commonwealth, and the empire. Well down the hill on the land axis the temporary Parliament House was opened on 9 May 1927 by another Duke of York, second son of the man who had opened the parliament in Melbourne, who was now George V. At the foot of Mount Ainslie in 1941 the city's first and still largest memorial was opened—a memorial to war. Cabinet had agreed to the design in 1928, and Griffin, no longer in charge of the project, had endorsed it as a suitable monument to close his land axis. The building of the memorial was so long delayed because of the Depression.[58]

The design brief for this monument required that all the names of the dead should appear. They are listed by fighting unit in alphabetical order with no indication of rank. The dead of the 1914–18 war were honoured democratically, and the war gave the nation an ordinary soldier as hero, the digger. War rather than politics produced the convincing democratic symbol. It had also, without planning as to location and date, given it a truly historic site and moment. Anzac Day, 25 April, marked the landing of Australian soldiers on a Turkish beach. Griffin's land axis as it leads up to the War Memorial is called Anzac Parade.

The common understanding became that the nation was born at Gallipoli. The political union of the colonies on 1 January 1901, even with the addition of the Boer War dead, had not been enough for nationhood. The attraction of death in battle as the test of national worthiness had been clear enough in 1901, and it seemed that satisfactory assurances had been given of the fighting prowess of Australians. However, fighting in World War I offered something more. The empire and hence Australia were in dire peril; the necessary sacrifices were much larger, terrifyingly large; Australians were fighting as a group rather than being distributed among British units, and in their first engagement at Gallipoli they won universal admiration.[59] Through their involvement in this war Australians became sure of their national status, but since the sacrifices had been made in defence of the empire, the ambiguities of a nation within an empire had been deepened rather than resolved.

The fourth structure on Griffin's land axis was a statue of a British monarch, George V, commissioned on his death in 1936 but not unveiled

A French architect's design for a Federation Monument in the national capital, something for which Australians have felt no need (part of Alfred Agache's entry to the competition for the planning of Canberra).

until 1953. It was placed in the centre of the lawn in front of the temporary Parliament House. Since this King as Duke of York had opened the first federal parliament, the base of his statue was thought to be an appropriate place to honour federation with a series of small portrait medallions: Parkes and Griffith for the 1891 Convention; the Duke and Duchess for the opening of the parliament; Barton as first Prime Minister. The elected Convention of 1897–98 is omitted, and there is no mention of the referendums. The statue is now located at the edge of the lawn.

The new permanent Parliament House was built not on Griffin's site but on top of the hill, or rather underneath it. Queen Elizabeth opened it in 1988. Within are Queen Victoria's table, Roberts' painting, and a good visual account of the history of federation on a huddle of display boards.

The founding fathers of federation are honoured in the names of Canberra's garden suburbs. This might make them memorable to Canberra's own residents; in the areas visited by citizen–tourists there are no monuments to them or to the people who voted for the constitution they wrote.[60]

Jubilee 1951

The Chifley Labor Government, which lost office in December 1949, had started planning for the celebrations of the fiftieth anniversary of federation. Menzies, the new Prime Minister, took a personal interest in them, but he flew out of Australia to London just as they began. He was attending a meeting of Commonwealth prime minsters to discuss the grave international situation. While the prime ministers conferred, the forces of the United Nations were retreating before the communists in Korea. It looked then as if the Cold War would soon be another, more terrifying world war. In planning for it, Australia was working closely with Britain. Australia's job in the event of war would be to defend the Middle East and keep its oil flowing to the West.[61]

Since its foundation the Labor Party had been suspicious of British imperialism. It had split over conscription for an imperial war in 1916. The short-lived Scullin Labor Government had appointed the first Australian-born Governor-General, Isaac Isaacs, in 1930. In the Second World War Curtin, the Labor leader, had looked to America to save Australia 'free of any pangs as to our traditional links or kinship with the United Kingdom'. But before the war was over Curtin was concerned at the rise of American power in the Pacific and was very keen to have Britain as counterweight. There was more hope of exercising influence over the British. He defied party policy and appointed the Duke of Gloucester as Governor-General.[62] Curtin's successor, Chifley, worked closely with Britain on economic and foreign policy and in doing so was dealing with a Labour government. Labor's support for the traditional link with Britain had never been stronger. It had no quarrel with Menzies going to London.

The jubilee celebrations began with a message from the King, which was played over loudspeakers to revellers on New Year's eve and printed in full next morning on the front pages of newspapers. His Majesty thanked Australians for giving men, money, and material for the causes of the motherland and told them that the whole British people took pride in their progress. The only reference to federation was to his father's opening the first parliament. As was proper for an independent nation, all this was written for him in Australia, including the personal touches about his fond memories of his own visit to open Parliament House in Canberra.[63]

Although the major parties differed over the nationalisation of the banks and the banning of the Communist Party, they were united in believing that on this anniversary Australia should celebrate its 'progress in the arts, learning, science, industrial development, agricultural expansion, as well as all types of sport'.[64] The most elaborate ceremonials of the year were the 'pageants of progress' through city streets, in which companies and public institutions displayed on floats their activities, past, present, and future.[65] So a float of oranges could find a place in the jubilee. Celebrating the achievement of federation barely rated in these festivities. In 1901 federation was cast as part of the story of progress; by 1951 it was only that, and the details of its accomplishment had almost totally disappeared.[66]

There was no social or institutional memory of these events; there was only personal or local memory. The Murray Valley remembered the Corowa conference. The Murray Valley Development League applied for funding to meet in Corowa on 31 July and 1 August, the dates of the conference that endorsed the scheme for a popular approach to federation. The application went to the national office of the jubilee organisation, which referred it to the New South Wales office, which referred it to its country section. Clearly no one dealing with this case had a clue about Corowa. By the time the League organised some political pressure, all the funds had been allocated.[67]

When Menzies was in London he received a letter from the cameraman who shot the film at the pavilion in Centennial Park fifty years before. He still remembered his skill or luck in getting a good shot of Hopetoun kissing the Bible. He suggested to Menzies that if the films could be found they would add interest to the current celebrations. A search for the forgotten 'historic' film then began, and 300 feet was discovered in the New South Wales Premier's Department.[68] The set of reels in their soldered tin box would have decomposed. Fortunately so many copies were made that an almost complete version has now been assembled.

Robert Garran, who was 26 when Barton recruited him for the Federation League, was still alive. He had retired as the Commonwealth's Solicitor-General in 1932. He was the major source of what little history of

The terrestrial globe on this float, sponsored by members of the Oil Industry of N.S.W., is surrounded by various forms of transport emphasising the importance of **OIL** in our daily life. The tank waggon and rail tank car at the rear are two means of transporting petroleum products, while on the skirts of the float are depicted scenes from transport, industry and agriculture all of which are dependent upon oil for their power and lubrication and efficient operation.

SUNSHINE is an appropriate theme for this float, sponsored by the Retail Traders' Association of New South Wales. It portrays the Commonwealth's progress over its first 50 years, expressed in the fashion evolution of the swimsuit—from the brave toe-dipping days of 1901 to the athletic sungathering of 1951.

Federation means progress: two floats in Sydney's 1951 jubilee procession.

federation was presented during the jubilee. He lectured in Canberra and on the ABC.[69] He had written the section on federation for the *Cambridge History of the British Empire* in 1933. This book was more readily available than his first history written with Quick and lodged in their legal text. But the organisers of these festivities were interested in him, not his history writing. For history, they had their simple tale of progress.

Even Menzies had no interest in the history of federation, although he was a constitutional lawyer who made his name winning the *Engineers* case. When he spoke to the state and federal officials involved in the jubilee he did not make a single reference to the event they were celebrating.[70] He was not keen about the civic component in Labor's plans: medals and books for school children and Australian flags for schools. He immediately lost the medal he had received in 1901, and he made an unsuccessful attempt to scrap medals this time round. The medal that was produced made no mention of federation.[71]

The book, *Commonwealth of Australia Jubilee 1901–1951*, had a good account of the constitution but dealt with the history of federation after 1889 in one paragraph without mentioning the elected Convention of 1897.[72] The distribution of flags did lead to the Australian flag becoming the official flag in place of the Union Jack.[73]

Menzies' conception of the jubilee was that the people, whatever their tastes or interests, should have some memorable experience. There should

The medal issued to school children in the 1951 jubilee makes no reference to federation.

be a good orchestra for music lovers, a distinguished judge to lecture to the lawyers, and carnivals for sport-lovers. The staging of some of these experiences involved 'bringing out' first-class performers. This was the one point of tension in the celebrations. Local performers and those who wanted to encourage them thought the cultural activities should be more Australian.[74] Labor had planned jubilee prizes for Australian literature, drama, and music.[75] These went ahead. There was no requirement that they have a civic or federation theme. To be Australian was sufficient honouring of a national festival when British cultural hegemony had not been broken. A new general history of Australia was commissioned; it was a good book written by several scholars, but it did not appear until 1955.[76]

Menzies' preferences are nicely revealed by his notations on a list of jubilee proposals. Besides 'Collection of biographies of prime ministers' he wrote: 'This leaves me cold.' Beside 'Re-enactment of Sturt's Murray trip' he wrote: 'I like this.'[77] He had a sure touch, for the journey of Sturt and his boat, which passed through three states and lasted for weeks, was the most popular event of the jubilee.[78] There was also much re-enacting of the deeds of explorers and pioneers in local communities. Suggestions for how to stage these were circulated: begin with the Aborigines in camp; if there are no Aborigines, begin with the pioneers.[79]

An interest in the federal story itself came from the Catholics. Always uneasy with the British cast of public ceremony, they regularly made heroic efforts to show that Irish Catholics had played an honourable part in Australia's history. On this occasion the Catholic Truth Society produced a booklet called *Catholics and the Commonwealth*, which gave a comprehensive account of the federal movement so that the role of individual Catholics could be highlighted.[80] At Mudgee the Catholic priest, Arthur Maher, wrote and produced the only federation play known to me. It is a terribly stilted drama. The narrator, who was relied on heavily, announced that its theme was the 'perseverance of the little people who forced those in high places to cease arguing and to trust the Australian democracy'.[81] This play was the only attempt in the whole jubilee to work the democratic myth. Maher gave strong roles to the Catholics involved in the Bathurst People's Convention and to Cardinal Moran, who had spoken there.

The Catholics were talking only to themselves. The nation found its strength without needing to celebrate its democratic origins. It was sustained by the belief in its progress, by the deeds of pioneers, explorers, and diggers, by the prowess of its sportsmen, and by its membership in difficult times of the empire that now had to be called the Commonwealth. It celebrated all these things in 1951 rather than the event whose jubilee it was.

In 1951 a profound change in the composition of Australia's population had begun. Non-British immigrants were arriving from Europe. The need to assimilate these 'new Australians' was one of the priorities of the jubilee.[82] If the nation had been celebrating the story of federation, it would have found it hard to give, say, the Poles a place. But a nation still developing and wanting everyone to participate in its festivals had no trouble. Members of Adelaide's Polish community, not three years after their arrival, marched in the city's pageant of progress, knowing no less about federation than the other participants.

The Polish community has a place in the 'pageant of progress', celebrating federation in Adelaide 1951.

The constitution was an object of attention at the jubilee and in the years before it, not to the people at large, but to state politicians and administrators, progressive academics, and defenders of freedom and free enterprise.[83] Their minds were focused by Labor's attempts in government to secure much wider powers for the Commonwealth. The High Court had upheld its uniform taxation legislation, which forced the states to abandon their income taxes, but it had ruled invalid Labor's nationalisation of the banks. At referendums the people had rejected sweeping new economic and social powers for the Commonwealth but had given it power over social security.

The spokesmen for the states insisted that they must regain their financial independence if Australia was to be a true federation. Menzies had promised to look into the matter. The supporters of free enterprise defended a federal constitution as a protection against Labor tyranny. The progressive academics took Labor's view that the federal constitution was a barrier to social reform and an artificial imposition on a unified country. Labor, not having been involved in making the constitution, always looked on it as a contrivance of the capitalist class. It was the party committed to the cultivation of an Australian sentiment but not to reverence for its constitution.

The views of the progressive academics were not without consequence. When interest in Australian history burgeoned in the 1950s and 1960s, they set the tone for the treatment of federation. Finlay Crisp, a political scientist who had worked for Chifley, wrote an influential textbook, which claimed that the founding fathers were 'men of property' defending the status quo.[84] He spent his retirement compiling a book entitled *Federation Fathers*, which honoured those who had opposed federation. His heroes were those who wanted a stronger and more democratic Commonwealth. It was he who, when compiling his useful bibliography of federation, decided to omit all references to federation poetry.

Bicentennial 1988

In 1988 there was no agreement on what multicultural Australia should celebrate. It was no longer a British society, and it had lost faith in progress. The organisers of the bicentennial festivities began with the theme 'Living Together'. Malcolm Fraser's Liberal Government made them change it to 'the Australian Achievement'. Bob Hawke's Labor Government reverted to 'Living Together'. The anniversary was of the arrival of the First Fleet, but the organisers refused to support the re-enactment of its voyage since it would offend Aborigines.[85]

As part of its honouring of the anniversary, the New South Wales Government decided to build a monument on the site of the inauguration of the Commonwealth in Centennial Park. It was not, of course, a special anniversary of federation, but it was a well-established tradition of Australian celebration that on a historical occasion any history would do.

The site of the inauguration was marked. In 1904 the stone on which the Governor-General had stood when he took the oath was set into the ground with the legend: 'On January 1st 1901 the Right Hon. the Earl of Hopetoun was sworn in as first Governor-General of the Australian Commonwealth on this hexagonal stone in the presence of the representatives of the six states.' Rising from the stone was a small six-sided plinth with the names of the six states and the date of their formation.

The Federation pavilion as designed (above) and built (below).

The government held a limited competition for a monument that was to incorporate this mini memorial. The winning entry by Alexander Tzannes was for a classical domed pavilion suggestive of the original plaster fantasy. It went though several revisions. In response to the criticism that it looked like a temple of doom, it was made lighter and more elegant. But revision continued, and that was not the version which was built. The steps leading up to the pavilion were removed so that the pillars sit directly on the ground, and the dome was replaced by a curved copper covering, akin to a flying saucer. A low encircling wall to mark off the monument was removed as it was considered likely to interfere with picnicking and cricket.

Originally the names of the states and the words 'The Continent of Light' (which federalists would have liked) appeared on the pediment. In the reworking of the design the architect consulted the doyen of Australian historians, Manning Clark, about inscriptions. Clark had no sympathy for federation, which appears in his *History of Australia* as a bourgeois plot. He suggested some words from a poem by Bernard O'Dowd who, as editor of the Labor paper *Tocsin*, had strenuously opposed federation. O'Dowd's 'Australia' is a good poem, not referring directly to federation, but asking whether Australia is to be a 'millennial Eden' or 'a new demesne for Mammon to infest'. The inscription became simply 'Mammon or Millennial Eden'. The letters are broadly spaced, running right around the monument, so that only a jogger with a good memory could take them in. There is no acknowledgment or explanation of the words.[86]

The domed ceiling within was decorated by Imants Tillers, a notable post-modern artist. The architect thought the federal stone was ugly and wanted to draw attention upwards. The theme of Tillers' decoration was the settlement of Australia, on which he had pronounced views. Geoffrey Blainey has called the highlighting of the dark side of Australian history the 'black armband' view. Tillers was in full mourning; he thought of genocidal Australia as 'the island of the dead'.[87] He also saw it as a deeply provincial society, taking its culture second-hand from elsewhere. This he illustrated by making the central figure in his decoration a copy of a work by the German painter Georg Baselitz, not a copy of the original, as he was at pains to stress, but a copy of a reproduction, which is how provincials get to see the great world. This huge, shambling, tortured, male figure appears amid a pattern of shapes and symbols taken from Aboriginal art. Across the torso of the figure are three labels bearing the words Faith, Hope, and Charity.

Tillers explained that the figure could stand for a pioneer, a rural worker, an explorer, an immigrant, or even a convict.[88] But not a federalist! His decoration has nothing to do with federation. A defender of his work wrote, 'That the new monument to Federation should express the themes

An unlikely federalist: the figure in Imants Tillers' decoration of the interior of the federation pavilion.

of pain, death and resurrection is appropriate. The settlement of Australia was a violent, bloody experience for Aboriginal and white men alike.'[89]

In 1901 and 1951 federation had been connected to the story of the exploration, settlement, and progress of the country. Now the connection had proved fatal. A peaceful, democratic movement was associated with violence and dispossession.

The monument was opened on 1 January 1988 by the Prime Minister and the Governor-General in the face of Aboriginal protest. The Aborigines had reason to protest at federation since the constitution said they were not to be counted in the census and the new Commonwealth deprived them of the vote. But in the bicentennial year the issue was invasion and land-taking. The Aborigines yelled as they stormed the dais: 'We are a sovereign people.'[90]

The monument shelters the tiny memorial within, but nowhere in its words and images does it speak of federation. The addition of the monument detracts from the minimalist message of the memorial by enveloping it in a great puzzle. What sort of nation is it that makes this the monument to its democratic foundations? When it is torn down, we will know that the story of federation has begun to matter.

16
Legacies

Australia is one of the few countries in the world where voting is compulsory and where citizens must be consulted on changes to the constitution. The founders of our nation expected that citizens would take an active interest in public affairs.

Constitutional Centenary Foundation 1991

Australia is governed by a constitution written in the 1890s. The constitution is not well known to the people; only half the people know that Australia has a written constitution.[1] The people nevertheless decide whether it is to be altered. Constitutional amendments are proposed by the parliament and then put to the people at referendum.

Griffith thought that the people could not cope with the complexities of constitutional amendment. His 1891 draft provided that the people in the states would elect conventions to consider proposals for amendment. Deakin argued that since the conventions would be saying only Yes or No to proposals this was something the people could do equally well at referendum. At the 1891 Convention the referendum was defeated 9 votes to 19.[2]

At the 1897–98 Convention there was much debate about the referendum, which was proposed as a mechanism for settling deadlocks between the Houses. For this it was defeated, with one argument being that the people could not make judgments on complex issues. There was virtually no opposition to the referendum being used for constitutional amendments. It was harder to argue against it for this purpose since the constitution was to be approved by the people at referendum.

At the time this ultra-democratic mechanism seemed likely to make the constitution easy to amend. During the campaign for its adoption objectors were told that whatever they disliked in the constitution could be readily changed. The people were in charge. Once Labor was established in Federal

Parliament some of its leaders hoped that they could put the whole Labor platform to the people and have it adopted as a constitutional amendment.[3]

Professor Harrison Moore, the foremost constitutional authority, predicted in 1902 that amendments would come from formal change rather than from interpretations of the High Court. Of course the reverse has happened.[4] Forty-four proposals have been put to the people, and only eight have been accepted.[5]

Billy Hughes was the politician who made the most heroic efforts to change the constitution by referendum. As Attorney-General in the Fisher Labor Government, he led the campaign for wider Commonwealth powers in 1911 and again in 1913, when he very nearly succeeded. He became Prime Minister in 1915 on Fisher's retirement and was expelled by the Labor Party in 1916 for supporting conscription. He and his supporters then combined with the Liberal Opposition to form the Nationalist Party. Hughes continued as Prime Minister and continued to hold to his Labor principles, one of which was larger economic and social powers for the Commonwealth. After the war Hughes again tried to acquire these powers at referendum. He had to water down his pre-war proposals to obtain the approval of his new allies, but he was defeated at the referendum by his old comrades. The Labor Party campaigned for No on the grounds that the traitor and class enemy should not be trusted with larger powers or that the powers asked for were not large enough.

It was here that the idea of a convention re-entered federal politics. If the people were guided by the parties, and if one party would always oppose what the other proposed, then a new bipartisan body of high standing was needed to propose change. Hughes planned for a constitutional convention with thirty-six delegates from federal and state parliaments and seventy-five elected delegates, one from each federal electorate, who might be the member or someone else. Members of parliament were less than enthusiastic, and the plan was dropped.[6]

Since then a 'convention' has regularly been part of plans for constitutional change. In the 1920s and 1930s the advocates of new states in New England and the Riverina called their gatherings conventions. In 1933 the people of Western Australia could vote at a referendum in favour of secession from the Commonwealth or for a new convention to revise the Constitution. They took the radical option and voted for secession. One of the Federal Government's responses to this dissatisfaction with itself was a plan for a convention where it would have as many delegates as all the states combined. The states rejected the offer.

In 1942 in the depth of the war the Labor Government called a convention to obtain agreement that the wide powers it enjoyed during the war should continue so that it could organise post-war reconstruction. The Convention was attended by twelve federal parliamentarians and the Premier and Leader of the Opposition of each state. It would not support Labor's plans but undertook to have the states refer the necessary powers to the Commonwealth. Not all states did so. The government then pressed on with plans for a referendum in 1944, which it lost. In this case, as in many others, the voting pattern was perverse. In the two states that had been willing to refer powers the vote was No; in the two states whose premiers were most opposed to the proposals, the vote was Yes.[7]

The Liberal Government elected in 1949 was opposed to Labor's centralism, but it nevertheless made use of the powers that the Commonwealth had accumulated through its financial predominance and the favourable interpretations of the High Court. The Liberal Premier of Victoria, Sir Henry Bolte, was frequently in bitter conflict with the federal Liberal Government over its financial control. He planned a constitutional convention, which in the first instance only the states would attend.[8] Since the Commonwealth alone can propose alterations to the constitution, the plan was sensibly changed to include the Commonwealth from the outset. There were twelve delegates elected by the state parliaments and sixteen from the Commonwealth. Three delegates represented local government in each state. The Governor-General opened the Convention in Sydney in 1973.

This was the first full-blown constitutional convention since the 1890s, and it was conscious of its illustrious predecessors. Its aim was to review the whole constitution. The Convention had been some time in the planning so by the time it met the long Liberal rule in Canberra had ended and Labor's Gough Whitlam was Prime Minister. He told the Convention on its first day that there was no possibility of the Commonwealth giving up the power it had under section 96 of granting of money to the states on the terms and conditions it set. He saw this power as the central device for implementing the Labor program, although on this occasion he defended it as following in the footsteps of Sir Robert Menzies. His vision of constitutional reform was of the states and local government cooperating with the Commonwealth to deliver better services to the people. The states were clearly not going to gain their central point, but there was much else to talk about. The Convention continued to meet off and on for eleven years.[9]

Until the 1970s the central argument over the constitution had been the relative powers of the Commonwealth and the states. Labor openly sought more power for the Commonwealth and was officially committed to abolishing the states. Its opponents were defenders of the states officially; in practice they were ready to make use of the Commonwealth's powers and occasionally to propose their increase. After the constitutional crisis of

1975 and the dismissal of the Whitlam Government by the Governor-General, the central constitutional issues became the power of the Senate to block supply (which had precipitated the crisis) and the reserve powers of the Governor-General (which had been used to resolve it). Labor wanted to curb the powers of the Senate and of the Governor-General, to which their opponents were not likely to agree since they had used the Senate's powers and benefited by the use of the Governor-General's.

After Labor returned to office in 1983 it closed down the Constitutional Convention, which was never going to agree to the sorts of changes it wanted, and appointed instead an expert commission to examine the constitution. The commission undertook a full review and made many recommendations, including a limitation of the Senate's power to block supply. Early in 1988 the Labor Attorney-General, wanting to begin the process of constitutional change in the bicentennial year, urged the commission to report immediately on less controversial matters.[10] He put four issues to referendum, hoping they would be readily accepted and so accustom the people to considering and amending their constitution. The changes concerned parliamentary terms, fair elections, local government, and rights and freedoms. The Liberal Party opposed them all. Some of its members were ready to support one or two of the proposals, but they were persuaded that the best campaign strategy was No No No No. The Catholic bishops opposed religious freedom, fearing for the effects on their government-funded schools. The result was the lowest vote ever for constitutional change.

What happens after the politicians fail? The people take over. On the hundredth anniversary of the 1891 Convention two professors of constitutional law brought the leaders of the people together. Representatives of business, trade unions, and the Aborigines met with bureaucrats, lawyers, judges, academics, journalists, and politicians to consider the constitution and how to promote its amendment. Like the 1973 Constitutional Convention, it met in the very chamber where the 1891 Convention had sat. Unlike that body, it deliberated in secret to encourage the meeting of minds and discourage polarisation.[11]

It was now easier to achieve agreement across political party lines. For a number of reasons Labor's long antagonism to the constitution was over: the High Court had given the Commonwealth new powers; the party had abandoned its wish to control the economy and was committed to deregulation and the selling of government enterprises; and progressive opinion was becoming suspicious of big government and more sympathetic to the division of powers and to state and local governments as being closer to the people.[12] Labor's resentment at its treatment in 1975 had also weakened as the moderate, electorally successful Labor governments of the 1980s were never in danger of having their supply blocked by the Senate.

The plan of the 1991 conference was not to propose changes but to identify areas where the constitution had become inadequate and where it could be improved. It envisaged a long period of public debate over these matters before a revised constitution could be put to the people to mark the hundredth anniversary of federation. The key factor to ensure success was that the people should be educated about the constitution and the options for changing it. On the recommendation of the conference, a Constitutional Centenary Foundation was established to perform this task. The Foundation was an independent bipartisan body, chaired by the former Governor-General, Sir Ninian Stephen, and financed by the Commonwealth and state governments. It was not itself to advocate any specific changes but to assist citizens to do so. The Foundation was vigorous and imaginative in its approach. It produced easy-to-read guides and option papers, provided forums for discussion, ran programs in schools, and established a 'constitution awareness' week. How large a dent it made in public ignorance is difficult to say.[13]

It is very hard to educate people about the constitution. Barton thought the constitution could be readily understood by any man of ordinary intelligence.[14] Its language is mostly plain and free of legalistic contortions. The most tortuous passage is that added to section 15 in 1977 to provide that if a senator dies or retires the replacement senator should be of the same political party. The matter is complex, but Griffith would have done much better. He would have winced at some of the language in the republican proposals defeated in 1999.

The difficulty is not chiefly in the language. Partly it arises from modern citizens not knowing what citizens of 1901 knew. The most progressive provision of the constitution was a democratically elected upper house. If you look at the provision for the election of the Senate, it says the electorate will be the same as for the House of Representatives; if you look at that provision it says the electors of the Representatives will be the same as for the lower house in the states. Who now knows what that was? It no longer matters because these provisions only applied until the Commonwealth set its own uniform franchise. It did so in 1902 giving all men and women the vote. That democratic provision is not in the constitution at all.

Persons of average intelligence reading the constitution will get the wrong idea unless they know the decisions of the High Court. They can read the list of the Commonwealth's powers, set out very clearly in section 51, but will they realise that item 29 'external affairs' now gives the Commonwealth the right to legislate on any internal affair that is the subject of an external treaty?

Or that the power over corporations, item 20, is wide enough for the Commonwealth to pass laws on consumer protection? Or that the innocuous section 96, several pages away, allows the Commonwealth to make policy on any matter for which it supplies the states with funds?

Nor can the constitution be correctly read without the 1931 British Statute of Westminster being read as well. The statute gave full independence to the dominions and so rendered some parts of the constitution dead letters. A nation that took its political independence seriously would have removed these provisions. Surely on this there could be no No campaign. But they are still there to surprise the modern reader: the monarch can give instructions to the Governor-General, and the monarch can disallow any Act passed by the Commonwealth Parliament.

The greatest difficulty in understanding the constitution has been there from the beginning. It gives executive power to the monarch and the Governor-General. Ministers are mentioned almost as if they are optional extras. The Governor-General chooses them, but there is no stipulation that ministers must have the support of parliament or that the Governor-General must act in normal circumstances on their advice. Neither Griffith nor Barton would attempt to write these provisions into the constitution since they were matters of convention rather than law. They might have been right that any such attempt would have been rejected in Britain, but the result was that Australia, unlike Britain, equipped itself with a written constitution that trumpets monarchical power. This boasted democratic document omits the very provisions that make our constitutional monarchy a democracy.

These sections of the constitution were responsible for much opposition to the Bill in the 1890s, especially from the Labor Party. Highly suspicious of federation in any case, it was dismayed to find that the Governor-General was to be head of the armed forces and head of the government. They were mocked for their ignorance: the veriest tyro at the Mechanics Institute knew the Governor-General, like the governors, would act on advice. That was not quite correct. The Governor-General would retain the reserve powers of the Crown so that in some circumstances some of the large powers given to him would be his to exercise alone. The constitution does not indicate what the reserve powers are.

No written constitution works in practice exactly according to its words. In this constitution, however, the words are directly contrary to practice, and so more than most it needs a specialist training to understand it. If Australian citizens should begin to read their constitution, they would be more ignorant of their system of government than they are now. The nation lives with this dilemma: the people can't be educated in the constitution until it is rewritten to reflect practice, but it can't be rewritten unless the people agree.

If the adults can't be reached, concentrate on the children. Acting on a report commissioned by the Keating Labor Government, the Howard Liberal Government instituted a program to enhance the teaching of civics in schools. Its aim was that students should understand the system of government under which they live. Those in charge of the program had high ambitions, but they decided that the constitution itself was not a fit document to be placed in the hands of children.[15]

There was no general review of the constitution in the 1990s. The one change in which citizens took an active interest was the creation of a republic. The Australian Republican Movement, formed in Sydney in 1991, was very different from the republicans of the 1880s.[16] They had been outsiders and radicals; the republicans of the 1990s came from Sydney's new elite of business, arts, and the media, and they proposed only a minimal disturbance to the existing constitution. They wanted to replace the Governor-General with a president to be elected by a two-thirds vote at a joint sitting of the Federal Parliament. In 1993 the Labor Prime Minister, Paul Keating, committed his government to the creation of an Australian republic of this sort. Those who wanted a complete overhaul of the constitution thought these republican proposals were dealing with symbolism rather than substance: it would be more useful to sort out the responsibilities of federal and state governments so that the people would know which government to blame for the shortage of hospital beds and school teachers.

The Liberal Party was divided on the republic. Prime Minister Keating, ignoring the conventional wisdom that constitutional change needs bipartisan support, derided them for their division and indecision—and with good effect. To protect themselves from the Keating onslaught, they announced that if they won government a constitutional convention, partly elected by the people, would decide the issue. They depicted themselves as democrats in contrast to an arrogant Prime Minister forcing his republic on the people.

John Howard, who became Prime Minister after the 1996 election, was a staunch monarchist, but he kept scrupulously to the promise to allow the people to decide the issue. So out of the exigencies of party warfare, elections for a convention were held in 1997, a hundred years after Australians had elected the Convention that wrote their constitution. This time proportional voting operated, as in elections for the Senate, and so a wider range of candidates was successful. A little more than half those elected were republicans, about a third monarchists, and the rest uncommitted. Of the republicans, three-fifths came from the Australian Republican Movement and two-fifths were of a more radical stamp, wanting a directly elected president.

Only half the members were elected; the rest were nominated by the government. Republicans demanded that all members be elected, but the government said it would make the Convention more representative by nominating women, immigrants, and Aborigines, who would probably be underrepresented in a solely elected convention. The government also appointed federal and state politicians, who were prohibited from being elected by the people. These notions of representation would have been totally abhorrent to the democrats of the 1890s, who believed election was the only test of legitimacy. The views of the nominated members were divided in the same way and in roughly the same proportion as the elected delegates.

The Convention was rated a great success. Its debates were lively and well conducted and, since their outcome was unknown, they aroused much more interest than those in the parliament. People queued to gain admission. Newspapers followed the convention closely, and the proceedings were broadcast live on radio and TV.

The delegates voted 89 to 52 in favour of a republic. Most of the time of the Convention was devoted to resolving the differences over the nature of the republic. To placate the supporters of a directly elected president, the Republican Movement delegates agreed that nominations for the president could be made by any individual or group; these would be sifted by a representative committee and then the Prime Minister would put one name to a joint sitting for its endorsement. Although this scheme did not quite gain majority support, the Prime Minister declared that he would put it to the people.[17]

At the referendum in November 1999 the proposal was rejected; the national vote was 45 per cent Yes, with no state recording a majority in favour. The No side was made up of monarchists and supporters of direct election, an unholy alliance of the sort that campaigned for No at the 1890s referendums and in most referendums since. The result was certainly not an endorsement of the Queen as monarch of Australia. During the campaign support for the republic in principle rose. If the monarchists defended the Queen, it was as no more than a useful cog in what they call an unrivalled constitution. Mostly they did not defend the Queen; they protected her with the cry that the people should elect their president.

The advocates of a parliamentary election for the president argued that a directly elected president would disturb the Westminster system and, far from giving the people control over the office, would hand it to those who had the means to run presidential election campaigns. But many who voted

No wanted to disturb the existing system, for which they had no respect, and were very receptive to the cry that the scheme was a politicians' republic, not a people's republic. This populist upsurge had not been envisaged by those planning a minimalist republic. There is a great gulf between what elite opinion-makers regard as sensible and useful reforms and what these people want. This difference is a stronger barrier to constitutional change than mere ignorance.

There was plenty of ignorance evident during the campaign, which the No side exploited in the usual way. One bogey was that all Crown land would pass to the Aborigines if the monarchy were removed. The republicans faced the difficulty of proposing a new method of creating the head of state when the present arrangements were poorly understood. For these the constitution is no help. On the appointment and dismissal of the Governor-General it says very little; on the powers of the Governor-General it speaks falsely. After the poll, the republicans urged the need for public education.

It is notable that the Convention carried little authority in the campaign. The politicians were said to be foisting on the people, without adequate consultation, a republic in which they were to control the president. This view overlooked the fact that the scheme was adopted by a convention in which there were few politicians and half the delegates had been elected by the people. The people had never been more directly involved in the development of a constitutional amendment—or at least those who wanted to be. Voting for the Convention was voluntary, although for the referendum it was compulsory. Even the losers in this campaign were willing to accept that the matter had been rushed and spoke of the need to proceed next time first by an indicative plebiscite on the principle of whether there should be a change to a republic—something on which the Convention had given a very clear answer. At the time of the Convention it seemed that Australia was re-establishing a worthy practice in constitution-making, but the loss of the referendum took the gloss off the convention idea.

So at the hundredth anniversary of federation Australia remains a federation under the Crown. The British Empire has gone and Australia has become an independent country, but this part of the constitution stands. The wearer of the Crown is called Queen of Australia, but she is so because she is Queen of the United Kingdom. This is the last surviving link with the 'mother country'.

Since I am a republican I might have shown some disappointment at the federalists allowing their project to be so fully enveloped in the British Empire. I beg their pardon. That Australians were all British had always been part of the reason why they should come together. It happened as they came together that Britain seemed to be offering a new partnership within the empire and so the imperial connection became more alluring. Of course the federalists were wrong to think that it could be an equal partnership, but it seemed to offer both safety and an escape from the inferiority of being colonial. And to belong to the British Empire was to be part of something grand and noble since this empire provided British justice to all its subjects and to Britons overseas the full rights of self-government.

It is absurd to wish that our forebears had rejected these opportunities. We must simply be clear-minded about the course of our national history. The nation was formed not against the empire but within it and was more admiring of Britain for allowing it to be a nation. The nation never resolved to leave the empire or break all ties with Britain; rather the empire collapsed and Britain abandoned its responsibilities to the dominions. The ties with Britain were broken piecemeal, with one tie still remaining. Thus there never was a moment when Australians claimed their political independence and made it the touchstone of their nationhood. They did define themselves as against Britain but in other spheres: by boasting that their society was much more open, by beating the English at cricket, and by producing superior soldiers.

Australians' civic understanding was closely related to their Britishness. Their rights and liberties and law courts and parliaments were British; the political history they knew was how British liberty had been established in Britain; they were citizens not merely of Australia but also of an empire. Paradoxically, as the nation has broken its ties with Britain and become independent, its civic consciousness has become impoverished.

It could be that the centenary of federation will help to awaken Australians to their own civic achievements in the 1890s. There is certainly at this anni-versary far more interest in the details of the story of federation than there was at the fiftieth jubilee. The centenaries of all the key moments have been acknowledged, not only the official conventions but also the meetings at Corowa, Bathurst, and Bendigo. In 1993 Prime Minister Keating attended the Corowa celebrations and linked the popular movement for federation to the campaign for a republic.[18] The board he appointed to advise on the centenary recommended that the first priority was for Australians to understand what they were celebrating. It suggested that every child receive not a medal but a golden CD telling the federation story.[19] Courtesy of the civics program, each school does now have a CD on federation called 'One Destiny'.

The organisers of the celebrations are encouraging localities not to stage a pageant of progress, but to find out how federation was fought out in their area. They are assisting the publication and distribution of books on federation—like this one. They have run TV advertisements to inform Australians about their federation history. They began with Barton, not with his deeds in the federation campaign, but to introduce him to Australians as their first Prime Minister. What sort of country is it, the advertisement asked, that does not know the name of its first Prime Minister? The answer is a country that is not quickly going to place Barton and Deakin alongside its real heroes: Ned Kelly, Phar Lap, and Don Bradman—a bushranger, a horse, and a cricketer.

Notes

The following abbreviations have been used in the Notes:

AA	Australian Archives
AGPS	Australian Government Publishing Service
CO	Colonial Office
ML	Mitchell Library
MS	manuscript
NLA	National Library of Australia
SMH	*Sydney Morning Herald*
V. and P.	*Votes and Proceedings*

Introduction

1 *Advertiser* (Adelaide), 1 Feb. 1897.

1 Destiny

1 Fully worked studies that take this view are Ronald Norris, *The Emergent Commonwealth*, Melbourne University Press, Melbourne, 1975, and W. G. McMinn, *Nationalism and Federalism in Australia*, Oxford University Press, Melbourne, 1994.

2 Al Gabay, *The Mystic Life of Alfred Deakin*, Cambridge University Press, Melbourne, 1992.

3 Gabay, *Mystic Life*, pp. 77, 79, 83, 84.

4 Alfred Deakin, *The Federal Story: The Inner History of the Federal Cause 1880–1900*, Melbourne University Press, Melbourne, 1963, p. 34.

5 *Daily Telegraph*, 20 April 1898.

6 R. Ely, *Unto God and Caesar: Religious Issues in the Emerging Commonwealth 1891–1906*, Melbourne University Press, Melbourne, 1971.

7 R. Pesman Cooper, 'Garibaldi E L'Australia', *Rassegna Storica del Risorgimento*, vol. 20, no. 11, 1985, pp. 205, 207 (translation kindly supplied by Professor Pesman Cooper).

8 Pesman Cooper, 'Garibaldi', pp. 210–11.

9 Newspaper cutting pasted in diary for 1883, Deakin Papers, NLA MS 1540/4/585.

10 *The Lyceum Leader, compiled from the Lyceum Guide for the Melbourne Progressive Lyceum, by the Conductor*, Melbourne, 1877 (in the Deakin Papers, NLA MS1540/4/585), pp. 43–4.

11 Marcus Haward and James Warden (eds), *An Australian Democrat: The Life, Work and Consequences of Andrew Inglis Clark*, University of Tasmania, Hobart, 1995.

12 This and the other poems cited are in the Clark Papers, University of Tasmania Archives, C4/H8.

13 J.A. La Nauze, *The Making of the Australian Constitution*, Melbourne University Press, Melbourne, 1972, p. 76.

14 Blotto to Clark, 27 August 1873, 17 November 1874, Clark Papers, C4/C/17.

15 Gabay, *Mystic Life*, p. 83; *Argus*, 12 July 1887.

16 See chap. 5, 'Prophet'.

17 John Reynolds, *Edmund Barton*, Angus & Robertson, Sydney, 1948, p. 96.

18 Commonwealth *Parliamentary Debates*, vol. 1, 1901, p. 21.

19 Haward and Warden (eds), *Australian Democrat*, pp. 93 (Michael Roe), 134 (Warden); John Henry, *Address to the Electors of Tasmania on the Federal Constitution Bill*, Devonport, n.d., pp. 11–12.

20 In 'Locksley Hall', line 128.

21 George D. Dean, *A Handbook on E. W. Cole, His Book Arcade, Tokens and Medals*, published by the author, 1988, copy in ML; Cole Turnley, *Cole of the Book Arcade*, Cole Publications, Melbourne, 1974, chap. 18.

22 The poems are scattered through newspapers, periodicals, and sheet music; collections are found in 'Federation Songs', an exercise book of newspaper cuttings, created by J. Plummer, ML QA 821. 08/35; 'Literature on Federation', NLA MS 5911; Australasian Federation League of Victoria, *Songs of Union*, Melbourne 1899, held in Deakin Papers, NLA MS 1540/11/172, 178; for a listing of songs see Georgina M. Binns, 'Patriotic and nationalistic song in Australia to 1919: A study of the popular sheet music genre', Master of Music thesis, University of Melbourne, 1988.

23 L.F. Crisp, *Federation Fathers*, Melbourne University Press, Melbourne, 1990, p. 370.

24 Cecil Hadgraft, *James Brunton Stephens*, University of Queensland Press, St Lucia, 1969, pp. 79–80, 85.

25 C.M.H. Clark, *Select Documents in Australian History 1851–1900*, Angus & Robertson, Sydney, 1955, pp. 467–70.

26 22 Oct. 1889.

27 *Queenslander*, 25 Jan. 1890, p. 168.

28 Deakin, *Federal Story*, pp. 177–9; see also 'The third of June', *Review of Reviews*, June 1898, p. 702.

29 Al Gabay, 'William Gay, the Bendigo poet and federation', *New Federalist*, no. 2, Dec. 1998, pp. 47–54.

30 Gay to Deakin, 5 Feb. 1896, Deakin Papers, NLA MS1540/4/738.

31 Gay to Deakin, 14 May 1895, 17 Jan., 7 May 1897, Deakin Papers, NLA MS 1540/1/284, 359, 364.

32 Vane Lindesay, *Aussie-osities*, Greenhouse, Richmond, Vic., 1988. I have been assisted on mottoes and coats of arms by the late Dr John Tregenza of Adelaide.

33 See editorial in *Brisbane Courier*, 2 Jan. 1901.

34 There is a memoir of Farrell by Bertram Stevens in *My Sundowner and Other Poems*, Angus & Robertson, Sydney, 1904.
35 Farrell to Parkes, 6 June 1889, 7 June 1890, Parkes Correspondence, ML, vol. 13, pp. 187–9, 337–41.
36 Griffith to Farrell, 3 Aug. 23 Sept. 1890, in John Farrell, Manuscript poems, ML A86.
37 The poem first appeared in the *Bulletin*, 18 Aug. 1883, p. 5, and was reprinted in J. Farrell, *How He Died and Other Poems*, Tusner & Henderson, Sydney, 1887, pp. 29–35.
38 J.A. La Nauze, 'The name of the Commonwealth of Australia', *Historical Studies*, vol. 15, no. 57, Oct. 1971, pp. 59–71.
39 NSW *Parliamentary Debates*, 1897, vol. 89, pp. 2989–94.
40 J.A. Agnew to Griffith, 9 June 1891, 23 Sept. 1896, 14 Oct., 2 Dec. 1897, Griffith Papers, ML MS Q188/91, Q189/183, 365–7, 381.
41 Evans to Deakin, 4, 14, 22, 25 Oct. 1900, Deakin Papers, NLA MS 1540/4/759, 763, 767, 771.
42 H.G. Turner and A. Sutherland, *The Development of Australian Literature*, George Robertson, Melbourne, 1898, pp. 43–53; Essex Evans, 'The poetry of Brunton Stephens', *Lone Hand*, Jan. 1908, pp. 340–3; Hadgraft, *Stephens*, p. 58; Gay to Deakin, newspaper reviews, Deakin Papers, NLA MS 1540/4/724, 725.
43 *Brisbane Courier*, 1 Jan. 1901.
44 McMinn judges the nationalism of politicians by how far they conform to the attitudes epitomised by the *Bulletin* school of writers; see *Nationalism and Federalism*, pp. 113, 129.
45 Brunton Stephens, Essex Evans to Griffith, 28 Nov., 14 Dec. 1898, Griffith Papers, ML MS Q189/589, 639.
46 Gay to Deakin, 24 Feb. 1896, Deakin Papers, NLA MS 1540/1/314.
47 *The Commonwealth and the Empire*, George Robertson, Melbourne, 1895.

2 Identity

1 Ignazio Silone, *The Living Thoughts of Mazzini*, Cassell, London, 1939, p. 30.
2 Frederick Hertz, *Nationality in History and Politics: A Psychology and Sociology of National Sentiment and Nationalism*, Routledge & Kegan Paul, London, 1944, p. 21.
3 The first Australian study to highlight these forces is Robert Birrell, *A Nation of Our Own: Citizenship and Nation-building in Federation Australia*, Longman Cheshire, Melbourne, 1995, a much underrated work that brings a sociologist's insights to nation-building.
4 Roger Joyce, *Samuel Walker Griffith*, University of Queensland Press, St Lucia, 1984, was reduced from a much longer manuscript, which I have also consulted at the National Library (NLA MS 7691).
5 The phrase is La Nauze's; see his *Making of the Australian Constitution*, p. 76.
6 J. Tighe Ryan, 'Australian character sketches', *Review of Reviews*, July 1894, p. 180.
7 This was the theme of his speeches to the Queensland Legislative Assembly, 9 July 1890, *Debates*, vol. 61, p. 193; at the Convention and inauguration banquets, *SMH*, 3 March 1891, 2 Jan. 1901; and of his article in the Brisbane *Courier*, 1 Jan. 1901.
8 Victoria *Parliamentary Debates*, 1884, p. 388; Frank Crowley, *Colonial Australia 1841–1874*, Nelson, Melbourne, 1980, pp. 633–4.

9 Queensland *Parliamentary Debates*, 1890, vol. 61, p. 193; for the image of children see also Geoffrey Serle, 'Victoria's campaign for federation', p. 17 in *Essays in Australian Federation* (ed. A.W. Martin), Melbourne University Press, Melbourne, 1969; K.S. Inglis, *The Rehearsal: Australians at War in the Sudan 1885*, Rigby, Adelaide, 1985, p. 22.

10 Francis Adams, *The Australians: A Social Sketch*, T. Fisher Unwin, London, 1893, p. 60; Thomas Bavin, *Sir Henry Parkes: His Life and Work*, Angus & Roberston, Sydney, 1941, pp. 32–3.

11 *The Federal Government of Australasia: Speeches Delivered on Various Occasions*, Sydney, 1890, pp. 25–6 (changed into direct speech).

12 The draft is published in J. Reynolds, 'A.I. Clark's American sympathies and his influence on Australian federation', *Australian Law Journal*, vol. 32, July 1958, pp. 67–75.

13 Sydney Convention 1891, *Debates*, pp. 767–76.

14 Reynolds, 'Clark's American sympathies', p. 67.

15 Adelaide Convention 1897, *Debates*, p. 981.

16 Sydney Convention 1891, *Debates*, pp. 33–4.

17 Service (*National Australian*, 11 March 1886); Deakin to Griffith, 23 May 1888, Griffith Papers, ML MSQ 187/354.

18 Manning Clark, *History of Australia*, vol. 2, Melbourne University Press, Melbourne, 1968, pp. 52–3.

19 Peter Cunningham, *Two Years in New South Wales*, Henry Colburn, London, 1827, vol. 2, p. 57.

20 There were some positive views, but in Victoria a spate of negative views; see Richard White, *Inventing Australia*, Allen & Unwin, Sydney 1981, chap. 5; D. Walker, 'Concept of "The Australian" ', in *The Australian People* (ed. James Jupp), Angus & Robertson, Sydney, 1988, pp. 864–8.

21 *Ballarat Courier*, 10 July 1879.

22 W. Sowden, *Australia: A Native's Standpoint*, Melbourne 1893, reprinted in *An Australian Native's Standpoint*, Macmillan, London, 1912; G. Meudell, 'Australia for the Australians', H.D'E. Taylor, 'Our future rulers', *Melbourne Review*, 1882, pp. 315–24, 418–36.

23 *Charlton Independent*, 19, 29 Jan., 2, 12, 19 Feb. 1886.

24 I have drawn heavily on the still unaccountably unpublished PhD thesis of Marian Aveling, 'A history of the Australian Natives Association 1871–1900', Monash University, 1970, pursuing some issues in greater depth through the leads she provides. The records and newspapers of the Association are held at the offices of Australian Unity, Albert Park, Melbourne.

25 J.E. Menadue, *A Centenary History of the Australian Natives Association 1871–1971*, Horticultural Press, Melbourne, 1971, pp. 27–9.

26 Aveling, 'Natives Association', appendix IIA; Birrell, *Nation of Our Own*, p. 91.

27 *General Laws for the Government of the Australian Natives Association*, Ballarat, 1885.

28 Aveling, 'Natives Association', pp. 6, 15; Birrell, *Nation of Our Own*, pp. 113–14; Geoffrey Serle, *The Rush to be Rich: A History of the Colony of Victoria 1883–1889*, Melbourne University Press, Melbourne, 1971, p. 311.

29 Birrell, *Nation of Our Own*, p. 92; *Review of Reviews*, July 1899, p. 31; *Argus*, 16 March 1900.

30 Australian Natives Association, Newscuttings, p. 33.
31 Bendigo Branch minutes, 1 June 1899.
32 *Advance Australia*, April 1898, report of Annual Conference; Menadue, *Centenary History*, pp. 203–7.
33 Aveling, 'Natives Association', p. 93.
34 Birrell, *Nation of Our Own*, p. 95.
35 Aveling, 'Natives Association', pp. 201–5; Serle, *Rush to be Rich*, p. 312.
36 Aveling, 'Natives Association', pp. 190–1.
37 *Argus*, 18 Feb. 1887; *Ballarat Courier*, 18 Feb. 1887.
38 Menadue, *Centenary History*, p. 311.
39 The Association's monthly *National Australian* carried views on this issue from Nov. 1885 to July 1886; for Conference decision, *Ballarat Courier*, *Age*, 18 Feb. 1887; see also *Advance Australia*, May, June 1899.
40 Aveling, 'Natives Association', pp. 193–8.
41 Deakin, *Federal Story*, pp. 167–70.
42 Fowler to Deakin, 1 May 1900, Deakin Papers, NLA MS 1540/11/482.
43 Deakin Papers, NLA MS 1540/11/220.
44 *Advance Australia*, April 1897, quoted by Birrell, *Nation of Our Own*, p. 96.
45 *Australian Native*, 13 Feb. 1883, report of Annual Conference.
46 Aveling, 'Natives Association', pp. 242–5; Menadue, *Centenary History*, has chapters on each state branch.
47 Aveling, 'Natives Association', pp. 214–17; *National Australian*, Nov. 1885, *Australian*, May 1888; Minutes of the Sydney Branch in Dowling Papers, NLA MS 47 series 2.
48 Janet Pettman, 'The Australian Natives Association and federation in South Australia', in *Essays* (ed. Martin).
49 Barton to Dowling, 19 Sept. 1893, Dowling Papers, NLA MS 47/1/253.
50 Birrell, *Nation of Our Own*, pp. 89–90.

3 Barriers

1 Australasian Federation League of Victoria, *Songs of Union*, Melbourne, 1899, in Deakin Papers, NLA MS 1540/11/178.
2 J.M. Ward, *Earl Grey and the Australian Colonies 1846–57*, Melbourne, Melbourne University Press, 1958.
3 Inter Colonial Conference, Report and Minutes, Customs Duties, Murray River, Victoria *V. and P.*, 1862–63, vol. 1; the agreed tariff can be found in ibid., vol. 2; *Argus*, 5 June 1863; *Register* (Adelaide), 3 June 1863.
4 C.D. Allin, *A History of the Tariff Relations of the Australian Colonies*, University of Minnesota, Minneapolis, 1918; G.D. Patterson, 'The Murray River customs dispute, 1853–1880', *Business Archives and History*, vol. 2, no. 2, 1962, pp. 122–36.
5 Select Committee on the Riverine Districts, Victoria, *V. and P.*, 1862–63, vol. 2.
6 Border Customs Duties, Victoria *V. and P.*, 1864–65.
7 *Riverine Herald*, 21 Sept. 1864.
8 F.A. Hare, *The Last of the Bushrangers: An Account of the Capture of the Kelly Gang*, Hurst & Blackett, London, 1892, pp. 51–4.
9 *Argus*, 26 Sept. 1864; *Riverine Herald*, 28 Sept. 1864.
10 *Argus*, 11 Oct., 8 Nov. 1864, 18, 21, 25 March, 12 April 1865.

11 Barton to Parkes, 28 Feb. 1891, Parkes Correspondence ML A919, vol. 49; Henry Parkes, *Fifty Years in the Making of Australian History*, Longmans Green, London, 1892, pp. 603–8.

12 C.D.W. Goodwin, *Economic Enquiry in Australia*, Duke University Press, Durham, NC, 1966, pp. 24–5.

13 Stuart Macintyre, *A Colonial Liberalism: The Lost World of Three Victorian Visionaries*, Oxford University Press, Melbourne, 1991.

14 R. Gollan, *Radical and Working Class Politics: A Study of Eastern Australia 1850–1910*, Melbourne University Press, Melbourne, 1960, chap. 3.

15 G.D. Patterson, *The Tariff in the Australian Colonies 1856–1900*, Cheshire, Melbourne, 1968.

16 Goodwin, *Economic Enquiry*, chaps 1, 2.

17 Border Customs Correspondence, Victoria, *V. and P.*, 1879, no. 58; Melbourne Conference 1890, *Debates*, p. 229.

18 Inter Colonial Conference Report and Minutes, Victoria, *V. and P.*, 1870, vol. 2.

19 Inter Colonial Conference Minutes, Victoria, *V. and P.*, 1880, no. 46, 1880–81, no. 62.

20 C.D. Allin, *Australasian Preferential Tariffs and Imperial Free Trade*, University of Minnesota, Minneapolis, 1929.

21 Victoria and Tasmania, Treaty for Intercolonial Free Trade, Victoria, *V. and P.*, 1884, vol. 4; Victoria *Parliamentary Debates*, 1885, pp. 1775–87; Premier Service reported on this defeat to the Chamber of Commerce, 16 Feb. 1893, Minutes, La Trobe Library, MS 10917.

22 Gillies to Griffith, 21 Aug. 1886, Griffith Papers, ML MS Q186; Queensland, *Parliamentary Debates*, 1886, pp. 728–37, 754–8, 1221–2.

23 Reciprocity Agreement with New Zealand, South Australia, *V. and P.*, 1895, vol. 3; *Parliamentary Debates*, 1895, pp. 2771–88.

24 Benjamin Cowderoy, *A Nonagenarian and His Friends*, Melbourne, 1902, p. 3; *Melbourne's Commercial Jubilee*, Melbourne, 1901, pp. 108–10.

25 *Reciprocal Tariffs and Intercolonial Trade*, Melbourne, 1883.

26 Melbourne Chamber of Commerce Minutes, La Trobe Library, MS 10917, Meeting 11 Dec. 1882, Annual Report 1884.

27 Even as careful a historian as Geoffrey Serle conflates a customs union with federation; see his *Rush to be Rich*, pp. 193, 314–15, and 'Victoria's campaign for federation', p. 44.

28 H.R. Reid, *A Customs Union for Australasia*, Melbourne, 1883; the annual reports of the Chamber of Commerce included in the Minutes record their activities for a customs union and their response to federation (as late as 1895 they were urging a customs union rather than federation).

29 See below, chap. 6.

30 Chamber of Commerce Minutes, 11 May 1893, Annual Report.

31 *Report of Proceedings at the Intercolonial Free Trade Conference of Delegates from the Chambers of Manufactures*, Melbourne, 1887.

32 *Report of Proceedings of the Congress of Chambers of Commerce of the Australasian Colonies*, Melbourne, 1889.

33 *Intercolonial Conference of Chamber of Commerce Representatives: Report of Proceedings*, Sydney, 1869, bound in Melbourne Chamber of Commerce Minutes.

4 Movement

1 Marjorie Jacobs, 'Bismarck and the annexation of New Guinea', *Historical Studies*, vol. 5, no. 17 (1951), pp. 14–26, and 'The Colonial Office and New Guinea', *Historical Studies*, vol. 5, no. 18 (1952), pp. 106–18. The following account of the annexation campaign and the formation of the Federal Council is taken from Serle, 'Victoria's campaign for federation'.

2 On the varieties of attachment see C. S. Blackton, 'Australian nationality and nationalism: The imperial federationist interlude 1885–1901', *Historical Studies*, vol. 7, no. 25, 1955, pp. 1–16; Noel McLachlan, *Waiting for the Revolution: A History of Australian Nationalism*, Penguin, Melbourne, 1989, chaps 4 and 5.

3 Imperial Federation League Minutes, 19 June 1885, Deakin Papers, NLA MS 1540/12/90.

4 Imperial Federation League Minutes, 26 June 1885, Deakin Papers, NLA MS 1540/12/90.

5 See its Melbourne meetings, *Argus*, 6 June 1885, 16 July 1889; George R. Parkin, *Imperial Federation: The Problem of National Unity*, Macmillan, London, 1892.

6 Mark McKenna, *The Captive Republic: A History of Republicanism in Australia 1788–1996*, Cambridge University Press, Melbourne, 1996, p. 187.

7 McKenna, *Captive Republic*, chaps 7 and 8; G. Davison, 'Sydney and the bush', *Historical Studies*, vol. 18, no. 71, 1978, pp. 191–209.

8 Imperial Federation League, List of subscribers to bring Mr Parkin, Deakin Papers, NLA MS 1540/12/76.

9 NSW *Parliamentary Debates*, vol. 16, 1885, pp. 262–76.

10 NSW *Parliamentary Debates*, vol. 15, 1884, pp. 6170–231.

11 Annexation of Islands in the Pacific Ocean, Vic. *V. and P.*, 1883, vol. 2, no. 23, pp. 4, 11.

12 Deakin, *Federal Story*, pp. 24–5.

13 Serle, 'Victoria's campaign for federation', pp. 19, 31.

14 This account is based on K.S. Inglis, *The Rehearsal: Australians at War in the Sudan 1885*, Rigby, Adelaide, 1985.

15 Sylvia Lawson, *The Archibald Paradox: A Strange Case of Authorship*, Allen Lane, Melbourne, 1983.

16 NSW *Parliamentary Debates*, vol. 29, 1887, p. 1538; vol. 35, 1888, p. 591; Queensland *Parliamentary Debates*, vol. 53, 1887, pp. 1783–90.

17 Gabay, *Mystic Life*, p. 52.

18 Queensland *Parliamentary Debates*, vol. 53, 1887, p. 1756.

19 Deakin, *Federal Story*, p. 23.

20 Serle, *Rush to be Rich*, pp. 302–7; *Argus*, 12 July 1887 (Deakin).

21 *Bulletin*, 7 May 1887, p. 4.

22 Garrick to Griffith, 25 Nov. 1887, Griffith Papers, ML MSQ 187/228.

23 NSW *Parliamentary Debates*, vol. 29, 1887, pp. 1529–1652; *SMH*, 28 Nov. 1887; Queensland *Parliamentary Debates*, vol. 53, 1887, pp. 1694–1721, 1730–59, 1763–91, 1827–9.

24 Serle, 'Victoria's campaign for federation', p. 20.

25 Garrick to Griffith 25 Nov. 1887, Griffith Papers, ML, MS Q187/228.

26 The manifestos of the two leaders are in the *Courier*, 8, 14 March 1888.
27 Francis Adams, *The Australians: A Social Sketch*, T. Fisher Unwin, London, 1893, prints the platform in Appendix B.
28 McKenna, *Captive Republic*, pp. 171–2; R. Thomson prints a photo of McIlwraith as frontispiece of his *Australian Nationalism: An Earnest Appeal to the Sons of Australia in Favour of the Federation and Independence of the States of Our Country*, Moss Bros, Sydney, 1888; Adams, *The Australians*, pp. 75–8.
29 Aveling, 'Natives Association', p. 219.

5 Prophet

1 W.G. McMinn, ' "Politics or Statesmanship": George Reid and the failure of the 1891 Federal Bill', *Papers on Parliament*, No. 13, Senate, Canberra, 1991.
2 McKenna, *Captive Republic*, pp. 136–50.
3 Parkes to Froude, 16 Aug. 1889, Parkes Papers ML A916.
4 A. Oldfield, *Woman Suffrage in Australia: A Gift or a Struggle?*, Cambridge University Press, Melbourne, 1992, pp. 70–1.
5 Louisa Lawson to Parkes, 15, 20 Aug., 10 Sept. 1889, Parkes Papers, ML A924, A892.
6 Barbara Penny, 'The Blake case', *Australian Journal of Politics and History*, vol. 6, no. 2, 1962, pp. 176–89; NSW *Parliamentary Debates*, vol. 35, 1888, pp. 553–603.
7 Geoffrey Serle, *The Rush to be Rich*, Melbourne University Press, Melbourne, 1971, pp. 307–8.
8 Henry Parkes, *Fifty Years in the Making of Australian History*, Longmans Green, London, 1892, vol. 2, p. 221.
9 *SMH*, 17 May 1888.
10 NSW *Parliamentary Debates*, vol. 35, 1888, pp. 558, 565; vol. 40, 1889, pp. 3817, 3822; Deakin, *Federal Story*, p. 30.
11 Thomson to Parkes, n.d. (1889?), Parkes Papers, ML A910. 69.
12 *SMH*, 24 May 1888 (McMillan).
13 *Bulletin*, 23 July 1887, p. 4.
14 NSW *Parliamentary Debates*, vol. 40, 1889, p. 3813.
15 NSW *Parliamentary Debates*, vol. 35, 1888, p. 553; Henry Parkes, *Federal Government of Australasia*, Sydney, 1890, pp. 48, 72–3.
16 Parkes to Salisbury, 2 Nov. 1889, 14 Feb 1890, Parkes Papers, ML A932, reproduced in *Sir Henry Parkes' Federation Scheme: Extract from Lord Carrington's Diary*, Confidential Print, Sydney 1889, pp. 32–5 (copies in Mitchell Library and NSW State Archives); Parkes to Hopetoun, 3 Jan. 1891, ML A1050(1); Parkes to Froude, 16 Aug. 1889, ML A916; Minute for Governor, Col. Sec. 5/5961, NSW State Archives. I owe the latter two references to Luke Trainor whose interpretation of Parkes's behaviour I have extended; see Trainor, *British Imperialism and Australian Nationalism*, Cambridge University Press, Melbourne, 1994, pp. 98–9, 105–6. To elucidate the letters, I have also drawn on Parkes's federation speeches; see below.
17 Parkes, *Federal Government*, passim.
18 NSW *Parliamentary Debates*, vol. 15, 1884, p. 6199; vol. 29, 1887, p. 1516.
19 Angus McIntyre (ed.), *Aging and Political Leadership*, Oxford University Press, Melbourne, 1988, chap. 7.

20 Parkes, *Fifty Years*, vol. 1, pp. 159–67, 239–42.
21 The negotiations with the other premiers are most comprehensively charted in *Sir Henry Parkes' Federation Scheme.*
22 Parkes Papers, ML A997, contains press cuttings of the Brisbane visit.
23 Thomas Bavin, *Sir Henry Parkes: His Life and Work*, Angus & Robertson, Sydney, 1941, p. 53; a plaque on the Tenterfield School of Arts asserts that the speech 'set in motion the popular movement for federation' (A.G.L. Shaw, 'Centennial reflections on Sir Henry Parkes' Tenterfield Oration', *Canberra Historical Journal*, new series, no. 25, March 1990, p. 3).
24 *Sir Henry Parkes' Federation Scheme*, p. 7.
25 They were collected in his book, *Federal Government.*
26 This correspondence is collected in one volume of the Parkes Papers at the Mitchell Library, A991.
27 SA *Parliamentary Debates*, 1889, cols 1725–8.
28 See the embarrassment at English press support in *Argus*, 7 Nov. 1889; *Courier*, 7 Nov. 1889.
29 The party's response to Parkes's initiative can be followed in the *Australian Star.*
30 See chap. 6, 'Limbo'.
31 *Australian Star*, 9 Nov. 1889.
32 The Parkes–Barton exchange has been printed from their correspondence in a typescript at NLA, MS 292/1, which was prepared for John Reynolds when he was writing his biography *Edmund Barton*, in which some of it appears.
33 Parkes, *Federal Government*, p. 24.
34 *SMH*, 9 Nov. 1889.
35 Ibid., 23 Nov. 1889 (Parkes); *Australian Star*, 27 Nov. 1889 (Barton).
36 Carrington to Parkes, 8 Nov. 1889, Parkes Correspondence, ML A991.
37 The *Age* refused to take Parkes seriously until he supported a protective tariff for the new nation; see *Age*, 11 Nov. 1889. Press views that the fiscal difficulty was still the obstacle continued to be put after the St Leonards speech; see *Argus*, 20 Nov.; *Mercury*, 29 Nov.; *West Australian*, 19 Nov.
38 *Sir Henry Parkes' Federation Scheme*, pp. 11, 18, 20, 22.
39 W. McMinn, 'Sir Henry Parkes as a federalist', *Historical Studies*, vol. 12, no. 47, Oct. 1966, pp. 405–16; A.W. Martin, 'Parkes and the 1890 conference', Senate, *Papers on Parliament*, no. 9. Canberra, 1990, and ' "*It would be a glorious finish to your life*": Federation and Henry Parkes', in *Makers of Miracles* (ed. David Headon and John Williams), Melbourne University Press, Carlton, Vic., 2000; Shaw, 'Centennial reflections', pp. 2–10.
40 For press reporting see *Daily Telegraph* (Melbourne), 15, 17 Feb. 1890.
41 Deakin, *Federal Story*, pp. 30–1.
42 Salisbury to Parkes, 23 Dec. 1889, Parkes Papers, ML A928.
43 *Argus*, 7 Feb. 1890.
44 Deakin, *Federal Story*, p. 27.
45 Melbourne Conference 1890, *Debates*, pp. 77–81.
46 Melbourne Conference 1890, *Debates*, p. 111; E.A. Freeman, 'Sentimental and practical politics', *Princeton Review*, vol. 1, March 1879, p. 316.
47 Melbourne Conference 1890, *Debates*, p. 228.

48 Melbourne Conference 1890, *Debates*, pp. 61, 210.
49 Sydney Convention 1891, *Debates*, pp. 51, 71–2, 131–2, 368–70, 793–4.
50 Parkes to Ponsonby, 18 April 1891, Parkes Papers, ML A1007.
51 Sydney Convention 1891, *Debates*, pp. 185–7.

6 Limbo

1 *SMH*, 26 Feb., 17 April 1891; NSW *Parliamentary Debates*, vol. 51, 1891 pp. 44–62.
2 *SMH*, 25 April 1891.
3 Deakin, 28 April 1891; Griffith, 6 May 1891 to Barton, Barton Papers, NLA, MS 51/1/157, 160.
4 *SMH*, 5 May 1891.
5 Parkes to Jersey, 24 April 1891, Parkes Papers, ML A 1007; NSW *Parliamentary Debates*, vol. 57, 1892, p. 5875.
6 Dibbs's proposal and the response to it are dealt with in L.F. Crisp, *Federation Fathers*, Melbourne University Press, Melbourne, 1990, pp. 77–105.
7 Minutes, La Trobe Library MS 10917, 7, 16 Feb., 7 March, 18 April 1893; *Argus*, 22, 30 March 1893; *Age*, 30 March 1893.
8 *Argus*, 29 May 1893.
9 This account is taken from Aveling, 'Natives Association', pp. 308–32.
10 *Argus*, 3 July 1894.
11 *Age*, 17 March 1894.
12 Sydney Convention 1891, *Debates*, p. 785.
13 Adelaide Chamber of Commerce Minutes, Mortlock Library, SRG 78, Box 1.
14 Register, 26 Jan. 1895; *Australasian Federation League, Report of the Inaugural Meeting in South Australia*, Adelaide 1895; Janet Pettman, 'The Australian Natives Association and federation in South Australia', pp. 132–3 in *Essays* (ed. Martin).
15 Sydney Chamber of Commerce Minutes, ML MS 5706, 15, 22, 28 Feb, 2 March 1893; *SMH*, 3 March 1893.
16 NSW *Parliamentary Debates*, vol. 57, 1892, p. 5885.
17 NSW *Parliamentary Debates*, vol. 61, 1892, p. 2085–6.
18 NSW *Parliamentary Debates*, vol. 57, 1892, p. 5888; vol. 61, pp. 2295–310.
19 *SMH*, 15 Nov. 1892; Melbourne Chamber of Commerce, Annual Meeting, Minutes, 11 May 1893.
20 E. Wilson to Barton, 16 March, 13, 30 June 1893, Dowling Papers, NLA MS 47/1/2704, 2705, 2710.
21 J. Tighe Ryan to Deakin, 19 March 1893, Deakin Papers, NLA MS 1540/200b reports Barton's intention; later Dowling and others claimed the chief spur on Barton was a deputation from the Natives. The press report of their deputation to him does not mention founding a league (see *Australian Star*, 13 May 1893), although their minutes do; see Dowling Papers, NLA MS 47, series 2, 30 May 1893.
22 Edward Dowling, *Australia and America in 1892: A Contrast*, Government Printer, Sydney, 1893, p. 71.
23 *SMH*, 23 June 1893.
24 McMillan to Parkes, 21 June 1893, Parkes Papers, vol. 14, ML A884; McMillan to W. Manning, 31 May 1894, Dowling Papers, 47/1/1497.
25 *Rules and Proposals of the Australasian Federation League*, Sydney, 1894.

26 *SMH*, 4 July 1893; the dodger that Labor used to rally its troops is in the opening pages of the League Minutes, Dowling Papers, 47/2, vol. 40.
27 A.W. Martin, 'Economic influences in the new federation movement', *Historical Studies*, vol. 6, no. 21, 1953, pp. 64–71.
28 Literature on Federation, NLA MS 5911/39, 42, 44.
29 Attendances are given in Minutes MS 47, series 2, vol. 40; the lawyers were A.P. Canaway, W.P. Cullen, F.B. Freehill (also company director), Robert Garran, F.D. Kent, Edward Scholes, P.W. Street, and J. Williamson.
30 The builder was John Young.
31 Minutes, 11 Sept., 6 Oct. 1893, 5 Jan. 1894.
32 Subscriptions to the League 1893–99, Dowling Papers NLA MS 47, Series 3, folder 55 (the seven donors listed gave seven pounds or more).
33 Balance sheets are included in the League's printed annual reports.
34 W. Dixon, 24 Sept. 1893, John Richards, 1 July 1896 to Dowling, 47/1/650, 2022; Minutes, 6 Oct. 1893, 17, 31 Aug. 1894, 11 Jan. 1895.
35 Dowling told the New Zealand Royal Commission on Federation that he had spent hundreds of pounds; see *House of Representatives Journal*, 1901, Appendices, vol. 1, p. 528.
36 *Commonwealth* (the League's journal), no. 1, Oct. 1894, p. 8, 1 June 1895, p. 11.
37 W.A. Murphy, J.R. Talbot, J.E. West, P.J. Brennan.
38 Barton to Dowling, 17, 18 July 1893, Dowling Papers 47/ 1/247, 250.
39 John Reynolds, *Edmund Barton*, Angus & Robertson, Sydney, 1948, p. 96.
40 Cowderoy in his report to the Chamber of Commerce Annual Meeting, Minutes, 26 April 1894.
41 Report to Chamber of Commerce, Minutes, 3 Aug. 1893.
42 See the report of C.H. Grondona, 4 Aug. 1893, Dowling Papers, 47/1/924.
43 The rival claimant was H. D'E. Taylor; see Helen Irving, 'When Quick met Garran: The Corowa plan', *The People's Conventions: Corowa (1893) and Bathurst (1896)*, Papers on Parliament, No. 32, Senate, Canberra, 1998.
44 The Bendigo Federation League published press accounts of Quick's campaign and responses to his plan in *The New Federation Movement*, Bendigo, 1894; see also *Bendigo Advertiser* report in Central League Minutes, 5 Jan. 1894, Dowling Papers, 47/Series 2, vol. 40.

7 Revival

1 Gordon S. Wood, *The Creation of the American Republic 1776–1787*, University of North Carolina Press, Chapel Hill, NC, 1969, chap. 8.
2 G.M. Parssinen, 'Association, convention, and anti-parliament in British radical politics 1771–1848', *English Historical Review*, vol. 88, 1973, pp. 504–33.
3 Gladstone and other admirers are quoted in R. Thomson, *Australian Nationalism: An Earnest Appeal to the Sons of Australia in Favour of the Federation and Independence of the States of Our Country*, Moss Bros, Sydney, 1888, pp. 154–7.
4 James Bryce, *The American Commonwealth*, Macmillan, London, 1888, vol. 1, p. 34.
5 NSW *Parliamentary Debates*, 1895, vol. 80, p. 2365, vol. 81, p. 2428.
6 Correspondence re Australasian Convention, Victoria *V. and P.*, 1883, vol. 3; Australasian Convention 1883, minutes, 28 Nov., Victoria, *V. and P.*, 1884, vol. 2;

Victoria *Parliamentary Debates*, 1884, pp. 242–3, 322; NSW *Parliamentary Debates* 1884, vol. 15, p. 6174.

7 Quick's draft Bill and the League's report on it are in *Rules and Proposals of Australasian Federation League*, Sydney, 1894. For the League's debate on the proposals see *SMH*, 16 March 1894, reprinted in *The New Federation Movement*, compiled and published by the Bendigo Federation League, 1894, which brings together press responses to Quick's plan.

8 *SMH*, 13 Nov. 1894.

9 NSW *Parliamentary Debates*, 1895, vol. 80, p. 1919; vol. 81, pp. 2470–1.

10 NSW *Parliamentary Debates*, 1895, vol. 80, pp. 1921–2.

11 I assume the adjournment plan was adopted in Hobart and not brought there by Reid because it does not appear in the press reports of the meeting until late, on 7 Feb. 1895, although Reid claimed that the Hobart plan was the same as had been adopted by his cabinet; see note 10 above. On the conference generally see Stuart Macintyre, 'After Corowa', *Victorian Historical Journal*, vol. 62, Oct. 1994, pp. 98–112.

12 Federal Council, *Debates*, 1895, p. 90.

13 NSW *Parliamentary Debates*, vol. 57, 1892, pp. 5878, 5916.

14 Parkes to Barton, 18, 22 March 1895, Barton Papers, ML MS 249/3.

15 Federation League Minutes, Dowling Papers, NLA MS 47/2, vol. 40, 31 May 1895.

16 *Daily Telegraph*, 23 Sept. 1895, quoted in A.W. Martin, 'Political developments in New South Wales 1894–6', MA thesis, University of Sydney, 1953, p. 202.

17 *SMH*, 11 July 1895; Reid and Parkes disputed how much money; see *SMH* 16, 20 July 1895.

18 *SMH*, 25 March 1895.

19 *SMH*, 20 July 1895.

20 *SMH*, 16 July 1895.

21 Victoria *Parliamentary Debates*, 1895, p. 4951.

22 NSW *Parliamentary Debates*, 1895, vol. 81, pp. 2470–2; Victoria *Parliamentary Debates*, 1895, pp. 4442–61; SA *Parliamentary Debates*, 1895, pp. 2850–1, 2882–4.

23 NSW *Parliamentary Debates*, 1895, vol. 80, pp. 2236–45.

24 SA *Parliamentary Debates*, 1895, pp. 2838–41.

25 'The conference of premiers at Hobart', *Review of Reviews*, Feb. 1895, pp. 149–53.

26 NSW *Parliamentary Debates*, 1895, vol. 80, p. 1919.

27 NSW *Parliamentary Debates* 1895, vol. 80, pp. 2305–6, 2356; Colonists Anti-Convention Bill League, manifesto, Literature on Federation, NLA MS 5911/59; *Daily Telegraph* (Sydney), 23 April 1898 (article by Judex).

28 NSW *Parliamentary Debates*, 1895, vol. 80, p. 2376.

29 The term is Crisp's, a view examined in Birrell; see *Nation of Our Own*, pp. 123–4.

30 *Courier*, 25 Feb. 1896; Queensland *Parliamentary Debates*, vol. 75, 1896, p. 158.

31 The long debates on the Enabling Bill, *Parliamentary Debates*, vols 75, 76, 1896, detail in injured tones the southern interference; Kingston's views were published in the *Review of Reviews*, Feb. 1896, and reprinted as *The Democratic Element in Australian Federation*, Adelaide, 1897; J. Bannon, *The Crucial Colony: South Australia's Role in Reviving Federation 1891 to 1897*, Federalism Research Centre, Canberra, 1994, chap. 7.

32 Queensland *Parliamentary Debates*, vol. 75, 1896, p. 137.
33 Queensland *Parliamentary Debates*, vol. 75, 1896, pp. 134–9.
34 *Proceedings People's Federal Convention, Bathurst, November, 1896*, Sydney 1897; there are several essays on the Convention in *The People's Conventions: Corowa (1893) and Bathurst (1896)*, Papers on Parliament no. 32, Senate, Canberra 1998.
35 Australasian Federation League, Minutes, Dowling Papers, NLA MS 47/2 23 Oct. 1896.
36 Astley to Dowling, 5, 31 Oct. 1896, Dowling Papers, NLA MS 47/1; Federation League Minutes, 6 Oct. 1896; Tessa Milne, 'Barton at Bathurst', Papers on Parliament no. 32.
37 Barton to Dowling 8, 12 July 1894, Dowling Papers NLA MS 47/1/264, 265; J. Tighe Ryan, *Federation. The Attitude of the Catholic Church: A Special Interview with His Eminence Cardinal Moran*, Sydney, 1894.
38 He described it as the most independent colony after New South Wales; see *SMH*, 5 May 1891.
39 This account is taken from *Courier*, 8–14 Dec. 1896; *SMH*, 9–12 Dec. 1896.
40 W.G. McMinn, *George Reid*, Melbourne University Press, Melbourne, 1989, p. 128, suggests that Queensland was attractive to Reid because it might, on some issues at the Convention, vote as a large state. It had given no indication of this, and it was becoming increasingly defensive of its own interests. What Reid stressed was its resources and potential, which leads me to infer that its likely adherence to free trade interested him more.
41 *SMH*, 14, 19 Dec. 1896.
42 Bannon, *Crucial Colony*, pp. 44–5.

8 Convention

1 See Rosemary Pringle, 'The 1897 convention elections in New South Wales: A milestone', *Journal Royal Australian Historical Society*, vol. 58, pt 3, Sept. 1972, pp. 217–25; Kathleen Dermody, 'The 1897 federal election convention: Success or failure', in *The Constitution Makers*, Papers on Parliament, No. 30, Senate, Canberra, 1997; *Review of Reviews*, Feb. 1897, pp. 131–4, March 1897, pp. 254–5.
2 *Age*, 6 March 1897, reported that all the Victorian delegates were protectionists.
3 L.F. Heydon, *Prudence in Federation*, Sydney, 1897.
4 *Advertiser*, 10 March 1897.
5 Australasian Federation League of New South Wales, *Annual Report*, 1896–97.
6 John Reynolds, *Edmund Barton*, Angus & Robertson, Sydney, 1948, p. 100; George Reid, *My Reminiscences*, Cassell, London, 1917, p. 132.
7 Arthur Patrick, *Christianity and Culture in Colonial Australia: Selected Catholic, Anglican, Wesleyan and Adventist Perspectives, 1891–1900*, Newcastle, 1991, chap. 5.
8 *SMH*, 16, 17, 23 Feb. 1897.
9 *Tenterfield Star*, 26 Oct. 1889.
10 *SMH*, 29 Jan., 19 Feb. 1897.
11 Susan Magarey, *Unbridling the Tongues of Women: A Biography of Catherine Helen Spence*, Hale & Iremonger, Sydney, 1985.
12 Judith A. Allen, *Rose Scott: Vision and Revision in Feminism*, Oxford University Press, Melbourne, 1994.

13 Jan Roberts, *Maybanke Anderson: Sex, Suffrage and Social Reform*, Hale & Iremonger, Sydney, 1993.
14 J.T. Walker, Diary, ML MS 2729, 19–21 March 1897; B.R. Wise, *The Making of the Australian Commonwealth, 1889–1900: A Stage in the Growth of the Empire*, Longmans Green, London, 1913, p. 229; *SMH*, 19, 20 March 1897; *Argus*, 22 March 1897.
15 Margaret Glass, *Charles Cameron Kingston: Federation Father*, Melbourne University Press, Melbourne, 1997.
16 *Australasian Insurance and Banking Record*, May 1895, pp. 287–8; June 1895, pp. 364–5; *Review of Reviews*, July 1897, p. 126; A.R. Hall, *The London Capital Market and Australia 1870–1914*, Social Science Monograph, Australian National University, Canberra, 1963, p. 173.
17 Adelaide Convention 1897, *Debates*, p. 302.
18 Gabay, *Mystic Life*, p. 84.
19 Adelaide Convention 1897, *Debates*, p. 284.
20 Adelaide Convention 1897, *Debates*, pp. 272, 274, 281.
21 Adelaide Convention 1897, *Debates*, pp. 1098–9.

9 Constitution

1 Adelaide Convention 1897, *Debates*, pp. 670–2.
2 Dobson to Griffith, 23 Dec. 1897, Griffith Papers, ML MS Q189/385.
3 Baker at Mount Gambier, newspaper cutting, Baker Papers, Mortlock Library PRG 38/1 vol. 9; Adelaide Convention 1897, *Debates*, p. 521.
4 This is section 84; see Adelaide Convention 1897, *Debates*, pp. 1044–51, Melbourne 1898, *Debates*, pp. 990–8, 1899–1901.
5 This is section 85 (ii); see Melbourne Convention 1898, *Debates*, p. 998.
6 See J.A. La Nauze, 'A little bit of lawyers' language: The history of "absolutely free"', in *Essays* (ed. Martin).
7 This phrase was Playford's. Sydney Convention 1891, *Debates*, p. 784.
8 Forrest said that the Commonwealth would use the power more moderately than the states and appeared to think that if the Commonwealth had the power the states would not; see Melbourne Convention 1898, *Debates*, p. 210; see also La Nauze's discussion in *Making of the Australian Constitution*, p. 208.
9 Melbourne Convention 1898, *Debates*, p. 20.
10 La Nauze, *Making of the Australian Constitution*, pp. 204–6.
11 See Cheryl Saunders, 'The hardest nut to crack: The financial settlement in the Commonwealth Constitution', in *Official Record of the Debates of the Australasian Federal Convention*, vol. 6: *The Convention Debates 1891–1898: Commentaries, Indices and Guide* (ed. Greg Craven), Legal Books, Sydney, 1986.
12 Melbourne Convention 1898, *Debates*, pp. 1247–9, 1611, 1633.
13 See R.R. Garran's discussion in *The Coming Commonwealth: An Australian Handbook of Federal Government*, Angus & Robertson, Sydney, 1897, pp. 163–6.
14 Melbourne Convention 1898, *Debates*, pp. 1633–53.
15 He lists all his board memberships in his Diary, 25 Dec. 1897, ML MS 2729; see also Sydney Convention 1897, *Debates*, p. 11.

16 Subscriptions to the League 1893–99, Dowling Papers NLA MS 47/3/55; Black to Barton 21 June 1893, Dowling Papers 47/1.
17 *Journal of the Institute of Bankers of New South Wales* carries Walker's paper in Dec. 1896 and the debate on it in Jan. 1897; *Australian Economist* carries papers by Black in March 1895, R.R. Garran in Oct. 1896, and Walker in Jan. 1897, and further papers and discussion monthly until Aug. 1897; R.L. Nash, *Federal Finance*, Sydney, 1897.
18 See B. Galligan and J. Warden, 'The Senate' in *Convention Debates* (ed. Craven).
19 Sydney Convention 1891, *Debates*, p. 755.
20 NSW *Debates* 1897, vol. 87, pp. 591, 594, 647–8, 653–4, 704, 882; vol. 88, p. 2129; vol. 89, pp. 2333–4, 2629, 2647, 2906; see also W.M. Hughes and W.T. Dick, *Federation as Proposed by the Adelaide Convention*, Sydney, 1897.
21 Melbourne Convention 1898, *Debates*, pp. 2140–1.
22 Melbourne Convention 1898, *Debates*, p. 2155.
23 Melbourne Convention 1898, *Debates*, p. 2163.
24 Deakin, *Federal Story*, p. 88.
25 Heydon, *Prudence in Federation*, p. 13.
26 McMinn, *Nationalism and Federalism*, chap. 10.

10 No–Yes

1 R. Norris, 'Economic influences on the 1898 South Australian referendum', in *Essays* (ed. Martin).
2 John Craig, 'Tasmania and the federal movement', *Tasmanian Historical Research Association, Papers and Proceedings*, vol. 22, no. 1, March 1975, pp. 7–48.
3 C.C. Kingston and F.W. Holder, *To the Electors of South Australia*, Adelaide, 1898; Commonwealth League, *Benefits of Federation*, Baker Papers, Mortlock Library PRG 38/1 vol. 9.
4 *Age*, 1, 2, 7, 12 March 1898; Deakin, *Federal Story*, pp. 92–3.
5 Deakin records the inside story of the conversion of the *Age* and Turner's government in *Federal Story*, chap. 14.
6 *Advance Australia*, 1 April 1898; J. Hume Cook, *ANA: An Historical Survey of its Genesis and Development*, Horticultural Press, Melbourne, 1931, pp. 14–15; Aveling, 'Natives Association', pp. 380–9.
7 The speech is reprinted in *Federal Story*, pp. 177–9.
8 This passage occurs in the version purchased by the League (see below); it does not occur in the *Federal Story* version.
9 Conference and Board of Directors Reports, vol. 4, p. 262, Special meeting, 30 March 1898, p. 6; the speech is at p. 213.
10 Aveling, 'Natives Association', pp. 390–2.
11 *Age*, 1 April 1898.
12 *Age*, 19 March 1898.
13 Elizabeth Pillar, 'Victorian opposition to federation 1880–1900', BA thesis, University of Melbourne, 1966.
14 John Rickard, *H.B. Higgins: The Rebel as Judge*, Allen & Unwin, Sydney 1984, pp. 99–105.
15 Hugh Anderson (ed.), *Tocsin: Radical Arguments against Federation 1897–1900*, Drummond, Melbourne, 1977.

16 B.R. Wise, *The Making of the Australian Commonwealth, 1889–1900: A Stage in the Growth of the Empire*, Longmans Green, London, 1913, pp. 328–9.
17 Deakin records the offer in *Federal Story*, pp. 88–9, 175; Reid confirms it in *McLeay Argus*, 21 Sept. 1898.
18 Deakin, *Federal Story*, pp. 64, 89.
19 Glenn Rhodes reports the attitude of MPs in all colonies in 'The Australian federation referenda 1898–1900: A spatial analysis of voting behaviour', PhD thesis, London School of Economics, 1988 (copy held at NLA MS 7630), pp. 342–4.
20 *SMH*, *Daily Telegraph*, 29 March 1898.
21 29 March 1898.
22 NSW *Parliamentary Debates*, 1898, vol. 92, p. 391.
23 *SMH*, 12 July 1898.
24 *Daily Telegraph*, 21 May 1898; the actual words are reported by Barton, *SMH*, 13 July 1898.
25 R.R. Garran, 'Memories of Federation', *Listener*, 17 May 1951, p. 793.
26 The *Daily Telegraph* of 14 April 1898 lists the leading members of the Anti-Bill league. Even at the second referendum J.T. Walker estimated that barely a third of the members of the Union and Australian Clubs, the gathering places of Sydney's wealthy, were for the Bill; see Diary, 17 Aug. 1900, ML MS 2729. The Sydney Chamber of Commerce was divided and took no position; see Rough Minutes, 25 April, 5 & 20 May 1898, ML MS 5706.
27 Helen Irving, *To Constitute a Nation*, Cambridge University Press, Melbourne, 1997, pp. 183–6.
28 *Daily Telegraph*, *Australian Star*, 4 June 1898.
29 Rhodes, 'Federation referenda', pp. 506–11, gives percentages for both referenda for capital city, country, and colony.
30 Australasian Federation, Copies of Telegrams, NSW *V. and P.*, 1898 (18th Parliament), vol. 2.
31 What follows is based on this correspondence in the Barton Papers, NLA MS 51/1, and Deakin Papers, NLA MS 1540/1, 11; see also Barton to Baker, 24 June 1898, Baker Papers, Mortlock Library PRG 38/1 vol. 9: Wise to Symon, 5 June 1898, Deakin to Symon, 6 & 9 June 1898, Turner to Symon, 10 Aug. 1898, Symon Papers NLA MS 1736/9/89, 94, 99, 111.
32 Turner and Deakin defended this approach in Victoria, *Parliamentary Debates*, 1898, vol. 88, pp. 963–78.
33 *Australian Federalist*, 9 July 1898.
34 *SMH*, 20 June 1898.
35 Included in the special election issue (King division) of the *Daily Telegraph*, July 1898, bound in the Mitchell Library with *Clarion Call*, the Barton paper.
36 *Daily Telegraph* and *SMH*, 6 June 1898, give slightly different figures.
37 The Dowling Correspondence, NLA MS 47/1, includes many letters on this election: see 160, 237, 796, 802, 1171, 1175, 1176, 1555, 1571, 1573, 1764, 1930, 2366, 2372, 2812; *Federalist*, 20 July 1898; on anti-federationists in the Protection Party see *Daily Telegraph*, 23, 25 July 1898.
38 See the hagiography produced for the Hastings-Macleay election, *Clarion Call, Supplement to Macleay Chronicle,* 15 Sept. 1898.
39 Deakin to Barton, 27 July 1898, Barton Papers, NLA MS 51/1/313

40 *Daily Telegraph*, 15 Sept. 1898; Reid to Barton, 23 June 1893, Barton Papers, NLA MS 51/201; Reid, *Reminiscences*, p. 268; Downer to Griffith, 25 May 1897, Griffith Papers, ML MS Q189.
41 Robert Pyers to Barton, 30 July 1898, Bruce Smith to Barton, 26 Aug 1898, Barton Papers, NLA MS 51/1/321, 324.
42 *Macleay Argus* covers the election from 10 Sept. 1898; the three Sydney dailies sent correspondents. There is a collection of newspaper cuttings in the Barton Papers, NLA MS 51/9/1060.
43 *Macleay Argus*, 21 Sept. 1898; *Daily Telegraph*, 15 Sept. 1898.
44 *Daily Telegraph*, 12 Sept. 1898.
45 Deakin to Barton, 25 Sept. 1898, Barton Papers, NLA MS 51/1/ 329.
46 Bede Nairn, *Civilising Capitalism: The Labor Movement in New South Wales 1870–1900*, Australian National University Press, Canberra 1973, chaps 13–16.
47 Sydney Convention 1897, *Debates*, p. 506; Melbourne Convention 1898, *Debates*, p. 2203.
48 *SMH*, 2 May 1899; *Worker* (Brisbane), 13 May 1899; J.T. Walker, Diary, 1 May 1899, ML MS 2729.
49 NSW *Parliamentary Debates*, vol. 100, 1899, pp. 1141–2, 1212–36.
50 This is how I interpret the comment: 'this Lord Chesterfield of high politics can use the language of the pot-house when it suits him'. *Parliamentary Debates*, vol. 100, p. 1226.
51 Barton to Deakin, 18 Sept. 1899, Deakin Papers, NLA MS 1540/11/112.

11 Continental

1 Lord John Russell, *Recollections and Suggestions*, 2nd edn, Longmans Green, London, 1875, p. 238.
2 Cited on title page of R.R. Garran, *The Coming Commonwealth*, Angus & Robertson, Sydney, 1897.
3 H. Willoughby, *Transportation: The British Convict in Western Australia*, London, 1865; for the extent of the anti-transportation movement see Geraldine Suter, *Index to the Argus*, 1864–65, under 'Convicts'.
4 British *Parliamentary Papers*, Western Australia: Further Correspondence re Introduction of Responsible Government, 1889 Cmd 5752, 1890 Cmd 5919.
5 Forrest used this phrase in his *Speech … Recommending the People of Western Australia to Join the Australian Commonwealth*, Perth, 1900, p. 5. To Barton he wrote of England, 8 March 1900, 'our Island Home is best' (Barton Papers, NLA MS 51/1/383).
6 As Parkes did in 'An Australian Nation', *Melbourne Review*, No. 16, Oct. 1879.
7 *Review of Reviews*, June 1898, p. 668.
8 See on regionalism and separation R.G. Neale, 'The new state movement in Queensland', *Historical Studies*, vol. 4, no. 15, Nov. 1950, pp. 198–213; G.C. Bolton, *A Thousand Miles Away: A History of North Queensland to 1920*, Australian National University Press, Canberra, 1963; Christine Doran, *Separatism in Townsville, 1884–1894*, James Cook University, Townsville, 1981; Lorna McDonald, *Rockhampton: A History of City and District*, University of Queensland Press, St Lucia, 1981.

9 Parkes, *Fifty Years*, pp. 571–2.

10 There is a revealing exchange over the issue between Nelson and Glassey in Queensland *Parliamentary Debates*, vol. 75, 1896, pp. 287–9. That the fear of interference with coloured labour was at the root of Queensland's hesitancy was the view of Drake, the leader of the opposition liberals (*Courier*, 28 Feb. 1896) and Kingston of South Australia (press cutting, Dowling Papers, NLA MS 47/1/2301).

11 J. Hume Cook, *ANA: An Historical Survey of Its Genesis and Development*, Horticultural Press, Melbourne 1931, pp. 12–13; Toutcher to Dowling, 7 May 1896, Dowling Papers, NLA MS 47/1/2339.

12 Federal Council, *Debates*, 1897, pp. 77–93.

13 Federal Council, *Debates*, 1897, p. 146.

14 Melbourne Convention 1898, *Debates*, pp. 1191–1238.

15 Tozer to Griffith, 31 March 1899, Griffith Papers, ML MSQ 189/725.

16 James Walker was the Queensland advocate at the Convention (oddly for both the government and the Rockhampton separationists). His diary records meetings with Nelson and Tozer and contains newspaper articles in which he floated the black line proposal, Diary, ML MS 2729, 16 March 1897, 6, 7 March 1898, and for cuttings, see vol. 65 pp. 79, 84; Queensland *Parliamentary Debates*, vol. 81, 1899, p. 38 (Plunkett on trip south); Sydney Convention 1897, *Debates*, p. 272; Melbourne Convention 1898, *Debates*, p. 230.

17 *Worker* (Brisbane), 14 May 1898.

18 Adelaide Convention 1897, *Debates*, pp. 409–10; Melbourne Convention 1898, *Debates*, pp. 1690–1702, 2171, 2398–400.

19 Ronald Lawson, *Brisbane in the 1890s*, University of Queensland Press, St Lucia, 1973, pp. 56–9.

20 Abbott caused a stir when he accused Queensland of trifling with the Convention; see Sydney Convention 1897, *Debates*, pp. 774–6, 1098–101; Melbourne Convention 1898, *Debates*, pp. 124, 293–5.

21 To Griffith from Baker, April 1897; from Deakin, 21 May 1897; from Downer, 29 April 1897, Griffith Papers, ML MSQ 189/281, 305, 309.

22 Adelaide Convention 1897, *Debates*, pp. 96, 647, 1007–10; Sydney Convention 1897, *Debates*, pp. 232–6, 394–415.

23 Sydney Convention 1897, *Debates*, p. 400.

24 Deakin, *Federal Story*, p. 112.

25 Queensland *Parliamentary Debates*, vol. 81, 1899, pp. 55–6; *Courier*, 8 Aug. 1899, Federal Supplement, p. 1, 4 Sept. 1899 (victory speech).

26 Queensland *Parliamentary Debates*, vol. 81, 1899, p. 60.

27 Queensland *Parliamentary Debates*, vol. 81, 1899, pp. 94, 102–3, 119.

28 *Courier*, 8, 14 Aug., 1 Sept. 1899.

29 This was the view of Dickson's erstwhile colleague, Tozer to Griffith, 31 March 1899, Griffith Papers, ML MSQ 189/725.

30 Queensland *Parliamentary Debates*, vol. 81, 1899, p. 347; Australian Federation: Volume of Handbills, Newspaper Cuttings issued in Queensland 1899 [central region], ML.

31 *Courier*, 8 Aug. 1899, Federal Supplement, p. 7; *Cairns Post*, 28 June 1899, reproduced in *Courier*, 5 July 1899, Bolton, *A Thousand Miles Away*, pp. 209–11.

32 Forrest's correspondence with the premiers is at WA Public Record Office, 1496/1443/1899.
33 Leake to Kirwan, 22 Dec. 1899, 15 June 1900, Kirwan Papers NLA MS 277/59, 92; Leake to Deakin, 27 July 1899, Deakin Papers, NLA MS1540/11/107.
34 Press cutting, Griffith Papers, ML MSQ 189/875.
35 Kingston to Kirwan, 3 Jan. 1900, Kirwan Papers NLA MS 279/67; John Kirwan, 'How Western Australia joined the Commonwealth', *WA Historical Society Journal*, vol. 4, part 2, 1950, p. 16.
36 *SMH*, 5 Feb. 1900.
37 Forrest to Barton, 8 March 1900, Barton Papers, NLA MS 51/1/383.
38 Barton to James, 22 July 1899, Deakin to James, 4 Aug. 1899, James Papers NLA MS 296.
39 See Barton's annotation on James to Barton, 15 Aug. 1899, Barton Papers, NLA MS 51/1/367.
40 Deakin to James, 10 July, 6 Sept., 19 Oct., 28 Nov. 1899, James Papers, NLA MS 296.
41 Forrest to Griffith, 22 Feb. 1900, Griffith Papers, ML MSQ 189/935.
42 *Albany Advertiser*, 15 Feb. 1900, cutting in Griffith Papers, ML MSQ 189/911.
43 Keith Sinclair, 'Why New Zealanders are not Australians' in *Tasman Relations: New Zealand and Australia, 1788–1988* (ed. Sinclair), Auckland University Press, Auckland, 1988.
44 Rollo Arnold, 'Some Australasian aspects of New Zealand life, 1890–1913', *New Zealand Journal of History*, vol. 4, no. 1, April 1970.
45 Miles Fairburn, 'New Zealand and Australasian federation, 1883–1901', *New Zealand Journal of History*, vol. 4, no. 2, Oct. 1970, pp. 154–5. Much of the goods passing across colonial borders in Australia did not have to pay duty as they were either exports for overseas or overseas imports being sent on to another colony. The best test of the extent to which colonial tariffs interfered with intercolonial trade is the amount of duty collected by the various colonies on the products of the others. The 1891 Convention published these figures for the seven colonies in its *Proceedings and Debates*, Report of Finance Committee, p. clv, which is Appendix B to the Report from Committee on Constitutional Machinery. The figures show that for 1889 the amount of duties collected on New Zealand goods by the other colonies was the second highest in the group (after those of New South Wales). Certainly the amounts varied; for a much lower figure for New Zealand for 1894 see Statistical Tables Bearing on the Question of Federation, p. 13, in *Papers on Federation Circulated on Consideration of the Draft Federal Constitution 1897 by the Legislature of Victoria*, Melbourne, 1897. Once Sydney became a free port, these figures are not good indicators of the extent of trade that would have benefited from federation; rather the fear became that with federation New Zealand's growing trade with Sydney would face tariffs again. For the extent of this trade see H.J. Mahon, 'Australasian Federation', in *New Zealand Illustrated Magazine*, Nov. 1899, pp. 91–2.
46 R.M. Burdon, *King Dick: A Biography of Richard John Seddon*, Whitcombe & Tombs, Christchurch, 1955, pp. 194–5, 222.
47 Sinclair, 'Why New Zealanders are not Australians', p. 99–100, which correctly notes that the two economies were competitive rather than complementary, but wrongly assumes the reverse was true of the different colonies within Australia.

Had it been so, there would not have been the difficulty in arranging reciprocal agreements between colonies (see above, chap. 3, 'Barriers').

48 New Zealand *House of Representatives Journal*, 1901, Appendices, vol. 1.

49 *Representatives Journal*, Appendices, vol. 1, pp. 112, 462–3; Sinclair, 'Why New Zealanders are not Australians', p. 102; Keith Sinclair, *A Destiny Apart*, Allen & Unwin, Wellington, 1986, pp. 119–20.

50 This is the judgment of Keith Sinclair in the two works cited above.

12 Empire

1 Richard Jay, *Joseph Chamberlain*, Oxford University Press, Oxford, 1981, p. 3.

2 In 'The English Flag'. All quotations of Kipling are taken from *Rudyard Kipling's Verse, Definitive Edition*, Doubleday, New York, 1940.

3 Marghanita Laski, *From Palm to Pine: Rudyard Kipling Abroad and at Home*, Sidgwick & Jackson, London 1987.

4 Harold Orel (ed.), *Kipling: Reviews and Recollections*, Barnes & Noble, Tetowa, 1983, vol. 2, pp. 271–6.

5 Trumpeter McKenzie describes his experiences in an unsourced cutting in James Walker, Diary 1898, ML MS 2729.

6 This account is from *SMH*, 21–24 June 1897.

7 *The Times*, 23 June 1897, p. 14.

8 *Report of a Conference between Right Hon. Joseph Chamberlain MP and the Premiers of the Self Governing Colonies of the Empire*, Confidential Print, Colonial Office 1897; see esp. pp. 100, 107–8. J.L. Garvin, *The Life of Joseph Chamberlain*, Macmillan, London, vol. 3, 1934, p. 193.

9 This account is taken from B.K. de Garis, 'The Colonial Office and the Commonwealth Constitution Bill' (quotation is at p. 111), in *Essays* (ed. Martin). Among the reasons de Garis suggests for the choice of Reid as intermediary, he does not include the one identified above.

10 This was the motive ascribed to him by his enemies; see letters to Samuel Way from Murray Smith and Darley in Way's Correspondence on Clause 74, Mortlock Library PRG 30/4/32, 73, 223, which seems to be confirmed by the animus he showed Griffith when he was appointed Chief Justice (see his drafts for Dawn of Federation in Symon Papers NLA MS 1736/29).

11 Melbourne Convention 1898, *Debates*, pp. 2295–309; *The Australian Commonwealth Bill: The Spectator's Criticism: A Reply*, Adelaide, 1900; 'The Privy Council Appeal', typescript in Symon Papers, NLA MS 1736/9/49–60.

12 Keith Dunstan, *The Paddock that Grew: The Story of the Melbourne Cricket Club*, Hutchinson, Sydney, 1988 (2nd edn), pp. 76–9; Melbourne Convention 1898, *Debates*, p. 2111; James Walker, Diary, ML MS 2729, 29, 31 Jan., 1 Feb. 1898; *Daily Telegraph*, 1 Feb., 4 March 1898; *Age*, 3, 19 March 1898.

13 W.F. Mandle, 'Cricket and Australian nationalism in the nineteenth century', *Journal of the Royal Australian Historical Society*, vol. 59. pt 4, Dec. 1973, pp. 225–46.

14 *Review of Reviews*, Feb. 1900, p. 157.

15 C.N. Connolly, 'Manufacturing "spontaneity": The Australian offers of troops for the Boer War', *Historical Studies*, vol. 18, no. 70, April 1978, pp. 106–17.

16 British *Parliamentary Debates*, 4th series, vol. 75, 1899, cols 702–3.

17 This account is based on Barbara Penny, 'Australia's reactions to the Boer War: A study in colonial imperialism', *Journal of British Studies*, vol. 7, no. 1, Nov. 1967, pp. 97–130; L. M. Field, *The Forgotten War: Australian Involvement in the South African Conflict of 1899–1902*, Melbourne University Press, Melbourne, 1979.
18 Garvin, *Joseph Chamberlain*, vol. 3, pp. 543–4.
19 Russel Ward in *The Australian Legend*, Oxford University Press, Melbourne, 1958, exaggerates the rapidity of the legend's acceptance. He does not mention the Boer War. The participation of bushmen in this conflict does not fit his characterisation of the legend as radical.
20 A. B. Paterson, *Singer of the Bush: Complete Works 1885–1900*, Lansdowne, Sydney, 1983, pp. 478, 554, 577.
21 Paterson, *Singer of the Bush*, pp. 582–6.
22 See Richard White, *Inventing Australia*, Allen & Unwin, Sydney, 1981, pp. 79–84.
23 Paterson, *Singer of the Bush*, pp. 689–90.
24 *The Times*, 1 May 1900, p. 6.
25 My interpretation of Chamberlain differs from that of de Garis, who considers that the interest of investors was paramount for him; see 'British influence on the federation of the Australian colonies 1880–1901', DPhil, University of Oxford, 1965, pp. 397–402.
26 A. J. Hannan, *The Life of Chief Justice Way*, Angus & Robertson, Sydney 1960, chap. 10. The project was being advanced by Halsbury, the Lord Chancellor, with whom Way exchanged letters on 1 March and 26 April 1900; Way Correspondence, Mortlock Library, PRG 30/4/175, 178.
27 For Griffith's continuing interest in this project see Joyce, *Griffith*, pp. 322, 351–2.
28 Sydney Convention 1891, *Debates*, pp. 33–4.
29 British *Parliamentary Papers*, Further Papers re Australian Federation, 1900 Cmd 158, pp. 79–81.
30 Deakin, *Federal Story*, p. 153.
31 Further Papers re Australian Federation, pp. 35–47.
32 Deakin, *Federal Story*, p. 163.
33 Salmon to Deakin 16 May 1900, Deakin Papers, NLA MS 1540/11/481; Natives Assoc to Symon 16, 18 June 1900, Symon Papers, NLA MS 1736/9/420, 422.
34 The exchanges between the delegates and the premiers are in the Deakin Papers, NLA MS 1540/11/527–554.
35 Forrest to Governor, 2 May 1900, and press statement of same day, WA PRO, Premier's Dept. Acc. 1496/198.
36 de Garis, 'British influence', pp. 364–9.
37 Further papers re Australian Federation, p. 53; Wittenoom to Forrest, 9 Feb. 1900 in WA PRO, Premier's Dept. Acc. 1496/198 1900.
38 Further Papers re Australian Federation, pp. 71–2.
39 Forrest to Deakin, 20 Aug. 1900, Deakin Papers, NLA MS 1540/11/165.
40 Bryce to Deakin, 26 March, 6 April, 10 May 1900; Massingham to Deakin, 4 April, n.d., 9 May 1900, Deakin Papers, NLA MS 1540/11/ 401, 416, 419, 444, 448, 450.
41 Mitchell Library Newspaper Cuttings, vol. 203 Q342. 901/N, collected by Barton, which throws doubt on Deakin in *Federal Story*, p. 154.
42 14 May 1900, p. 15; 17 May, p. 6; 22 June, p. 4.

43 The preoccupations of the two sides can be followed in the correspondence of the chief protagonists, Way's Correspondence on Clause 74, Mortlock Library PRG 30/4; Symon Papers, NLA MS 1736/9.
44 Deakin, *Federal Story*, pp. 158–9.
45 This was the view of Australians on both sides of the dispute: see Kingston to Symon, 5 July 1900, Symon Papers NLA MS 1736/9/460; Way to Walker, 1 June 1900, Way Papers, Mortlock Library, PRG 30/4/297.
46 Deakin, *Federal Story*, p. 166; La Nauze, *Making of the Australian Constitution*, pp. 263–4.
47 Deakin, *Federal Story*, pp. 162, 171.
48 The draft of the lecture is in the Barton Papers, NLA MS 51/5/977; *SMH*, *Daily Telegraph*, 12 Dec. 1900.
49 Barton to Lyne, 16 June 1900, Barton Papers, NLA MS 51/1/469.
50 White to Barton, 6, 9 April 1900, Barton Papers, NLA MS 51/1/604, 607; *Academy*, 7, 14 April 1900, pp. 296–7, 319.
51 C. Carrington, *Rudyard Kipling*, Macmillan, London, 1955, pp. 258–9; 'The young Queen' appeared in *The Times*, 4 Oct. 1900 and in the Australian press 3 Nov.; see editorial in *SMH*, 6 Nov.
52 *Mercury*, 2 Jan. 1901 (street decorations Sydney), *SMH*, 20 May 1898 (design of federal badge); *Leader*, 22 Dec. 1900 (cover).
53 *Bulletin*, 23 Dec. 1899, p. 7 (I owe this reference to Field, *Forgotten War*, p. 50).
54 See Margaret Anderson (ed.), *When Australia was a Woman*, Western Australian Museum, Perth 1998.

13 Ways and Means

1 Stuart Macintyre has given a critical assessment of the invocation of the people in 'Corowa and the voice of the people' and 'The idea of the people' in *The People's Conventions: Corowa (1893) and Bathurst (1896)*, Papers on Parliament, No. 32, Department of the Senate, Canberra 1998.
2 Donald Creighton, *The Road to Confederation: The Emergence of Canada 1863–1867*, Macmillan, Toronto, 1964.
3 P. B. Waite, *The Life and Times of Confederation 1864–1867*, University of Toronto Press, Toronto, 1962.
4 *Sir Henry Parkes' Federation Scheme: Extracts from Lord Carrington's Diary*, Confidential Print, Sydney, 1889, pp. 3, 7 (copies at ML and NSW Archives).
5 15, 17 Feb. 1890.
6 *Daily Telegraph*, 29 March 1898; *Review of Reviews*, April 1898, pp. 383–4.
7 The Queensland Bill is in Griffith to Barton, 7 May 1891, Barton Papers, NLA MS 51/6/991, 991a.
8 NSW *Parliamentary Debates*, 1891, vol. 51, p. 45.
9 Quick and Garran refer to the 1890 Natives conference and record the names of the delegates, although it is at odds with their interpretation of a two-fold federation movement, admittedly more stark in Garran's *Prosper the Commonwealth*, Angus & Robertson, Sydney, 1958, than in the *Annotated Constitution*.
10 Memo to Potter, Government Printer, 18, 26 March 1890, Parkes Papers, ML A 932; Barton to Dowling, 21 July 1897, 17 March 1898, Dowling Papers, NLA MS 47/1/279, 281.

11 For activities during the referendum campaigns see Odgers to Baker, 1 Aug. 1899, Baker Papers, Mortlock Library, PRG 38/1 vol. 9; *Daily Telegraph*, 3 May 1898 (Randwick, Woollahra, Waverley, and Lawson debating societies), 5 May (Surry Hills), 16 May (Tamworth), 28 May (Toxteth).
12 H. Ashworth to Dowling, 28 April 1898, Dowling Papers, NLA MS 47/1.
13 Derek Drinkwater, 'Federation through the eyes of a South Australian model parliament', *The Constitution Makers*, Papers on Parliament, no. 30, Senate, Canberra, 1997.
14 *SMH*, 30 Jan. 17, 18, 19 Feb. 1897.
15 Prospectus bound with Mitchell Library's copy of the later *Federalist* 1898; ANA Sydney Committee Minutes, 30 May, 9 June 1890, Dowling Papers, NLA MS 47/2.
16 No. 2, Nov. 1894, pp. 11–12, 14–15.
17 In issues of Feb., April, May, June 1895.
18 No. 5, Feb. 1895, p. 14, no. 9 June 1895, p. 11; Federation League Minutes, 10, 17, 31 Aug. 1894, 27 Sept. 1895, Dowling Papers, NLA MS 47/2 vol. 40.
19 Al Gabay, 'William Gay, the Bendigo poet and federation', *The New Federalist*, no. 2, Dec. 1998, pp. 47–54.
20 W. Gay and M. E. Sampson, *The Commonwealth and the Empire*, George Robertson, Melbourne, 1895, pp. 19–20, 25.
21 No. 8, May 1895, p. 2.
22 Adelaide Convention 1897, *Debates*, p. 289.
23 Feb. 1898, p. 137.
24 No. 5, Feb. 1895, p. 2.
25 Dowling Papers, NLA MS 47/1/977.
26 Dowling Papers, 47/1/1772.
27 Dowling Papers, 47/1/1296, 1303.
28 Dowling Papers, 47/1/679, 898, 1900.
29 Dowling Papers, 47/1/2156, 2394, 2404.
30 Dowling Papers, 47/1/534, 987, 898, 1255.
31 Irving, *To Constitute a Nation*, pp. 184–6; Dowling Papers, 47/1/2674 et seq.
32 A. A. Dangar, who gave £50 himself, complained to Barton about how few were giving; see Dowling Papers, 47/1/746.
33 Scott Bennett, *Federation*, Cassell, Melbourne, 1975, p. 167.
34 J. B. Hirst, *Adelaide and the Country*, Melbourne University Press, Melbourne, 1973, p. 49.
35 Bennett, *Federation*, p. 85.
36 Financial records are in United Federal Executive, Finance Committee Minutes, Dowling Papers, 47/2 vol. 45.
37 The Finance Minutes need to be supplemented by letters from J. S. Horsfall and Samuel McCaughey, who acted as bagmen in the Riverina and collected from Melbourne donors; see Dowling Papers 47/1/1261–3, 1265, 1649, 1652, 1662. For contributions from Victoria and South Australia to the 1898 election in New South Wales see letters to Symon from Lilian Wise, 13 July 1898, and Deakin, 15 July 1898, Symon Papers, NLA MS 1736/9/105, 113.
38 *Daily Telegraph*, 23 May 1898 (Norton), 26 May (E. M. Clark), 1 June (Want); Wise to James, 10 Jan. 1899, James Papers, NLA MS 296/19.

39 Bennett, *Federation*, p. 167.
40 Dowling Papers, 47/1/1827; *Daily Telegraph*, 26 May 1898.
41 *Advance Australia*, June 1898, p. 6.
42 Dowling Papers, 47/1/2650, 2653, 2675.
43 Minutes of the ANA Geelong Branch, 3, 7 June 1898, held at Australian Unity, South Melbourne; *Geelong Advertiser*, 7 June 1898.
44 Dowling Papers, 47/1/678, 987, 1390, 1754, 2080, 2082, 2394, 2810.
45 *SMH*, 18, 20 May 1898.
46 Dowling Papers, 47/1/898.
47 *Daily Telegraph*, 15 April 1898 (Want); Dowling Papers, 47/1/2100; Home Rule scare in Queensland, *Light*, no. 3, 12 Aug. 1899; *Courier*, Federal Supplement, 8 Aug. 1899, p. 8.
48 Dowling Papers, 47/1/2414.
49 Barton to Baker, 9 June 1898, Baker Papers, Mortlock Library PRG 38/1 vol. 9; *Daily Telegraph*, 7 April 1898 (Barton at Balmain).
50 Dowling Papers, 47/1/620, *Federalist*, 18 June 1898.
51 Linda Grant De Pauw, *The Eleventh Pillar: New York State and the Federal Constitution*, Cornell University Press, Ithaca, NY, 1966, chap. 7.
52 Wise, *Making of the Commonwealth*, p. 356 (usually rendered as if it were a transcript of a real speech; it was remembered half jokingly long after the campaign. Note that Lyne received his knighthood only in 1900).
53 R. S. Parker, 'Australian federation: The influence of economic interests and political pressures', *Historical Studies*, vol. 4, no. 13, Nov. 1949, pp. 1–24, and a Comment in no. 15, Nov. 1950, pp. 238–40; R. Norris, 'Economic influences in the 1898 South Australian federation referendum' in Martin (ed.), *Essays*, and *The Emergent Commonwealth: Australian Federation, Expectations and Fulfilment 1889–1910*, Melbourne University Press, Melbourne, 1975.
54 Rhodes, 'Federation referenda', pp. 482, 488.
55 Geoffrey Blainey made this point in 'The role of economic interests in Australian federation', *Historical Studies*, vol. 4. no. 15, Nov. 1950, pp. 224–37.
56 *Daily Telegraph*, 21 May 1898 (Higgins), 7 April, 1 June 1898 (Hughes), 2 June (Notes of Day on campaign).
57 Wise, *Making of the Commonwealth*, p. 354; John Craig, 'Tasmania and the federal movement', *Tasmanian Historical Research Association*, vol. 22, no. 1, March 1975, p. 27; *Review of Reviews*, June 1898, p. 709; *SMH*, 1 June 1898; *Daily Telegraph*, 30 May 1898 (introduction of song).
58 *Argus*, 1 June 1898; the song is printed in *Songs of Union*, Australasian Federation League, Melbourne 1899 (copy in Deakin Papers, NLA MS 1540/11/178).
59 Hugh Anderson (ed.), *Tocsin: Radical Arguments against Federation*, Drummond, Melbourne, 1977, pp. 6, 31, 34, 38–9, 63, 66, 70, 83, 141.
60 *The Commonwealth*, No. 1, Oct. 1894, pp. 3–4 (Andrew Garran), 4–5 (Quick); Gay and Sampson, *Commonwealth and Empire*, pp. 14–15 (Robert Garran); *Daily Telegraph*, 14 April 1898 (Barton).
61 *To the Electors of South Australia*, 2 June 1898.
62 They appear in *Review of Reviews* May 1898 and are examined in Rhodes, 'Federation referenda', vol. 2, pp. 91–3.

63 *Review of Reviews*, March 1898, pp. 313–14 (Wise); *Courier* (Brisbane), Federal Supplement, 8 Aug. 1899, p. 8 (Rutledge); Queensland *Parliamentary Debates*, vol. 81, 1899, p. 443 (Allan), p. 452 (Norton); Helen Irving (ed.), *A Woman's Constitution? Gender and History in the Australian Commonwealth*, Hale & Iremonger, Sydney, 1996, p. 9.

64 'The sentiment of federation' by L.B., 21 May 1898.

14 Beginning

1 *Songs of Union*, Melbourne, 1899, held in Deakin Papers, NLA MS 1540/11/172, 178.

2 *SMH*, 30 Oct. 1900; *Argus*, 3 Nov. 1900.

3 *SMH*, 30 Oct., 1 Dec. 1900.

4 J. T. Walker to Symon, 20 Dec. 1899, Symon Papers, NLA MS 1736/9/144.

5 Barton to Deakin, 5 Nov. 1900, Deakin Papers, NLA MS 1540/14/6.

6 On the planning for the first government and the Governor-General's choice of prime minister I have, except where indicated, drawn on the evidence supplied by J. A. La Nauze in *The Hopetoun Blunder: The Appointment of the First Prime Minister of the Commonwealth of Australia December 1900*, Melbourne University Press, Melbourne, 1957, while not accepting its interpretation.

7 Deakin to Barton, 14 Nov. 1900, Barton Papers, NLA MS 51/1/725; Barton to Deakin, 20 Nov. 1900, Deakin Papers, 1540/14/10.

8 Barton to Deakin, 14 Dec. 1900, Deakin Papers, 1540/14/31.

9 Roger Pegrum, *The Bush Capital: How Australia Chose Canberra as its Federal City*, Hale & Iremonger, Sydney, 1983, chap. 1.

10 *Argus*, 26 Jan., 24 Dec. 1900.

11 Chamberlain to Hopetoun, 30 Nov. 1900, in Cabinet Papers, Australian Archives, CRS A6006.

12 Tighe Ryan to Deakin, 14 Oct. 1900, Deakin Papers, 1540/14/2.

13 *Australian Star*, 17, 18, 19 Dec. 1900; *Daily Telegraph*, 11, 12, 14, 17 Dec. 1900.

14 Mennell to Deakin, 18, 25 Sept. 1900, Deakin Papers, 1540/1/550, 554; *SMH*, *Daily Telegraph*, 20 Dec. 1900 (Reid's statement).

15 Kingston to Deakin, 20 Dec. 1900, Deakin Papers, 1540/14/35.

16 Reid, *Reminiscences*, p. 4; *SMH*, 26 June 1897.

17 Philip Mennell, a confidant of both Reid and Deakin, wrote to Deakin: 'Reid has done marvels in manipulating that small brained Hopetoun to his purposes'; see 28 Dec. 1900, Deakin Papers, 1540/1/581.

18 *SMH*, 17 Dec. 1900.

19 *Argus*, 22 Dec. 1900.

20 Hopetoun to Chamberlain, 25 Dec. 1900, CO 418/8/521.

21 *SMH*, 21 Dec. 1900, reports on national opinion.

22 Here I follow closely La Nauze's account in *Hopetoun Blunder*.

23 Reid tried this line in the election (see *SMH*, 5 Feb. 1900) and could have made more use of it if Barton had been chosen first.

24 *Daily Telegraph*, 20 Dec. 1900.

25 Hopetoun to Chamberlain, 25 Dec. 1900, CO 418/8/521. In an exchange of letters with Lyne, Hopetoun put on the record that he had chosen Barton on his advice; see 26, 27 Dec. 1900, Lyne Correspondence, NLA MS 129.

26 *SMH*, 18 Jan. 1901.
27 *SMH*, 23 Feb., 14 March 1900.
28 The following account has drawn chiefly on La Nauze, *Alfred Deakin: A Biography*, Melbourne University Press, Melbourne, 1965; Geoffrey Sawer, *Australian Federal Politics and Law 1901–1929*, Melbourne University Press, Melbourne, 1956; R. Norris, *The Emergent Commonwealth*, Melbourne University Press, Melbourne, 1975; Birrell, *Nation of Our Own*.
29 *SMH*, 18 Jan. 1901.
30 Patricia Grimshaw, 'A white woman's suffrage', in *A Woman's Constitution?* (ed. Irving). Aborigines who already had the vote for state elections were entitled to keep it for Commonwealth under section 41, but many lost it by administrative measures; see Pat Streeton and Christine Finnimore, 'Black fellow citizens: Aborigines and the Commonwealth franchise', *Historical Studies*, vol. 25, no. 101, Oct. 1993, pp. 521–35.
31 Audrey Oldfield deals with both issues in *Woman Suffrage in Australia: A Gift or a Struggle?*, Cambridge University Press, Melbourne, 1992.
32 SA *Parliamentary Debates*, 1900, pp. 433–4, 1002–3. A similar plan for a convention was introduced in Victoria and not proceeded with; see *Parliamentary Debates*, 1901, vol. 97, pp. 374–83, vol. 98, pp. 2574–5.
33 Reid, *Reminiscences*, pp. 211–12.
34 For two years goods imported before this date still paid the Commonwealth tariff less any duty paid to the state if they crossed a state border, and the border customs houses remained for ten years to collect statistics of interstate trade to provide the evidence for assessing the financial reimbursements to the states; see David Day, *Contraband and Controversy: The Customs History of Australia from 1901*, AGPS Press, Canberra, 1996, pp. 34–6.
35 Deakin, *Federated Australia: Selections from Letters to the Morning Post 1900–1910* (ed. J.A. La Nauze), Melbourne University Press, Melbourne, 1968, p. 97.
36 Deakin to Griffith, 21 Feb., 17 April 1901, Griffith Papers, ML MS Q190/1/233, 281.
37 See Deakin's description of him in this role, *Federated Australia*, p. 113.
38 La Nauze, *Alfred Deakin*, details Lyne's ambitions; his denunciation of Deakin is at pp. 562–6.
39 Gabay, *Mystic Life*, chap. 8.

15 Forgetting

1 Taken from the poem that precedes the play by Arthur W. Maher, 'Founders of Federation', 1951, typescript ML.
2 *From Colony to Commonwealth: Being a Brief History of Federation, Together with a Record of the Festivities and Ceremonies which took place in the City of Sydney on the Occasion of the Proclamation of the Commonwealth in January 1901*, William Brooks Ltd, Sydney, 1901, pp. 7–8.
3 *Advertiser*, 2 Jan. 1901.
4 Barton's is held at the National Library, Plate 25620.
5 Dowling Papers, NLA MS 47/1/990, Minutes 47/2 vol. 40, 15 Dec. 1900; the Minutes here mention a work being printed, which might have been *From Colony to Commonwealth*, see note 2 above.

6 *Argus*, 9 May 1901 (Natives propose Parkes's health); *Australian Star*, 4 June 1898 (Barton when he thought referendum won); *SMH*, 2, 4 Jan. 1901 (Barton proposes Parkes's health at banquet and Council lunch); *SMH*, 21 Nov. 1896 (Reid at Bathurst), 30 Jan. 1897 (Reid offering Parkes presidency of the 1897 Convention).
7 *SMH*, 29 Dec. 1900, 3 Jan. 1901.
8 The preparations for the festivities are fully reported in the press; the Mitchell Library Newspaper Cuttings vols 260 and 261 provide a good coverage; for organisational structure see *SMH*, 23 Oct. 1900; composite photo of Organising Committee is held at NLA Image 16300.
9 *SMH*, 26, 30 Oct. 1900.
10 Irving, *To Constitute a Nation*, pp. 11–13.
11 M. Tsiatsias, 'A celestial parade: The Chinese celebration of Australian nationhood, Melbourne, May 1901', BA hons thesis, La Trobe University, 1999.
12 *SMH*, 2 Jan. 1901, p. 13.
13 Richard Ely, *Unto God and Caesar: Religious Issues in the Emerging Commonwealth 1891–1906*, Melbourne University Press, Melbourne, 1976, chap. 14.
14 Hicks Beach to Chamberlain, 6, 10 Sept. 1900, Bigge to Chamberlain, 19 Oct. 1900 and Chamberlain's minute thereon, Chamberlain Papers 16/6/30, 31, 74, Joint Copying Project.
15 Lyon Harvey, *Commonwealth Day, or Sydney en Fête: A Metrical Souvenir of the Federal Celebrations*, Sydney, 1901, p. 10.
16 NSW *Parliamentary Debates*, 1900, vol. 107, pp. 5216, 5642, 5793, 5888, 5892, 6362.
17 W.M. Hughes, *Policies and Potentates*, Angus & Robertson, Sydney, 1950, pp. 42–3.
18 *Australian Field*, 5 Jan. 1901, p. 39; *SMH*, 2 Jan. 1901; *Bulletin*, 5 Jan. 1901, p. 24.
19 Chamberlain to Barton, 9 July 1900; Ampthill to Barton, 19 July 1900; Barton to Art Gallery, 6 Sept. 1900; Art Gallery to Barton, 7 Sept. 1900, Barton Papers NLA MS 51/1/688, 690, 708, 710. It is not absolutely clear that the request to the Queen was Barton's idea; he certainly took it up enthusiastically.
20 *SMH*, 5 Dec. 1900.
21 Holder to Forrest, 10 Sept. 1900, Date of Establishment of Commonwealth, Western Australia PRO, Premiers 1496/898 1900.
22 *Australasian*, 5 Jan. 1901, p. 24.
23 There are two accounts of this incident or something similar might have happened twice see *Mercury* (Hobart), 2 Jan. 1901; *Week* (Brisbane), 4 Jan. 1901.
24 For Brassey's arrival see *Argus*, 26 Oct. 1895; for Beauchamp's, *SMH*, 19 May 1899.
25 *Leader*, 5 Jan. 1901.
26 *Argus*, 9 May 1901.
27 Newspaper Cuttings vol. 260 ML.
28 The Mitchell Library has a two-volume collection of Australian Weekly Papers, Commonwealth Numbers, F990. 1/C, which report on the event in detail.
29 *Argus*, 2 Jan. 1901; see also the trouble the Archbishop had with his vestments, as depicted in the film taken at the time; available in *Federation Films*, National Film and Sound Archive, Canberra, 1992.
30 *Bulletin*, 5 Jan. 1901, p. 12.
31 *Truth*, 6 Jan. 1901, bound in Newspaper Cuttings, vol. 261 ML.
32 *Age*, 2 Jan. 1901.

33 *SMH*, 2 Jan. 1901.
34 *SMH*, 2 Jan. 1901; *Mercury* (Hobart), 8 Jan. 1901; *Australasian*, 5 Jan. 1901.
35 *SMH*, 27 Dec. 1900.
36 *SMH*, 8 Jan. 1901; *Town and Country Journal*, 19 Jan. 1901, p. 23; a printed program for this event is held at the Powerhouse Museum, Sydney.
37 *SMH*, 12 Nov. 1900.
38 *SMH*, 15 Jan. 1901.
39 *SMH*, 4 Jan. 1901.
40 *SMH*, 12 Jan. 1901.
41 Chris Long, 'Australia's first films', part 10: Federation, *Cinema Papers*, no. 101, Oct. 1994, pp. 56–61, 82–3.
42 Letter of Robert Sandall, Jan. 1952, Australian Archives, Commonwealth Jubilee Celebrations, PM A461/7, CB 317/1/6.
43 Forrest to Holder, 11 Sept. 1900, in Date of Establishment of Commonwealth, PRO Western Australia, Premiers Acc. 1496/898 1900; this and the file 1496/198 contain the exchanges between the premiers. See also *Argus*, 3, 7, 8, 12 Sept. 1900.
44 Stewart Firth and Jeanette Hoorn, 'From Empire Day to Cracker Night', in *Out of Empire: The British Dominion of Australia* (ed. John Arnold, Peter Spearritt, and David Walker), Mandarin, Melbourne, 1993.
45 Chamberlain to Salisbury, 22 Jan. 1900, Salisbury to Chamberlain, 29 Aug. 1900, Chamberlain Papers, Joint Copying Project; Governor of New South Wales to Colonial Office, 13 Sept. 1900, and Chamberlain's minutes thereon, CO 201/68.
46 *Argus*, 6 May 1901.
47 Harold Nicolson, *King George the Fifth*, Constable, London, 1952, pp. 66–8.
48 Quoted in Ian Turner, *The Australian Dream*, Sun Books, Melbourne, 1968, p. 256.
49 *Argus*, *Age*, 3 May 1901; information supplied by Bruce Davidson, Parliamentary Librarian.
50 *Argus*, 9 May 1901.
51 *Argus*, 9 May 1901.
52 *Argus*, 20, 21, 24, 26 Sept. 1900; *Age*, 24 Sept. 1900.
53 *Review of* Reviews, May 1901, pp. 502–14, and *Mercury* (Hobart), 14 May 1901.
54 Humphrey McQueen, *Tom Roberts*, Macmillan, Sydney, 1996, p. 474; Gavin Souter, *Lion and Kangaroo: Australia 1901–1919, the Rise of a Nation*, Collins, Sydney, 1976, chap. 4.
55 Carol Foley, *The Australian Flag: Colonial Relic or Contemporary Icon?*, Federation Press, Sydney, 1996.
56 Roger Pegrum, *The Bush Capital: How Australia Chose Canberra as its Federal City*, Hale & Iremonger, Sydney, 1983, chap. 2; Peter Harrison, *Walter Burley Griffin: Landscape Architect*, National Library of Australia, Canberra, 1995, p. 3.
57 John W. Reps, *Canberra 1912: Plans and Planners of the Australian Capital Competition*, Melbourne University Press, Melbourne, 1997, pp. 140–6; K.S. Inglis, 'Ceremonies in a capital landscape', in *Australia: The Daedalus Symposium* (ed. Stephen R. Graubard), Angus & Robertson, Sydney, 1985.
58 K.S. Inglis, *Sacred Places: War Memorials in the Australian Landscape*, Melbourne University Press, Melbourne, 1998, pp. 336–47.

59 Inglis, *Sacred Places*, pp. 60–6, discusses why the Boer War did not take hold in Australian consciousness.

60 There is a statue to Barton on the approach to the suburb that bears his name, looking (as Graeme Davison says) as if he is waiting for a taxi; Davison, 'The use and abuse of Australian history', *Historical Studies*, vol. 23, no. 91, Oct. 1988, p. 64.

61 A.W. Martin, *Robert Menzies*, vol. 2, Melbourne University Press, Melbourne, 1999, pp. 164, 175–9.

62 David Day, *John Curtin: A Life*, Harper Collins, Sydney, 1999, chap. 38.

63 Message from King, AA PM A461/7, CY 317/1/6.

64 *Commonwealth of Australia, Jubilee Celebrations 1901–1951, Official Programme*, Part 2, 1 April to 31 December, p. 8 (copy in Jubilee Press Clippings, Parts 6–8, AA CP133 S4).

65 There were pageants in Sydney on 29 Jan. (see *Cavalcade of Jubilee, Australia Day, January 1951*) and in Adelaide, Hobart, and Launceston on 9 May; Melbourne's was a static performance in the Exhibition Building on 9 May.

66 Of the metropolitan papers only the *Canberra Times* gave substantial attention to the history of federation on the anniversaries of 1 Jan. and 9 May.

67 Commonwealth Jubilee, Anniversary of Border Federation League, AA PM A461/7, AV 317/1/6.

68 Commonwealth Jubilee, State Government Plans and Organisation, NSW, AA PM A461/7, CB317/1/6.

69 *SMH*, 2 Jan. 1951, p. 3; typescripts of the broadcasts are in Garran Papers, NLA MS 2001/7.

70 Conference of Representatives of Commonwealth and State Governments on Jubilee Celebrations, Parliament House, Canberra, 20 March 1950, typescript, Menzies Papers, NLA MS 4936/37/548/38.

71 Issue of Jubilee Medals, AA PM A461/7, M317/1/6.

72 *Commonwealth of Australia Jubilee 1901–1951*, copy in Jubilee Press Clippings Parts 6–8, AA CP 133 S4.

73 Elizabeth Kwan, 'Which flag? Which country? An Australian dilemma, 1901–1951', PhD thesis, ANU, 1995, chap. 8.

74 See Minutes, State Arts Committee for the Commonwealth Jubilee Celebrations, NSW State Archives, Premier's Dept 5/1315, and controversy on 'Hiawatha' K/W 3/5639.

75 Cultural Activities, Recommendations of Inter-Departmental Sub Committee 8 Dec. 1949, in Commonwealth Jubilee Celebrations Policy, AA PM 461/7, B317/1/6.

76 Gordon Greenwood (ed.), *Australia: A Social and Political History*, Angus & Robertson, Sydney, 1955.

77 Commonwealth Jubilee Celebrations, Prime Minister's Decisions, AA PM 461/7, BU317/1/6.

78 This re-enactment was proposed and organised by the ABC; see Ken Inglis, *This is the ABC*, Melbourne University Press, Melbourne, 1983, pp. 168–9.

79 'Pageantry Comes to Town', Jubilee Celebrations, States Arts Committee Correspondence, Premier's Dept, NSW State Archives K/W 3/5640.

80 James G. Murtagh, *Catholics and the Commonwealth*, Australian Catholic Truth Society, Melbourne, 1951.

81 'Founders of Federation', typescript ML; the play was performed at the Mudgee Town Hall, 9 and 10 May 1951.
82 Meeting of Executive Committee, 3 July 1950, Notes for Prime Minister's Opening Address, Commonwealth Jubilee Celebrations Policy, AA PM A461/7, B317/1/6; *Commonwealth of Australia, Jubilee Celebrations 1901–1951, Official Programme*, Part 2, 1 April to 31 December, p. 8 (copy in Jubilee Press Clippings Parts 6–8, AA CP 133, S4).
83 There was a series of conferences on the constitution the proceedings of which are reported in Geoffrey Sawyer et al., *Federalism in Australia: Papers Read at the Fifteenth Summer School of the Australian Institute of Political Science*, Cheshire, Melbourne, 1949; F.A. Bland (ed.), *Changing the Constitution*, NSW Constitutional League, Sydney, 1950; Geoffrey Sawer (ed.), *Federalism: An Australian Jubilee Study*, Cheshire, Melbourne, 1952; see also Gordon Greenwood, *The Future of Australian Federalism*, Melbourne University Press, Melbourne, 1946.
84 *The Parliamentary Government of the Commonwealth of Australia*, Melbourne, 1949 (later reissued as *Australian National Government*).
85 Peter Spearritt, 'Celebration of a nation: The triumph of spectacle', *Historical Studies*, vol. 23, no. 91, Oct. 1988, pp. 3–20.
86 'Federation Pavilion: Sydney's new classicism', *Architecture Bulletin*, Sept. 1985; 'The Federation Pavilion competition', *Architecture Bulletin*, Feb. 1986; Charmaine Chan, 'Centennial Park's new Federation Pavilion', *Heritage Australia*, vol. 8, no. 3, Spring 1989; Philip Drew, 'Seeking a symbol of Commonwealth', *Business Review Weekly*, 15 Jan. 1988, pp. 100–1; there is a model of the elegant version at ML XR20.
87 *Australian* Magazine, 6–7 Sept. 1986, p. 11.
88 *Australian* Magazine, 7–8 Nov. 1987, pp. 11–12.
89 Nicholas Baume, 'Learning from the Dreamtime', *Art and Australia*, vol. 26, no. 1, Spring 1988, p. 83.
90 *SMH*, 2 Jan. 1988.

16 Legacies

1 Final Report of the Constitutional Commission, vol. 1, p. 43, reports a survey taken in April 1987 when 53. 9 per cent of the people knew that there was a written constitution; see Commonwealth *Parliamentary Papers*, 1988, vol. 22.
2 Sydney Convention 1891, *Debates*, pp. 894–7.
3 Deakin, *Federated Australia: Selections from Letters to the Morning Post 1900–1910* (ed. J.A. La Nauze), Melbourne University Press, Melbourne, 1968, pp. 55–6.
4 La Nauze, *Making of the Australian Constitution*, p. 287.
5 Brian Galligan, 'The 1988 referendums and Australia's record on constitutional change', *Parliamentary Affairs*, vol. 43, no. 4, Oct. 1990, pp. 497–506.
6 L.F. Fitzhardinge, *The Little Digger 1914–1952*, Angus & Robertson, Sydney, 1979, pp. 425–7, 440–1.
7 Paul Hasluck, *The Government and the People 1942–1945*, Australian War Memorial, Canberra, 1970, pp. 524–40.
8 The scheme was first proposed by a Labor MP and then taken up by the Liberal Government; see Victoria *Parliamentary Debates*, vol. 295, 1969–70, pp. 422–5, 624–30, 738–41.

9 *Proceedings of the Australian Constitutional Convention, 1973–1985.*
10 Final Report of Constitutional Commission, vol. 1, pp. 46–8.
11 *SMH*, 3, 4, 6 April 1991; *Australian*, 2, 4, 5, 6–7 April 1991.
12 Brian Galligan and Cliff Walsh, 'Australian federalism—yes or no', in *Australian Federation: Towards the Second Century* (ed. Greg Craven), Melbourne University Press, Melbourne, 1992.
13 The Foundation issued newsletters and an annual report.
14 Melbourne Convention 1898, *Debates*, pp. 2466–7.
15 *Whereas the People: Civics and Citizenship Education*, AGPS, Canberra, 1994. The Curriculum Corporation, Melbourne, issued the materials to schools; see *Discovering Democracy*, Primary and Secondary Kit, 1998.
16 John Hirst, 'Towards the republic', in *The Australian Century* (ed. Robert Manne), Text Publishing, Melbourne, 1999.
17 *Report of the Constitutional Convention 2–13 February 1998*, Commonwealth of Australia, Canberra, 1998.
18 'The Prime Minister's Centenary Dinner Speech—Corowa, 31 July 1993', *The People's Conventions: Corowa (1893) and Bathurst (1896)*, Papers on Parliament, no. 32, Senate, Canberra, 1998.
19 *2001: A Report from Australia*, AGPS, Canberra, 1994, pp. 11–13.

Sources

Bibliographies

There are two invaluable bibliographies to the printed and manuscript material:

Federation: The Guide to Records, compiled by S.G. Foster, Susan Marsden, and Roslyn Russell, Australian Archives, Canberra, 1998.

Federation Bibliography, Part 1, Newspapers and Printed Sources, compiled by Pam Crichton, Patsy Hardy, and Marion Stell, Australian National University, Canberra, 1992.

The use I have made of the sources recorded in these volumes will be evident in the Notes. I have not made detailed references in the Notes to the works listed below under 'The constitution' and 'Biographies'.

The constitution

The standard works on the writing of the document, the constitution of the Commonwealth of Australia, are:

Quick, John, and Garran, Robert R., *The Annotated Constitution of the Australian Commonwealth*, Angus & Robertson, Sydney, 1901, reprinted by Legal Books, Sydney, 1995.

La Nauze, J.A., *The Making of the Australian Constitution*, Melbourne University Press, Melbourne, 1972.

La Nauze's book is a work of profound scholarship, but he would have been the first to admit that it does not supersede Quick and Garran, which also has an account of the wider federation movement. The Australasian Federation Conference of 1890 and the Australasian Federal Conventions of 1891 and 1897–98 published their *Debates*, to which there is a composite index: Greg Craven (ed.), *The Convention Debates 1891–1898*, Legal Books, Sydney, 1986.

Biographies

There are good biographies of the leading federation fathers:

Bolton, Geoffrey, *Edmund Barton*, Allen & Unwin, Sydney, 2000.

Joyce, Roger, *Samuel Walker Griffith*, University of Queensland Press, St Lucia, 1984.
La Nauze, J.A., *Alfred Deakin: A Biography*, Melbourne University Press, Melbourne, 1965.
McMinn, W.G., *George Reid*, Melbourne University Press, Melbourne, 1989.
Martin, A.W., *Henry Parkes: A Biography*, Melbourne University Press, Melbourne, 1980.

First-hand accounts

Four of the founding fathers left their own accounts:

Deakin, Alfred, *The Federal Story: The Inner History of the Federal Cause 1880–1900*, Melbourne University Press, Melbourne, 1963.
Parkes, Henry, *Fifty Years in the Making of Australian History*, Longmans Green, London, 1892.
Reid, George, *My Reminiscences*, Cassell, London, 1917.
Wise, Bernhard, *The Making of the Australian Commonwealth, 1889–1900*, Longmans Green, London, 1913.

Significant works

The following are works I have turned to frequently:

Aveling, Marian, 'A history of the Australian Natives Association 1871–1900', PhD thesis, Monash University, 1970.
Birrell, Robert, *A Nation of Our Own: Citizenship and Nation-building in Federation Australia*, Longman, Melbourne, 1995.
Gabay, Al, *The Mystic Life of Alfred Deakin*, Cambridge University Press, Melbourne, 1992.
Irving, Helen, *To Constitute a Nation: A Cultural History of Australia's Constitution*, Cambridge University Press, Melbourne, 1997.
McMinn, W.G., *Nationalism and Federalism in Australia*, Oxford University Press, Melbourne, 1994.
Martin, A.W. (ed.), *Essays in Australian Federation*, Melbourne University Press, Melbourne, 1969 (particularly Geoffrey Serle's 'The Victorian Government's campaign for federation 1883–1889').
Rhodes, Glenn, 'The Australian federation referenda 1898–1900: A spatial analysis of voting behaviour', PhD thesis, London School of Economics, 1988 (copy held in National Library of Australia, MS 7630).

Centenary works

The forthcoming centenary of federation has prompted the publication of a number of works, not all of them books:

Evans, Raymond et al., *1901: Our Future's Past: Documenting Australia's Federation*, Macmillan, Sydney, 1997.
Federation, 3-part TV series, Video, Film Australia, Sydney, 1999.

Headon, David, and Williams, John (eds), *Makers of Miracles: The Cast of the Federation Story*, Melbourne University Press, Carlton, Vic., 1999.
Irving, Helen (ed.), *The Centenary Companion to Australian Federation*, Cambridge University Press, Melbourne, 1999 (contains accounts of the federal movement in each state).
Matthews, Brian, *Federation*, Text Publishing, Melbourne, 1999.
One Destiny: The Federation Story, CD ROM, Global Vision, Melbourne, 1998.
Russell, Roslyn, and Chubb, Philip, *One Destiny! The Federation Story: How Australia Became a Nation*, Penguin, Melbourne, 1998.

Illustrations

Australian Archives (Canberra): pp. 321, 325
Australian Unity (ANA Archives), South Melbourne: p. 42
Lieutenant Colonel Simon Hearder: p. 289
National Library of Australia: pp. 6, 11, 18, 35, 41, 50, 54, 57, 65, 68, 71 (Louisa Lawson), 82, 90, 95, 100, 103, 109, 119, 128, 130, 133, 140, 145, 153, 155, 166, 169, 173, 185, 189, 190, 193, 197, 206, 210, 212, 216, 217, 236, 240, 246, 252, 253, 254, 258, 263, 264, 267, 268, 270, 278, 286, 298, 305, 327, 329 (pavilion as designed)
Oxley Library, Brisbane: p. 27
State Library of New South Wales (Mitchell and Dixson collections): pp. 7, 8, 14, 71 (Henry Lawson), 75, 110, 150, 151, 196, 220, 234, 242, 245, 280, 299, 301, 303, 307, 308, 310, 324
State Library of South Australia: pp. 20, 164
State Library of Victoria: pp. 22, 60, 106, 143, 230, 292, 318
Sungravure: p. 240
Tasmanian State Library: p. 266
University of Melbourne Archives: p. 46.

Index